IMMANUEL KANT
Critique of Practical Reason

IMMANUEL KANT

Critique of Practical Reason

And Other Writings in Moral Philosophy

Translated and Edited with an Introduction by
LEWIS WHITE BECK

THE UNIVERSITY OF CHICAGO PRESS
CHICAGO · ILLINOIS

THE UNIVERSITY OF CHICAGO PRESS, CHICAGO 37
Cambridge University Press, London, N.W. 1, England
W. J. Gage & Co., Limited, Toronto 2B, Canada

Copyright 1949 by The University of Chicago. All rights reserved. Published 1949. Composed and printed by THE UNIVERSITY OF CHICAGO PRESS, *Chicago, Illinois, U.S.A.*

TRANSLATOR'S PREFACE

THIS volume contains complete translations of Kant's most important ethical writings with the exception of the *Observations on the Feeling of the Beautiful and Sublime* and the *Metaphysics of Morals*. Excerpts from the latter, however, have been included. Since several of these works have hitherto been generally unavailable in English and others are not now in print,[1] the present translations may fill an important gap in the literature of ethics.

The translations, with one exception, are based on *Immanuel Kants Werke*, edited by Ernst Cassirer (Berlin: Bruno Cassirer, 1922-23). Departures from the Cassirer text are indicated in footnotes, with the name of the editor who originally suggested the emendation. In these notes the frequent references to Vorländer are to the critical editions he prepared for the Philosophische Bibliothek (Leipzig: Meiner). The Cassirer edition does not contain *On a Supposed Right To Lie;* for this work, the edition of the Prussian Academy of Sciences (Berlin, 1902 *et seq.*) was used. For the sake of uniformity, the approximate pagination of the Academy edition is given in the running heads.

All footnotes originating with the translator are numbered; Kant's own footnotes are marked with asterisks. Material added to the text is inclosed in square brackets. Occasionally paragraphs have been divided differently from the original. I have not followed Kant's extravagant use of spaced type (corresponding to our italics), but passages italicized in the translation are in spaced type in the original.

Many persons have given me much assistance with this work, and I wish to express my thanks to them. Especially do I wish to thank my wife, who gave me aid from the very first day of work; Professor Helmut Kuhn, who critically examined the entire manuscript and made innumerable suggestions for its improvement; Professor Paul Weiss; and Miss Eleanora Duggan, who typed the manuscript.

I now give brief accounts of the works, in chronological order,

1. *Kant's Critique of Practical Reason and Other Works on the Theory of Ethics,* translated into English by Thomas Kingsmill Abbott (London: Longmans, Green & Co., 1879; 6th ed., new impression, 1923), has been out of print for a number of years.

TRANSLATOR'S PREFACE

which are included in this volume. Much of this information is taken from the excellent introductions which Vorländer prefixed to his critical editions of Kant's works and from the notes included in the Prussian Academy edition.

An Inquiry into the Distinctness of the Fundamental Principles of Natural Theology and Morals (*Untersuchung über die Deutlichkeit der Grundsätze der natürlichen Theologie und der Moral*) was published in 1764. In 1763 the Classe der tiefsinnigen Philosophie of the Royal Academy of Sciences in Berlin had proposed the following question for a prize essay: "Whether metaphysical truths generally, and in particular the fundamental principles of natural theology and morals, are not capable of proofs as distinct as those of geometry;[2] and if they are not, what is the true nature of their certainty, to what degree can this certainty be developed, and is this degree sufficient for conviction?" The prize was won by Moses Mendelssohn with his *Treatise on Evidence in the Metaphysical Sciences*, in which he argued that metaphysics is capable of the same kind of certainty but not of the same ready comprehensibility as geometry. The Academy praised Kant's essay, however, in which quite different conclusions were reached, saying that it was almost the equal of Mendelssohn's; and it was decided that the two works should be published together. Kant's essay had been written in obvious haste, and he requested time to revise it. This was granted, but he did not make any changes in the text.

An English translation appeared in *Kant's Essays and Treatises* (2 vols.; London, 1798–99). This edition was published by William Richardson in London, and probably is his own translation.[3]

---

[2]. The mathematical background of Kant's essay is conveniently summarized by Ernst Cassirer, *Substance and Function; and Einstein's Theory of Relativity*, trans. W. C. and M. C. Swabey (Chicago: Open Court Publishing Co., 1923), pp. 351–52. Kant's thesis that there is a fundamental difference between mathematical and philosophical thinking is in anticipation of his future break with rationalism, as this occurred in the *Dissertation* of 1770. See also the section of the *Critique of Pure Reason* entitled "The Discipline of Pure Reason" and the interesting commentary on it by C. D. Broad, "Kant's Theory of Mathematical and Philosophical Reasoning," *Proceedings of the Aristotelian Society, 1941–42*, pp. 1–24.

[3]. Cf. René Wellek, *Immanuel Kant in England, 1793–1838* (Princeton: Princeton University Press, 1932). It was attributed to one Anthony F. M. Willich by Creighton and Lefevre in the bibliography to their translation of Paulsen's *Immanuel Kant, His Life and Doctrine* (New York: Charles Scribner's Sons, 1902).

TRANSLATOR'S PREFACE

What Is Enlightenment? (*Zur Beantwortung der Frage: Was ist Aufklärung?*) was published in the *Berlinische Monatsschrift* for December, 1784. Nothing is known of the origin and occasion of this stimulating essay. In some respects it anticipates the *Strife of Faculties*. Its conclusion, on treating man as a being of worth instead of as a machine, anticipates the distinction between man and things in the chief ethical works. As a *Tendenzschrift* it is one of the best programs for the work which Kant and his century undertook—the century which he calls in the first *Critique* the "age of criticism." It is historically significant that this essay appeared between the American and the French revolutions.

It was done into English by the anonymous translator of the *Essays and Treatises* (1798–99).

Foundations of the Metaphysics of Morals (*Grundlegung zur Metaphysik der Sitten*) was published in Riga in 1785, and a corrected edition appeared in 1786. It was the outcome of work begun much earlier, and we find references in 1771 to a work on the metaphysics of morals that Kant was planning. It is known that the earlier drafts of the *Prolegomena* (published in 1784) contained some of the material which later appeared in the *Foundations*. Although the *Foundations*, unlike the *Prolegomena*, shows no signs of being directed explicitly at Christian Garve, the author of the review which aroused Kant to re-write the *Prolegomena*, the polemical tone of the *Foundations*, especially in its second section, may best be understood in the light of the popular philosophy represented by Garve.

It has been translated into English by the anonymous translator of *Essays and Treatises* (1798–99), by J. W. Semple (Edinburgh, 1836; 4th ed., 1886), by T. K. Abbott, and by Otto Manthey-Zorn (New York: Appleton-Century Co., 1938).

What Is Orientation in Thinking? (*Was heisst: Sich in Denken Orientieren?*) was published in the *Berlinische Monatsschrift* for October, 1786. To understand this highly polemical essay, it is necessary to know something of the controversy which occasioned it.

Shortly before Lessing's death, Friedrich Heinrich Jacobi concluded from a conversation with him that Lessing had become a Spinozist, and after Lessing's death he published this opinion. (At that time Spinoza was held in little esteem, and Voltaire's judgment, *moins lu que cité*, was correct.) Moses Mendelssohn attempted to defend Lessing from this accusation, and a lengthy polemic ensued. (The chief works on both sides are cited by Kant and need not be listed here.)

During this controversy both antagonists attempted to draw Kant into the argument. As usual, he was reluctant; but he inevitably became involved, since both parties to the conflict were making use of certain portions of his philosophy and claiming his support. During the controversy, however, Mendelssohn sadly admitted his divergence from Kant, calling him by the now famous name of *der alles Zermalmende* and expressing the hope that Kant would build up as skilfully as he had torn down.

In brief, Mendelssohn had argued that, whenever metaphysics comes into conflict with sound common sense, the philosopher must orient himself by the latter, for experience shows it to be generally right. For Jacobi, on the other hand, feeling was the ultimate criterion. When Mendelssohn therefore accused him of atheism because he denied the rational arguments for the existence of God, Jacobi appealed to Kant's refutations of these arguments.

When Kant finally entered the controversy, which was causing a tempest in German intellectual circles, he asserted that reason, though not competent to establish metaphysical knowledge, has its own a priori needs and that orientation should be about these and not about the subjective needs of feeling. He then went on to point out the social implications of Jacobi's antirationalism.

The only previous translation is that in the *Essays and Treatises*.

Critique of Practical Reason (*Kritik der praktischen Vernunft*) was published in Riga in 1788. This, the central work of Kant's ethics, was planned as the revision to the sections on practical philosophy in the second edition of the *Critique of Pure Reason* (1787). The relationship between the first and second *Critiques* and the *Foundations* is discussed fully in my Introduction.

Previously the only full translation in English was that of Abbott.

Perpetual Peace: A Philosophical Sketch (*Zum ewigen Frieden: Ein philosophischer Entwurf*) was published in Königsberg in 1795. A second edition, containing the section on secret articles, was issued the following year. This hortatory work is a classic forerunner of modern peace plans and a sharp indictment of European government and diplomacy. It shows Kant's interest in the American and French revolutions. The Preface is an intimation of Kant's difficulties with the censor.

Kant's attitude to war is complex, because he combines a high appreciation of its historical function with insistence upon its moral reprehensibility. These two points of view are nicely balanced in this essay, which develops ideas he had earlier put forward in his *Idea of a Universal Cosmopolitical History*. Some of the section titles, or theses, of this earlier work aptly summarize the two points of view and may serve as a synopsis of *Perpetual Peace*. "The means which nature employs to bring about the development of all the capacities implanted in man, is their mutual antagonism in society, but only as far as this antagonism becomes at length the cause of an order among them that is regulated by law.... The greatest practical problem for the human race, to the solution of which it is impelled by nature, is the establishment of a civil society, universally administering right according to law.... The problem of the establishment of a perfect civil constitution is dependent on the problem of the regulation of the external relations between the states conformably to law; and without the solution of this latter problem it cannot be solved.... The history of the human race, viewed as a whole, may be regarded as the realization of a hidden plan of nature to bring about a political constitution ... as the only state in which all the capacities implanted by her in mankind can be fully developed."[4] *Perpetual Peace* adds to these some important considerations concerning forms of governments and concludes that only republicanism can guarantee peaceful international relations. The work contains few new ideas of a philosophical nature. Most of the ethical matters in it had been developed before, while the moral case against war, in contrast to the legalistic and utilitarian argument of this book, appears in the *Metaphysics of Morals*.

Many English translations exist. The earliest is *Project for a Perpetual Peace*, translated anonymously and published in London "by Couchman for Vernor, 1796." This was republished, with the original orthography, and with an Introduction by Nicholas Murray Butler, by the United States Library Association in 1932 (reissued in 1939 by Columbia University Press). It was also included in *Essays and Treatises* (1798-99). W. Hastie translated it in his *Kant's Principles of Politics* (Edinburgh, 1891). Other translations are by Benjamin F. Trueblood (Boston, 1897), Mary Campbell Smith (London: Allen & Unwin, 1915;

---

4. Translation by W. Hastie, *Kant's Principles of Politics* (Edinburgh, 1891), pp. 9-10, 12, 15, 21.

TRANSLATOR'S PREFACE

Macmillan & Co., 1917; contains a scholarly introduction), Helen O'Brien (London: Sweet & Maxwell, 1927), and C. J. Friedrich (Cambridge: Harvard University Press, 1948).

On a Supposed Right To Lie from Altruistic Motives (*Über ein vermeintes Recht aus Menschenliebe zu lügen*) was published in *Berlinische Blätter*, September, 1797. This short essay shows Kant in his most rigoristic role. Kant here allows the categorical imperative to function as an abstract universal, though a more fruitful application of it was possible without compromising the formalistic insights developed in the earlier works. Considered in the light of various well-known anecdotes about Kant in his old age, this essay reveals perhaps more about him than about his philosophy at its highest stages.

It was translated by A. E. Kroeger in the *Journal of Speculative Philosophy* (St. Louis), 1873, and by Abbott.

Less rigoristic applications of Kant's principles, which are perhaps even more harmonious with the general spirit of his mature philosophy, can be found in *Lectures on Ethics*, translated by Louis Infield (New York and London: Appleton-Century Co., n.d.). The original edition is entitled *Eine Vorlesung Kants über Ethik*, ed. Paul Menzer (Berlin: Pan-Verlagsgesellschaft, 1924).

Metaphysics of Morals (*Metaphysik der Sitten*) was published in 1797 in two parts, "Metaphysical Foundations of Jurisprudence" and "Metaphysical Foundations of the Doctrine of Virtue." More than any other of Kant's ethical treatises, this is an encyclopedic work, wherein the "architectonic" features of Kant's thinking are most salient. The reason for this is to be sought in the title of the work, which must be understood in the strict Kantian sense. "Metaphysical foundations" does not refer to ontological presuppositions, as one might think. This work is metaphysical in the only sense in which Kant, in the *Prolegomena*, admitted that metaphysics might be "scientific"; that is, it is a complete systematic elaboration of a priori judgments. Because of this, perhaps the work as a whole is of less interest to the modern reader than the more exploratory works covering much of the same material, i.e., the *Foundations* and the *Critique of Practical Reason*. Of the two parts, the first is probably the more important, since it is Kant's only complete statement of his legal theory. Part II is concerned chiefly with the elucidation of specific human virtues and duties.

The two excerpts translated here are important as expanding certain parts of Kant's theory which are not given full treatment

TRANSLATOR'S PREFACE

elsewhere. The first selection is the conclusion to the section entitled "Public Law" in Part I, the title used here having been supplied by me. The passage is important for its presentation of Kant's moral case against war, the argument in *Perpetual Peace* having been more largely political and utilitarian.

The second selection is taken from the Introduction to the "Doctrine of Virtue." It is exceedingly important inasmuch as it formulates most clearly the concept of moral teleology as an essential aspect of formalism, which has often been interpreted as excluding consideration of any ends whatsoever.

There is a translation by "the translator of *Kant's Essays and Treatises*" (London, 1799) in two volumes. The first part of this work was translated as *The Philosophy of Law* by W. Hastie (Edinburgh, 1887) and the second by Semple (Edinburgh, 1836). The Introduction to the entire work and the Preface and Introduction to the second part were also translated by Abbott.

L. W. B.

University of Delaware
June 7, 1948

CONTENTS

INTRODUCTION 1

KANT AND HIS PREDECESSORS 1
THE ETHICAL IMPORT OF THE "CRITIQUE OF PURE REASON" . 8
APPROACH TO THE "CRITIQUE OF PRACTICAL REASON" . . . 16
THE PHENOMENON OF MORALITY 18
HUMAN NATURE AND FREEDOM 28
THE CHARACTER OF MAN 40
RATIONAL FAITH 45

I. FOUNDATIONS OF THE METAPHYSICS OF MORALS 50

PREFACE 50
FIRST SECTION. TRANSITION FROM THE COMMON RATIONAL KNOWLEDGE OF MORALS TO THE PHILOSOPHICAL . 55
SECOND SECTION. TRANSITION FROM THE POPULAR MORAL PHILOSOPHY TO THE METAPHYSICS OF MORALS . . . 66
THIRD SECTION. TRANSITION FROM THE METAPHYSICS OF MORALS TO THE CRITICAL EXAMINATION OF PURE PRACTICAL REASON 101

II. CRITIQUE OF PRACTICAL REASON 118

PREFACE 118
INTRODUCTION. OF THE IDEA OF A "CRITIQUE OF PRACTICAL REASON" 128
PART I. DOCTRINE OF THE ELEMENTS OF PURE PRACTICAL REASON 130

Book I. Analytic of Pure Practical Reason 130
    Chapter I. Principles of Pure Practical Reason . . 130
    Chapter II. The Concept of an Object of Pure Practical Reason 166
    Chapter III. The Incentives of Pure Practical Reason 180

CONTENTS

    Book II. Dialectic of Pure Practical Reason 212
        Chapter I. A Dialectic of Pure Practical Reason in General 212
        Chapter II. The Dialectic of Pure Reason in Defining the Concept of the Highest Good 214
    Part II. Methodology of Pure Practical Reason . . 249
    Conclusion 258

III. AN INQUIRY INTO THE DISTINCTNESS OF THE PRINCIPLES OF NATURAL THEOLOGY AND MORALS 261
    Introduction 261
    First Reflection. General Comparison of the Way of Attaining Certainty in Mathematical Knowledge with That in Philosophical Knowledge . . 262
    Second Reflection. The Sole Method of Achieving the Greatest Possible Certainty in Metaphysics . 269
    Third Reflection. Of the Nature of Metaphysical Certainty 276
    Fourth Reflection. Of the Distinctness and Certainty of Which the Primary Grounds of Natural Theology and Morals Are Capable . . . 281
    Postscript 285

IV. WHAT IS ENLIGHTENMENT? 286

V. WHAT IS ORIENTATION IN THINKING? . . 293

VI. PERPETUAL PEACE: A PHILOSOPHICAL SKETCH 306
    Introduction 306
    Section I. Containing the Preliminary Articles for Perpetual Peace among States 306
    Section II. Containing the Definitive Articles for Perpetual Peace among States 311
    First Supplement. Of the Guarantee for Perpetual Peace 322
    Second Supplement. Secret Article for Perpetual Peace 329

[xiv]

CONTENTS

    APPENDIX I. ON THE OPPOSITION BETWEEN MORALITY AND POLITICS WITH RESPECT TO PERPETUAL PEACE . . 331

    APPENDIX II. OF THE HARMONY WHICH THE TRANSCENDENTAL CONCEPT OF PUBLIC RIGHT ESTABLISHES BETWEEN MORALITY AND POLITICS 340

VII. ON A SUPPOSED RIGHT TO LIE FROM ALTRUISTIC MOTIVES 346

VIII. SELECTIONS FROM *THE METAPHYSICS OF MORALS* 351

    PERPETUAL PEACE AS A MORAL AND POLITICAL IDEAL . . 351

    EXPOSITION OF THE CONCEPT OF AN END WHICH IS ALSO A DUTY 352

BIBLIOGRAPHICAL NOTE 358

INDEX 363

INTRODUCTION

KANT AND HIS PREDECESSORS

THERE is a saying among philosophers, "You can philosophize with Kant or against Kant, but you cannot philosophize without him." Much truth lies in this adage, even though few thinkers today would call themselves Kantians without much redefinition and qualification. Nor is its truth greatly diminished by the fact that idealism, as it developed from Kant's philosophy, has been on the defensive for nearly a century. But, inasmuch as Kant saw more clearly than anyone else the ultimate problem of modern thought, and devoted to its solution the greatest philosophical genius of modern times, any thinker who ignores Kant proceeds at unnecessary risk.

The ultimate issue which Kant faced consists in the logical incompatability between the objective and subjective conditions of scientific knowledge. It is the disharmony between the object of science and the human ends it is made to serve. In the Renaissance, after Galilei, Descartes, and Newton had banished purpose from nature, nature came to be seen as a vast mechanism. With the replacement of Aristotelian ideas by mechanistic conceptions, science began to achieve unprecedented control over nature. A similar change of viewpoint in Hobbes, Spinoza, and Harvey with regard to man's own body and mind opened the way for analogous advances in the control of man.

But control for what? It is man who develops science and who through it controls nature for his own purposes. There lies the paradox: man is understood as a machine, but the use of his knowledge of himself and of the external world is thoroughly purposive. The problem is more urgent than any other in modern philosophy because the two incompatible convictions —the idea of the world as a vast impersonal order and the idea of knowledge as power—are fundamental to our world view and equally deep-rooted. To the extent that Western civilization is based on science, it rests on a paradox.

Philosophers before Kant who were aware of this problem attempted to solve it in a variety of ways, and many who were not explicitly conscious of its full implications nevertheless developed philosophies which even now sometimes serve as frameworks for attempted solutions. These ventures involved one of four strategies:

1. The problem was denied by exempting man from the laws of nature through *ad hoc* hypotheses (Descartes, many orthodox Christian philosophers).
2. The problem was declared irresolvable and transferred to a higher court of faith (Malebranche, sometimes Descartes, and many orthodox Christian philosophers).
3. The problem was declared illusory because purpose is not ultimate even in man (Spinoza and Hobbes).
4. The problem was declared illusory because mechanism is not ultimate even in nature (Leibniz and Berkeley).

All these strategies have one failing in common. Each allays the conflict only by weakening one or both of the contending forces. None of them accepts with "natural piety" the competing claims of man as knower and agent and of nature (including man) as known and mechanical.

Kant's consummate greatness as a thinker is nowhere shown more indubitably than in his acceptance of both knower and known as facts not to be compromised. Though in his philosophy there are elements of each of these four inadequate attempts, they are integrated into a new philosophy which does justice to their antagonistic demands.

In the eighteenth century, the Age of Enlightenment, the main stream of thought was guided by a faith in human reason. It was intellectualistic in its attitude toward revelation and tradition and skeptical of things irrational; it was little interested in the past and exceedingly optimistic about the future.

Kant was in many respects an exemplary philosopher of the Enlightenment. His *What Is Enlightenment?* is a document of much diagnostic value to the historian of ideas. Yet he was also the nemesis of Enlightenment as a historical epoch. More than any other philosopher, he placed limits on knowledge without falling into the irrationalism of the forerunners of Romanticism. He exposed the superficiality of the humanistic and intellectualistic optimism of the time without becoming an apologist for the past.

Together with Hume and Rousseau, he subjected current ideas to a searching examination and found them wanting. Hume's demonstration of the nonintellectual foundations of science and Rousseau's nullification of contemporary institutions prepared the way for fundamental changes. These two

INTRODUCTION

critics, however, did not constructively replace what they had rejected. Hume was finally left with only a contemplative skepticism, which Kant turned into a justification of science; Rousseau prepared men's minds for the Revolution, but it was Kant's deepening of Rousseau's criticism of law imposed from above that gave philosophical dignity to *liberté, egalité, fraternité*.[1] Indeed, George Herbert Mead, in his *Movements of Thought in the Nineteenth Century*, gave to Kant the title usually reserved for Rousseau, "the philosopher of the Revolution."[2]

This dual relationship of Kant's thinking to Enlightenment can best be accounted for by his two dominant interests—by his interest in natural science and by his religious allegiance.

More than any other philosopher of the period except perhaps Leibniz, Kant was attentive to the results of the scientific exploration of nature. Even when placing restrictions on science, he seems always to have thought as a scientist. His earliest works were purely scientific in character, and the number of times he compares his procedure to that of the scientist is remarkable. The *Critique of Pure Reason* is a criticism of the metaphysical claims of science, but it is also a defense of it against its internal enemies.

The counterweight to science in Kant's thought is religion. Pietism, an anticlerical movement founded by Spener in the seventeenth century, emphasized the religious and moral responsibility of the individual, the directness of his contact with God, and the importance of good works and quiet faith over ritual and dogma. This religious attitude was instilled into young Kant by his Pietistic parents. But at the same time he learned to dislike

1. Kant formulates these ideals as liberty, equality, and independence. See *On the Saying, "That May Be True in Theory But It Does Not Hold in Practice,"* II (Cassirer ed., VI, 373 ff.; Hastie, *Kant's Principles of Politics*, p. 35).

2. Kant's attitude toward the French and American revolutions is complex because his rejection of violent revolution in general (see Hastie, pp. 50–56) went with an enthusiastic approval of the ends sought in these revolutions (see *Strife of Faculties*, II, §6 [Cassirer ed., 398]). His position with regard to the French Revolution has been pictured in detail by Karl Vorländer, "Kants Stellung zur französischen Revolution," *Philosophische Abhandlungen Hermann Cohen...dargebracht* (Berlin: B. Cassirer, 1912), pp. 246–81; and by Paul Schrecker, "Kant et la Révolution Française," *Revue philosophique*, XXVIII (1939), 394–425. Schrecker says: "The Revolution and even more the echo it set up in the world are to the Kantian ethics what the discovery of the circulation of the blood is to the mechanism of Descartes: a confirmation, as it were, an experimental confirmation, of the fundamental principles of the theory."

[3]

the externalized type of Pietism with which he became painfully acquainted in school. Much of his later religious and ethical thought can be understood as a revolt against the externalized and formal Pietism of the Collegium Fridericianum as well as a defense of the sturdy and unpretentious devotion of his family.

For a proper appreciation of Kant's historical position it is necessary to understand his relation not only to these dominant cultural factors but also to four previous philosophies—the rationalism of the Leibniz-Wolff school, German "popular philosophy," British psychological ethics, and the unclassifiable philosophy of Rousseau.[3]

Kant's philosophical training was that of a Wolffian. Christian Wolff, professor of philosophy in the University of Halle, had developed the rationalism of Leibniz into an elaborate and comprehensive system of ideas. Although Kant was almost never an encyclopedic systematizer in Wolff's manner, his formalistic emphasis is undoubtedly in part attributable to his training. Much of his terminology is derived from textbooks of the Wolffian school, regularly used by him for his own lectures. His marginalia to the textbooks of Alexander Baumgarten, a leading Wolffian, are important sources of information on Kant's development.

However, the substance of Kant's philosophy differs widely from that of Wolff. The *Inquiry* of 1764 renounces the Wolffian method of synthesis, and the *Dissertation* of 1770 restricts the scope of metaphysics as conceived by Wolff. It is this kind of metaphysics which is repudiated in the first *Critique*. In ethics Kant rejects the empty formalism, the perfectionistic ideal, and the utilitarian basis of Wolff's system.

The followers of Wolff, the so-called "academic philosophers," were opposed by the "popular philosophers" who rejected the logical rigor of the academic philosophy. Though some of them, influenced by the "encyclopedic" tradition, retained elements of rationalistic metaphysics, they generally preferred appeals to feeling, common sense, and "sound human reason" as criteria of truth. Through their eclecticism and their uncritical enthusiasm for progress and enlightenment, they gained acclaim and popular following. Windelband correctly

---

3. The extremely important relationship between Hume and Kant will be discussed in the following section. The relation to Rousseau has been brilliantly treated by Ernst Cassirer, *Rousseau, Kant, Goethe,* trans. J. Gutmann, P. O. Kristeller, and J. H. Randall, Jr. (Princeton: Princeton University Press, 1945).

INTRODUCTION

remarks that the emptier and more superficial their metaphysics became, the greater the role they ascribed to utility; and, as a result, they fell into "the most jejune philistinism and sensible, prosaic commonplace."[4] Kant, especially in the second part of the *Foundations* and in *What Is Orientation in Thinking?* opposed this group even more vigorously than the Wolffians did.

British psychological moralists appealed so greatly to Kant that he has often been regarded as their disciple.[5] But his early acceptance of their theories was not that of a disciple, and the changes he introduced were of central significance. His later rejection of their theory of moral sense and his radically new orientation to moral feeling are apparent throughout the ethical works of the critical period. Kant's relation to Shaftesbury and Hutcheson is somewhat like that of Socrates to the Sophists. Both the British moralists and Kant based their ethics on human nature. But Kant, like Socrates, searched for the essential character of man's nature, a universal law determining its particular manifestations.[6] In the announcement of his lectures for the winter semester of 1765–66, he says this explicitly:

> I shall make distinct the method by which man must be studied, not just man as he is distorted by the variable form which his chance condition impresses upon him and as he has almost always been misjudged even by philosophers,[7] but rather the abiding nature of man and its unique position in creation....[8]

This "abiding nature of man," differently conceived, becomes the central topic in Kant's later ethical works.

The philosopher who had the greatest influence on Kant's ethics was undoubtedly Rousseau. Kant's admiration for Rousseau is most clearly expressed in unpublished fragments in which he speaks of Rousseau's "noble sweep of genius" and of the beauty of the style as so disturbing that he has to read him a long

---

4. Wilhelm Windelband, *A History of Philosophy*, trans. James Hayden Tufts (2d ed.; New York: Macmillan Co., 1919), p. 507.
5. As late as 1771, his friend and former pupil, Marcus Herz, wrote that Adam Smith was said to be Kant's "favorite" (Cassirer ed., IX, 101; Academy ed., X, 121). The degree to which Kant was a disciple has, however, been exaggerated. For a critical evaluation of the relationship see Paul Arthur Schilpp, *Kant's Precritical Ethics* (Chicago: Northwestern University, 1938), and below, pp. 25 ff.
6. Later, in the *Critique of Pure Reason* (A314f–B371f), he expresses his admiration for this feature of the Socratic-Platonic philosophy.
7. The allusion is clearly to Shaftesbury and Hutcheson, whose views he has just previously said are incomplete.
8. Vorländer ed., V, 158–59.

time before he can be reasonable in his approach.[9] According to a well-known anecdote, Kant missed his customary walk on the day *Émile* arrived. Although the published writings on moral philosophy mention Rousseau only a few times, and in the works in the broader field of social philosophy explicit references to him are generally somewhat critical, Rousseau's influence on Kant is obvious.

Hendel finds the dominant motifs of Rousseau's philosophy and life in the "ideas of obligation, contract, equality, freedom."[10] These are likewise central in Kant. For both, the social contract is not a historical fact but a principle of justification, a political postulate.[11] Freedom for both is not just political freedom but a symptom of reason's dominance and, as such, inseparable from moral obligation. Rousseau describes immoral action as a violation of the contract by which the individual is bound to the whole. Immoral action restricts equality by partiality, and it is possible because reason does not free man from the importunities of the senses. The will which engenders moral actions must be independent of personal contingencies. This, for Kant, is the good will, and it is clearly anticipated in Rousseau's general will.

These two analogous concepts reveal at the same time a marked difference in point of view. For Rousseau, the general will is a political ideal which is to serve as a check upon the will of the majority. This ideal underlies the original contract itself, and from it all positive laws derive their justification. In its capacity as the ultimate legal norm, the general will corresponds to "the right" in Kant's philosophy, to which all positive laws must be accommodated. But the good will has a far wider competence than the general will, and this wider competence befits its higher metaphysical status as a fact of pure reason. It is the direct evidence for and the sole condition of morality. Its expression is the categorical imperative and (in politics) the criterion of publicity.[12]

Each of these points of agreement between Rousseau and Kant involves both the universality neglected by British moralists and

---

9. *Ibid.*, III, 267.

10. Charles William Hendel, *Jean-Jacques Rousseau, Moralist* (London: Oxford University Press, 1934), II, 165.

11. See *On the Saying, "That May Be True in Theory But It Does Not Hold in Practice,"* II (Cassirer ed., VI, 380; Academy ed., VIII, 297; Hastie, p. 49).

12. See below, p. 341.

INTRODUCTION

the concreteness lacking in Wolff's universals. Rousseau sought to discover man's nature by historical analysis. As Kant says, he did not so much wish that man should return to the state of nature as that, from his present position, he should look back upon his natural condition as a means of discovering in himself the universal—the essence of what he is, apart from the various distortions introduced by society.[13] In this way Rousseau succeeded at the precise point where Kant had found Hutcheson and Shaftesbury wanting:

> Among the multitude of forms assumed by man, Rousseau first discovered man's deeply hidden nature and the concealed law by the observation of which providence is justified.... God is justified by Newton and Rousseau, and more than ever is Pope's thesis true.[14]

Kant's indebtedness to Rousseau is best stated in a fragment probably dating from the sixties:

> By inclination I am an inquirer. I feel a consuming thirst for knowledge, the unrest which goes with the desire to progress in it, and satisfaction at every advance in it. There was a time when I believed this constituted the honor of humanity, and I despised the people, who know nothing. Rousseau corrected me in this. This blinding prejudice disappeared. I learned to honor man, and I would find myself more useless than the common laborer if I did not believe that this attitude of mine [as an investigator] can give a worth to all others in establishing the rights of mankind.[15]

In this fragment Kant reflects Rousseau's conviction of the superiority of uncorrupted natural feeling over vain pride of intellect, his pessimism concerning progress through enlightenment, and his faith in democracy founded upon moral egalitarianism. It also foreshadows Kant's doctrines of the limits of human reason. The idea of limits of human reason is to be interpreted morally as the primacy of practical reason, a possession of all men and not just of the enlightened few.

From the concept of the limits of human reason—fully developed only twenty years later—flows the philosophical justification for the other views Kant shared with Rousseau. First among these is the moral argument for the existence of God

---

13. *Anthropology*, II, E (Cassirer ed., VIII, 221; Academy ed., VII, 326).
14. Vorländer ed., VIII, 280.
15. *Ibid.*, p. 273. This revealing passage has been subjected to an exhaustive analysis from the existential standpoint by Gerhart Krüger, *Philosophie und Moral in der Kantischen Kritik* (Tübingen: Mohr, 1931), pp. 60 ff.

[7]

anticipated in *Émile*. In order to voice his protest against contemporary naturalism, Rousseau, lacking speculative power, had to fall back on personal faith. Kant, by formulating and defending a metaphysics that was both a priori and practical, developed Rousseau's insight into an indispensable part of his own more critical philosophy.

In the 1760's, when Kant was studying Hutcheson and Rousseau, he was working on what he intended to be his definitive treatise on ethics, which, with characteristic optimism in matters of authorship, he expected soon to finish. From the fragments that have come down to us we might reasonably suppose that it would apply the method of the *Inquiry*, searching out by analysis the hidden nature of man of which he speaks in the announcement of his lectures for 1765–66. We might expect that the projected work would emphasize the indemonstrability of the ultimate principles of ethics and would support them by arguments not unlike those found in Hutcheson and Rousseau. Or Kant might have developed a speculative metaphysics, also in the manner of the *Inquiry*, which would provide a context for the more empirical ethics.

But something unexpected happened. Kant read Hume, and, before he could go forward with his ethical works, ultimate questions had to be answered. The competence of reason had been radically questioned, and, before the mind could enjoy the luxury of metaphysics, or the security of rational certainty in science or of moral certainty in religion, reason's authority in experience and science's relation to the spirit had to be determined. Only upon a basis so secured would it be possible to found an ethics more than merely edifying. The result of this fundamental investigation was the *Critique of Pure Reason*.

THE ETHICAL IMPORT OF THE
CRITIQUE OF PURE REASON

The explicit task of Kant's first *Critique* was to answer the question—restated in more exact terms—which had occupied him in the *Inquiry* of 1764: "How are synthetic judgments a priori possible?" Since all rational knowledge consists of a priori synthetic judgments, failure to answer this question could not but affect every department of thought.

A synthetic judgment is one whose predicate is not contained in the concept of its subject. It *synthesizes* diverse elements into one proposition. For instance, "This table is of oak" is a synthetic judgment, while "This table is a piece of furniture" is analytic, because we find the predicate of the latter by merely analyzing the concept of table.

An a priori[16] judgment is one which applies to all possible experience of a relevant kind without being derived from any particular experience. If a judgment is derived from particular experiences, i.e., if it is a posteriori, we cannot know that it is universally and necessarily true. Now, since mathematics and natural science make statements which we accept as being universally true, their validity cannot be derived from experiences, however often repeated.

All this was well known to Kant's predecessors in the rationalistic school. But Kant discovered that the basic propositions in these fields of knowledge were both synthetic—going beyond the subject—and a priori—requiring no experience to amplify the concept of the subject. Before Kant, "a priori synthetic judgment" would have been considered a *contradictio in adjecto*. If a judgment was synthetic, experience seemed necessary to lead us beyond the concept of its subject. In order to find out what predicate not included actually qualifies it, the object denoted by the subject of the proposition would have to be given in perception. That is to say, a synthetic proposition would have to be an empirical, an a posteriori, proposition.

On the other hand, if a judgment was a priori, it was thought that it had to be analytic, for only by analysis of a given concept could a judgment be made which did not require experience. Thus the rationalistic philosophers who emphasized reason's faculty of reaching true conclusions without sense experience were forced to the conclusion that all final knowledge is analytic.

Kant, originally trained in the rationalistic philosophy of Wolff and himself an able practicing mathematician, only gradually perceived the inadequacies of this view. In the *Inquiry* of 1764 he saw the divergence between mathematical and metaphysical knowledge and made the first hesitant step toward coming to terms with empiricism. In the *Dissertation* of 1770 he discovered that mathematics—the paradigm of rationalistic certainty—was concerned only with appearances. This was a radical change of view which foreshadowed the further retrenchment of speculation in the *Critique of Pure Reason* eleven years later.

Probably it was only after Kant had begun what might be

---

16. "A priori" was originally used in formal logic to denote the evidence for a deduction, wherein the conclusion is known from prior grounds. A more critical account of Kant's concept is given below, pp. 21–22.

called his own "palace revolution" within rationalism that he came to know of Hume's work. Hume awoke him from his "dogmatic slumber"—Kant's term for his early faith in the power of reason to give metaphysical knowledge. Yet even if he had not accepted Hume's argument against the possibility of metaphysics, it is probable that Hume's strictures on natural science would have aroused him. For both rationalism and empiricism, if carried to the ultimate, deny the necessity and universality of natural science, and Kant's conviction of the certainty of Newtonian mechanics was too deep to be shaken by any negative conclusions drawn from speculations concerning the human mind. Kant asked *how* synthetic judgments a priori are possible, but *that* they are possible he never seems to have questioned. Instead, he revised the principles of both rationalism and empiricism in the light of a hard fact to which these two schools had not given due regard—the validity and certainty of the synthetic judgments of geometry and physics.

This revision Kant made in his well-known "Copernican Revolution." In a famous passage in the Preface to the second edition of the *Critique of Pure Reason*, Kant compares his new epistemology to the Copernican hypothesis. The predecessors of Copernicus had had difficulty in explaining the apparent motions of the planets on the supposition that they all revolved around the earth. Before Kant, it was similarly impossible in philosophy to explain how there could be a priori knowledge of things on the assumption that knowledge is passive conformity to the object. "Failing of satisfactory progress in explaining the movements of the heavenly bodies on the supposition that they all revolved round the spectator," Kant says, "he [Copernicus] tried whether he might not have better success if he made the spectator to revolve and the stars to remain at rest."[17] Similarly, if the phenomenal characteristics of objects are explained in terms of the behavior of the knowing mind, it is possible to see how

17. *Critique of Pure Reason,* trans. Norman Kemp Smith (2d ed.; London: Macmillan & Co., 1933), B, xvi. It has appeared to some that Kant's procedure could be more aptly compared to that of Ptolemy, since Kant placed the spectator in the center of the epistemological world. Kant, however, was interested in explaining what we may by analogy call the "apparent motions" of the object, and in doing this it is important, as Copernicus showed, to consider the real nature ("motion") of the spectator. Hence the Copernican Revolution itself implies the distinction between appearance and reality, just as Copernican astronomy distinguished real from apparent motion. See H. J. Paton, *Kant's Metaphysic of Experience* (New York: Macmillan Co., 1936), I, 75–76.

INTRODUCTION

knowledge of them can be a priori, for, as objects of knowledge, they must conform to the structure and activity of the knowing mind which make knowledge possible.

One advantage claimed for the rationalistic method lay in the fact that, whereas empiricism had to stop at the limits of sense experience, rationalism was perhaps even more fruitful beyond these boundaries. Under the influence of Hume's criticism of causation, Kant discovered that the rationalistic method accomplished too much: it not only proved theses which transcended possible experience; with equal cogency it proved their antitheses too. The discovery of these antinomies (i.e., conflicts of principles) was the true beginning of Kant's new philosophical development. The antinomies arise from the inadequacy of reason to meet its own demands on thought. Let us see how these antinomies result from the diversity of our cognitive faculties and what they imply concerning the limits of knowledge.

The mind has three cognitive faculties: sensibility, understanding, and reason. Sensibility supplies empirical content or sensation. Understanding links sensations into perceptions and these into objects of knowledge and series of objective events. Sensibility and understanding supply us with a constellation of phenomena under laws; the experience formed by them is empirical nature. Nature comprises series of phenomena in space and time, and these series can and indeed must be infinitely extendable, for every phenomenon has other phenomena as its conditions. There is, in sensibility and understanding and in the world of experience they underlie, no way to arrest this infinite regress of conditions. Reason, however, demands a totality of these conditions, for otherwise all is contingent. This demand cannot be met by a faculty which, like understanding, merely seeks out proximate causes, and proximate causes of proximate causes, and so on. Extending the phenomenal series infinitely (in the antitheses of the four antinomies) is met by the demonstration (in the theses) that the extension under the rules of understanding is inadequate to reason's needs; and, if reason is to reach satisfaction, it must speculate *beyond any possible experience* to find the unconditioned.

In this speculation, reason negates the restriction of the categories to the world of possible experience. A category and its schema are *constitutive* of nature, for nature is simply phenomena under the laws of understanding; but the object of speculation cannot be in time, and therefore the schemata of the categories do not apply to it. It cannot be in time, for then it would be conditioned in an infinite regress; but, as it is not in time, the categories cannot *constitute* it. In spite of this, the categories control our thought about it and are consequently in this function called *regulative ideas*. If the difference between the constitutive categories and the regulative ideas is overlooked, the antinomies cannot be resolved. The rationalistic philosophers had not drawn this distinction, and therefore their speculative metaphysics was ripe for the Kantian critique, which really commences with the demonstration of the antinomies.

While the Copernican Revolution alone might have strengthened Kant's predisposition toward rationalism, discovery of the antinomies showed this philosophy to be inadequate at its crucial point. The Copernican Revolution is a confession that the object is not the determining factor in knowledge; the natural dialectic of reason is proof that speculative theory is not the determining feature in metaphysics. If the object determined knowledge, a priori knowledge would be impossible, and scientific knowledge would be out of the question. If theoretical reason were the only faculty, a true and adequate metaphysics would be impossible, and the supersensuous world would be a mere extension of the world of appearances. And, if this were the true state of affairs, morality would be impossible. For morality, Kant argues, makes demands on men as free agents—demands at variance with the mechanistic world picture of science. It makes demands conflicting a fortiori with a supersensuous world conceived of as a mere extension of nature. The antinomies show that this extension is impossible, and for that reason Kant regarded them as the "most fortunate perplexity"[18] into which pure reason could ever fall.

The antinomies strictly limit theoretical reason to the world of space and time, nullifying all speculative flights from the results of science and all attempts to use scientific method in speculation beyond the limits of sense. But their resolution permits an altogether different use of reason. The occurrence of the antinomies is indicative of reason's broader competence as a faculty not exclusively devoted to cognition.

This is very clear in the third antinomy, the one most directly concerned with ethics. This antinomy arises from the conflict in the idea of causality and is resolved by the distinction between the world of appearances and that of things as they are in themselves. Kant made the discovery that the thesis, which asserts the reality of nonmechanical causes, and its antithesis, which asserts

18. See below, p. 212.

INTRODUCTION

the sufficiency of natural causality, may each be true if their respective scopes are sharply distinguished.

The field of application of each is defined by the nature of the argument supporting it, and neither can be validly employed beyond the area to which the respective proofs extend. The proof of the thesis presents the claim of reason, which requires a sufficient cause of every phenomenon. This sufficient cause cannot be found within phenomena, because a phenomenal cause is the effect of prior events and hence not by itself a sufficient explanation of subsequent phenomena. The proof of the antithesis, on the other hand, represents the interest of the understanding in applying the law of causality to a series of events in time. The argument shows that the assumption of a free cause among phenomena would interrupt the continuity required by natural law. There is no contradiction, however, when the thesis is applied to the relationship between noumena (things-in-themselves) and phenomena (appearances) and the antithesis to relations among phenomena. These separate and distinct but compatible applications are all that is legitimized by these two proofs.

The solution to the third antinomy, therefore, is achieved through a distinction between the world of appearance and the world of supersensuous reality. *This dualism is the necessary presupposition of Kant's ethical theory.* Without it, science would be the only occupation of reason. With it, science is limited in two respects: a boundary is fixed beyond which scientific knowledge cannot aspire and the possibility is established that natural law may not be the only form of causality.

First, by rejecting the presumptions of theoretical reason to a scientific metaphysics, a practical extension of pure reason is made possible. "I have therefore found it necessary," Kant says, "to deny *knowledge,* in order to make room for *faith.* The dogmatism of metaphysics ... is the source of all that unbelief, always very dogmatic, which wars against morality."[19]

The limitation he places upon theory may be taken negatively or affirmatively, with respect to what it forbids or what it permits. Negatively, it means that reason is incapable of knowledge of God, freedom, and immortality. Regarded in isolation, this stricture has been the occasion of positivistic and fictionalistic interpretations of Kant—the belief that reason's true vocation is found in knowledge and that whatever is assumed in the light of

19. *Critique of Pure Reason,* B, xxx (Smith trans.).

practical demands is fictional and subjective. Yet such interpretations are in complete discord both with the general character of Kant's philosophy and with his personality as a man of deep faith.

In his ethical and religious works, however, the affirmative interpretation—the emphasis on "making room for faith" instead of on "denying knowledge"—is of more central importance. Morality, even in the *Critique of Pure Reason,* is a given fact whose necessity and universality require legitimation just as the apriority of science does. The denial of the possibility of knowledge is not a reluctant admission of reason's impotence but an expression of the moral injunction that we *ought not* to know.[20] Knowledge of the intelligible world would destroy the possibility of free actions and of the faith that moral demands can be met. Thus instead of providing us in a "stepmotherly fashion with a faculty needed for our end," "inscrutable wisdom is not less worthy of veneration in respect to what it denies us than in what it has granted to us," for only through our theoretical ignorance of our destiny is there proper scope for our practical faith.[21]

The second way in which science is limited is by defending a causality not under natural law. The resolution of the antinomy of causality is necessary for Kant's ethics, for the antithesis, which implies the impossibility of morality, is the inevitable consequence to which theoretical understanding, unrestrained by criticism, leads us. Indeed, Kant says that, if the antinomy could not be resolved, it would be morality and not nature that we should have to surrender.[22] With the demonstration that natural causality is not the only thinkable kind of causality, Kant voided the chief argument against freedom; but this refutation is not by itself enough to establish freedom. The reality of freedom must be shown by indicating it as a necessary a priori condition of a type of experience. In this case the experience to be considered is morality with its universal and necessary injunctions. Morality must be defended against subversive empiricism in the same way mathematics and physics were defended.

This mode of arguing for freedom as the *ratio essendi* of morality is in its turn a Copernican Revolution in ethics. There is a perfect parallelism between the mode of argument and the conclusions in the theoretical and practical phases of Kant's philoso-

20. See Richard Kroner, *Kants Weltanschauung* (Tübingen: Mohr, 1914), p. 20.
21. See below, pp. 247–49.
22. *Critique of Pure Reason,* B xxix, A537–B565.

INTRODUCTION

phy. In both, reason appears as the lawgiver and as bound by the laws which it gives. Kant clearly compares these two legislative functions: "The legislation of human reason (philosophy) has two objects, nature and freedom, and therefore contains not only the law of nature, but also the moral law, presenting them at first in two distinct systems, but ultimately in one single philosophical system. The philosophy of nature deals with all *that is*, the philosophy of morals with that which *ought to be*."[23]

Apriority of knowledge can be maintained only by rooting it in understanding; apriority of duty can be preserved only by basing it on an equally pure, but acting, reason. Just as empiricism in epistemology destroys certainty, so empiricism in morality destroys its obligatory character. Any ethics deriving from the idea of the good as happiness dislodges the person from his autonomous position as legislator and destroys both the dignity of the agent and the necessity inherent in moral law.

Hence, in order to justify the phenomenon of moral necessitation, moral will must be identified with pure but practical reason. This pure reason is the same reason that was discovered in the *Critique of Pure Reason*, but it is here acting in a different capacity. It is no longer theoretical, no longer loses itself in transcendent speculation. Only in action can it be adequately manifested. The ideas of reason remain transcendent and problematical to thought, while in action they are concretely effective. Kant says that in the "ought" reason "frames to itself with perfect spontaneity an order of its own according to ideas."[24] Caird has succinctly stated the continuity and difference between the two functions of reason: "Just because reason cannot find its ideal realized in the world, it seeks to realize that ideal for itself."[25]

Not only does the first *Critique* thus erect the framework in which all Kant's subsequent thought naturally fits, but there are several clear indications in it of the specific ethical theses developed later. In 1781 Kant had already passed beyond the moral doctrines of the precritical period, though this transition was a gradual evolution rather than a radical change. The following specific ethical doctrines are anticipated in the first *Critique*:

23. *Ibid.*, A840–B868 (Smith trans.).
24. *Ibid.*, A548–B576 (Smith trans.). See below, p. 158.
25. Edward Caird, *The Critical Philosophy of Immanuel Kant* (New York: Macmillan Co., 1889), II, 164. Kant asserts this continuity throughout the second *Critique*. Note especially his statement that all interest, even that of theoretical reason, is ultimately practical (below, p. 225).

1. Moral laws are principles of the possibility of experience, the imperatives being objective laws of freedom.[26]
2. The laws of morality are not empirical and prudential, i.e., they do not show how happiness is obtained, but they contain the a priori conditions of worthiness to be happy. This worthiness, unlike happiness itself, necessarily constitutes a system, a *"corpus mysticum* of the rational beings in it [the world]."[27]
3. The highest good, defined as the proper proportion between happiness and virtue, gives practical confirmation to other ideas that were only problematical to speculative reason, viz., the existence of God and the immortality of the soul. The way in which immortality is postulated in the first *Critique* should be particularly noted: happiness and virtue do not correspond in this life, though reason demands that they should; hence there must be another life. In the second *Critique*, however, the argument is more strictly moral: we are required by moral law to be perfect, and, as this is impossible for a finite sensuous being, a continuation of moral progress *in infinitum* is postulated—a consequence of Kant's view that an obligation is invalid unless it can be fulfilled.[28]

APPROACH TO THE *CRITIQUE OF PRACTICAL REASON*

Kant's chief works on ethics—the *Foundations of the Metaphysics of Morals* and the *Critique of Practical Reason*—may almost be said to be afterthoughts. The *Critique of Pure Reason*, as first planned in 1772 and published nine years later, was designed to lay the foundation of philosophy in its entirety—for a metaphysics of nature as well as for a metaphysics of morals. But, instead of following the order of development as foreshadowed in the first *Critique*, Kant first wrote a *Foundations of the Metaphysics of Morals* (1785), and then, as though the work of laying foundations were still unfinished, a *Critique of Practical Reason* (1788) followed. This duplication or triplication is all the more surprising as Kant, while developing the concept of practical

---

26. *Critique of Pure Reason*, A802–B830, A807–B835.
27. *Ibid.*, A808–B836.
28. In this change, Kant has anticipated the objection often made that happiness, being a state in which all desires are satisfied, is conceivable only for a sensuous being and hence is incompatible with the idea of immortality. The moral argument for the existence of God undergoes an analogous refinement in the *Opus postumum*. See below, p. 48.

INTRODUCTION

reason in the *Foundations*, denied the necessity of a critique of practical reason. In 1797 the *Metaphysics of Morals*—the book that might have been expected to follow on the heels of the *Critique of Pure Reason*—at last appeared. But this final work turned out to be less significant than its predecessors.

These changes in Kant's plans require some explanation. The most obvious change in thought occurs between the first *Critique* and the *Foundations*. In the former, ethics is not a part of transcendental philosophy; in spite of its a priori form, it must have reference to particular empirical conditions in man which we cannot suppose to be universal and necessary characteristics of rational beings generally. These conditions are feelings of pleasure and pain and desire. It was to be the task of the *Metaphysics of Morals* to take the a priori forms enunciated in the *Critique* and apply them to the empirical nature of man, just as the *Metaphysical Foundations of Natural Sciences* did this for nature in general. The *Foundations*, however, begins from quite a different point of view: a metaphysics of ethics is developed wholly a priori. Later, the applicability of this metaphysics to man is proved in the *Critique of Practical Reason*. Here Kant asks how pure reason can be practical.

The *Foundations* follows the analytic method outlined by Kant in the *Inquiry*. It reproduces the natural order of thought by beginning with a phenomenon that requires explanation, whereas the *Critiques* begin with principles and "elements" and only subsequently arrive at the experiences to be explained.

Why was the second *Critique* written? The most obvious reason is that Kant wished to answer various critics of his ethical theory as previously expounded. Since Kant was not given to petty polemics, a reply to each critic on each point did not appeal to him. The objections indicated that his work had not been understood; the *Critique of Practical Reason* may be considered as Kant's new attempt to explain his ethics from the ground up. This is borne out by evidence that the work we now know as the *Critique of Practical Reason* grew out of the revisions Kant projected for, but did not include in, the second edition of the *Critique of Pure Reason*.

But of more importance than any answers to criticism are the problems which, in Kant's own opinion, must have needed more explanation and development than they had previously received. These may be listed as follows:

1. The phenomenon of morality and the necessity expressed

by the imperative are simply accepted in the first *Critique* as facts. The full seriousness of this acceptance is not evident until we reach the somewhat exhortatory tone of the *Foundations*.

2. How man as a member of the world of sense can take an interest in morality, i.e., how the moral law can be effective, is hardly discussed at all in the first *Critique*, though a framework for an answer to such a question was provided. Therefore, the *Critique of Practical Reason* asks explicitly: How can pure reason be practical? This was regarded as an empirical question in the first *Critique*, but the *Foundations* showed how it could be treated as a transcendental question. It required an answer before the *Metaphysics of Morals* with its encyclopedic delineation of human duties could be written.

3. While the conflict of theoretical and practical claims is solved—in principle, at least—in the *Critique of Pure Reason* and presupposed in the *Foundations*, the essay *What Is Orientation in Thinking?* and the second *Critique* provide the definitive exposition of the doctrine of the primacy of practical reason over theoretical reason. The problem of the identity of reason in its dual employment, explicitly excluded from discussion in the *Foundations*,[29] is of central importance in the *Critique of Practical Reason*.

4. The doctrine of immortality, inadequately developed and defended in the first *Critique*, undergoes a thorough revision in the second.

These various points must be examined in the light of the whole system of which they are integral parts.

THE PHENOMENON OF MORALITY

The use of the transcendental method characterizes all phases of Kant's work. He begins like a scientist examining an object or an experience. He notes what aspects are explicable in terms of what is given and sets out to find a reason for those aspects not adequately explained in these terms. That is, he makes a regress upon the conditions of the datum, requiring that the conditions explain adequately the peculiarities of the conditioned. In the first *Critique* he investigates the contents of the sciences and finds that their a posteriori material and their a priori form require quite different modes of derivation and explanation. And in turn the a priori conditions, which cannot be empirically

---

29. See below, p. 54.

INTRODUCTION

given, require a justification (a "deduction") to show that they actually serve as conditions of this experience. Through this dialectical development, the original experience becomes clarified, the a priori form becomes more explicit and highly articulated, and the whole experience grows richer in implications. The *Critique of Practical Reason* does not reveal this method as clearly as the *Foundations of the Metaphysics of Morals*. The former begins with definitions and theorems, and seems, at first, to "deduce" morality in the ordinary sense of deduction—i.e., to derive it from something more universal. But, farther on, the reader comes upon Kant's repeated assertions that we cannot answer the question as to why man should be moral. This shows that the deduction actually goes in the other direction, from the phenomenon to the transcendental conditions which underlie it. Though the moral phenomenon, "chill duty," may be, as Hegel says, "the revelation given to reason," it is not "the final undigested lump left in the stomach"[30] but rather the starting-point of the investigation.

For this reason Kant places a high value on the ordinary moral convictions of mankind. Though innocence may be misled, in moral matters it is a useful guide. Duty, being obligatory upon men, cannot lie beyond their comprehension. Thus Kant takes his departure from the ordinary practical knowledge of morality. Philosophy is to elucidate moral common sense and to strengthen it by distinguishing its essential from its accidental features.

"Concerning the ruling ideas in the practical part of Kant's system," said Schiller, "only philosophers disagree, but men have always been unanimous."[31] These ideas, summarized in the first section of the *Foundations*, are basic to Christian ethics, especially to Pietism.

---

30. *Lectures on the History of Philosophy*, trans. E. S. Haldane and F. H. Simpson (3 vols.; London, 1892–96), III, 461. There is Kantian authority for this Hegelian judgment. When Kant says that deduction of the categorical imperative is impossible, he is thinking of an ideal that he did not reach even in the first *Critique*; in both *Critiques* deduction is the exhibition of a formal supreme principle as underlying an actual experience. Messer, in pointing out this fact, remarks that while Kant is usually criticized for forcing a parallelism on the arguments of the two *Critiques*, here is an actual parallel that he ignores or denies (August Messer, *Kants Ethik: Eine Einführung in ihre Hauptprobleme und Beiträge zu deren Lösung* [Leipzig: Veit, 1904], p. 109).
31. Quoted in Kroner, *op. cit.*, p. 17. See below, pp. 147, 252.

[19]

In this section Kant gives an unusually concise anatomy of morality. A moral action, he asserts, is one done solely from duty, not for any specific purpose. This is the most remarkable and also the most debatable of his basic ideas. Benevolent actions are enjoined by Christianity, and they were made the basis of those British ethical systems which remained closest to common sense. Why, then, does Kant deny moral value to actions motivated by a feeling of altruism, animated as they are by a worthy motive?

Although benevolent actions are obligatory, their moral value lies in submitting to the obligation, not in actually achieving the end.[32] If the end of the benevolent action were the root of the obligation, failure to achieve it would nullify the morality of the action regardless of the intention. The English philosophers remained close to common sense in not actually drawing this conclusion. Kantianism drew the conclusions latent at this point in their philosophy.

Kant's conception of the nature of man would not permit him to derive man's obligation from anything in the world of sense. By doing so, he would surrender the apriority of duty. The a priori character of morality, however, is not just an implication of Kant's system, and, in insisting upon it, he is not a mere stickler for principles. Rather, the moral a priori indicates a fact largely overlooked by the ancient writers and explained away by Kant's forerunners, viz., obligatoriness constitutes the essence of morality. To explain this hard fact of moral obligation, Kant requires a Copernican Revolution in ethics. This revolution re-

---

32. See below, pp. 145, 222. An alternative to the dichotomy between actions for ends and actions from specifically moral motives has often been suggested in recent British ethics. This concept of prima facie duties has been proposed as a way out of a peculiar problem in Kant's ethics: since a certain motive involving a specific attitude toward obligation constitutes the necessary condition of morality, we cannot have an obligation to be moral, for that would be an obligation to have an obligation, and so on *in infinitum*. Moreover, the *feeling* that we have an obligation is not a feeling that can be commanded. Kant's answer to this problem is more abstract than that of his British critics, since he makes the phenomenon of constraint in general the basis of specific duties, while they begin with intuitions of particular duties. But, in finding distinct sources for the goodness and rightness of an action, their assumption of the quality of goodness is not unlike Kant's own, and their ascription of rightness is not immune to Kant's criticism of teleological theories. There is a brief, but excellent, comparison of Kant with his British critics in H. J. Paton's *The Categorical Imperative: A Study in Kant's Moral Philosophy* (Chicago: University of Chicago Press, 1948), pp. 110–12.

sults in the doctrine of moral autonomy—man gives the law to himself. He can do so because he exists as sovereign in the intelligible world, and, even while a subject in the world of sense, he may respect both himself and his fellow-men as pure noumena, pure rational beings. This constraint of self by self is obligation; subjectively, it is respect for the law.

Action from respect for law is the key to the universality and necessity of moral precepts, which would be variable and contingent if they depended upon particular ends, however general they might be. Universality and necessity are the marks of apriority. And just as necessity which would bind thought could come only from the mind itself, so the moral law which is a priori must be dictated by the reason which is to fulfil it. Otherwise this reason would not be free and would have to be encouraged to obedience by incentives of reward and punishment.

Reason, unaffected by individual differences, gives only the universal form, not the particular material. From the analysis of the apriority of duty follow both the formula of morality and the chief characteristic of Kant's system: *it is subjective a priori formalism*. This characterization of his ethics has often been taken lightly, as if by itself it constituted a sufficient criticism of his system. When properly interpreted, it is its truth and strength.

At this point it is well to see what is *not* involved in the concept of the formal a priori character of duty. First, that which is a priori is not prior in time. The moral law is not inborn, nor is it given by outer fiat. On the other hand, it is found not by induction from experience but by a critical analysis of the conditions of experience, commencing from what is implicit in any moral experience. Moral education is a process of developing the child's mind toward perceiving the essential features of morality. Though Kant's ethics claims universal validity, the fact that there is no universal agreement on ethical principles constitutes no objection to his theory. Ethical universality does not entail anthropological uniformity.

Second, though all experience must conform to the a priori, no experience is adequate to its universality. Because of this, Kant can disapprove of the appeal to examples for ethical theory and yet use them in ethical training.

Third, the a priori is not a supreme principle from which deductions can be made as if it were a mathematical axiom. In the *Inquiry* Kant defined the true function of formal principles. He says: "Just as nothing follows from the primary formal principles of our judgments of truth except when primary material grounds are given, so also no particular definite obligation follows from these two [formal] rules except when indemonstrable material principles of practical knowledge are connected with them."[33] It has always been objected that the categorical imperative gives no specific moral guidance. Hegel's objection, for instance, is that only when an institution (say, property) is universalized can the categorical imperative indicate a condition which a moral action must meet. Yet the function of a formula is not to supply the variables but to provide the procedure toward a solution; it is the necessary but not sufficient condition for a given solution.[34]

But should not the condition defined by the formula be the sufficient condition, assuming that moral action is action done only from respect for law? This is a difficult question, to which Kant gives no univocal answer. Yet, I think, the objection that a formal principle cannot have particular material consequences may be answered in perfect harmony with Kant's ethics as a whole. He denies that the moral law could be derived from some one final goal of life, such as happiness.[35] In questions of morality we should simply give no regard to particular motives of happiness, though they may be occasions of the moral problem. The

---

33. See below, pp. 283–84. Later, in the period of the *Dissertation* (1770), he wrote: "The supreme principles *diiudicationis moralis* are, it is true, rational, but they are only *principia formalia*. They do not determine any specific purpose, but merely the moral form of every purpose; therefore, *in concreto principia prima materialia* occur according to this form" (Fragment 6633, Academy ed., XIX, 120; quoted from Schilpp, *op. cit.*, pp. 105–6).

34. See below, p. 123 n. Broad defends Kant from such criticisms by suggesting that the categorical imperative might better be called the "supreme principle of categorical imperatives." It is, he says, a second-order principle which states the necessary and sufficient conditions to be fulfilled by any first-order principle qualifying as a categorical imperative. He compares it to one of the valid modes of the syllogism, not to a true major premise (C. D. Broad, *Five Types of Ethical Theory* [New York: Harcourt, Brace & Co., 1930], pp. 120–21, 123). If this view had been followed consistently by Kant, however, conflicts between duties could have been honestly admitted, and this he does not do in *On a Supposed Right To Lie from Altruistic Motives*. See also William David Ross, *Foundations of Ethics* (Oxford: Clarendon Press, 1939), pp. 173, 313.

35. *On the Saying, "That May Be True in Theory But It Does Not Hold in Practice,"* I (Cassirer ed., VI, 361; Academy ed., VIII, 279).

moral problem arises as a problem of the whole man; moral law is a formula, a procedure[36] for its solution.

Human beings are ends in themselves and fulfil their destiny by being worthy of happiness. But the moral law, Kant affirms, is the only factor which should be regarded in making a decision, though it is obvious that the problem to be solved by the agent is not posed by moral law alone but rather by the tension between law and natural inclinations. In excluding the ends of inclinations from moral legislation, moral law does not degrade morality to a mere mechanical routine of carrying out abstract rules. Rather, it indicates the way to achieve specifically moral goals, which must be defined a priori without reference to the contingencies of experience and man's partiality toward himself or others.

The formal element, implicit in ordinary morality, is separated and purified and then seen as the basis for widening the moral claims beyond the phenomenon in which they were discovered. Kant correctly compares[37] his procedure to that of the chemist who analyzes a complex mixture. With pure principles, as with pure substances, procedures which have heretofore been "empirical" can be made rational and comprehensible, and new relationships can be uncovered which are a priori conditions of a broader experience and permit a more penetrating insight.

So much, then, for the straightforward analysis to which Kant subjects the moral phenomenon. Since man is obligated by laws which flow from his own reason, the elucidation of these laws presents no great difficulty. The distinction between the hypothetical and categorical imperatives, and between legality and morality, and the gradual process by which the categorical imperative becomes more and more concrete until finally it is a definition of the unique ends of moral action, are clearly and systematically presented in the works translated in this volume.

Criticism of the foundations of Kant's ethics has not been lacking. In spite of the variety of arguments employed, they may be divided into two types—those that reject moral value as a sepa-

36. Schilpp, in his excellent analysis of Kant's early works, has especially developed the "procedural aspect" of formalism in which "rational reflection, creative construction, and transition [are] the only *method* capable of coping successfully with the exigencies of human experience and with the needs of moral obligation" (*op. cit.*, p. 173). That formalism has been quite differently interpreted, and that this interpretation has had serious historical consequences, is argued by F. S. C. Northrop, *The Meeting of East and West* (New York: Macmillan Co., 1946), pp. 201, 217, etc.

37. See below, pp. 198, 260.

rate species and those that accept moral value as irreducible yet localize it in a way incompatible with Kantianism.

The doctrines which deny the specificity and irreducibility of moral value—whether they arise in Marxian, Darwinian, theological, or utilitarian philosophies—use one or both of two tactics. They deny the phenomenon of obligation as anything more than a myth, fiction, or mistaken feeling; or they accept it as a prima facie fact to be justified on their own assumptions.

Against the first tactic, Kant did nothing and could do nothing except exhibit the phenomenon of morality and show that its interpretation as a natural fact (the theory advanced by his opponents) is incompatible with their own teleological theory of nature. He points out that, if moral injunctions were part of natural economy, nature would have done better by leaving decisions to instinct. On the other hand, if the conception of nature is not one based on design and if no supranatural source of morals is postulated, the phenomenon of morality becomes an illusion, to be explained in the light of a mechanistic natural science. Kant rejects this theory for the same reason that he rejected Hume's conclusion in science: it flies in the face of facts which should be explained, not explained away. For him, moral constraint is the starting-point, which cannot be justified except by its philosophical fruits—the intelligibility of the world revealed through its analysis. Just as Aristotle waited until moral character was formed before teaching the theory of morals to the young, so Kant presupposes the acceptance, in broad outlines, of a Christian-humanistic moral attitude and speaks only to those who share it.

The second tactic fails for the same reason that the various naturalistic explanations of the logical a priori failed in the nineteenth century. In each case a speculative cosmological system is made the foundation of rational necessity, and the results of science are made fundamental to the process by which they are discovered. This is a vicious epistemological circle. The a posteriori cart is placed before the a priori horse. One of Kant's greatest contributions was his demonstration of the inevitability of skepticism, once knowledge is regarded as a natural fact on the same level with its object. Similarly, moral relativism and skepticism must result from ethics which derives the concept of what ought to be from that of existence as it seems to be in the light of contemporary scientific knowledge. And this moral skepticism is equally self-refuting, because science has its moral foundations just as it has its rational presuppositions in the narrower sense of theoretical rationality.

The criticism to which we now turn is of greater philosophical interest. Accepting moral value as an irreducible and unique fact, the German phenomenologists, the British analytical moralists, and their many fellow-workers throughout the world renounce Kant's transcendental subjective formalism and yet seek to preserve the apriority of moral law or moral values discovered through some kind of intuition or immediate rational insight. To evaluate this criticism, we must first review Kant's own attitude toward the moral sense and then examine one of these counter-movements.

In the beginnings of modern European philosophy, Christian dualism had kept the senses in a secondary position in morals long after the importance of sense perception to scientific knowledge had been re-established. But it was inevitable that the increasing secularization and naturalization of thought should bring with it a reorientation to natural man. This change of outlook was associated with a rejection of the moral precepts involved in Christian dualism; in time of change it is not easy to separate the central elements from the peripheral ones in opposing views. The revolution, therefore, resulted not in a naturalistic ethics but in an amoralism, whose greatest exponent was Thomas Hobbes. After Hobbes a reaction came; the main trend of British ethics was to reconcile an ethics of natural man with Christian tradition.

Within the naturalistic framework, Shaftesbury, with his concept of "disinterestedness" of the senses, contrived an escape from amoralistic conclusions. Like Locke, he held that the senses are capable of reflecting upon themselves and thus of becoming free from domination by the object of desire to which they are normally directed. Shaftesbury says:

> In a creature capable of forming general notions of things, not only the outward beings which offer themselves to the sense, are the objects of the affection; but the very actions themselves, and the affections of pity, kindness, gratitude, and their contraries, being brought into the mind by reflection, become objects. So that by means of this reflected sense, there arises another kind of affection toward those very affections themselves, which have already been felt, and are now become the subject of a new liking or dislike.[38]

38. *Inquiry concerning Virtue* in L. A. Selby Bigge, *The British Moralists* (Oxford: Clarendon Press, 1897), I, 11. (I have modernized the spelling here and in the following passage.)

Hutcheson, developing Shaftesbury's idea, held that something absolutely good is apprehended in actions. This good, in his philosophy, is benevolence, or that which tends to promote "public natural happiness." The perception of moral excellence is different from perception of an object of desire, and thus the sense for natural good is distinct from that for moral good.[39] It is not itself the incentive to moral action (this being benevolence) but the source of approbation or disapproval: "This moral sense, either of our own actions, or of those of others, has this in common with our other senses, that however our desire of virtue may be counterbalanced by interest, our sentiment or perception of its beauty cannot; as it certainly might be, if the only ground of our approbation were views of advantage."[40]

In his precritical period Kant seems to have inclined toward such a view in his *Observations on the Feeling of the Sublime and the Beautiful,* which is composed in the manner of Shaftesbury. Kant speaks, in the *Distinctness of the Fundamental Principles of Natural Theology and Morals*,[41] of "sensations of the good" and of feeling as the "faculty of sensing the good." Nevertheless, in his critical writings, he completely rejects the concept of moral sense, though he attempts to reconstruct the concept of moral feeling.[42] It is easy to see why his critical system demands this rejection. The mind is receptive rather than spontaneous in assimilating sensory material, and any knowledge resulting from receptivity is a posteriori. Hence the theory of moral sense would vitiate the autonomy of reason and destroy the apriority of morals.

With the modern phenomenological approach, however, the old issue has been reopened on a level not anticipated by Kant. The phenomenologists claim for intuition what is specifically denied to it by Kant—an a priori insight into content (material) and not merely formal conditions. Phenomenology thus represents a Counter-Copernican Revolution in philosophy, locating the a priori in the essential relationships between experiential objects grasped through immediate insight. At the same time the a priori ceases to be a manifestation of a transcendental subject; it is the basic structure of any possible object of experience.

39. Concerning Moral Good and Evil, ibid., pp. 78, 159.
40. Ibid., p. 78.
41. See below, p. 284.
42. *Metaphysics of Morals,* Part II, Introduction, V, XII. See below, pp. 184, 221.

INTRODUCTION

This powerful method[43] offers a new alternative to Kant's formalism. Hartmann agrees that if Kant's disjunction between "nature" and "reason" is exhaustive, then Kant's formalism must be accepted as the only alternative to an a posteriori naturalism. But he and other phenomenologists deny the exhaustiveness of this disjunction, asserting that there is a realm of values into which we have an a priori insight. On this foundation, it is claimed, an ethics which is both material and a priori can be erected.

It is profitless to argue, outside of a general treatise on metaphysics, concerning the relative merits of two such radically different approaches to philosophy. Nor is it possible to borrow a little from Kant and a little from Scheler and Hartmann to piece out an eclectic system—a method repeatedly repudiated by Kant with impatience and irony. Nevertheless, in some respects, especially in ethics, these two approaches are complementary; and, while it is out of the question to make a system of them, it is important to notice how they supplement each other.

The Kantian ethics is weak in two respects. First, the manner in which moral concern comes into experience is never satisfactorily examined. Kant often speaks of the "fact" of obligation, and he calls the moral law the "sole fact of pure reason." Yet the sense in which it is a "fact" is never made clear; it is the starting-point, but the analysis of it leads away from its factuality. Second, "monotony" arises in the Kantian ethics from the attempt to discover everywhere the same basic pattern in all actions having moral worth. Naturally, every ethical theory must seek the highest common factor, but in Kant's writing the road back to the rich and variegated complexity of the moral phenomenon is seldom followed. The store of ethical phenomenology found in the *Observations on the Feeling of the Sublime and the Beautiful* was never put to use in Kant's mature philosophy.

On the other hand, it is precisely the factuality and empirical variety of the moral phenomenon which have attracted the closest attention of Scheler, Hartmann, Ross, and others who are

---

43. Any of the standard treatises on phenomenology should be consulted on these fundamental conceptions, e.g., Marvin Farber, *The Foundations of Phenomenology* (Cambridge: Harvard University Press, 1943). The account given here is based principally on Max Scheler's *Der Formalismus in der Ethik und die materiale Wertethik* (Halle: Niemeyer, 1916), I, 47 ff., and Nicolai Hartmann's *Ethics*, trans. Stanton Coit (New York: Macmillan Co., 1932), Vol. I, chaps. xi, xii, xiii.

phenomenological or "analytic" in their approach. Though their picture lacks the logical and metaphysical simplicity of the Kantian, it is much more subtle in its portrayal of the facts of the moral life. For this richness it must pay by an occasionally uncritical assumption of faculties and principles.[44]

Finally, phenomenology, with all its emphasis on the a priori, is unable to give as convincing an account as Kant does of the necessity inherent in moral imperatives. Kant states that an ethics beginning from the good necessarily leads to heteronomy and to hypothetical imperatives. To attribute to the object (the good) a character of "obligatoriness" in its relation to human action, as some phenomenologists do, is to make use of an *ad hoc* hypothesis which may well be discarded without making the phenomenon unintelligible. On the other hand, the Kantian conception of the relation of the good to obligation is simple, clear, and cogent. The *logique du cœur* of the phenomenologists seems to be a poor foundation for imperious duty exalted by Kant.

HUMAN NATURE AND FREEDOM

Kant repeatedly refers to his theory of morality as the "ethics of intention," and moral personality is everywhere the center of his thought. Only the good will is good; every rational being is an end in itself; humanity in man must be treated as an end and never as a means only; and our own moral perfection and the happiness of others are ends which are also duties. Kant's theory, however, legitimizes the moral command for rational beings in general. Morality cannot be derived from the empirical nature of man, nor should it be applied to man alone. It lies in the essence of rationality itself and applies to all rational beings.

Man, however, is not merely a rational being; and his peculiar position in the world, as a rational being affected by sensuous needs, creates special problems for him. It requires special efforts on Kant's part to show how man as a citizen of the sensuous world can fulfil his destiny in the intelligible world. The problem of *human* morals is thus resolvable into two questions: How can man be a member of the intelligible world? How can the demands made upon his intelligible nature be met in the world of

---

44. Although the following story may be apocryphal, it represents an impatience which is often created in a reader by the elaboration and overelaboration of entities in phenomenology. It is said that, when Scheler first read Hartmann's *Ethik,* he exclaimed, "My colleague Hartmann believes he can take a stroll through the realm of values as though it were Cologne!"

sense? The first is the problem of freedom; the second, that of the empirical character which is obligated to act morally.

The moral law is the "sole fact of pure reason."[45] But freedom is the "*ratio essendi* of morality" and "the keystone of the whole structure of pure reason."[46] It is the central problem of Kant's entire work and, as such, appears in various perspectives and at various strata within his philosophy.

There is, first of all, freedom of choice, which in one place[47] is said to be independent of transcendental freedom, the truly metaphysical concept springing from the third antinomy. Then there is the metaphysical concept itself, fully developed by means of the distinction between phenomena and noumena. This metaphysical concept of freedom is worked out problematically in the theoretical phases of the system and is asserted practically in the great ethical treatises. Finally, there is the concept of freedom which results from the faculty of judgment as the mediator between the worlds of appearance and reality. This is the latest of the three, elaborated in full in the *Critique of Judgment*.

Freedom on the first level is empirically given. It is freedom from the immediate importunities of sense. Kant is correct in saying that its reality is independent of the answer to the speculative problem of whether or not the will whose fredom is thus assured is ultimately a part of the mechanism of nature. He is not consistent, however, in his statement that this freedom is adequate to the requirements of morality as he expounds them in the remainder of his work. Nevertheless, this rudimentary concept of freedom helps us understand how the empirical personality can act morally.

Wholly within the realm of appearance, then, there is in man a faculty which can be called empirically free—the faculty of

---

45. See below, pp. 143, 157. The difference between the two passages cited ("*Faktum*," "*gleichsam ein Faktum*") is of interest. The former passage states that it is not an empirical fact, and the latter hesitates to call it a fact at all. In modern terminology Kant might call it a construct in both passages. Alfred Hegler (*Die Psychologie in Kants Ethik* [Freiburg i.B.: Mohr, 1891], p. 92) writes that the moral law is *Faktum* "because it shows itself as real in maxims determined by it, and constitutes an ultimate possession of consciousness not reducible to any other," and that it is *gleichsam ein Faktum* "because it is not a single empirical datum (*Thatsache*) in consciousness, like some presentation or volition; it is not an empirical fact, but the sole fact of pure reason."

46. See below, p. 118.

47. *Critique of Pure Reason*, A803–B831.

choice.[48] Choice "is the faculty of desire so far as it is connected with the consciousness of the competence of its action to produce its object."[49] It is free to the extent that choice is determined by reason (considered simply as the highest faculty of the mind which in its turn is a part of nature) and is contrasted with the animal will (*arbitrium brutum*), which is exercised without this control.[50] Choice can thus be considered, within the one world of nature, to be both free and necessitated.[51]

Such freedom, however, is of "limited liability." It is not capable of freeing man from all his yesterdays. Because it leaves man finally a part of nature, it does not justify us in imputing a man's actions to him as if he, and not nature, where the author of his works. It is freedom only in the legal sense. Freedom, Kant says elsewhere, cannot be understood psychologically; it is the stumbling block of all empiricism and cannot be salvaged if time is the mode of existence of things-in-themselves. Empirically, it is at most a partial manifestation of true freedom.

Freedom of choice with respect to human actions as phenomenon consists in the capacity of choosing between two opposing things, the lawful and the unlawful. Herein man regards himself as phenomenon, but as noumenon he himself is theoretically and practically legislative for objects of choice. In this respect he is free, but he has no choice.[52]

These two concepts—choice without true freedom and freedom which is conformity with the law prescribed by reason—are contrasted as the negative and positive concepts of freedom.[53] The former is freedom *from* something; it is arbitrary and lawless in itself, for reason as its determining ground is as yet undefined. Reason might conceivably be merely the name of a transcendent thought-process directed ultimately to the satisfaction of the senses which are unable to command the faculty of choice

48. *Willkür*. In Kant this word does not have the implication of willfulness that it possesses in modern German, where it implies some degree of arbitrariness and irresponsibility. Abbott translates it as "elective will," which conveys the meaning very well but has the disadvantage of rendering a common everyday German word by a technical philosophical term.
49. *Metaphysics of Morals*, Part I: "Introduction to the Metaphysics of Morals," I (Cassirer ed., VII, 13; Academy ed., VI, 213).
50. *Critique of Pure Reason*, A534–B562.
51. *Lose Blätter* (Reicke ed.), II, 28.
52. *Ibid.*, pp. 139–40. See below, p. 158.
53. *Metaphysics of Morals*, Part I: "Introduction to the Metaphysics of Morals," I. See below, pp. 102, 158.

INTRODUCTION

directly. But even though such a faculty of thought might transcend the ordinary laws of psychology, so long as its goals were in nature it would be restricted by man's empirical character as a being of wants and needs. Hence to be free from the senses in an unqualified way requires something more than the possibility of enlightened choice between alternatives. A determining ground of choice is required which will legislate for it directly, not indirectly through its objects. This determining ground must be independent of the entire world of sense. Only then can freedom *from* the world of sense become freedom *to* something else positively defined. If we could see freedom as an efficient cause, Kant affirms, we could also see that the practical law (reason's legislation) is the supreme law for choice, for it is the efficient cause issuing from rational beings.[54]

But Kant does not make the transition from the negative to the positive concept of freedom in this way, since we cannot perceive the freedom of an efficient cause.[55] Rather, he seems to make a fresh start. This phase of the argument has two distinct parts—one which shows freedom, positively defined, to be possible, and one which shows it to be real. Taken together, they constitute the transcendental-practical doctrine of freedom universally associated with Kant's name.

The argument begins with the third antinomy, whose antithetical propositions, we remember, may both be true provided their respective scopes are defined. Thus nature as existing in time is determined under the category of causality. It is, however, possible to think (though we cannot know) noumena—things-in-themselves—which are not in time and are therefore independent of the law of nature. Hence, if man is not merely a phenomenon but also a noumenon, then he may be free as noumenon (in accordance with the thesis) without ceasing to be mechanically determined in his role as temporal phenomenon (as the antithesis asserts).

Evidence for this dual character, apart from its being sug-

54. See below, pp. 158, 169, 199.
55. In one place Kant writes as if we might make such a transition, though what he says will also bear a different interpretation. He says that the positive concept of freedom is "the capacity of pure reason to be practical of itself. This, however, is not possible except through the subjection of the maxims of any action to the condition of the worthiness of these maxims to serve as universal law" (*Metaphysics of Morals*, Part I: "Introduction to the Metaphysics of Morals," I [Cassirer ed., VII, 14; Academy ed., VI, 213]).

[31]

gested by the fact that we possess a priori knowledge and are thus free of the time order in knowing, is found in obligation. Obligation is characterized by subjective necessity, the objective counterpart of which is moral law. Neither obligation nor the law can be derived from experience, for experience establishes no necessity. The moral law requires man to act from a rational principle and not from an inclination to an object in the sensuous world, no matter how desirable. It therefore implies that man must be capable of actions free from any inclinations and determined only by reason. Thus his absolute spontaneity as a being outside of time and his membership in a completely determined temporal order are jointly guaranteed without any mutual interference.

These two human roles are distinguished as the rational and the empirical character or as will in contrast to choice. "Will is the faculty of desire not with respect to action (as in the case of choice) but with respect to the determining ground of choice to an action. Of itself it has really no determining ground. It is practical reason itself so far as reason can determine choice."[56] To the extent that reason is autonomous (i.e., determines its own ends in a categorical imperative instead of being merely the guardian of the senses),[57] it constrains the empirical personality to respect and obey its law. This it does even though the law may be broken—indeed, may never have been truly fulfilled.

[Practical freedom] presupposes that although something has not happened, it *ought* to have happened, and that its cause, [as found] in the [field of] appearance, is not, therefore, so determining that it excludes a causality of our will—a causality which, independently of those natural causes, and even contrary to their force and influence, can produce something that is determined in the time-order in accordance with empirical laws, and which can therefore begin a series of events *entirely of itself*.[58]

Why man is free is a question as unanswerable as why he should be moral or why he is rational. How is man free, as a theoretical question, is likewise unanswerable. It is a speculative question, lying beyond the scope of theory. At most, speculative reason can answer the question negatively by showing how the contradiction between the causality of freedom and that of nature is only apparent. If the alleged contradiction could not

56. *Ibid.* 57. See below, p. 222.
58. *Critique of Pure Reason*, A534–B562 (Smith trans.).

be resolved, Kant confesses that freedom would have to be surrendered in favor of natural necessity. But just as the *Critique of Pure Reason* limited knowledge in order to make a place for faith, it limited temporal causality to give a place to causality of freedom, or—what is the same thing—it limited nature for the sake of morality. While we cannot show in any theoretical or empirical way *how* freedom is possible, we can prove *that* it is possible, and we can show how faith in freedom functions in our moral convictions and conduct. Man is in the world but not of it. This concept, tenuous as it is, is superior, even from a moral point of view, to those ancient and modern conceptions which leave man in the world as a natural being while exempting him from its laws.[59] For these speculative conceptions end with an indeterminism which is of no greater moral utility and comfort than mechanism itself.

Yet the theoretical questions insist upon an answer. We want an intellectual justification for faith. To be told that one ought to have done otherwise, when a satisfactory psychological investigation convinces us that one could not have been expected to do otherwise, seems often—as Kant admits—to "conflict with equity."[60] To have acted "otherwise"—i.e., spontaneously to have commenced a new causal series—is in conflict with the Analogy of Experience,[61] which treats the entire world of sense as a causal system. The initiation of a new series cannot be interpreted as an *influxus mysticus* without surrendering the category of causality. Kant says that, in a given case, reason could not otherwise determine action except by making the empirical character itself different,[62] and this in turn would require a change in the entire causal order so that sufficient empirical conditions could be found for its alternative state. Hence a causally integrated totality of appearances would require a completely integrated noumenal order which, in the case in point, would have had to be different from what it actually is. If these two orders are independent of each other, it is impossible to see how the manifestation of the rational character could be considered a spontaneous initiation of a causal chain within the empirical

---

59. In the ancient world Lucretius, and in the contemporary world those physicists who seek comfort in the Heisenberg principle, would give man a freedom he could not manage. Scientific unpredictability would not imply moral freedom so much as a hazardous irresponsibility.
60. See below, p. 205.
61. *Critique of Pure Reason*, A211–B256.   62. *Ibid.*, A556–B584.

world. The consequence seems to be Spinozism: nothing can be different from what it is.

The mere possibility of evil in a world which is supposed to be the appearance of the world of reason, the source of all morality, presents a difficult problem for the theory. The actuality of evil actions accentuates this difficulty. If we grant that the first two *Critiques* sufficiently justify the possibility of moral actions, they do not explain how actions which ought to be morally good can fail to be so. The existence of evil is incompatible with a pure will which is free but without choice. Evil cannot be regarded simply as phenomenal, for then it would not be imputable as *moral* evil.[63] It is rather a mistaken subordination of pure and empirical maxims in the empirical character, and the theory of freedom is still unable to justify the claim that one might have refrained from an evil action which actually was performed.

These and similar difficulties are unavoidable in the second phase of Kant's conception of freedom because the argument is still on a theoretical level. They are irresolvable for two reasons.

First, the concept of freedom at this level, though distinguishing between appearance and reality, does not adequately define their relationship. It leaves morality and science each claiming its own concept of causality, and these concepts are kept from open conflict only by a strict definition of areas of application. But when the two kinds of causality are applied to a specific moral action or character, their claims again inevitably conflict. Nevertheless, it is one reality in its several manifestations that we need to judge in order to bring peace and not just a truce to philosophy. Until the harshness of the distinction is tempered without loss to the positive results of the two *Critiques*, such contradictions will occur in every specific judgment. Though the first two *Critiques* established an "impassable chasm" between the two realms "as though they were so many different worlds," the law of freedom, Kant says, "ought to have an influence" on the world of sense.[64] The problems arising from the "two-world theory" can be solved only when the relationship between the two worlds is developed affirmatively.

Second, the claims of reason and those of understanding are

---

63. *Religion within the Limits of Reason Alone*, trans. Theodore M. Greene and Hoyt H. Hudson (Chicago: Open Court Publishing Co., 1934), p. 17.

64. *Critique of Judgment*, Introduction, II, IX (Cassirer ed., V, 244, 264).

at variance, yet each is sovereign in its own sphere. Neither is capable of extending its claims at the expense of the other. But, more significantly, neither is competent to apply its own principles directly to its object. These principles are without exception formal. The problems, however, are not formal but material, arising from the rival but justified claims of these two faculties to the phenomenon whose true estimation is in dispute. For the adjudication of these claims, a mediating faculty is required.

This faculty is judgment, and the third *Critique* presents the last and most profound treatment of freedom to be found in Kant's works. It is also the most difficult, because freedom itself is seldom the center of his attention. Rather, Kant turns primarily to consider a different, but related, problem—that of purpose.

The *Critique of Pure Reason* requires the formal unity of the a priori laws of nature, but it does not establish the idea of an equally inclusive system of individual objects. Nature, Kant says, constitutes a system by its transcendental laws, but "there is such an infinite multitude of empirical laws and so great a heterogeneity of the forms of nature ... that the concept of a system according to these empirical laws must be wholly alien to the understanding, and neither the possibility nor even less the necessity of such a whole can be conceived."[65] This concept of an empirical whole is nevertheless demanded as an ideal, as a regulative concept giving sense and direction to the search for interrelationships among the phenomena of nature. This interrelationship is provided by the faculty of judgment which subsumes particulars under given universals or finds universals that fit given particulars. In carrying out this function, judgment presupposes a "formal design" in nature, i.e., an all-pervasive, comprehensible order.

We are never excused from searching for a mechanical explanation of any single fact (including human actions), yet at the same time we cannot anticipate a "Newton of a blade of grass." The mechanistic theory does not lead us from the parts which it investigates to the whole of its organization. This limitation is particularly relevant to human actions, even though they are in principle, Kant says, as predictable as astronomical events.

The idea of formal design is of pre-eminent importance in the case of man, for man's character is purposive in the sense that all

65. *First Introduction to the Critique of Judgment*, II (Cassirer ed., V, 185).

parts are to be properly subordinated to the whole; moreover, man's moral conduct understood as conformity with his own internal law transcends mechanical causality, in which causes are external to the acting character.[66] For these reasons it is proper to judge man by the regulative idea of his design and purpose, which is moral, and we can do so without prejudice to a mechanistic explanation of nature.

Because both of these ideas, purposive design and mechanism, function methodologically without interfering with each other, we see how the ends of freedom may be thought of as possible within the system of nature. The existence of natural purposes in the world indicates the heuristic inadequacy of the category of mechanical causality. The existence of organisms does not prove conclusively that there is an over-all design in the world and that man is the purpose of creation. But it shows something very important about the constitution of the mind. The mind, we are made to see, because of the nature of its operations, must apply the causal concept and also supplement it with the concept of purpose.

In contrasting moral necessity as dictated by duty with factual necessity as determined by nature, we contrast action as something which ought to be done with action as simply occurring. But, says Kant, it is because of the constitution of the mind that moral law must be represented as a command, i.e., as pre-

66. William T. Jones, "Purpose, Nature, and the Moral Law," in *The Heritage of Kant* (Princeton: Princeton University Press, 1939), pp. 229-42, and *Morality and Freedom in the Philosophy of Immanuel Kant* (London: Oxford University Press, 1940), has emphasised this point. He denies the validity of the concept of noumenal causality and denies that the third *Critique* can bridge the gap between theory and practice by its attempted proof that the highest good is possible in nature. In fact, he goes further and says that this attempt is itself incompatible with the deepest insights of Kant's system concerning the true relation between morality and nature. He holds that the existence of the organism permits a constitutive use of the category of purpose (which is, of course, denied by Kant), and that it supplies an analogon by which we can see the supplementation to natural necessity required for the achievement of the highest moral end. Mr. Jones quite correctly sees in the organism not a natural purpose requiring a peculiarly transcendent cause but an objective analogon of morality itself. "The peculiar kind of order which distinguishes organisms from other natural objects," he says, "is identical with the order which, we find, connects motive and act in morally good action and which distinguishes it from all other action" (*The Heritage of Kant*, p. 240). Thus freedom (but not freedom of choice) is found in an order of being to which mechanistic explanation is simply irrelevant.

scribing what ought to be done whether it is actually done or not. The necessity of dutiful action cannot be represented as a mode of physical being, but only as an ought-to-be; but this would not be so if reason alone were legislative in the world of appearance. For then the world of appearance would be a perfect representation of reason's practical conception of reality. The idea of duty is a practical conception, an ideal which would then have as much power as it has "manifest authority." The conflict is not between two worlds but between two subjectively necessary modes of viewing the world. The mind is unable to think purposively and mechanically, or practically and theoretically, at the same time. But the characteristic of the finite human mind should not be attributed to its objects.[67]

Design, or organization, we seem to find everywhere in nature. It is the dependence of all the parts upon all the others and hence upon the whole. In an organism, as a natural organization, every part is both cause and effect of all the others. The understanding, however, because its procedure is discursive, is unable to make theoretical use of this concept of mutuality. Understanding arrives at universals through particulars, thus achieving an abstract universal from which the particulars cannot again be derived. Yet they seem, in the case of an organism, to be derived from the concrete universal which is the organized whole itself. The categories of the understanding cannot be formulated as rules for this kind of synthesis. We can comprehend the observed dependence of part upon whole not through a category of purpose or wholeness—as many biologically oriented writers on Kant have proposed—but only through a regulative idea, *by analogy with our own technique*. As technicians, we do combine parts into wholes and order means to ends in the light of a guiding idea, a concept of the whole. By analogy, we think of a *technique of nature*, as though nature worked for certain ends in the light of a guiding idea, i.e., as created or as creating with a design. But in nature it is not the whole as such which is the condition of the parts (for the parts are parts of physical nature and are under the condition of time and efficient causation). It is rather the *idea* of the whole which conditions their relationships as we see them. Purpose, however, is the concept of an object so far as the concept contains the ground of the reality of the object itself.[68] Hence the discursive nature of human understanding makes concrete constitutive in-

67. *Critique of Judgment*, §77.   68. *Ibid.*, Introduction, IV.

sight into the organization of nature impossible and compels us to interpret design, in a merely regulative manner, as a consequence of purpose. We have, thus, only an abstract insight into nature's structure, and our concrete insight into nature's relationships is always constituted by the category of causation in time.

But it is possible to think of another kind of understanding, one free from human limitations, an "intuitive understanding." Such an understanding would proceed from an intuition of the whole to its parts, thereby reversing the procedure of the human understanding, which can only construct a whole out of its parts. This superhuman understanding would, by directly intuiting wholes, see wholes as the efficient causes of parts. Our intuition presents us with conditioned wholes which, in the order of time and efficient causation, are the effects, not the causes, of their parts. We can think abstractly of an absolute and unconditioned whole, but we cannot intuit it. As our conception of it is abstract, we comprehend it only by an analogy, in which the *concept* of the whole is seen as the condition of the particular constellation of its parts. This is precisely what we mean by design or purpose. Therefore it lies in the nature of the human mind to think in teleological as well as in mechanical terms. The mechanical pattern, in which the category of causality has a schema in time, is constitutive of the world of experience, while the teleological procedure, without a temporal form, is regulative of our search for the order between various causal sequences.

Freedom, like purpose, is a regulative idea. It posits a design, and this design does not lie in the constitution of nature. As purpose is regulative of our theoretical judgment, so freedom is regulative of practice. Purpose and freedom are not constitutive, and the world of nature is not the world of morality. But just as the *Critique of Judgment* permits us to guide our thought by the idea of purpose, the *Critique of Practical Reason* states as the typic of the moral law the injunction: act as though the moral law could become a law of nature.

The faculty of ideas—pure reason—thus becomes practical. Morality and freedom are the positing of a regulative idea as an ideal to be achieved and the conduct of reason so as to achieve it. The regulative idea of the unconditioned condition which functions theoretically in the teleological judgment now becomes practical.

INTRODUCTION

That which is regulative always has direct relevance to the practical. All practical ideas are regulative not merely of thought but of conduct. It means little or nothing to demand that the practical be constitutive—man's reach should exceed his grasp.[69] For an intuitive understanding, design, purpose, and even freedom might be constitutive categories, and they would not in the least conflict with the demands of mechanism. For us, there is an antinomy between freedom and efficient causation when both are taken constitutively, and this conflict can be resolved by us only by considering freedom and design to be regulative. The conflict holds between our diverse procedures, not in reality.

The *Critique of Judgment*, while not breaking down the distinction between appearance and reality, thus points the way to a *de facto* justification of the judgment of freedom. Without making freedom a category of nature, this *Critique* explains how the realm of nature is conceivable as harmonious, or at least compatible, with the ends of freedom. But then there must be *a* purpose. The eighteenth-century optimists had little hesitation in seeing man and his welfare, considered eudemonistically, as this all-justifying end, for purpose was still, in principle, a constitutive concept of their cosmology. But Kant could not identify this purpose with man as a part of nature. A regulative teleology and a formal morality, however, stand together:

If things in the world, which are dependent in their existence, need a supreme cause acting toward ends, then man is the final end of creation; for without him the chain of graduated ends would not be perfectly grounded, and only in man (but in him only as subject to morality) is there unconditional legislation with respect to ends. This alone makes him capable of being a final end, to which all nature is teleologically subordinated.[70]

---

69. The answer to the question, "What ought I to do?" "consists of *one* presupposition and *one* inference. The presupposition: It must be proved (and the two *Critiques* do prove) that the unconditioned is not impossible, that there is some hope of its achievement and realization, small though it be. For no man could knowingly and without reserve throw himself into something conceded impossible and indeed apodictically impossible. The inference: If there is the slightest hope that the Absolute can ever be realized in the intelligible world, then so act as if the maxim of your action should become, by your will, a law of nature" (Lucien Goldmann, *Mensch, Gemeinschaft und Welt in der Philosophie Immanuel Kants* [Zürich and New York: Europa Verlag, 1945], pp. 173-74).

70. *Ibid.*, §84.

It is in the light of this consideration that "ends that are also duties," in the language of the *Metaphysics of Morals*, are comprehensible. They are the ends of free, and therefore moral, beings.

THE CHARACTER OF MAN

Man is considered in two roles in Kant's ethics—man as the moral ideal and man as an empirical character trying to achieve personality. Man in the first role is the archetype for man in the second role. Empirical man always has an obligation to respect personality in the former sense, to serve and promote it.

This introduces a definitely teleological element into Kant's otherwise formalistic ethics. Can this "moral purpose" be made consistent with Kant's assertions that moral actions are actions done without regard to ends to be achieved? An affirmative answer to this question is self-evident when it is realized that the idea of purpose is itself involved in the doctrine of autonomy.

We have seen in the preceding section that purpose and freedom are two aspects of a causality which is not mechanical. Rational nature exists as an end in itself, says Kant; any other end would be heteronomous. This end is not imposed upon the self by an alien universe but is the very nature of the self. This immanent teleology of moral obligation is expressed in an early fragment: "If there is any science man really needs, it is the one I teach: how he may properly fill the place assigned to him in creation. From it he may learn what he must be, in order to be a man."[71]

But how different from the ideal of man is actual man! Man is a creature of needs, the satisfaction of which gives pleasure. This pleasure is the only natural incentive to action. Consequently, all theories of human nature which place the driving force of conduct in the satisfaction of needs are ultimately forms of hedonism. Moreover, ethical theories based on them are heteronomous, since they view reason at most as a guide to the successful attainment of the ends of desire and not as active on its own account. Happiness as an ideal is the satisfaction of all desires. Though technical imperatives can be formulated for the achievement of pleasure arising from the satisfaction of an immediate need, happiness is a concept of such fluctuating content that no definite imperative can be derived from it.

71. *Fragmente aus dem Nachlasse* (Kirchmann ed.), p. 323.

INTRODUCTION

The moral law, however, lays down a rule without exceptions, giving commands instead of counsels. Before its majesty the senses are humiliated. This humiliation awakens respect for the law. Respect thus functions as moral feeling. It is the subjective aspect, not the cause, of morality. It is painful as an arrest of the natural inclination but akin to pleasure in presenting a moral goal which every man can achieve out of the inward resources of his rational nature, irrespective of his position in the world. The moral law, as a universal principle integrating the diverse forces in man's nature, is the basis of what is commonly called "character." The inner form of character is virtue, or "the moral disposition in conflict" with the wayward and chaotic inclinations. In building his character, man develops a genuine interest in his own perfection as a moral goal. This interest, combined with faith, gives strength and substance to character by awakening hope of the highest good in the world.

Such are the central features of Kant's account of human nature as presented in the works here translated and in the *Metaphysics of Morals*. Two criticisms of it are sufficiently important to require examination: that Kant's theory does not give sufficient scope to human emotions and is "false to human nature" and that Kant's supposition that all natural motivation is egoistic and hedonistic forces his own theory into an extreme and untenable position.

It is easy to dispose of the first criticism, once we decide what is meant by being "false to human nature." Kant expressed his impatience with criticism of what ought to be in the light of what is when he wrote his essay *On the Saying, "That May Be True in Theory But It Does Not Hold in Practice."* In ethics it is human nature itself which is on trial. When theory does not apply to practice, two courses are open: either we may do as the scientist often does and add to our theory those special conditions which will close the gap between abstract theoretical and concrete empirical propositions or we may force the fact, so far as it is under our control, to conform to the criterion we erect. Naturally, if ethics has any normative function, the latter must be the procedure of the moralist.

This criticism, however, might better be rephrased as follows: Kant's theory, because it is exclusively rationalistic, is not adequate to what enlightened moral persons find worthy in human nature. Human actions and virtues have an emotional setting which is not accidental to them but constitutes a part of their essential character, and this is ignored by Kant. The critic can find evidence that seems to justify this criticism. There is a rigoristic "Prussian" trend in Kant's writings and in his personality as we know it through various anecdotes. This often causes a modern reader to lose patience with the great philosopher, and it has even caused another philosopher to make an invidious comparison between "Kantian morals" and "human morals." Schiller, who knew better, satirized Kant in a verse famous as a paradigm of this kind of criticism:

"Gladly I serve my friends, but, alas, from inclination,
And often I'm troubled because I am not good."

"Nothing else will do: You must try to despise them,
And with revulsion do what Duty orders you."

Although this picture of Kant's ethics is incomplete, it is easy to see how it came about. Almost everyone else at that time was accentuating feeling at the expense of reason in morality; Kant's aim, on the contrary, was to establish reason as the exclusively legislative moral faculty. Therefore, even when he acknowledged the contribution of feeling to character, it was not his purpose to emphasize it, and for obvious polemical reasons he often slighted it. Nevertheless, feeling did not cease to play a role in his ethics after 1770. Schilpp has adequately shown that in the earlier period Kant was never an uncritical disciple of the Shaftesbury-Hutcheson school,[72] and it is equally true that in his later period he was not the cold thinking machine he is often pictured. Though he never admitted that feelings could generate a genuine moral disposition, or desire for happiness could function as a moral motive, Kant was quite aware of the "synergistic" relationships between reason and empirical character. The careful reader of the works in this volume will readily perceive this, and I shall merely cite some collateral evidence from Kant's other writings.

In the 1770's Kant wrote to Herz: "The supreme ground of morality must not merely allow us to reach delight; it must itself delight in the highest degree, for it is not just a speculative conception, but must have a moving force. Though it is indeed intellectual, it must have a direct relation to the basic incentives

72. *Op. cit.,* p. 35.

INTRODUCTION

of the will."[73] During the same period Kant was formulating his own concept of moral feeling and defined "moral incentives" as inclinations arising from feelings which are self-consistent and therefore the basis for orderly, integrated activity.[74] Such feelings might be called the material causes of morality. Alone they have no moral worth, but they are the material which reason fashions into character.

Later, in the *Critique of Judgment*, Kant describes and commends certain sentiments which attune man to morality, compares the "moral feeling" to the aesthetic feeling, and regards the beautiful as a "symbol" of the moral.[75] The *Metaphysics of Morals*, in which man as a sensuous being is always the center of attention, does much to counteract what is perhaps one-sided in the *Foundations* and in the second *Critique*, where the argument attempts to establish an objective law valid for every rational being as such.[76]

A long footnote in *Religion within the Limits of Reason Alone* supplies further evidence—if it is needed—that Kant's refusal to place feeling in the center of ethical consideration does not mean that it can be disregarded. Schiller had objected to Kant's rigorism and lack of emphasis on the "graceful" attributes of morality, and Kant answered that "grace" can come after duty but should replace it or be mixed with it as one of the moral motives. He then says:

> Now if one asks, What is the aesthetic character, the temperament, so to speak, of virtue, whether courageous and hence joyous or fear-ridden and dejected, an answer is hardly necessary. This latter slavish frame of mind can never occur without a hidden hatred of the law. And a heart which is happy in the performance of its duty (not merely complacent in the recognition thereof) is a mark of genuineness in the virtuous spirit—of genuineness even in piety, which does not consist in the self-inflicted torment of a repentant sinner (a very ambiguous state of mind, which ordinarily is nothing but inward regret at having infringed upon the rules of prudence), but rather in the firm resolve to do better in the future. This resolve, then, encouraged by

---

73. Cassirer ed., IX, 116; Academy ed., X, 138.
74. Reflections, Nos. 6690, 6696 (Academy ed., XIX, 134, 135).
75. *Critique of Judgment*, §§86, 29, 59, etc.
76. There is an exhaustive collection of passages showing the relations between morality and happiness, duty and inclinations, in Paton, *The Categorical Imperative*, appendix to chap. 3, pp. 55-57.

good progress, must needs beget a joyous frame of mind, without which man is never certain of having really attained a love for the good, i.e., of having incorporated it into his maxim.[77]

Without being a hedonist, one cannot go further.

The second objection to Kant's psychology is that, as psychology, it is too narrowly hedonistic. In rightly denying the ethical adequacy of nonrational incentives, he came to deny to empirical motivation any value whatever—a mistake indicative of a defective theory of human desires.

Kant's psychology on this question, we admit, is often confused and occasionally wrong. To begin with, it is obvious that Kant has not learned the lesson Butler taught Kant's British contemporaries,[78] namely, that inclinations are disinterested in respect to persons. Inclinations are, as Butler rightly saw, aimed simply at their own satisfaction, and where this primary satisfaction lies—in myself or in others—is not determined by the nature of the particular passion but by its circumstances, its direction either toward myself or toward others. The satisfaction "belongs" to me in the sense that it is my desire which is satisfied, but this does not imply that it was a desire *for* my satisfaction. Rather, whatever satisfaction I get out of the action is due to the fact that my desire has met *its* satisfaction. To infer that the desire itself was a desire for my satisfaction simply and immediately is to equivocate on the term "satisfaction."

Still another equivocation is involved in the argument. "Satisfaction" may indicate either the fruition and fulfilment of a need, or it may mean simply pleasure or agreeableness. Now it is true that pleasure is usually associated with satisfaction in the former sense. When, however, it is rightly stated that satisfaction is the goal of a need or a desire and of the action they engender, it is often erroneously supposed that satisfaction is being taken in the second sense, and the argument for hedonism becomes a tautology. In the former sense, "Satisfaction is the object of desire" is a definition; in the latter sense, however, it is an empirical proposition with little or no psychological evidence to support it. Yet most arguments for psychological hedonism depend upon interpreting the subject of the proposition, "Satisfaction is the object of desire," as equivalent to pleasure. Kant him-

---

77. *Religion within the Limits of Reason Alone*, p. 19 n. (Greene and Hudson trans.). (Italics omitted.)

78. There is no evidence that Kant had ever heard of Joseph Butler.

self generally does this, and he can find no material for a precept which is not thus reducible to pleasure.[79] In order to break the bond of pleasure, therefore, he is forced entirely out of the empirical realm.

Nowhere in Kant is there a clear-cut analysis of the pattern of desire. He generally argues that all principles built on empirically given interests are finally forms of the principle of self-love and one's own happiness; but, in the light of Butler's conclusive analysis, this argument must be rejected.

However, the consequences of these errors are not such as to require any fundamental revision of Kant's position as a whole. Butler's analysis may serve to refute Hobbes, but not Kant. For Kant's objection to the principle of private happiness is not that it is selfish in a disparaging sense. It is rather that this principle gives no universal precepts and can furnish no transcendental justification to the moral imperative. The whole problem of selfishness lies this side of the essential moral question which Kant alone among his contemporaries was discussing. The entire argument on altruism versus egoism is not, according to Kant, a moral problem at all; at most, it belongs to casuistry.

The same is true of the consequences of the second equivocation. For though Kant's argument for psychological hedonism as a purely descriptive theory is invalid, his rejection of empirical motivation in morals is not predicated upon the specific character of the goal, whether it be pleasure or satisfaction in some broader sense. He rejects pleasure and the pursuit of happiness not because either is ordinarily immoral per se but because it lies beyond their power, as empirical, to deliver moral imperatives. Character built on them has no stability or dignity. With respect to them, man is passive, not active and free. Hence the argument does not concern their specific features; their empirical status condemns them.

Such equivocations would be fatal to any ethics derived from natural man. But, since Kant's ethics is not empirically derived, these errors do not infect the system as a whole.

RATIONAL FAITH

Morality stands independent in Kant's philosophy. The contributions made to it by theology are at most supplements. In establishing the principle of morality, even the "highest good"—

79. See below, pp. 132, 151–52; cf. pp. 123 n., 220.

faith in which implies practical-metaphysical propositions—can be completely disregarded.[80]

Nevertheless, morality has metaphysical implications and at least one presupposition. If human reason were capable of theoretical certainty in metaphysics, and were able to demonstrate the falsity of the collateral propositions of theology and metaphysics, then morality would assert its claim in vain. Reason, however, lacks this capacity. Its impotence seemed to some of Kant's contemporaries to open the gate to irresponsible speculation. The consequence was enthusiasm, fanaticism (*Schwärmerei*), and superstition. "Flights of genius" start from subjective sentiments which are inadequate to attain objective status even in the world of sense—let alone in the supersensuous realm of speculation, where, Kant says, they beat their wings in empty space.[81] Reason needs to supplement its conditional knowledge with unconditionally certain knowledge; this is both theoretically[82] and practically necessary. Yet to mere theory this is impossible, as the *Critique of Pure Reason* shows.

Kant's argument against both camps of his opponents—those who anticipated positivism and those who drew their inspiration from Romanticism and its cult of feeling—is found in his essay on *What Is Orientation in Thinking?* Kant shows that reason has its own needs independent of those of feeling and that it is able to satisfy them by deducing the necessity of certain a priori metaphysical postulates. But the crucial point of his discovery is that apriority extends beyond the scope of knowledge; there is a *moral necessity* in certain propositions which we cannot claim for them as parts of knowledge. This moral necessity is subjective in the sense that it is not based on or directed to objects of knowledge but is objective in the sense that it is not restricted by particular conditions in any subject.

With this concept of an a priori faith, Kant is victor over dogmatic theology, which claims knowledge of the supersensuous; over the philosophy of feeling, which bases metaphysics on our subjective and contingent wants; and over skepticism, which disclaims interest in the supersensuous. The consequences of all

---

80. *On the Saying, "That May Be True in Theory But It Does Not Hold in Practice,"* I (Cassirer ed., VI, 362; Academy ed., VIII, 280).

81. See below, p. 116; *Critique of Pure Reason*, B 9.

82. Reason's need to extend itself even in speculation is ultimately a practical need. See below, pp. 114 n., 225. We have already seen that all practical principles are regulative, not constitutive; here is the converse of that.

INTRODUCTION

three are equally inadequate for practice and untenable in theory. We have seen that if reason could proceed in a purely speculative way, metaphysics would be merely an extension of physics, and freedom would be impossible. Thus dogmatic metaphysics, developed as a rigorous science, would destroy its chief partisans, the theologians. Aware both of man's need for metaphysics and of the impossibility of certainty in speculation, the philosophers of Storm and Stress, like practitioners of *Lebensphilosophie*, today, let the a posteriori subjective wants of men guide their reason. Kant refused to do this on theoretical grounds, and in some of the most eloquent passages of his works he points out the ruinous practical consequences of such a tendency.

While rational faith is compatible with a doctrine that denies metaphysical knowledge, a faith conjoined to a metaphysics which denies the object of rational faith (as Kant holds Spinozism to do) can be only an irrational faith.[83] This degrades reason, and Kant exhorts his opponents to consider the practical and political consequences of their irrationalism. No duty can be acknowledged unless reason is legislative, and, if reason does not legislate, force will replace it, nullifying the Romanticist's sublime dreams.

Against the skeptics, Kant's argument is less explicit, inasmuch as his whole philosophy is an examination of their limitations. Skepticism is a dogmatic disbelief and suffers from all the ills of dogmatism, in addition to those brought about by failure to seek unconditional certainty or to justify it where it is found in both science and morals.

Against all these theories, Kant puts forward rational faith—a faith which demands the same degree of assent required for theoretical knowledge and yet avoids the speculative claims of those who believe metaphysics to be a theoretical science.

The Supreme Being is the proper object of rational faith. We have seen already that the view that immortality is necessary to the highest good gave way to the belief that it is necessary to morality itself. A similar development occurs later in the postulate of the existence of God. This development is in the direction of an increasing immanence of God in the practical sphere. In the first *Critique*, Kant speaks of moral laws as commands associated a priori with promises and threats, an association which can occur only if there is a supreme intelligence as the moral gover-

---

83. See below, p. 302.

[47]

nor of the world. And he states that to reject belief in God and immortality would overthrow the moral principles themselves.[84]

In the second *Critique* God appears as necessary to the existence of the *summum bonum*. God is the being that guarantees happiness in proportion to virtue; and moral laws, in whose fulfilment lies man's worthiness to be happy, can be looked upon as divine commands. Their acceptance is defined as religion. Finally, a still further revision is made in the *Opus postumum*, in which God is identified with the moral law itself. "God is not a being outside me, but merely a thought in me. God is the morally practical reason legislating for itself. Therefore there is only one God in me, about me, above me."[85]

Kant was aware of the antinomic relationship between belief in a commanding, rewarding, and forgiving God and the autonomy of the moral agent. This is undoubtedly the source of his final explicit rejection of any theology but a moral one and of his making that theology not so much an adjunct to his ethics as identical with it. God identified with the moral law is not the danger to moral autonomy that a God rewarding morality would be, for belief in the latter may destroy purity of motive.

Since it is practical and not speculative reason which finally warrants Kant's use of the concept of God, theology for him can have no theoretical content, and religion is only the attitude of performing all duties as divine commands. The judgment, "There is a God," is not a theoretical judgment; it is not a hypothesis in a theoretical context. It is a practical postulate, a point of orientation. In the ordinary sense of the word "know" we do not know that it is true,[86] yet there is an a priori guaranty for it. Nor would such knowledge, were it possible, be desirable, for it would be predicated upon an extension of mere theory, of that aspect of mind which leads to amoral dogmatism. "Inscrutable wisdom" in denying us this knowledge, says Kant, "is not less worthy of veneration in respect to what it denies us than in what it has granted to us."[87]

In view of these postulates which are conjoined to a denial of

84. *Critique of Pure Reason*, A811–B839, A828–B856. See also Fragment 6674 (Academy ed., XIX, 130), which states that all duties disappear if there is no God, and Fragment 6858 (*ibid.*, p. 181), which states that without religion there is no genuine incentive to morality.
85. *Kants Opus postumum*, ed. Erich Adickes (Berlin: Reuther & Reichard, 1920), p. 819.
86. *Critique of Pure Reason*, A829–B857.
87. See below, p. 249.

speculative metaphysics, attempts to label Kant's philosophy as a whole should perhaps follow Richard Kroner,[88] who considers Kant a radical voluntarist, not simply because he made the will basic (as Schopenhauer and Nietzsche were to do) but because he made the rational will the true organ of philosophy itself. While other voluntarists have developed their philosophies into theoretical appreciations of the will, Kant places the will beyond all theory. In its limited function as theoretical reason it judges nature and attempts to judge itself; as practical reason it leaves this kind of understanding behind. In its true nature it acts but it cannot be known, for all knowledge is theoretical limitation.

88. *Op. cit.*, chaps. i and iv.

I

FOUNDATIONS OF THE METAPHYSICS OF MORALS

PREFACE

ANCIENT Greek philosophy was divided into three sciences: physics, ethics, and logic. This division conforms perfectly to the nature of the subject, and one need improve on it perhaps only by supplying its principle in order both to insure its exhaustiveness and to define correctly the necessary subdivisions.

All rational knowledge is either material, and observes some object, or formal, and is occupied merely with the form of understanding and reason itself and with the universal rules of thinking without regard to distinctions between objects. Formal philosophy is called logic. Material philosophy, however, which has to do with definite objects and the laws to which they are subject, is itself divided into two parts. This is because these laws are either laws of nature or laws of freedom. The science of the former is called physics and that of the latter, ethics. The former is also called theory of nature and the latter, theory of morals.

Logic can have no empirical part—a part in which universal and necessary laws of thinking would rest upon grounds taken from experience. For in that case it would not be logic, i.e., a canon for understanding or reason which is valid for all thinking and which must be demonstrated. But, on the other hand, natural and moral philosophy can each have its empirical part. The former must do so, for it must determine the laws of nature as an object of experience, and the latter because it must determine the human will so far as it is affected by nature. The laws of the former are laws according to which everything happens; those of the latter are laws according to which everything should happen, but allow for conditions under which what should happen often does not.

All philosophy, so far as it is based on experience, may be called empirical; but, so far as it presents its doctrines solely on the basis of a priori principles, it may be called pure philosophy.

The latter, when merely formal, is logic; when limited to definite objects of understanding, it is metaphysics.

In this way there arises the idea of a twofold metaphysics—a metaphysics of nature and a metaphysics of morals. Physics, therefore, will have an empirical and also a rational part, and ethics likewise. In ethics, however, the empirical part may be called more specifically practical anthropology; the rational part, morals proper.

All crafts, handiworks, and arts have gained by the division of labor, for when one person does not do everything, but each limits himself to a particular job which is distinguished from all the others by the treatment it requires, he can do it with greater perfection and with more facility. Where work is not thus differentiated and divided, where everyone is a jack-of-all-trades, the crafts remain at a barbaric level. It might be worth considering whether pure philosophy in each of its parts does not require a man particularly devoted to it, and whether it would not be better for the learned profession as a whole to warn those who are in the habit of catering to the taste of the public by mixing up the empirical with the rational in all sorts of proportions which they do not themselves know and who call themselves independent thinkers (giving the name of speculator to those who apply themselves to the merely rational part). This warning would be that they should not at one and the same time carry on two employments which differ widely in the treatment they require, and for each of which perhaps a special talent is required, since the combination of these talents in one person produces only bunglers. I only ask whether the nature of the science does not require that a careful separation of the empirical from the rational part be made, with a metaphysics of nature put before real (empirical) physics and a metaphysics of morals before practical anthropology. These prior sciences[1] must be carefully purified of everything empirical so that we can know how much pure reason can accomplish in each case and from what sources it creates its a priori teaching, whether the latter inquiry be conducted by all moralists (whose name is legion) or only by some who feel a calling to it.

Since my purpose here is directed to moral philosophy, I narrow the proposed question to this: Is it not of the utmost necessity to construct a pure moral philosophy which is completely freed from everything which may be only empirical and thus

1. [Reading the plural with the Academy ed.]

belong to anthropology? That there must be such a philosophy is self-evident from the common idea of duty and moral laws. Everyone must admit that a law, if it is to hold morally, i.e., as a ground of obligation, must imply absolute necessity; he must admit that the command, "Thou shalt not lie," does not apply to men only, as if other rational beings had no need to observe it. The same is true for all other moral laws properly so called. He must concede that the ground of obligation here must not be sought in the nature of man or in the circumstances in which he is placed but sought a priori solely in the concepts of pure reason, and that every other precept which rests on principles of mere experience, even a precept which is in certain respects universal, so far as it leans in the least on empirical grounds (perhaps only in regard to the motive involved), may be called a practical rule but never a moral law.

Thus not only are moral laws together with their principles essentially different from all practical knowledge in which there is anything empirical, but all moral philosophy rests solely on its pure part. Applied to man, it borrows nothing from knowledge of him (anthropology) but gives him, as a rational being, a priori laws. No doubt these laws require a power of judgment sharpened by experience partly in order to decide in what cases they apply and partly to procure for them an access to man's will and an impetus to their practice. For man is affected by so many inclinations that, though he is capable of the idea of a practical pure reason, he is not so easily able to make it concretely effective in the conduct of his life.

A metaphysics of morals is therefore indispensable, not merely because of motives to speculate concerning the source of the a priori practical principles which lie in our reason, but also because morals themselves remain subject to all kinds of corruption so long as the guide and supreme norm of their correct estimation is lacking. For it is not sufficient to that which should be morally good that it conform to the law; it must be done for the sake of the law. Otherwise the conformity is merely contingent and spurious, because, though the unmoral ground may indeed now and then produce lawful actions, more often it brings forth unlawful ones. But the moral law can be found in its purity and genuineness (which is the central concern in the practical) nowhere else than in a pure philosophy; therefore, this (i.e., metaphysics) must lead the way, and without it there can be no moral philosophy. Philosophy which mixes pure principles with empirical ones does not deserve the name, for what distinguishes philosophy from common rational knowledge is its treatment in separate sciences of what is confusedly comprehended in such knowledge. Much less does it deserve the name of moral philosophy, since by this confusion it spoils the purity of morals themselves and works contrary to its own end.

It should not be thought that what is here required is already present in the celebrated Wolff's propaedeutic to his moral philosophy, i.e., in what he calls universal practical philosophy, and that it is not an entirely new field that is to be opened. Precisely because his work was to be universal practical philosophy, it deduced no will of any particular kind, such as one determined without any empirical motives but completely by a priori principles; in a word, it had nothing which could be called a pure will, since it considered only volition in general with all the actions and conditions which pertain to it in this general sense. Thus his prodaedeutic differs from a metaphysics of morals in the same way that general logic is distinguished from transcendental philosophy, the former expounding the actions and rules of thinking in general, and the latter presenting the particular actions and rules of pure thinking, i.e., of thinking by which objects are known completely a priori. For the metaphysics of morals is meant to investigate the idea and principles of a possible pure will and not the actions and conditions of the human volition as such, which are for the most part drawn from psychology.

That in general practical philosophy laws and duty are discussed (though improperly) is no objection to my assertion. For the authors of this science remain even here true to their idea of it: They do not distinguish the motives which are presented completely a priori by reason alone, and which are thus moral in the proper sense of the word, from the empirical motives which the understanding by comparing experiences elevates to universal concepts. Rather, they consider motives without regard to the difference in their source but only with reference to their greater or smaller number (as they are considered to be all of the same kind); they thus formulate their concept of obligation, which is anything but moral, but which is all that can be desired in a philosophy which does not decide whether the origin of all possible practical concepts is a priori or only a posteriori.

As a preliminary to a metaphysics of morals which I intend someday to publish, I issue these *Foundations*. There is, to be sure, no other foundation for such a metaphysics than a critical examination of a pure practical reason, just as there is no other foundation for metaphysics than the already published critical examination of the pure speculative reason. But, in the first place, a critical examination of pure practical reason is not of such extreme importance as that of the speculative reason, because the human reason, even in the commonest mind, can easily be brought to a high degree of correctness and completeness in moral matters, while, on the other hand, in its theoretical but pure use it is entirely dialectical. In the second place, I require of a critical examination of a pure practical reason, if it is to be complete, that its unity with the speculative be subject to presentation under a common principle, because in the final analysis there can be but one and the same reason which must be differentiated only in application. But I could not bring this to such a completeness without bringing in observations of an altogether different kind and without thereby confusing the reader. For these reasons I have employed the title, *Foundations of the Metaphysics of Morals*, instead of *Critique of Pure Practical Reason*.

Because, in the third place, a metaphysics of morals, in spite of its forbidding title, is capable of a high degree of popularity and adaptation to common understanding, I find it useful to separate this preliminary work of laying the foundation, in order not to have to introduce unavoidable subtleties into the later, more comprehensible work.

The present foundations, however, are nothing more than the search for and establishment of the supreme principle of morality. This constitutes a task altogether complete in its intention and one which should be kept separate from all other moral inquiry.

My conclusions concerning this important question, which has not yet been discussed nearly enough, would, of course, be clarified by application of the principle to the whole system of morality, and it would receive much confirmation by the adequacy which it would everywhere show. But I must forgo this advantage which would in the final analysis be more privately gratifying than commonly useful, because ease of use and apparent adequacy of a principle are not any sure proof of its correctness but rather awaken a certain partiality which prevents a rigorous investigation and evaluation of it for itself without regard to consequences.

I have adopted in this writing the method which is, I think, most suitable if one wishes to proceed analytically from common knowledge to the determination of its supreme principle, and then synthetically from the examination of this principle and its sources back to common knowledge where it finds its application. The division is therefore as follows:

1. First Section. Transition from the Common Rational Knowledge of Morals to the Philosophical
2. Second Section. Transition from the Popular Moral Philosophy to the Metaphysics of Morals
3. Third Section. Final Step from the Metaphysics of Morals to the Critical Examination of Pure Practical Reason

FIRST SECTION

TRANSITION FROM THE COMMON RATIONAL KNOWLEDGE OF MORALS TO THE PHILOSOPHICAL

NOTHING in the world—indeed nothing even beyond the world—can possibly be conceived which could be called good without qualification except a *good will*. Intelligence, wit, judgment, and the other talents of the mind, however they may be named, or courage, resoluteness, and perseverence as qualities of temperament are doubtless in many respects good and desirable. But they can become extremely bad and harmful if the will, which is to make use of these gifts of nature and which in its special constitution is called character, is not good. It is the same with the gifts of fortune. Power, riches, honor, even health, general well-being, and the contentment with one's condition which is called happiness make for pride and even arrogance if there is not a good will to correct their influence on the mind and on its principles of action, so as to make it universally conformable to its end. It need hardly be mentioned that the sight of a being adorned with no feature of a pure and good will yet enjoying uninterrupted prosperity can never give pleasure to a rational impartial observer. Thus the good will seems to constitute the indispensable condition even of worthiness to be happy.

Some qualities seem to be conducive to this good will and can facilitate its action, but, in spite of that, they have no intrinsic unconditional worth. They rather presuppose a good will, which limits the high esteem which one otherwise rightly has for them and prevents their being held to be absolutely good. Moderation in emotions and passions, self-control, and calm deliberation not only are good in many respects but even seem to constitute a part of the inner worth of the person. But however unconditionally they were esteemed by the ancients, they are far from being good without qualification. For, without the principles of a good will, they can become extremely bad, and the coolness of a villain makes him not only far more dangerous but also more directly abominable in our eyes than he would have seemed without it.

The good will is not good because of what it effects or accomplishes or because of its adequacy to achieve some proposed end; it is good only because of its willing, i.e., it is good of itself. And, regarded for itself, it is to be esteemed incomparably higher than anything which could be brought about by it in favor of any inclination or even of the sum total of all inclinations. Even if it should happen that, by a particularly unfortunate fate or by the niggardly provision of a stepmotherly nature, this will should be wholly lacking in power to accomplish its purpose, and if even the greatest effort should not avail it to achieve anything of its end, and if there remained only the good will (not as a mere wish but as the summoning of all the means in our power), it would sparkle like a jewel with its own light, as something that had its full worth in itself. Usefulness or fruitlessness can neither diminish nor augment this worth. Its usefulness would be only its setting, as it were, so as to enable us to handle it more conveniently in commerce or to attract the attention of those who are not yet connoisseurs, but not to recommend it to those who are experts or to determine its worth.

But there is something so strange in this idea of the absolute worth of the will alone, in which no account is taken of any use, that, notwithstanding the agreement even of common sense, the suspicion must arise that perhaps only high-flown fancy is its hidden basis, and that we may have misunderstood the purpose of nature in its appointment of reason as the ruler of our will. We shall therefore examine this idea from this point of view.

In the natural constitution of an organized being, i.e., one suitably adapted to life, we assume as an axiom that no organ will be found for any purpose which is not the fittest and best adapted to that purpose. Now if its preservation, welfare—in a word, its happiness—were the real end of nature in a being having reason and will, then nature would have hit upon a very poor arrangement in appointing the reason of the creature to be the executor of this purpose. For all the actions which the creature has to perform with this intention, and the entire rule of its conduct, would be dictated much more exactly by instinct, and that end would be far more certainly attained by instinct than it ever could be by reason. And if, over and above this, reason should have been granted to the favored creature, it would have served only to let it contemplate the happy constitution of its nature, to admire it, to rejoice in it, and to be grateful for it to its beneficent cause. But reason would not have been given in order that the being should subject its faculty of desire to that weak and delusive guidance and to meddle with the purpose of nature. In a word, nature would have taken care that reason did not break forth into practical use nor have the presumption, with its weak insight, to think out for itself the plan of happiness and the means of attaining it. Nature would have taken over not only the choice of ends but also that of the means and with wise foresight would have intrusted both to instinct alone.

And, in fact, we find that the more a cultivated reason deliberately devotes itself to the enjoyment of life and happiness, the more the man falls short of true contentment. From this fact there arises in many persons, if only they are candid enough to admit it, a certain degree of misology, hatred of reason. This is particularly the case with those who are most experienced in its use. After counting all the advantages which they draw—I will not say from the invention of the arts of common luxury—from the sciences (which in the end seem to them to be also a luxury of the understanding), they nevertheless find that they have actually brought more trouble on their shoulders instead of gaining in happiness; they finally envy, rather than despise, the common run of men who are better guided by mere natural instinct and who do not permit their reason much influence on their conduct. And we must at least admit that a morose attitude or ingratitude to the goodness with which the world is governed is by no means always found among those who temper or refute the boasting eulogies which are given of the advantages of happiness and contentment with which reason is supposed to supply us. Rather their judgment is based on the idea of another and far more worthy purpose of their existence for which, instead of happiness, their reason is properly intended, this purpose, therefore, being the supreme condition to which the private purposes of men must for the most part defer.

Reason is not, however, competent to guide the will safely with regard to its objects and the satisfaction of all our needs (which it in part multiplies), and to this end an innate instinct would have led with far more certainty. But reason is given to us as a practical faculty, i.e., one which is meant to have an influence on the will. As nature has elsewhere distributed capacities suitable to the functions they are to perform, reason's proper function must be to produce a will good in itself and not one good merely as a means, for to the former reason is absolutely essential. This will must indeed not be the sole and complete good but the highest good and the condition of all others, even of the desire for happiness. In this case it is entirely compatible with the wisdom of nature that the cultivation of reason, which is required for the former unconditional purpose, at least in this life restricts in many ways—indeed can reduce to less than nothing—the achievement of the latter conditional purpose, happiness. For one perceives that nature here does not proceed unsuitably to its purpose, because reason, which recognizes its highest practical vocation in the establishment of a good will, is capable only of a contentment of its own kind, i.e., one that springs from the attainment of a purpose, which in turn is determined by reason, even though this injures the ends of inclination.

We have, then, to develop the concept of a will which is to be esteemed as good of itself without regard to anything else. It dwells already in the natural sound understanding and does not need so much to be taught as only to be brought to light. In the estimation of the entire worth of our actions it always takes first place and is the condition of everything else. In order to show this, we shall take the concept of duty. It contains that of a good will, though with certain subjective restrictions and hindrances; but these are far from concealing it and making it unrecognizable, for they rather bring it out by contrast and make it shine forth all the brighter.

I here omit all actions which are recognized as opposed to duty, even though they may be useful in one respect or another, for with these the question does not arise at all as to whether they may be done *from* duty, since they conflict with it. I also pass over the actions which are really in accordance with duty and to which one has no direct inclination, rather doing them because impelled to do so by another inclination. For it is easily decided whether an action in accord with duty is done from duty or for some selfish purpose. It is far more difficult to note this difference when the action is in accordance with duty and, in addition, the subject has a direct inclination to do it. For example, it is in fact in accordance with duty that a dealer should not overcharge an inexperienced customer, and wherever there is much business the prudent merchant does not do so, having a fixed price for everyone, so that a child may buy of him as cheaply as any other. Thus the customer is honestly served. But this is far from sufficient to justify the belief that the merchant has behaved in this way from duty and principles of honesty. His own advantage required this behavior; but it cannot be assumed that over and above that he had a direct inclination to the purchaser and that, out of love, as it were, he gave none an advantage in price over another. Therefore the action was done neither from duty nor from direct inclination but only for a selfish purpose.

On the other hand, it is a duty to preserve one's life, and moreover everyone has a direct inclination to do so. But, for that reason, the often anxious care which most men take of it has no intrinsic worth, and the maxim of doing so has no moral import. They preserve their lives according to duty, but not from duty. But if adversities and hopeless sorrow completely take away the relish for life; if an unfortunate man, strong in soul, is indignant rather than despondent or dejected over his fate and wishes for death, and yet preserves his life without loving it and from neither inclination nor fear but from duty—then his maxim has a moral import.

To be kind where one can is duty, and there are, moreover, many persons so sympathetically constituted that without any motive of vanity or selfishness they find an inner satisfaction in spreading joy and rejoice in the contentment of others which they have made possible. But I say that, however dutiful and amiable it may be, that kind of action has no true moral worth. It is on a level with other inclinations, such as the inclination to honor, which, if fortunately directed to what in fact accords with duty and is generally useful and thus honorable, deserve praise and encouragement but no esteem. For the maxim lacks the moral import of an action done not from inclination but from duty. But assume that the mind of that friend to mankind was clouded by a sorrow of his own which extinguished all sympathy with the lot of others and that he still had the power to benefit others in distress, but that their need left him untouched because he was preoccupied with his own need. And now suppose him to tear himself, unsolicited by inclination, out of this dead insensibility and to do this action only from duty and without any inclination—then for the first time his action has genuine moral worth.

Furthermore, if nature has put little sympathy in the heart of a man, and if he, though an honest man, is by temperament cold and indifferent to the sufferings of others perhaps because he is provided with special gifts of patience and fortitude, and expects or even requires that others should have the same—and such a man would certainly not be the meanest product of nature—would not he find in himself a source from which to give himself a far higher worth than he could have got by having a good-natured temperament? This is unquestionably true even though nature did not make him philanthropic, for it is just here that the worth of the character is brought out, which is morally and incomparably the highest of all: he is beneficent not from inclination but from duty.

To secure one's own happiness is at least indirectly a duty, for discontent with one's condition under pressure from many cares and amid unsatisfied wants could easily become a great temptation to transgress duties. But, without any view to duty, all men have the strongest and deepest inclination to happiness, because in this idea all inclinations are summed up. But the precept of happiness is often so formulated that it definitely thwarts some inclinations, and men can make no definite and certain concept of the sum of satisfaction of all inclinations, which goes under the name of happiness. It is not to be wondered at, therefore, that a single inclination, definite as to what it promises and as to the time at which it can be satisfied, can outweigh a fluctuating idea, and that, for example, a man with the gout can choose to enjoy what he likes and to suffer what he may, because according to his calculations at least on this occasion he has not sacrificed the enjoyment of the present moment to a perhaps groundless expectation of a happiness supposed to lie in health. But, even in this case, if the universal inclination to happiness did not determine his will, and if health were not at least for him a necessary factor in these calculations, there yet would remain, as in all other cases, a law that he ought to promote his happiness, not from inclination but from duty. Only from this law would his conduct have true moral worth.

It is in this way, undoubtedly, that we should understand those passages of Scripture which command us to love our neighbor and even our enemy, for love as an inclination cannot be commanded. But beneficence from duty, also when no inclination impels it and even when it is opposed by a natural and unconquerable aversion, is practical love, not pathological love; it resides in the will and not in the propensities of feeling, in principles of action and not in tender sympathy; and it alone can be commanded.

[Thus the first proposition of morality is that to have moral worth an action must be done from duty.] The second proposition is: An action done from duty does not have its moral worth in the purpose which is to be achieved through it but in the maxim by which it is determined. Its moral value, therefore, does not depend on the reality of the object of the action but merely on the principle of volition by which the action is done without any regard to the objects of the faculty of desire. From the preceding discussion it is clear that the purposes we may have for our actions and their effects as ends and incentives of the will cannot give the actions any unconditional and moral worth. Wherein, then, can this worth lie, if it is not in the will in relation to its hoped-for effect? It can lie nowhere else than in the principle of the will irrespective of the ends which can be realized by such action. For the will stands, as it were, at the crossroads halfway between its a priori principle which is formal and its a posteriori incentive which is material. Since it must be determined by something, if it is done from duty, it must be determined by the formal principle of volition as such, since every material principle has been withdrawn from it.

The third principle, as a consequence of the two preceding, I would express as follows: Duty is the necessity of an action done from respect for the law. I can certainly have an inclination to the object as an effect of the proposed action, but I can never have respect for it precisely because it is a mere effect and not an activity of a will. Similarly, I can have no respect for any inclination whatsoever, whether my own or that of another; in the former case I can at most approve of it and in the latter I can even love it, i.e., see it as favorable to my own advantage. But that which is connected with my will merely as ground and not as consequence, that which does not serve my inclination but overpowers it or at least excludes it from being considered in making a choice—in a word, the law itself—can be an object of respect and thus a command. Now as an act from duty wholly excludes the influence of inclination and therewith every object of the will, nothing remains which can determine the will objectively except the law and subjectively except pure respect for this practical law. This subjective element is the maxim* that I should follow such a law even if it thwarts all my inclinations.

Thus the moral worth of an action does not lie in the effect which is expected from it or in any principle of action which has to borrow its motive from this expected effect. For all these effects (agreeableness of condition, indeed even the promotion of the happiness of others) could be brought about through other causes and would not require the will of a rational being, while the highest and unconditional good can be found only in such a will. Therefore, the pre-eminent good can consist only in the conception of the law in itself (which can be present only in a rational being) so far as this conception and not the hoped-for effect is the determining ground of the will. This pre-eminent good, which we call moral, is already present in the person who acts according to this conception, and we do not have to expect it first in the result.†

But what kind of a law can that be, the conception of which must determine the will without reference to the expected re-

---

* A maxim is the subjective principle of volition. The objective principle (i.e., that which would serve all rational beings also subjectively as a practical principle if reason had full power over the faculty of desire) is the practical law.

† It might be objected that I seek to take refuge in an obscure feeling behind the word "respect," instead of clearly resolving the question with a concept of reason. But though respect is a feeling, it is not one received through any [outer] influence but is self-wrought by a rational concept; thus it differs specifically from all feelings of the former kind which may be referred to inclination or fear. What I recognize directly as a law for myself I recognize with respect, which means merely the consciousness of the submission of my will to a law without the intervention of other influences on my mind. The direct determination of the will by the law and the consciousness of this determination is respect; thus respect can be regarded as the effect of the law on the subject and not as the cause of the law. Respect is properly the conception of a worth which thwarts my self-love. Thus it is regarded as an object neither of inclination nor of fear, though it has something analogous to both. The only object of respect is the law, and indeed only the law which we impose on ourselves and yet recognize as necessary in itself. As a law we are subject to it without consulting self-love; as imposed on us by ourselves, it is consequence of our will. In the former respect it is analogous to fear and in the latter to inclination. All respect for a person is only respect for the law (of righteousness, etc.) of which the person provides an example. Because we see the improvement of our talents as a duty, we think of a person of talents as the example of a law, as it were (the law that we should by practice become like him in his talents), and that constitutes our respect. All so-called moral interest consists solely in respect for the law.

sult? Under this condition alone the will can be called absolutely good without qualification. Since I have robbed the will of all impulses which could come to it from obedience to any law, nothing remains to serve as a principle of the will except universal conformity of its action to law as such. That is, I should never act in such a way that I could not will that my maxim should be a universal law. Mere conformity to law as such (without assuming any particular law applicable to certain actions) serves as the principle of the will, and it must serve as such a principle if duty is not to be a vain delusion and chimerical concept. The common reason of mankind in its practical judgments is in perfect agreement with this and has this principle constantly in view.

Let the question, for example, be: May I, when in distress, make a promise with the intention not to keep it? I easily distinguish the two meanings which the question can have, viz., whether it is prudent to make a false promise, or whether it conforms to my duty. Undoubtedly the former can often be the case, though I do see clearly that it is not sufficient merely to escape from the present difficulty by this expedient, but that I must consider whether inconveniences much greater than the present one may not later spring from this lie. Even with all my supposed cunning, the consequences cannot be so easily foreseen. Loss of credit might be far more disadvantageous than the misfortune I now seek to avoid, and it is hard to tell whether it might not be more prudent to act according to a universal maxim and to make it a habit not to promise anything without intending to fulfil it. But it is soon clear to me that such a maxim is based only on an apprehensive concern with consequences.

To be truthful from duty, however, is an entirely different thing from being truthful out of fear of disadvantageous consequences, for in the former case the concept of the action itself contains a law for me, while in the latter I must first look about to see what results for me may be connected with it. For to deviate from the principle of duty is certainly bad, but to be unfaithful to my maxim of prudence can sometimes be very advantageous to me, though it is certainly safer to abide by it. The shortest but most infallible way to find the answer to the question as to whether a deceitful promise is consistent with duty is to ask myself: Would I be content that my maxim (of extricating myself from difficulty by a false promise) should hold as a universal law for myself as well as for others? And could I say to myself that everyone may make a false promise when he is in a difficulty from which he otherwise cannot escape? I immediately see that I could will the lie but not a universal law to lie. For with such a law there would be no promises at all inasmuch as it would be futile to make a pretense of my intention in regard to future actions to those who would not believe this pretense or—if they overhastily did so—who would pay me back in my own coin. Thus my maxim would necessarily destroy itself as soon as it was made a universal law.

I do not, therefore, need any penetrating acuteness in order to discern what I have to do in order that my volition may be morally good. Inexperienced in the course of the world, incapable of being prepared for all its contingencies, I only ask myself: Can I will that my maxim become a universal law? If not, it must be rejected, not because of any disadvantage accruing to myself or even to others, but because it cannot enter as a principle into a possible universal legislation, and reason extorts from me an immediate respect for such legislation. I do not as yet discern on what it is grounded (a question the philosopher may investigate), but I at least understand that it is an estimation of the worth which far outweighs all the worth of whatever is recommended by the inclinations, and that the necessity of my actions from pure respect for the practical law constitutes duty. To duty every other motive must give place, because duty is the condition of a will good in itself, whose worth transcends everything.

Thus within the moral knowledge of common human reason we have attained its principle. To be sure, common human reason does not think it abstractly in such a universal form, but it always has it in view and uses it as the standard of its judgments. It would be easy to show how common human reason, with this compass, knows well how to distinguish what is good, what is bad, and what is consistent or inconsistent with duty. Without in the least teaching common reason anything new, we need only to draw its attention to its own principle, in the manner of Socrates, thus showing that neither science nor philosophy is needed in order to know what one has to do in order to be honest and good, and even wise and virtuous. We might have conjectured beforehand that the knowledge of what everyone is obliged to do and thus also to know would be within the reach of everyone, even the most ordinary man. Here we cannot but admire the great advantages which the practical faculty of judgment has over the theoretical in ordinary human understanding. In the theoretical, if ordinary reason ventures to go beyond the laws of experience and perceptions of the senses, it falls into sheer inconceivabilities and self-contradictions, or at least into a chaos of uncertainty, obscurity, and instability. In the practical, on the other hand, the power of judgment first shows itself to advantage when common understanding excludes all sensuous incentives from practical laws. It then becomes even subtle, quibbling with its own conscience or with other claims to what should be called right, or wishing to determine correctly for its own instruction the worth of certain actions. But the most remarkable thing about ordinary reason in its practical concern is that it may have as much hope as any philosopher of hitting the mark. In fact, it is almost more certain to do so than the philosopher, because he has no principle which the common understanding lacks, while his judgment is easily confused by a mass of irrelevant considerations, so that it easily turns aside from the correct way. Would it not, therefore, be wiser in moral matters to acquiesce in the common rational judgment, or at most to call in philosophy in order to make the system of morals more complete and comprehensible and its rules more convenient for use (especially in disputation) than to steer the common understanding from its happy simplicity in practical matters and to lead it through philosophy into a new path of inquiry and instruction?

Innocence is indeed a glorious thing, but, on the other hand, it is very sad that it cannot well maintain itself, being easily led astray. For this reason, even wisdom—which consists more in acting than in knowing—needs science, not so as to learn from it but to secure admission and permanence to its precepts. Man feels in himself a powerful counterpoise against all commands of duty which reason presents to him as so deserving of respect; this counterpoise is his needs and inclinations, the complete satisfaction of which he sums up under the name of happiness. Now reason issues inexorable commands without promising anything to the inclinations. It disregards, as it were, and holds in contempt those claims which are so impetuous and yet so plausible, and which will not allow themselves to be abolished by any command. From this a natural dialectic arises, i.e., a propensity to argue against the stern laws of duty and their validity, or at least to place their purity and strictness in doubt and, where possible, to make them more accordant with our wishes and inclinations. This is equivalent to corrupting them in their very foundations and destroying their dignity—a thing which even common practical reason cannot ultimately call good.

In this way common human reason is impelled to go outside its sphere and to take a step into the field of practical philosophy. But it is forced to do so not by any speculative need, which never occurs to it so long as it is satisfied to remain merely healthy reason; rather, it is so impelled on practical grounds in order to obtain information and clear instruction respecting the source of its principle and the correct determination of this principle in its opposition to the maxims which are based on need and inclination. It seeks this information in order to escape from the perplexity of opposing claims and to avoid the danger of losing all genuine moral principles through the equivocation in which it is easily involved. Thus when practical common reason cultivates itself, a dialectic surreptitiously ensues, which forces it to seek aid in philosophy, just as the same thing happens in the theoretical use of reason. In this case, as in the theoretical, it will find rest only in a thorough critical examination of our reason.

SECOND SECTION

TRANSITION FROM THE POPULAR MORAL PHILOSOPHY TO THE METAPHYSICS OF MORALS

IF WE have derived our earlier concept of duty from the common use of our practical reason, it is by no means to be inferred that we have treated it as an empirical concept. On the contrary, if we attend to our experience of the way men act, we meet frequent and, as we ourselves confess, justified complaints that we cannot cite a single sure example of the disposition to act from pure duty. There are also justified complaints that, though much may be done that accords with what duty commands, it is nevertheless always doubtful whether it is done from duty, and thus whether it has moral worth. There have always been philosophers who for this reason have absolutely denied the reality of this disposition in human actions, attributing everything to more or less refined self-love. They have done so without questioning the correctness of the concept of morality. Rather they spoke with sincere regret of the frailty and corruption of human nature, which is noble enough to take as its precept an idea so worthy of respect but which at the same time is too weak to follow it, employing reason, which should legislate for human nature, only to provide for the interest of the inclinations either singly or, at best, in their greatest possible harmony with one another.

It is in fact absolutely impossible by experience to discern with complete certainty a single case in which the maxim of an action, however much it may conform to duty, rested solely on moral grounds and on the conception of one's duty. It sometimes happens that in the most searching self-examination we can find nothing except the moral ground of duty which could have been powerful enough to move us to this or that good action and to such great sacrifice. But from this we cannot by any means conclude with certainty that a secret impulse of self-love, falsely appearing as the idea of duty, was not actually the true determining cause of the will. For we like to flatter ourselves with a pretended nobler motive, while in fact even the strictest examination can never lead us entirely behind the secret incentives, for, when moral worth is in question, it is not a matter of actions which one sees but of their inner principles which one does not see.

Moreover, one cannot better serve the wishes of those who ridicule all morality as a mere phantom of human imagination overreaching itself through self-conceit than by conceding to them that the concepts of duty must be derived only from experience (for they are ready to believe from indolence that this is true of all other concepts too). For, by this concession, a sure triumph is prepared for them. Out of love for humanity I am willing to admit that most of our actions are in accordance with duty; but, if we look closer at our thoughts and aspirations, we everywhere come upon the dear self, which is always salient, and it is this instead of the stern command of duty (which would often require self-denial) which supports our plans. One need not be an enemy of virtue, but only a cool observer who does not mistake even the liveliest aspiration for the good with its reality, to be doubtful sometimes whether true virtue can really be found anywhere in the world. This is especially true as one's years increase and the power of judgment is made wiser by experience and more acute in observation. This being so, nothing can secure us against the complete abandonment of our ideas of duty and preserve in us a well-founded respect for its law except the clear conviction that, even if there never were actions springing from such pure sources, our concern is not whether this or that was done but that reason of itself and independently of all appearances commands what ought to be done. Our concern is with actions of which perhaps the world has never had an example, with actions whose feasibility might be seriously doubted by those who base everything on experience, and yet with actions inexorably commanded by reason. For example, pure sincerity in friendship can be demanded of every man, and this demand is not in the least diminished if a sincere friend has never existed, because this duty, as duty in general, prior to all experience lies in the idea of a reason which determines the will by a priori grounds.

It is clear that no experience can give occasion for inferring the possibility of such apodictic laws. This is especially clear when we add that, unless we wish to deny all truth to the concept of morality and renounce its application to any possible object, we cannot refuse to admit that the law of this concept is of such broad significance that it holds not merely for men but for all rational beings as such; we must grant that it must be valid with absolute necessity and not merely under contingent conditions and with exceptions. For with what right could we bring into unlimited respect something that might be valid only under contingent human conditions? And how could laws of the determination of our will be held to be laws of the determination of the will of a rational being in general and of ourselves in so far as we are rational beings, if they were merely empirical and did not have their origin completely a priori in pure, but practical, reason?

Nor could one give poorer counsel to morality than to attempt to derive it from examples. For each example of morality which is exhibited to me must itself have been previously judged according to principles of morality to see whether it is worthy to serve as an original example, i.e., as a model. By no means could it authoritatively furnish the concept of morality. Even the Holy One of the Gospel must be compared with our ideal of moral perfection before He is recognized as such; even He says of Himself, "Why call ye Me (Whom you see) good? None is good (the archetype of the good) except God only (Whom you do not see)." But whence do we have the concept of God as the highest good? Solely from the idea of moral perfection which reason formulates a priori and which it inseparably connects with the concept of a free will. Imitation has no place in moral matters, and examples serve only for encouragement. That is, they put beyond question the practicability of what the law commands, and they make visible that which the practical rule expresses more generally. But they can never justify our guiding ourselves by examples and our setting-aside their true original which lies in reason.

If there is thus no genuine supreme principle of morality which does not rest merely on pure reason independently of all experience, I do not believe it is necessary even to ask whether it is well to exhibit these concepts generally (*in abstracto*), which, together with the principles belonging to them, are established a priori. At any rate, this question need not be asked if knowledge which establishes this is to be distinguished from ordinary knowledge and called philosophical. But in our times this question may perhaps be necessary. For if we collected votes as to whether pure rational knowledge separated from all experience, i.e., metaphysics of morals, or popular practical philosophy is to be preferred, it is easily guessed on which side the majority would stand.

This condescension to popular notions is certainly very commendable once the ascent to the principles of pure reason has been satisfactorily accomplished. That would mean the prior establishment of the doctrine of morals on metaphysics and then, when it is established, to procure a hearing for it through popularization. But it is extremely absurd to want to achieve popularity in the first investigation, where everything depends on the correctness of the fundamental principles. Not only can this procedure never make claim to that rarest merit of true philosophical popularity, since there is really no art in being generally comprehensible if one thereby renounces all basic insight; but it produces a disgusting jumble of patched-up observations and half-reasoned principles. Shallow pates enjoy this, for it is very useful in everyday chitchat, while the more sensible feel confused and dissatisfied without being able to help themselves. They turn their eyes away, even though philosophers, who see very well through the delusion, find little audience when they call men away for a time from this pretended popularization in order that they may rightly appear popular after they have attained a definite insight.

One need only look at the essays on morality which that popular taste favors. One will sometimes meet with the particular vocation of human nature (but occasionally also the idea of a rational nature in general), sometimes perfection, and sometimes happiness, here moral feeling, there fear of God, a little of this and a little of that in a marvelous mixture. However, it never occurs to the authors to ask whether the principles of morality are, after all, to be sought anywhere in knowledge of human nature (which we can derive only from experience). And if this is not the case, if the principles are completely a priori, free from everything empirical, and found exclusively in pure rational concepts and not at all in any other place, they never ask whether they should undertake this investigation as a separate inquiry, i.e., as pure practical philosophy or (if one may use a name so decried) a metaphysics* of morals. They never think of dealing with it alone and bringing it by itself to completeness and of requiring the public, which desires popularization, to await the outcome of this undertaking.

But a completely isolated metaphysics of morals, mixed with no anthropology, no theology, no physics or hyperphysics, and even less with occult qualities (which might be called hypophysical), is not only an indispensable substrate of all theoretically sound and definite knowledge of duties; it is also a desideratum of the highest importance to the actual fulfilment of its precepts. For the pure conception of duty and of the moral law generally, with no admixture of empirical inducements, has an influence on the human heart so much more powerful than all other incentives† which may be derived from the empirical field that reason, in the consciousness of its dignity, despises them and gradually becomes master over them. It has this influence only through

* If one wishes, the pure philosophy of morals (metaphysics) can be distinguished from the applied (i.e., applied to human nature), just as pure mathematics and pure logic are distinguished from applied mathematics and applied logic. By this designation one is immediately reminded that moral principles are not founded on the peculiarities of human nature but must stand of themselves a priori, and that from such principles practical rules for every rational nature, and accordingly for man, must be derivable.

† I have a letter from the late excellent Sulzer[2] in which he asks me why the theories of virtue accomplish so little even though they contain so much that is convincing to reason. My answer was delayed in order that I might make it complete. The answer is only that the teachers themselves have not completely clarified their concepts, and when they wish to make up for this by hunting in every quarter for motives to the morally good so as to make their physic right strong, they spoil it. For the commonest observation shows that if we imagine an act of honesty performed with a steadfast soul and sundered from all view to any advantage in this or another world and even under the greatest temptations of need or allurement, it far

2. [Johann Georg Sulzer (1720–79), an important figure at the court and in literary circles in Berlin. Cf. *Allgemeine deutsche Biographie*, XXXVII, 144–47.]

reason, which thereby first realizes that it can of itself be practical. A mixed theory of morals which is put together both from incentives of feelings and inclinations and from rational concepts must, on the other hand, make the mind vacillate between motives which cannot be brought under any principle and which can lead only accidentally to the good and often to the bad.

From what has been said it is clear that all moral concepts have their seat and origin entirely a priori in reason. This is just as much the case in the most ordinary reason as in reason which is speculative to the highest degree. It is obvious that they can be abstracted from no empirical and hence merely contingent cognitions. In the purity of their origin lies their worthiness to serve us as supreme practical principles, and to the extent that something empirical is added to them, just this much is subtracted from their genuine influence and from the unqualified worth of actions. Furthermore, it is evident that it is not only of the greatest necessity in a theoretical point of view when it is a question of speculation but also of the utmost practical importance to derive the concepts and laws of morals from pure reason and to present them pure and unmixed, and to determine the scope of this entire practical but pure rational knowledge (the entire faculty of pure practical reason) without making the principles depend upon the particular nature of human reason, as speculative philosophy may permit and even sometimes find necessary. But since moral laws should hold for every rational being as such, the principles must be derived from the universal concept of a rational being generally. In this manner all morals, which need anthropology for their application to men, must be completely developed first as pure philosophy, i.e., metaphysics, independently of anthropology (a thing which is easily done in such distinct fields of knowledge). For we know well that if we are not in possession of such a metaphysics, it is not merely futile to define accurately for the purposes of speculative judgment the moral element of duty in all actions which accord with duty, but impossible to base morals on legitimate principles for merely ordinary and practical use, especially in moral instruction; and it is only in this manner that pure moral dispositions can be pro-

---

surpasses and eclipses any similar action which was affected in the least by any foreign incentive; it elevates the soul and arouses the wish to be able to act in this way. Even moderately young children feel this impression, and one should never represent duties to them in any other way.

duced and engrafted on men's minds for the purpose of the highest good in the world.

In this study we do not advance merely from the common moral judgment (which here is very worthy of respect) to the philosophical, as this has already been done, but we advance by natural stages from a popular philosophy (which goes no further than it can grope by means of examples) to metaphysics (which is not held back by anything empirical and which, as it must measure out the entire scope of rational knowledge of this kind, reaches even ideas, where examples fail us). In order to make this advance, we must follow and clearly present the practical faculty of reason from its universal rules of determination to the point where the concept of duty arises from it.

Everything in nature works according to laws. Only a rational being has the capacity of acting according to the conception of laws, i.e., according to principles. This capacity is will. Since reason is required for the derivation of actions from laws, will is nothing else than practical reason. If reason infallibly determines the will, the actions which such a being recognizes as objectively necessary are also subjectively necessary. That is, the will is a faculty of choosing only that which reason, independently of inclination, recognizes as practically necessary, i.e., as good. But if reason of itself does not sufficiently determine the will, and if the will is subjugated to subjective conditions (certain incentives) which do not always agree with objective conditions; in a word, if the will is not of itself in complete accord with reason (the actual case of men), then the actions which are recognized as objectively necessary are subjectively contingent, and the determination of such a will according to objective laws is constraint. That is, the relation of objective laws to a will which is not completely good is conceived as the determination of the will of a rational being by principles of reason to which this will is not by nature necessarily obedient.

The conception of an objective principle, so far as it constrains a will, is a command (of reason), and the formula of this command is called an *imperative*.

All imperatives are expressed by an "ought" and thereby indicate the relation of an objective law of reason to a will which is not in its subjective constitution necessarily determined by this law. This relation is that of constraint. Imperatives say that it would be good to do or to refrain from doing something, but they say it to a will which does not always do something simply because it is presented to it as a good thing to do. Practical good is what determines the will by means of the conception of reason and hence not by subjective causes but, rather, objectively, i.e., on grounds which are valid for every rational being as such. It is distinguished from the pleasant, as that which has an influence on the will only by means of a sensation from merely subjective causes, which hold only for the senses of this or that person and not as a principle of reason which holds for everyone.*

A perfectly good will, therefore, would be equally subject to objective laws (of the good), but it could not be conceived as constrained by them to act in accord with them, because, according to its own subjective constitution, it can be determined to act only through the conception of the good. Thus no imperatives hold for the divine will or, more generally, for a holy will. The "ought" is here out of place, for the volition of itself is necessarily in unison with the law. Therefore imperatives are only formulas expressing the relation of objective laws of volition in general to the subjective imperfection of the will of this or that rational being, e.g., the human will.

All imperatives command either hypothetically or categorically. The former present the practical necessity of a possible action as a means to achieving something else which one desires (or which one may possibly desire). The categorical imperative would be one which presented an action as of itself objectively necessary, without regard to any other end.

Since every practical law presents a possible action as good and thus as necessary for a subject practically determinable by

* The dependence of the faculty of desire on sensations is called inclination, and inclination always indicates a need. The dependence of a contingently determinable will on principles of reason, however, is called interest. An interest is present only in a dependent will which is not of itself always in accord with reason; in the divine will we cannot conceive of an interest. But the human will can take an interest in something without thereby acting from interest. The former means the practical interest in the action; the latter, the pathological interest in the object of the action. The former indicates only the dependence of the will on principles of reason in themselves, while the latter indicates dependence on the principles of reason for the purpose of inclination, since reason gives only the practical rule by which the needs of inclination are to be aided. In the former case the action interests me, and in the latter the object of the action (so far as it is pleasant for me) interests me. In the first section we have seen that, in the case of an action done from duty, no regard must be given to the interest in the object, but merely in the action itself and its principle in reason (i.e., the law).

reason, all imperatives are formulas of the determination of action which is necessary by the principle of a will which is in any way good. If the action is good only as a means to something else, the imperative is hypothetical; but if it is thought of as good in itself, and hence as necessary in a will which of itself conforms to reason as the principle of this will, the imperative is categorical.

The imperative thus says what action possible to me would be good, and it presents the practical rule in relation to a will which does not forthwith perform an action simply because it is good, in part because the subject does not always know that the action is good and in part (when it does know it) because his maxims can still be opposed to the objective principles of practical reason.

The hypothetical imperative, therefore, says only that the action is good to some purpose, possible or actual. In the former case it is a problematical,[3] in the latter an assertorical, practical principle. The categorical imperative, which declares the action to be of itself objectively necessary without making any reference to a purpose, i.e., without having any other end, holds as an apodictical (practical) principle.

We can think of that which is possible through the mere powers of some rational being as a possible purpose of any will. As a consequence, the principles of action, in so far as they are thought of as necessary to attain a possible purpose which can be achieved by them, are in reality infinitely numerous. All sciences

3. [The *First Introduction to the Critique of Judgment* says: "This is the place to correct an error into which I fell in the *Foundations of the Metaphysics of Morals*. After I had stated that the imperatives of prudence commanded only conditionally, and indeed only under the condition of merely possible, i.e., problematic, ends, I called that kind of practical precept 'problematic imperatives.' But there is certainly a contradiction in this expression. I should have called them 'technical imperatives,' i.e., imperatives of art. The pragmatic imperatives, or rules of prudence which command under the condition of an actual and even subjectively necessary end, belong also among the technical imperatives. (For what is prudence but the skill to use free men and even the natural dispositions and inclinations of oneself for one's own designs?) Only the fact that the end to which we submit ourselves and others, namely, our own happiness, does not belong to the merely arbitrary ends [which we may or may not have] justifies a special name for these imperatives, because the problem does not require merely a mode of reaching the end, as is the case with technical imperatives, but also requires a definition of what constitutes this end itself (happiness). The end must be presupposed as known in the case of technical imperatives" (Cassirer ed., V, 183 n.).]

have some practical part which consists of problems of some end which is possible for us and of imperatives as to how it can be reached. These can therefore generally be called imperatives of skill. Whether the end is reasonable and good is not in question at all, for the question is only of what must be done in order to attain it. The precepts to be followed by a physician in order to cure his patient and by a poisoner in order to bring about certain death are of equal value in so far as each does that which will perfectly accomplish his purpose. Since in early youth we do not know what ends may occur to us in the course of life, parents seek to let their children learn a great many things and provide for skill in the use of means to all sorts of arbitrary ends, among which they cannot determine whether any one of them may later become an actual purpose of their pupil, though it is possible that he may someday have it as his actual purpose. And this anxiety is so great that they commonly neglect to form and correct their judgment on the worth of things which they may make their ends.

There is one end, however, which we may presuppose as actual in all rational beings so far as imperatives apply to them, i.e., so far as they are dependent beings; there is one purpose not only which they *can* have but which we can presuppose that they all *do* have by a necessity of nature. This purpose is happiness. The hypothetical imperative which represents the practical necessity of action as means to the promotion of happiness is an assertorical imperative. We may not expound it as merely necessary to an uncertain and a merely possible purpose, but as necessary to a purpose which we can a priori and with assurance assume for everyone because it belongs to his essence. Skill in the choice of means to one's own highest welfare can be called prudence* in the narrowest sense. Thus the imperative which refers to the choice of means to one's own happiness, i.e., the precept of prudence, is still only hypothetical; the action is not absolutely commanded but commanded only as a means to another end.

Finally, there is one imperative which directly commands a

* The word "prudence" may be taken in two senses, and it may bear the name of prudence with reference to things of the world and private prudence. The former sense means the skill of a man in having an influence on others so as to use them for his own purposes. The latter is the ability to unite all these purposes to his own lasting advantage. The worth of the first is finally reduced to the latter, and of one who is prudent in the former sense but not in the latter we might better say that he is clever and cunning yet, on the whole, imprudent.

certain conduct without making its condition some purpose to be reached by it. This imperative is categorical. It concerns not the material of the action and its intended result but the form and the principle from which it results. What is essentially good in it consists in the intention, the result being what it may. This imperative may be called the imperative of morality.

Volition according to these three principles is plainly distinguished by dissimiliarity in the constraint to which they subject the will. In order to clarify this dissimilarity, I believe that they are most suitably named if one says that they are either rules of skill, counsels of prudence, or commands (laws) of morality, respectively. For law alone implies the concept of an unconditional and objective and hence universally valid necessity, and commands are laws which must be obeyed, even against inclination. Counsels do indeed involve necessity, but a necessity that can hold only under a subjectively contingent condition, i.e., whether this or that man counts this or that as part of his happiness; but the categorical imperative, on the other hand, is restricted by no condition. As absolutely, though practically, necessary it can be called a command in the strict sense. We could also call the first imperative technical (belonging to art), the second pragmatic* (belonging to welfare), and the third moral (belonging to free conduct as such, i.e., to morals).

The question now arises: How are all these imperatives possible? This question does not require an answer as to how the action which the imperative commands can be performed but merely as to how the constraint of the will, which the imperative expresses in the problem, can be conceived. How an imperative of skill is possible requires no particular discussion. Whoever wills the end, so far as reason has decisive influence on his action, wills also the indispensably necessary means to it that lie in his power. This proposition, in what concerns the will, is analytical; for, in willing an object as my effect, my causality as an[4] acting subject, i.e., the use of the means, is already thought, and the imperative derives the concept of necessary actions to this end from

---

* It seems to me that the proper meaning of the word "pragmatic" could be most accurately defined in this way. For sanctions which properly flow not from the law of states as necessary statutes but from provision for the general welfare are called pragmatic. A history is pragmatically composed when it teaches prudence, i.e., instructs the world how it could provide for its interest better than, or at least as well as, has been done in the past.

4. [Reading *handelnde* with the Academy ed.; the Cassirer ed. has: "my causality as that of an acting subject."]

the concept of willing this end. Synthetical propositions undoubtedly are necessary in determining the means to a proposed end, but they do not concern the ground, the act of the will, but only the way to make the object real. Mathematics teaches, by synthetical propositions only, that in order to bisect a line according to an infallible principle, I must make two intersecting arcs from each of its extremities; but if I know the proposed result can be obtained only by such an action, then it is an analytical proposition that, if I fully will the effect, I must also will the action necessary to produce it. For it is one and the same thing to conceive of something as an effect which is in a certain way possible through me and to conceive of myself as acting in this way.

If it were only easy to give a definite concept of happiness, the imperatives of prudence would completely correspond to those of skill and would be likewise analytical. For it could be said in this case as well as in the former that whoever wills the end wills also (necessarily according to reason) the only means to it which are in his power. But it is a misfortune that the concept of happiness is such an indefinite concept that, although each person wishes to attain it, he can never definitely and self-consistently state what it is he really wishes and wills. The reason for this is that all elements which belong to the concept of happiness are empirical, i.e., they must be taken from experience, while for the idea of happiness an absolute whole, a maximum, of well-being is needed in my present and in every future condition. Now it is impossible even for a most clear-sighted and omnipotent but finite being to form here a definite concept of that which he really wills. If he wills riches, how much anxiety, envy, and intrigues might he not thereby draw upon his shoulders! If he wills much knowledge and vision, perhaps it might become only an eye that much sharper to show him as more dreadful the evils which are now hidden from him and which are yet unavoidable or to burden his desires—which already sufficiently engage him—with even more needs! If he wills a long life, who guarantees that it will not be long misery? If he wills at least health, how often has not the discomfort of the body restrained him from excesses into which perfect health would have led him? In short, he is not capable, on any principle and with complete certainty, of ascertaining what would make him truly happy; omniscience would be needed for this. He cannot, therefore, act according to definite principles so as to be happy, but only according to empirical counsels, e.g., those of diet, economy, courtesy, restraint, etc., which are shown by experience best to promote welfare on the average. Hence the imperatives of prudence cannot, in the strict sense, command, i.e., present actions objectively as practically necessary; thus they are to be taken as counsels (*consilia*) rather than as commands (*praecepta*) of reason, and the task of determining infallibly and universally what action will promote the happiness of a rational being is completely unsolvable. There can be no imperative which would, in the strict sense, command us to do what makes for happiness, because happiness is an ideal not of reason but of imagination,[5] depending only on empirical grounds which one would expect in vain to determine an action through which the totality of consequences—which is in fact infinite—could be achieved. Assuming that the means to happiness could be infallibly stated, this imperative of prudence would be an analytical proposition, for it differs from the imperative of skill only in that its end is given while in the latter case it is merely possible. Since both, however, only command the means to that which one presupposes, the imperative which commands the willing of the means to him who wills the end are both analytical. There is, consequently, no difficulty in seeing the possibility of such an imperative.

To see how the imperative of morality is possible is, then, without doubt the only question needing an answer. It is not hypothetical, and thus the objectively conceived necessity cannot be supported by any presupposition, as was the case with the hypothetical imperatives. But it must not be overlooked that it cannot be shown by any example (i.e., it cannot be empirically shown) whether or not there is such an imperative; it is rather to be suspected that all imperatives which appear to be categorical be yet hypothetical, but in a hidden way. For instance, when it is said, "Thou shalt not make a false promise," we assume that the necessity of this avoidance is not a mere counsel for the sake of escaping of some other evil, so that it would read, "Thou shalt not make a false promise so that, if it comes to light, thou ruinest thy

---

5. [The distinction between happiness and pleasure, which Kant says the followers of Epicurus confused, is explained in a fragment dating back to about 1775: "Happiness is not something sensed but something thought. Nor is it a thought which can be taken from experience but a thought which only makes its experience possible. Not as if one had to know happiness in all its elements, but [one must know] the a priori condition by which alone one can be capable of happiness" (*Lose Blätter* [Reicke ed.], trans. Schilpp, in *Kant's Precritical Ethics*, p. 129).]

credit;" we assume rather that an action of this kind must be regarded as of itself bad and that the imperative of the prohibition is categorical. But we cannot show with certainty by any example that the will is here determined by the law alone without any other incentives, even though this appears to be the case. For it is always possible that secretly fear of disgrace, and perhaps also obscure apprehension of other dangers, may have had an influence on the will. Who can prove by experience the nonexistence of a cause when experience shows us only that we do not perceive the cause? But in such a case the so-called moral imperative, which as such appears to be categorical and unconditional, would be actually only a pragmatic precept which makes us attentive to our own advantage and teaches us to consider it.

Thus we shall have to investigate purely a priori the possibility of a categorical imperative, for we do not have the advantage that experience would give us the reality of this imperative, so that the [demonstration of its] possibility would be necessary only for its explanation and not for its establishment. In the meantime, this much may at least be seen: the categorical imperative alone can be taken as a practical *law*, while all the others may be called principles of the will but not laws. This is because what is necessary merely for the attainment of an arbitrary purpose can be regarded as itself contingent, and we get rid of the precept once we give up the purpose, whereas the unconditional command leaves the will no freedom to choose the opposite. Thus it alone implies the necessity which we require of a law.

Secondly, in the case of the categorical imperative or law of morality, the cause of difficulty in discerning its possibility is very weighty. This imperative is an a priori synthetical practical proposition,* and, since to discern the possibility of propositions of this sort is so difficult in theoretical knowledge, it may well be gathered that it will be no less difficult in the practical.

In attacking this problem, we will first inquire whether the mere concept of a categorical imperative does not also furnish the formula containing the proposition which alone can be a

---

* I connect a priori the will, without a presupposed condition resulting from an inclination, with the action (though I do so only objectively, i.e., under the idea of a reason which would have complete power over all subjective motives). This is, therefore, a practical proposition which does not analytically derive the willing of an action from some other volition already presupposed (for we do not have such a perfect will); it rather connects it directly with the concept of the will of a rational being as something which is not contained within it.

categorical imperative. For even when we know the formula of the imperative, to learn how such an absolute law is possible will require difficult and special labors which we shall postpone to the last section.

If I think of a hypothetical imperative as such, I do not know what it will contain until the condition is stated [under which it is an imperative]. But if I think of a categorical imperative, I know immediately what it contains. For since the imperative contains besides the law only the necessity of the maxim* of acting in accordance with this law, while the law contains no condition to which it is restricted, there is nothing remaining in it except the universality of law as such to which the maxim of the action should conform; and in effect this conformity alone is represented as necessary by the imperative.[6]

There is, therefore, only one categorical imperative. It is: Act only according to that maxim by which you can at the same time will that it should become a universal law.

Now if all imperatives of duty can be derived from this one imperative as a principle, we can at least show what we understand by the concept of duty and what it means, even though it remain undecided whether that which is called duty is an empty concept or not.

The universality of law according to which effects are produced constitutes what is properly called nature in the most general sense (as to form), i.e., the existence of things so far as it is determined by universal laws. [By analogy], then, the universal imperative of duty can be expressed as follows: Act as though the maxim of your action were by your will to become a universal law of nature.

We shall now enumerate some duties, adopting the usual division of them into duties to ourselves and to others and into perfect and imperfect duties.†

---

*A maxim is the subjective principle of acting and must be distinguished from the objective principle, i.e., the practical law. The former contains the practical rule which reason determines according to the conditions of the subject (often its ignorance or inclinations) and is thus the principle according to which the subject acts. The law, on the other hand, is the objective principle valid for every rational being, and the principle by which it ought to act, i.e., an imperative.

6. [Following reading of Cassirer ed.]

† It must be noted here that I reserve the division of duties for a future *Metaphysics of Morals* and that the division here stands as only an arbitrary one (chosen in order to arrange my examples). For the rest, by a

1. A man who is reduced to despair by a series of evils feels a weariness with life but is still in possession of his reason sufficiently to ask whether it would not be contrary to his duty to himself to take his own life. Now he asks whether the maxim of his action could become a universal law of nature. His maxim, however, is: For love of myself, I make it my principle to shorten my life when by a longer duration it threatens more evil than satisfaction. But it is questionable whether this principle of self-love could become a universal law of nature. One immediately sees a contradiction in a system of nature, whose law would be to destroy life by the feeling whose special office is to impel the improvement of life. In this case it would not exist as nature; hence that maxim cannot obtain as a law of nature, and thus it wholly contradicts the supreme principle of all duty.

2. Another man finds himself forced by need to borrow money. He well knows that he will not be able to repay it, but he also sees that nothing will be loaned him if he does not firmly promise to repay it at a certain time. He desires to make such a promise, but he has enough conscience to ask himself whether it is not improper and opposed to duty to relieve his distress in such a way. Now, assuming he does decide to do so, the maxim of his action would be as follows: When I believe myself to be in need of money, I will borrow money and promise to repay it, although I know I shall never do so. Now this principle of self-love or of his own benefit may very well be compatible with his whole future welfare, but the question is whether it is right. He changes the pretension of self-love into a universal law and then puts the question: How would it be if my maxim became a universal law? He immediately sees that it could never hold as a universal law of nature and be consistent with itself; rather it must necessarily contradict itself. For the universality of a law which says that anyone who believes himself to be in need could promise what he pleased with the intention of not fulfilling it would make the promise itself and the end to be accomplished by it impossible; no one would believe what was promised to him but would only laugh at any such assertion as vain pretense.

3. A third finds in himself a talent which could, by means of

---

perfect duty I here understand a duty which permits no exception in the interest of inclination; thus I have not merely outer but also inner perfect duties. This runs contrary to the usage adopted in the schools, but I am not disposed to defend it here because it is all one to my purpose whether this is conceded or not.

some cultivation, make him in many respects a useful man. But he finds himself in comfortable circumstances and prefers indulgence in pleasure to troubling himself with broadening and improving his fortunate natural gifts. Now, however, let him ask whether his maxim of neglecting his gifts, besides agreeing with his propensity to idle amusement, agrees also with what is called duty. He sees that a system of nature could indeed exist in accordance with such a law, even though man (like the inhabitants of the South Sea Islands) should let his talents rust and resolve to devote his life merely to idleness, indulgence, and propagation—in a word, to pleasure. But he cannot possibly will that this should become a universal law of nature or that it should be implanted in us by a natural instinct. For, as a rational being, he necessarily wills that all his faculties should be developed, inasmuch as they are given to him for all sorts of possible purposes.

4. A fourth man, for whom things are going well, sees that others (whom he could help) have to struggle with great hardships, and he asks, "What concern of mine is it? Let each one be as happy as heaven wills, or as he can make himself; I will not take anything from him or even envy him; but to his welfare or to his assistance in time of need I have no desire to contribute." If such a way of thinking were a universal law of nature, certainly the human race could exist, and without doubt even better than in a state where everyone talks of sympathy and good will or even exerts himself occasionally to practice them while, on the other hand, he cheats when he can and betrays or otherwise violates the rights of man. Now although it is possible that a universal law of nature according to that maxim could exist, it is nevertheless impossible to will that such a principle should hold everywhere as a law of nature. For a will which resolved this would conflict with itself, since instances can often arise in which he would need the love and sympathy of others, and in which he would have robbed himself, by such a law of nature springing from his own will, of all hope of the aid he desires.

The foregoing are a few of the many actual duties, or at least of duties we hold to be real, whose derivation from the one stated principle is clear. We must be able to will that a maxim of our action become a universal law; this is the canon of the moral estimation of our action generally. Some actions are of such a nature that their maxim cannot even be *thought* as a universal law of nature without contradiction, far from it being possible that one could will that it should be such. In others this internal impossibility is not found, though it is still impossible to *will* that their maxim should be raised to the universality of a law of nature, because such a will would contradict itself. We easily see that the former maxim conflicts with the stricter or narrower (imprescriptable) duty, the latter with broader (meritorious) duty. Thus all duties, so far as the kind of obligation (not the object of their action) is concerned, have been completely exhibited by these examples in their dependence on the one principle.

When we observe ourselves in any transgression of a duty, we find that we do not actually will that our maxim should become a universal law. That is impossible for us; rather, the contrary of this maxim should remain as a law generally, and we only take the liberty of making an exception to it for ourselves or for the sake of our inclination, and for this one occasion. Consequently, if we weighed everything from one and the same standpoint, namely, reason, we would come upon a contradiction in our own will, viz., that a certain principle is objectively necessary as a universal law and yet subjectively does not hold universally but rather admits exceptions. However, since we regard our action at one time from the point of view of a will wholly conformable to reason and then from that of a will affected by inclinations, there is actually no contradiction, but rather an opposition of inclination to the precept of reason (*antagonismus*). In this the universality of the principle (*universalitas*) is changed into mere generality (*generalitas*), whereby the practical principle of reason meets the maxim halfway. Although this cannot be justified in our own impartial judgment, it does show that we actually acknowledge the validity of the categorical imperative and allow ourselves (with all respect to it) only a few exceptions which seem to us to be unimportant and forced upon us.

We have thus at least established that if duty is a concept which is to have significance and actual legislation for our actions, it can be expressed only in categorical imperatives and not at all in hypothetical ones. For every application of it we have also clearly exhibited the content of the categorical imperative which must contain the principle of all duty (if there is such). This is itself very much. But we are not yet advanced far enough to prove a priori that that kind of imperative really exists, that there is a practical law which of itself commands absolutely and without any incentives, and that obedience to this law is duty.

With a view to attaining this, it is extremely important to

remember that we must not let ourselves think that the reality of this principle can be derived from the particular constitution of human nature. For duty is practical unconditional necessity of action; it must, therefore, hold for all rational beings (to which alone an imperative can apply), and only for that reason can it be a law for all human wills. Whatever is derived from the particular natural situation of man as such, or from certain feelings and propensities, or, even, from a particular tendency of the human reason which might not hold necessarily for the will of every rational being (if such a tendency is possible), can give a maxim valid for us but not a law; that is, it can give a subjective principle by which we may act but not an objective principle by which we would be directed to act even if all our propensity, inclination, and natural tendency were opposed to it. This is so far the case that the sublimity and intrinsic worth of the command is the better shown in a duty the fewer subjective causes there are for it and the more they are against it; the latter do not weaken the constraint of the law or diminish its validity.

Here we see philosophy brought to what is, in fact, a precarious position, which should be made fast even though it is supported by nothing in either heaven or earth. Here philosophy must show its purity, as the absolute sustainer of its laws, and not as the herald of those which an implanted sense or who knows what tutelary nature whispers to it. Those may be better than no laws at all, but they can never afford fundamental principles, which reason alone dictates. These fundamental principles must originate entirely a priori and thereby obtain their commanding authority; they can expect nothing from the inclination of men but everything from the supremacy of the law and due respect for it. Otherwise they condemn man to self-contempt and inner abhorrence.

Thus everything empirical is not only wholly unworthy to be an ingredient in the principle of morality but is even highly prejudicial to the purity of moral practices themselves. For, in morals, the proper and inestimable worth of an absolutely good will consists precisely in the freedom of the principle of action from all influences from contingent grounds which only experience can furnish. We cannot too much or too often warn against the lax or even base manner of thought which seeks principles among empirical motives and laws, for human reason in its weariness is glad to rest on this pillow. In a dream of sweet illusions (in which it embraces not Juno but a cloud), it substitutes for morality a bastard patched up from limbs of very different parentage, which looks like anything one wishes to see in it, but not like virtue to anyone who has ever beheld her in her true form.*

The question then is: Is it a necessary law for all rational beings that they should always judge their actions by such maxims that they themselves could will to serve as universal laws? If it is such a law, it must be connected (wholly a priori) with the concept of the will of a rational being as such. But in order to discover this connection, we must, however reluctantly, take a step into metaphysics, although into a region of it different from speculative philosophy, i.e., the metaphysics of morals. In a practical philosophy it is not a question of assuming grounds for what happens but of assuming laws of what ought to happen even though it may never happen, that is to say, objective, practical laws. Hence in practical philosophy we need not inquire into the reasons why something pleases or displeases, how the pleasure of mere feeling differs from taste, and whether this is distinct from a general satisfaction of reason. Nor need we ask on what the feeling of pleasure or displeasure rests, how desires and inclinations arise, and how, finally, maxims arise from desires and inclination under the co-operation of reason. For all these matters belong to an empirical psychology, which would be the second part of physics, if we consider it as philosophy of nature so far as it rests on empirical laws. But here it is a question of objectively practical laws and thus of the relation of a will to itself so far as it determines itself only by reason; for everything which has a relation to the empirical automatically falls away, because if reason of itself alone determines conduct, it must necessarily do so a priori. The possibility of reason's thus determining conduct must now be investigated.

The will is thought of as a faculty of determining itself to action in accordance with the conception of certain laws. Such a faculty can be found only in rational beings. That which serves the will as the objective ground of its self-determination is an end, and, if it is given by reason alone, it must hold alike for all rational beings. On the other hand, that which contains the

---

* To behold virtue in her proper form is nothing else than to exhibit morality stripped of all admixture of sensuous things and of every spurious adornment of reward or self-love. How much she then eclipses everything which appears charming to the senses can easily be seen by everyone with the least effort of his reason, if it be not spoiled for all abstraction.

ground of the possibility of the action, whose result is an end, is called the means. The subjective ground of desire is the incentive,[7] while the objective ground of volition is the motive. Thus arises the distinction between subjective ends, which rest on incentives, and objective ends, which depend on motives valid for every rational being. Practical principles are formal when they disregard all subjective ends; they are material when they have subjective ends, and thus certain incentives, as their basis. The ends which a rational being arbitrarily proposes to himself as consequences of his action are material ends and are without exception only relative, for only their relation to a particularly constituted faculty of desire in the subject gives them their worth. And this worth cannot, therefore, afford any universal principles for all rational beings or valid and necessary principles for every volition. That is, they cannot give rise to any practical laws. All these relative ends, therefore, are grounds for hypothetical imperatives only.

But suppose that there were something the existence of which in itself had absolute worth, something which, as an end in itself, could be a ground of definite laws. In it and only in it could lie the ground of a possible categorical imperative, i.e., of a practical law.

Now, I say, man and, in general, every rational being exists as an end in himself and not merely as a means to be arbitrarily used by this or that will. In all his actions, whether they are directed to himself or to other rational beings, he must always be regarded at the same time as an end. All objects of inclinations have only a conditional worth, for if the inclinations and the needs founded on them did not exist, their object would be without worth. The inclinations themselves as the sources of needs, however, are so lacking in absolute worth that the universal wish of every rational being must be indeed to free themselves completely from them. Therefore, the worth of any objects to be obtained by our actions is at all times conditional. Beings whose existence does not depend on our will but on nature, if they are not rational beings, have only a relative worth as means and are therefore called "things"; on the other hand, rational beings are designated "persons," because their nature indicates that they are ends in

7. [*Triebfeder* in contrast to *Bewegungsgrund*. Abbott translates the former as "spring," but "urge" might better convey the meaning. I follow Greene and Hudson's excellent usage in their translation of the *Religion*.]

themselves, i.e., things which may not be used merely as means. Such a being is thus an object of respect and, so far, restricts all [arbitrary] choice. Such beings are not merely subjective ends whose existence as a result of our action has a worth for us but are objective ends, i.e., beings whose existence in itself is an end. Such an end is one for which no other end can be substituted, to which these beings should serve merely as means. For, without them, nothing of absolute worth could be found, and if all worth is conditional and thus contingent, no supreme practical principle for reason could be found anywhere.

Thus if there is to be a supreme practical principle and a categorical imperative for the human will, it must be one that forms an objective principle of the will from the conception of that which is necessarily an end for everyone because it is an end in itself. Hence this objective principle can serve as a universal practical law. The ground of this principle is: rational nature exists as an end in itself. Man necessarily thinks of his own existence in this way; thus far it is a subjective principle of human actions. Also every other rational being thinks of his existence by means of the same rational ground which holds also for myself;* thus it is at the same time an objective principle from which, as a supreme practical ground, it must be possible to derive all laws of the will. The practical imperative, therefore, is the following: Act so that you treat humanity, whether in your own person or in that of another, always as an end and never as a means only. Let us now see whether this can be achieved.

To return to our previous examples:

First, according to the concept of necessary duty to one's self, he who contemplates suicide will ask himself whether his action can be consistent with the idea of humanity as an end in itself. If, in order to escape from burdensome circumstances, he destroys himself, he uses a person merely as a means to maintain a tolerable condition up to the end of life. Man, however, is not a thing, and thus not something to be used merely as a means; he must always be regarded in all his actions as an end in himself. Therefore, I cannot dispose of man in my own person so as to mutilate, corrupt, or kill him. (It belongs to ethics proper to define more accurately this basic principle so as to avoid all misunderstanding, e.g., as to the amputation of limbs in order to pre-

---

* Here I present this proposition as a postulate, but in the last section grounds for it will be found.

serve myself, or to exposing my life to danger in order to save it; I must, therefore, omit them here.)

Second, as concerns necessary or obligatory duties to others, he who intends a deceitful promise to others sees immediately that he intends to use another man merely as a means, without the latter containing the end in himself at the same time. For he whom I want to use for my own purposes by means of such a promise cannot possibly assent to my mode of acting against him and cannot contain the end of this action in himself. This conflict against the principle of other men is even clearer if we cite examples of attacks on their freedom and property. For then it is clear that he who transgresses the rights of men intends to make use of the person of others merely as a means, without considering that, as rational beings, they must always be esteemed at the same time as ends, i.e., only as beings who must be able to contain in themselves the end of the very same action.*

Thirdly, with regard to contingent (meritorious) duty to one's self, it is not sufficient that the action not conflict with humanity in our person as an end in itself; it must also harmonize with it. Now in humanity there are capacities for greater perfection which belong to the end of nature with respect to humanity in our own person; to neglect these might perhaps be consistent with the preservation of humanity as an end in itself but not with the furtherance of that end.

Fourthly, with regard to meritorious duty to others, the natural end which all men have is their own happiness. Humanity might indeed exist if no one contributed to the happiness of others, provided he did not intentionally detract from it; but this harmony with humanity as an end in itself is only negative rather than positive if everyone does not also endeavor, so far as he can, to further the ends of others. For the ends of any person, who is an end in himself, must as far as possible also be my end, if that conception of an end in itself is to have its full effect on me.

This principle of humanity and of every rational creature as

* Let it not be thought that the banal "*quod tibi non vis fieri, etc.*" could here serve as guide or principle, for it is only derived from the principle and is restricted by various limitations. It cannot be a universal law, because it contains the ground neither of duties to one's self nor of the benevolent duties to others (for many a man would gladly consent that others should not benefit him, provided only that he might be excused from showing benevolence to them). Nor does it contain the ground of obligatory duties to another, for the criminal would argue on this ground against the judge who sentences him. And so on.

an end in itself is the supreme limiting condition on freedom of the actions of each man. It is not borrowed from experience, first, because of its universality, since it applies to all rational beings generally, and experience does not suffice to determine anything about them; and, secondly, because in experience humanity is not thought of (subjectively) as the end of men, i.e., as an object which we of ourselves really make our end. Rather it is thought of as the objective end which should constitute the supreme limiting condition of all subjective ends, whatever they may be. Thus this principle must arise from pure reason. Objectively the ground of all practical legislation lies (according to the first principle) in the rule and in the form of universality, which makes it capable of being a law (at most a natural law); subjectively, it lies in the end. But the subject of all ends is every rational being as an end in itself (by the second principle); from this there follows the third practical principle of the will as the supreme condition of its harmony with universal practical reason, viz., the idea of the will of every rational being as making universal law.[8]

By this principle all maxims are rejected which are not consistent with the universal lawgiving of will. The will is thus not only subject to the law but subject in such a way that it must be regarded also as legislative and only for this reason as being subject to the law (of which it can regard itself as the author).

In the foregoing mode of conception, in which imperatives are conceived universally either as conformity to law by actions—a conformity which is similar to a natural order—or as the prerogative of rational beings as such, the imperatives exclude from their legislative authority all admixture of any interest as an incentive. They do so because they were conceived as categorical. They were only assumed to be categorical, however, because we had to make such an assumption if we wished to explain the concept of duty. But that there were practical propositions which commanded categorically could not here be proved independently, just as little as it can be proved anywhere in this section. One thing, however, might have been done: to indicate in the imperative itself, by some determination which it contained, that in volition from duty the renunciation of all interest is the specific mark of the categorical imperative, distinguishing it from the hypothetical. And this is now being done in the third formulation of the principle, i.e., in the idea of the will of every rational being as a will giving universal law. A will which stands under laws can

8. [Following the suggestion of Paton, *op. cit.*, p. 180.]

be bound to this law by an interest. But if we think of a will giving universal laws, we find that a supreme legislating will cannot possibly depend on any interest, for such a dependent will would itself need still another law which would restrict the interest of its self-love to the condition that [the maxims of this will] should be valid as universal law.

Thus the principle of every human will as a will giving universal laws in all its maxims* is very well adapted to being a categorical imperative, provided it is otherwise correct. Because of the idea of universal lawgiving, it is based on no interest, and, thus of all possible imperatives, it alone can be unconditional. Or, better, converting the proposition: if there is a categorical imperative (a law for the will of every rational being), it can only command that everything be done from the maxim of its will as one which could have as its object only itself considered as giving universal laws. For only in this case are the practical principle and the imperative which the will obeys unconditional, because the will can have no interest as its foundation.

If we now look back upon all previous attempts which have ever been undertaken to discover the principle of morality, it is not to be wondered at that they all had to fail. Man was seen to be bound to laws by his duty, but it was not seen that he is subject only to his own, yet universal, legislation, and that he is only bound to act in accordance with his own will, which is, however, designed by nature to be a will giving universal laws. For if one thought of him as subject only to a law (whatever it may be), this necessarily implied some interest as a stimulus or compulsion to obedience because the law did not arise from his will. Rather, his will was constrained by something else according to a law to act in a certain way. By this strictly necessary consequence, however, all the labor of finding a supreme ground for duty was irrevocably lost, and one never arrived at duty but only at the necessity of action from a certain interest. This might be his own interest or that of another, but in either case the imperative always had to be conditional and could not at all serve as a moral command. This principle I will call the principle of *autonomy* of the will in contrast to all other principles which I accordingly count under *heteronomy*.

The concept of each rational being as a being that must regard

* I may be excused from citing examples to elucidate this principle, for those which have already illustrated the categorical imperative and its formula can here serve the same purpose.

itself as giving universal law through all the maxims of its will, so that it may judge itself and its actions from this standpoint, leads to a very fruitful concept, namely, that of a *realm of ends*.

By "realm" I understand the systematic union of different rational beings through common laws. Because laws determine ends with regard to their universal validity, if we abstract from the personal difference of rational beings and thus from all content of their private ends, we can think of a whole of all ends in systematic connection, a whole of rational beings as ends in themselves as well as of the particular ends which each may set for himself. This is a realm of ends, which is possible on the aforesaid principles. For all rational beings stand under the law that each of them should treat himself and all others never merely as means but in every case also as an end in himself. Thus there arises a systematic union of rational beings through common objective laws. This is a realm which may be called a realm of ends (certainly only an ideal), because what these laws have in view is just the relation of these beings to each other as ends and means.

A rational being belongs to the realm of ends as a member when he gives universal laws in it while also himself subject to these laws. He belongs to it as sovereign when he, as legislating, is subject to the will of no other. The rational being must regard himself always as legislative in a realm of ends possible through the freedom of the will, whether he belongs to it as member or as sovereign. He cannot maintain the latter position merely through the maxims of his will but only when he is a completely independent being without need and with power adequate to his will.

Morality, therefore, consists in the relation of every action to that legislation through which alone a realm of ends is possible. This legislation, however, must be found in every rational being. It must be able to arise from his will, whose principle then is to do no action according to any maxim which would be inconsistent with its being a universal law and thus to act only so that the will through its maxims could regard itself at the same time as universally lawgiving. If now the maxims do not by their nature already necessarily conform to this objective principle of rational beings as universally lawgiving, the necessity of acting according to that principle is called practical constraint, i.e., duty. Duty pertains not to the sovereign in the realm of ends, but rather to each member, and to each in the same degree.

The practical necessity of acting according to this principle, i.e., duty, does not rest at all on feelings, impulses, and inclinations; it rests merely on the relation of rational beings to one another, in which the will of a rational being must always be regarded as legislative, for otherwise it could not be thought of as an end in itself. Reason, therefore, relates every maxim of the will as giving universal laws to every other will and also to every action toward itself; it does so not for the sake of any other practical motive or future advantage but rather from the idea of the dignity of a rational being, which obeys no law except that which he himself also gives.

In the realm of ends, everything has either a *price* or a *dignity*. Whatever has a price can be replaced by something else as its equivalent; on the other hand, whatever is above all price, and therefore admits of no equivalent, has a dignity.

That which is related to general human inclinations and needs has a market price. That which, without presupposing any need, accords with a certain taste, i.e., with pleasure in the mere purposeless play of our faculties, has an *affective price*. But that which constitutes the condition under which alone something can be an end in itself does not have mere relative worth, i.e., a price, but an intrinsic worth, i.e., dignity.

Now morality is the condition under which alone a rational being can be an end in itself, because only through it is it possible to be a legislative member in the realm of ends. Thus morality and humanity, so far as it is capable of morality, alone have dignity. Skill and diligence in work have a market value; wit, lively imagination, and humor have an affective price; but fidelity in promises and benevolence on principle (not from instinct) have intrinsic worth. Nature and likewise art contain nothing which could replace their lack, for their worth consists not in effects which flow from them, nor in advantage and utility which they procure; it consists only in intentions, i.e., maxims of the will, which are ready to reveal themselves in this manner through actions even though success does not favor them. These actions need no recommendation from any subjective disposition or taste in order that they may be looked upon with immediate favor and satisfaction, nor do they have need of any immediate propensity or feeling directed to them. They exhibit the will which performs them as the object of an immediate respect, since nothing but reason is required in order to impose them on the will. The will is not to be cajoled into them, for this, in the case of duties, would be a contradiction. This esteem lets the worth of such a turn of mind be recognized as dignity and puts it infinitely beyond any price, with which it cannot in the least be brought into competition or comparison without, as it were, violating its holiness.

And what is it that justifies the morally good disposition or virtue in making such lofty claims? It is nothing less than the participation it affords the rational being in giving universal laws. He is thus fitted to be a member in a possible realm of ends to which his own nature already destined him. For, as an end in himself, he is destined to be legislative in the realm of ends, free from all laws of nature and obedient only to those which he himself gives. Accordingly, his maxims can belong to a universal legislation to which he is at the same time also subject. A thing has no worth other than that determined for it by the law. The legislation which determines all worth must therefore have a dignity, i.e., unconditional and incomparable worth. For the esteem, which a rational being must have for it, only the word "respect" supplies a suitable expression. Autonomy is thus the basis of the dignity of both human nature and every rational nature.

The three aforementioned ways of presenting the principle of morality are fundamentally only so many formulas of the very same law, and each of them unites the others in itself. There is, nevertheless, a difference in them, but the difference is more subjectively than objectively practical, for it is intended to bring an idea of reason closer to intuition (by means of a certain analogy) and thus nearer to feeling. All maxims have:

1. A form, which consists in universality; and in this respect the formula of the moral imperative requires that the maxims be chosen as though they should hold as universal laws of nature.

2. A material, i.e., an end; in this respect the formula says that the rational being, as by its nature an end and thus as an end in itself, must serve in every maxim as the condition restricting all merely relative and arbitrary ends.

3. A complete determination of all maxims by the formula that all maxims which stem from autonomous legislation ought to harmonize with a possible realm of ends as with a realm of nature.*

* Teleology considers nature as a realm of ends; morals regards a possible realm of ends as a realm of nature. In the former the realm of ends is a theoretical idea for the explanation of what actually is. In the latter it is a practical idea for bringing about that which is not actually real but which can become real through our conduct, and which is in accordance with this idea.

There is a progression here like that through the categories of the unity of the form of the will (its universality), the plurality of material (the objects, i.e., the ends), and the all-comprehensiveness or totality of the system of ends. But it is better in moral evaluation to follow the rigorous method and to make the universal formula of the categorical imperative the basis: Act according to the maxim which can at the same time make itself a universal law. But if one wishes to gain a hearing for the moral law, it is very useful to bring one and the same action under the three stated principles and thus, so far as possible, to bring it nearer to intuition.

We can now end where we started, with the concept of an unconditionally good will. That will is absolutely good which cannot be bad, and thus it is a will whose maxims, when made a universal law, can never conflict with itself. Thus this principle is also its supreme law: Always act according to that maxim whose universality as a law you can at the same time will. This is the only condition under which a will can never come into conflict with itself, and such an imperative is categorical. Because the validity of the will, as a universal law for possible actions, has an analogy with the universal connection of the existence of things under universal laws, which is the formal element of nature in general, the categorical imperative can also be expressed as follows: Act according to maxims which can at the same time have themselves as universal laws of nature as their object. Such, then, is the formula of an absolutely good will.

Rational nature is distinguished from others in that it proposes an end to itself. This end would be the material of every good will. Since, however, in the idea of an absolutely good will without any limiting condition of the attainment of this or that end, every end to be effected must be completely abstracted (as any particular end would make each will only relatively good), the end here is not conceived as one to be effected but as an independent end and thus merely negatively. It is that which must never be acted against, and which must consequently never be valued as merely a means but in every volition also as an end. Now this end can never be other than the subject of all possible ends themselves, because this is at the same time the subject of a possible will which is absolutely good; for the latter cannot be made secondary to any other object without contradiction. The principle: Act with reference to every rational being (whether yourself or another) so that it is an end in itself in your maxim, is thus basically identical with the principle: Act by a maxim which involves its own universal validity for every rational being.

That in the use of means to every end I should restrict my maxim to the condition of its universal validity as a law for every subject is tantamount to saying that the subject of ends, i.e., the rational being itself, must be made the basis of all maxims of actions and thus be treated never as a mere means but as the supreme limiting condition in the use of all means, i.e., as an end at the same time.

It follows incontestably that every rational being must be able to regard himself as an end in himself with reference to all laws to which he may be subject, whatever they may be, and thus as giving universal laws. For it is just the fitness of his maxims to a universal legislation that indicates that he is an end in himself. It also follows that his dignity (his prerogative) over all merely natural beings entails that he must take his maxims from the point of view which regards himself, and hence also every other rational being, as legislative. (The rational beings are, on this account, called persons.) In this way, a world of rational beings (*mundus intelligibilis*) is possible as a realm of ends, because of the legislation belonging to all persons as members. Consequently, every rational being must act as if he, by his maxims, were at all times a legislative member in the universal realm of ends. The formal principle of these maxims is: So act as if your maxims should serve at the same time as the universal law (of all rational beings). A realm of ends is thus possible only by analogy with a realm of nature. The former, however, is possible only by maxims, i.e., self-imposed rules, while the latter is possible by laws of efficient causes of things externally necessitated. Regardless of this difference, by analogy we call the natural whole a realm of nature so far as it is related to rational beings as its end; we do so even though the natural whole is looked at as a machine. Such a realm of ends would actually be realized through maxims whose rule is prescribed to all rational beings by the categorical imperative, if they were universally obeyed. But a rational being, though he scrupulously follow this maxim, cannot for that reason expect every other rational being to be true to it; nor can he expect the realm of nature and its orderly design to harmonize with him as a fitting member of a realm of ends which is possible through himself. That is, he cannot count on its favoring his expectation of happiness. Still the law: Act according to the maxims of a universally legislative member of a merely potential realm of ends, remains in full force, because it commands categorically. And just in this lies the paradox that merely the dignity of humanity as rational nature without any end or advantage to be gained by it, and thus respect for a mere idea, should serve as the inflexible precept of the will. There is the further paradox that the sublimity and worthiness of every rational subject to be a legislative member in the realm of ends consists precisely in independence of maxims from all such incentives. Otherwise he would have to be viewed as subject only to the natural law of his needs.[9] Although the realm of nature as well as that of ends would be thought of as united under a sovereign, so that the latter would no longer remain a mere idea but would receive true reality, the realm of ends would undoubtedly gain a strong urge in its favor, but its intrinsic worth would not be augmented. Regardless of this, even the one and only absolute legislator would still have to be conceived as judging the worth of rational beings only by the disinterested conduct which they prescribe to themselves merely from the idea [of dignity]. The essence of things is not changed by their external relations, and without reference to these relations a man must be judged only by what constitutes his absolute worth; and this is true whoever his judge is, even if it be the Supreme Being. Morality is thus the relation of actions to the autonomy of the will, i.e., to possible universal lawgiving by maxims of the will. The action which can be compatible with the autonomy of the will is permitted; that which does not agree with it is prohibited. The will whose maxims necessarily are in harmony with the laws of autonomy is a holy will or an absolutely good will. The dependence of a will not absolutely good on the principle of autonomy (moral constraint) is *obligation*. Hence obligation cannot be applied to a holy will. The objective necessity of an action from obligation is called *duty*.

From what has just been said, it can easily be explained how it happens that, although in the concept of duty we think of subjection to law, we do nevertheless ascribe a certain sublimity and dignity to the person who fulfils all his duties. For though there is no sublimity in him in so far as he is subject to the moral law, yet he is sublime in so far as he is legislative with reference to the law and subject to it only for this reason. We have also shown above how neither fear of nor inclination to the law is the incentive which can give a moral worth to action; only respect

9. [Reading plural with Vorländer.]

for it can do so. Our own will, so far as it would act only under the condition of a universal legislation rendered possible by its maxims—this will ideally possible for us is the proper object of respect, and the dignity of humanity consists just in its capacity of giving universal laws, although with the condition that it is itself subject to this same legislation.

THE AUTONOMY OF THE WILL AS THE SUPREME PRINCIPLE OF MORALITY

Autonomy of the will is that property of it by which it is a law to itself independently of any property of objects of volition. Hence the principle of autonomy is: Never choose except in such a way that the maxims of the choice are comprehended in the same volition as a universal law. That this practical rule is an imperative, that is, that the will of every rational being is necessarily bound to it as a condition, cannot be proved by a mere analysis of the concepts occurring in it, because it is a synthetical proposition. To prove it, we would have to go beyond the knowledge of objects to a critical examination of the subject, i.e., of the pure practical reason, for this synthetical proposition which commands apodictically must be susceptible of being known completely a priori. This matter, however, does not belong in the present section. But that the principle of autonomy, which is now in question, is the sole principle of morals can be readily shown by mere analysis of concepts of morality; for by this analysis we find that its principle must be a categorical imperative and that the imperative commands neither more nor less than this very autonomy.

THE HETERONOMY OF THE WILL AS THE SOURCE OF ALL SPURIOUS PRINCIPLES OF MORALITY

If the will seeks the law which is to determine it anywhere else than in the fitness of its maxims to its own universal legislation, and if it thus goes outside itself and seeks this law in the property of any of its objects, heteronomy always results. For then the will does not give itself the law, but the object through its relation to the will gives the law to it. This relation, whether it rests on inclination or on conceptions of reason, only admits of hypothetical imperatives: I should do something for the reason that I will something else. The moral, and therewith categorical, imperative, on the other hand, says I should act this or that way even though I will nothing else. For example, the former says I should not lie if I wish to keep my reputation. The latter says I should not lie even though it would not cause me the least injury. The latter, therefore, must disregard every object to such an extent that it has absolutely no influence on the will, so that practical reason (will) not merely may minister to an interest not its own but rather may show its commanding authority as the supreme legislation. Thus, for instance, I should seek to further the happiness of others, not as though its realization was any concern of mine (whether because of direct inclination or of some satisfaction related to it indirectly through reason); I should do so merely because the maxim which excludes it from my duty cannot be comprehended as a universal law in one and the same volition.

CLASSIFICATION OF ALL POSSIBLE PRINCIPLES OF MORALITY FOLLOWING FROM THE ASSUMED PRINCIPLE OF HETERONOMY

Here as everywhere in the pure use of reason so long as a critical examination of it is lacking, human reason at first tries all possible wrong ways before it succeeds in finding the one true way.

All principles which can be taken in this point of view are either empirical or rational. The former, drawn from the principle of happiness, are based on physical or moral feeling; the latter, drawn from the principle of perfection, are based either on the rational concept of perfection as a possible result or on the concept of an independent perfection (the will of God) as the determining cause of our will.

Empirical principles are not at all suited to serve as the basis of moral laws. For if the basis of the universality by which they should be valid for all rational beings without distinction (the unconditional practical necessity which is thereby imposed upon them) is derived from a particular tendency of human nature or the particular circumstance in which it is found, that universality is lost. But the principle of one's own happiness is the most objectionable of all. This is not merely because it is false and because experience contradicts the supposition that well-being is always proportional to good conduct, nor yet because this principle contributes nothing to the establishment of morality, inasmuch as it is a very different thing to make a man happy from making him good, and to make him prudent and farsighted for his own advantage is far from making him virtuous. Rather, it is because this principle supports morality with incentives which undermine it and destroy all its sublimity, for it puts the motives to virtue and those to vice in the same class, teaching us only to make a better calculation while obliterating the specific difference between them. On the other hand, there is the alleged special sense,* the moral feeling. The appeal to it is superficial, since those who cannot think expect help from feeling, even with respect to that which concerns universal laws; they do so even though feelings naturally differ so infinitely in degree that they are incapable of furnishing a uniform standard of the good and bad, and also in spite of the fact that one cannot validly judge for others by means of his own feeling. Nevertheless, the moral feeling is nearer to morality and its dignity, inasmuch as it pays virtue the honor of ascribing the satisfaction and esteem for her directly to morality, and does not, as it were, say to her face that it is not her beauty but only our advantage which attaches us to her.

Among the rational principles of morality, there is the ontological concept of perfection. It is empty, indefinite, and consequently useless for finding in the immeasurable field of possible reality the greatest possible sum which is suitable to us; and, in specifically distinguishing the reality which is here in question from all other reality, it inevitably tends to move in a circle and cannot avoid tacitly presupposing the morality which it ought to explain. Nevertheless, it is better than the theological concept, which derives morality from a most perfect divine will. It is better not merely because we cannot intuit its perfection, having rather to derive it only from our own concepts of which morality itself is foremost, but also because if we do not so derive it (and to do so would involve a most flagrant circle in explanation), the only remaining concept of the divine will is made up of the attributes of desire for glory and dominion combined with the awful conceptions of might and vengeance, and any system of ethics based on them would be directly opposed to morality.

* I count the principle of moral feeling under that of happiness, because every empirical interest promises to contribute to our well-being by the agreeableness that a thing affords, either directly and without a view to future advantage or with a view to it. We must likewise, with Hutcheson, count the principle of sympathy with the happiness of others under the moral sense which he assumed.

But if I had to choose between the concept of the moral sense and that of perfection in general (neither of which at any rate weakens morality, although they are not capable of serving as its foundations), I would decide for the latter, because it preserves the indefinite idea (of a will good in itself) free from corruption until it can be more narrowly defined. It at least withdraws the decision of the question from sensibility and brings it to the court of pure reason, although it does not even here decide the question.

For the rest, I think that I may be excused from a lengthy refutation of all these doctrines. It is so easy, and presumably so well understood even by those whose office requires them to decide for one of these theories (since the hearers would not tolerate suspension of judgment), that such a refutation would be only superfluous work. What interests us more, however, is to know that all these principles set up nothing other than the heteronomy of the will as the first ground of morality and thus necessarily miss their aim.

In every case in which an object of the will must be assumed as prescribing the rule which is to determine the will, the rule is nothing else but heteronomy. The imperative in this case is conditional, stating that if or because one wills this object, one should act thus or so. Therefore the imperative can never command morally, that is, categorically. The object may determine the will by means of inclination, as in the principle of one's own happiness, or by means of reason directed to objects of our possible volition in general, as in the principle of perfection; but the will in these cases never determines itself directly by the conception of the action itself but only by the incentive which the foreseen result of the action incites in the will—that is, "I ought to do something because I will something else." And here still another law must be assumed in my person as the basis of this imperative; it would be a law by which I would necessarily will that other thing; but this law would again require an imperative to restrict this maxim. Since the conception of an object commensurate to our power incites in the will an impulse according to the natural characteristic of our person, this impulse belongs to the nature of the subject (either to the sensibility, i.e., inclination and taste, or to understanding and reason which faculties, according to the particular constitution of their nature, take pleasure in exercising themselves on an object). If follows that it would be really nature that would give the law. As a law of nature, known and proved by experience, it would be contingent and therefore unfit to be an apodictical practical rule such as the moral rule must be. Such a law always represents heteronomy of the will; the will does not give itself the law, but an external impulse gives it to the will according to the nature of the subject which is adapted to receive it.

The absolutely good will, the principle of which must be a categorical imperative, is thus undetermined with reference to any objects. It contains only the form of volition in general, and this form is autonomy. That is, the capability of the maxims of every good will to make themselves universal laws is itself the sole law which the will of every rational being imposes on itself, and it does not need to support this on any incentive or interest.

How such a synthetical practical a priori proposition is possible and why it is necessary is a problem whose solution does not lie within the boundaries of the metaphysics of morals. Moreover, we have not here affirmed its truth, and even less professed to command a proof of it. We showed only through the development of the universally received concept of morals that autonomy of the will is unavoidably connected with it, or rather that it is its foundation. Whoever, therefore, holds morality to be something real and not a chimerical idea without truth must also concede its principle which has been adduced here. Consequently, this section was merely analytical, like the first. To prove that morality is not a mere phantom of the mind—and if the categorical imperative, and with it the autonomy of the will, is true and absolutely necessary as an a priori principle, it follows that it is no phantom—requires that a synthetical use of pure practical reason is possible. But we must not venture on this proof without first making a critical examination of this faculty of reason. In the last section we shall give the principal features of such an examination that will be sufficient for our purpose.

THIRD SECTION

TRANSITION FROM THE METAPHYSICS OF MORALS TO THE CRITICAL EXAMINATION OF PURE PRACTICAL REASON

THE CONCEPT OF FREEDOM IS THE KEY TO THE EXPLANATION OF THE AUTONOMY OF THE WILL

AS WILL is a kind of causality of living beings so far as they are rational, freedom would be that property of this causality by which it can be effective independently of foreign causes determining it, just as natural necessity is the property of the causality of all irrational beings by which they are determined to activity by the influence of foreign causes.

The preceding definition of freedom is negative and therefore affords no insight into its essence. But a positive concept of freedom flows from it which is so much the richer and more fruitful. Since the concept of a causality entails that of laws according to which something, i.e., the effect, must be established through something else which we call cause, it follows that freedom is by no means lawless even though it is not a property of the will according to laws of nature. Rather, it must be a causality according to immutable laws, but of a peculiar kind. Otherwise a free will would be an absurdity. Natural necessity is, as we have seen, a heteronomy of efficient causes, for every effect is possible only according to the law that something else determines the efficient cause to its causality. What else, then, can the freedom of the will be but autonomy, i.e., the property of the will to be a law to itself? The proposition that the will is a law to itself in all its actions, however, only expresses the principle that we should act according to no other maxim than that which can also have itself as a universal law for its object. And this is just the formula of the categorical imperative and the principle of morality. Therefore a free will and a will under moral laws are identical.

Thus if freedom of the will is presupposed, morality together with its principle follows from it by the mere analysis of its concept. But the principle is nevertheless a synthetical proposition; an absolutely good will is one whose maxim can always include itself as a universal law. It is synthetical because by analysis of the concept of an absolutely good will that property of the maxim cannot be found. Such synthetical propositions, however, are possible only by the fact that both cognitions are connected through their union with a third in which both of them are to be found. The positive concept of freedom furnishes this third cognition, which cannot be, as in the case of physical causes, the nature of the sensuous world, in the concept of which we find conjoined the concepts of something as cause in relation to something else as effect. We cannot yet show directly what this third cognition is to which freedom directs us and of which we have an a priori idea, nor can we explain the deduction of the concept of freedom from pure practical reason and therewith the possibility of a categorical imperative. For this some further preparation is needed.

FREEDOM MUST BE PRESUPPOSED AS THE PROPERTY OF THE WILL OF ALL RATIONAL BEINGS

It is not enough to ascribe freedom to our will, on any grounds whatever, if we do not also have sufficient grounds for attributing it to all rational beings. For since morality serves as a law for us only as rational beings, morality must hold valid for all rational beings, and since it must be derived exclusively from the property of freedom, freedom as the property of the will of all rational beings must be demonstrated. And it does not suffice to prove it from certain alleged experiences of human nature (which is indeed impossible, as it can be proved only a priori), but we must prove it as belonging generally to the activity of rational beings endowed with a will. Now I say that every being which cannot act otherwise than under the idea of freedom is thereby really free in a practical respect. That is to say, all laws which are inseparably bound with freedom hold for it just as if its will were proved free in itself by theoretical philosophy.* Now I affirm that we must necessarily grant that every rational being who has a will also has the idea of freedom and that it acts only under this idea. For in such a being we think of a reason which is practical, i.e., a reason which has causality with respect to its objects. Now we cannot conceive of a reason which consciously responds to a bidding from the outside with respect to its judgments, for then the subject would attribute the determination of its power of judgment not to reason but to an impulse. Reason must regard itself as the author of its principles, independently of foreign influences; consequently, as practical reason or as the will of a rational being, it must regard itself as free. That is to say, the will of a rational being can be a will of its own only under the idea of freedom, and therefore in a practical point of view such a will must be ascribed to all rational beings.

OF THE INTEREST ATTACHING TO THE IDEAS OF MORALITY

We have finally reduced the definite concept of morality to the idea of freedom, but we could not prove freedom to be real

---

* I follow this method of assuming that freedom only ideally assumed by rational beings as the basis of their actions is sufficient to our purpose, because I wish to avoid having to prove freedom also in its theoretical aspect. For if the latter is left unproved, the laws which would obligate a being who was really free would hold for a being who cannot act except under the idea of his own freedom. Thus we can escape here from the onus which presses on the theory.

in ourselves and in human nature. We only saw that we must presuppose it if we would think of a being as rational and conscious of his causality with respect to actions, that is, as endowed with a will; and so we find that on the very same grounds we must ascribe to each being endowed with reason and will the property of determining himself to action under the idea of freedom.

From presupposing this idea [of freedom] there followed also consciousness of a law to act so that the subjective principles of actions, i.e., maxims, in every instance must be so chosen that they can hold also as objective, i.e., universal, principles, and thus can serve as principles for the universal laws we give. But why should I subject myself as a rational being, and thereby all other beings endowed with reason, to this law? I will admit that no interest impels me to do so, for that would then give no categorical imperative. But I must nevertheless take an interest in it and see how it comes about, for this "ought" is properly a "would" that is valid for every rational being provided reason is practical for him without hindrance [i.e., exclusively determined his action]. For beings who like ourselves are affected by the senses as incentives different from reason and who do not always do that which reason for itself alone would have done, that necessity of action is expressed only as an "ought." The subjective necessity is thus distinguished from the objective.

It therefore seems that the moral law, i.e., the principle of the autonomy of the will, is, properly speaking, only presupposed in the idea of freedom, as if we could not prove its reality and objective necessity by itself. Even if that were so, we would have still gained something because we would at least have defined the genuine principle more accurately than had been done before. But with regard to its validity and to the practical necessity of subjection to it, we would not have advanced a single step, for we could give no satisfactory answer to anyone who asked us why the universality of our maxim as of a law had to be the restricting condition of our action. We could not tell on what is based the worth we ascribe to actions of this kind—a worth so great that there can be no higher interest, nor could we tell how it happens that man believes it is only through this that he feels his own personal worth, in contrast to which the worth of a pleasant or unpleasant condition is to be regarded as nothing.

We do find sometimes that we can take an interest in a personal quality which involves no [personal] interest in any [external] condition, provided only that [possession of] this quality makes us capable of participating in the [desired] condition in case reason were to effect the allotment of it. That is, mere worthiness to be happy even without the motive of participating in it can interest of itself. But this judgment is in fact only the effect of the already assumed importance of moral laws (if by the idea of freedom we detach ourselves from every empirical interest). But that we ought to detach ourselves, i.e., regard ourselves as free in acting and yet as subject to certain laws, in order to find a worth merely in our person which would compensate for the loss of everything which makes our situation desirable—how this is possible and hence on what grounds the moral law obligates us we still cannot see in this way.

We must openly confess that there is a kind of circle here from which it seems that there is no escape. We assume that we are free in the order of efficient causes so that we can conceive of ourselves as subject to moral laws in the order of ends. And then we think of ourselves as subject to these laws because we have ascribed freedom of the will to ourselves. This is circular because freedom and self-legislation of the will are both autonomy and thus are reciprocal concepts, and for that reason one of them cannot be used to explain the other and to furnish a ground for it. At most they can be used for the logical purpose of bringing apparently different conceptions of the same object under a single concept (as we reduce different fractions of the same value to the lowest common terms).

One recourse, however, remains open to us, namely, to inquire whether we do not assume a different standpoint when we think of ourselves as causes a priori efficient through freedom from that which we occupy when we conceive of ourselves in the light of our actions as effects which we see before our eyes.

The following remark requires no subtle reflection, and we may suppose that even the commonest understanding can make it, though it does so, after its fashion, by an obscure discernment of judgment which it calls feeling: all conceptions, like those of the senses, which come to us without our choice enable us to know the objects only as they affect us, while what they are in themselves remains unknown to us; therefore, as regards this kind of conception, even with the closest attention and clearness which understanding may ever bring to them we can attain only to knowledge of appearances and never to knowledge of things in themselves. As soon as this distinction is once made (perhaps merely because of a noticed difference between conceptions which are given to us from somewhere else and to which we are passive and those which we produce only from ourselves and in which we show our own activity), it follows of itself that we must assume behind the appearances something else which is not appearance, namely, things-in-themselves; we do so although we must admit that we cannot approach them more closely and can never know what they are in themselves, since they can never be known by us except as they affect us. This must furnish a distinction, though a crude one, between a world of sense and a world of understanding. The former, by differences in the sensuous faculties, can be very different among various observers, while the latter, which is its foundation, remains always the same. A man may not presume to know even himself as he really is by knowing himself through inner sensation. For since he does not, as it were, produce himself or derive his concept of himself a priori but only empirically, it is natural that he obtains his knowledge of himself through inner sense and consequently only through the appearance of his nature and the way in which his consciousness is affected. But beyond the characteristic of his own subject which is compounded of these mere appearances, he necessarily assumes something else as its basis, namely, his ego as it is in itself. Thus in respect to mere perception and receptivity to sensations he must count himself as belonging to the world of sense; but in respect to that which may be pure activity in himself (i.e., in respect to that which reaches consciousness directly and not by affecting the senses) he must reckon himself as belonging to the intellectual world. But he has no further knowledge of that world.

To such a conclusion the thinking man must come with respect to all things which may present themselves to him. Presumably it is to be met with in the commonest understanding which, as is well known, is very much inclined to expect behind the objects of the senses something else invisible and acting of itself. But such an understanding soon spoils it by trying to make the invisible again sensuous, i.e., to make it an object of intuition. Thus common understanding becomes not in the least wiser.

Now man really finds in himself a faculty by which he distinguishes himself from all other things, even from himself so far as he is affected by objects. This faculty is reason. As a pure spontaneous activity it is even elevated above understanding. For though the latter is also a spontaneous activity and does not, like sense, merely contain conceptions which arise only when one is affected by things, being passive, it nevertheless cannot produce by its activity any other concepts than those which serve to bring the sensuous conceptions under rules and thereby to unite them in one consciousness. Without this use of sensibility it would not think at all, while, on the other hand, reason shows such a pure spontaneity in the case of ideas that it[10] far transcends everything that sensibility can give to consciousness[10] and shows its chief occupation in distinguishing the world of sense from the world of understanding, thereby prescribing limits to the understanding itself.

For this reason a rational being must regard himself as intelligence (and not from the side of his lower powers), as belonging to the world of understanding and not to that of the senses. Thus he has two standpoints from which he can consider himself and recognize the laws of the employment of his powers and consequently of all his actions: first, as belonging to the world of sense, under laws of nature (heteronomy), and, second, as belonging to the intelligible world under laws which, independent of nature, are not empirical but founded only on reason.

As a rational being and thus as belonging to the intelligible world, man cannot think of the causality of his own will except under the idea of freedom, for independence from the determining causes of the world of sense (an independence which reason must always ascribe to itself) is freedom. The concept of autonomy is inseparably connected with the idea of freedom, and with the latter there is inseparably bound the universal principle of morality, which ideally is the ground of all actions of rational beings, just as natural law is the ground of all appearances.

Now we have removed the suspicion which we raised that there might be a hidden circle in our reasoning from freedom to autonomy and from the latter to the moral law. This suspicion was that we laid down the idea of freedom for the sake of the moral law in order later to derive freedom from it, and that we were thus unable to give any ground for the law, presenting it only as a *petitio principii* that well-disposed minds would gladly allow us but which we could never advance as a demonstrable proposition. But we now see that, if we think of ourselves as free,

---

10. [Kant wrote *er....ihm*, which gives no tenable meaning. Adickes suggested *sie....ihr = reason....to reason*. But as sensibility does not give material to reason, at least directly, Vorländer and the Cassirer ed. read *sie....ihm*, and they are followed here.]

we transport ourselves into the intelligible world as members of it and know the antonomy of the will together with its consequence, morality; while, if we think of ourselves as obligated, we consider ourselves as belonging both to the world of sense and at the same time to the intelligible world.

HOW IS A CATEGORICAL IMPERATIVE POSSIBLE?

The rational being counts himself, *qua* intelligence, as belonging to the intelligible world, and only as an efficient cause belonging to it does he call his causality a will. On the other side, however, he is conscious of himself as a part of the world of sense in which his actions are found as mere appearances of that causality. But we do not discern how they are possible on the basis of that causality which we do not know; rather, those actions must be regarded as determined by other appearances, namely, desires and inclinations, belonging to the world of sense. As a mere member of the intelligible world, all my actions would completely accord with the principle of the autonomy of the pure will, and as a part only of the world of sense would they have to be assumed to conform wholly to the natural law of desires and inclinations and thus to the heteronomy of nature. (The former actions would rest on the supreme principle of morality, and the latter on that of happiness.) But since the intelligible world contains the ground of the world of sense and hence of its laws, the intelligible world is (and must be conceived as) directly legislative for my will, which belongs wholly to the intelligible world. Therefore I recognize myself *qua* intelligence as subject to the law of the world of understanding and to the autonomy of the will. That is, I recognize myself as subject to the law of reason which contains in the idea of freedom the law of the intelligible world, while at the same time I must acknowledge that I am a being which belongs to the world of sense. Therefore I must regard the laws of the intelligible world as imperatives for me, and actions in accord with this principle as duties.

Thus categorical imperatives are possible because the idea of freedom makes me a member of an intelligible world. Consequently, if I were a member of only that world, all my actions *would* always be in accordance with the autonomy of the will. But since I intuit myself at the same time as a member of the world of sense, my actions *ought* to conform to it, and this categorical ought presents a synthetic a priori proposition, since besides my will affected by my sensuous desires there is added the idea of the will as pure, practical of itself, and belonging to the intelligible world, which according to reason contains the supreme condition of the former [sensuously affected] will. It is similar to the manner in which concepts of the misunderstanding, which of themselves mean nothing but lawful form in general, are added to the intuitions of the sensuous world, thus rendering possible a priori synthetic propositions, on which all knowledge of a system of nature rests.

The practical use of common human reason confirms the correctness of this deduction. When we present examples of honesty of purpose, of steadfastness in following good maxims, and of sympathy and general benevolence even with great sacrifice of advantages and comfort, there is no man, not even the most malicious villain (provided he is otherwise accustomed to using his reason), who does not wish that he also might have these qualities. But because of his inclinations and impulses he cannot bring this about, yet at the same time he wishes to be free from such inclinations which are burdensome even to himself. He thus proves that, with a will free from all impulses of sensibility, he in thought transfers himself into an order of things altogether different from that of his desires in the field of sensibility. He cannot expect to obtain by that wish any gratification of desires nor any condition which would satisfy his real or even imagined inclinations, for the idea itself, which elicits this wish from him, would lose its pre-eminence if he had any such expectation. He can expect only a greater inner worth of his person. He imagines himself to be this better person when he transfers himself to the standpoint of a member of the intelligible world to which he is involuntarily impelled by the idea of freedom, i.e., independence from the determining causes of the world of sense; and from this standpoint he is conscious of a good will, which on his own confession constitutes the law for his bad will as a member of the world of sense. He acknowledges the authority of this law even while transgressing it. The moral ought is therefore his own volition as a member of the intelligible world, and it is conceived by him as an ought only in so far as he regards himself at the same time as a member of the world of sense.

ON THE EXTREME LIMIT OF ALL PRACTICAL PHILOSOPHY

In respect to their will, all men think of themselves as free. Hence arise all judgments of actions as being such as ought to have been done, although they were not done. But this freedom is not an empirical concept and cannot be such, for it still remains even though experience shows the contrary of the demands which are necessarily conceived as consequences of the supposition of freedom. On the other hand, it is equally necessary that everything which happens should be inexorably determined by natural laws, and this natural necessity is likewise no empirical concept, because it implies the concept of necessity and thus of a priori knowledge. But this concept of a system of nature is confirmed by experience, and it is inevitably presupposed if experience, which is knowledge of the objects of the senses interconnected by universal laws, is to be possible. Therefore freedom is only an idea of reason whose objective reality in itself is doubtful, while nature is a concept of the understanding which shows and necessarily must show its reality by examples of experience.

There now arises a dialectic of reason, since the freedom ascribed to the will seems to stand in contradiction to natural necessity. At this parting of the ways reason in its speculative purpose finds the way of natural necessity more well-beaten and usable than that of freedom; but in its practical purpose the footpath of freedom is the only one on which it is possible to make use of reason in our conduct. Hence it is as impossible for the subtlest philosophy as for the commonest reasoning to argue freedom away. Philosophy must therefore assume that no true contradiction will be found between freedom and natural necessity in the same human actions, for it cannot give up the concept of nature any more than that of freedom.

Hence even if we should never be able to conceive how freedom is possible, at least this apparent contradiction must be convincingly eradicated. For if even the thought of freedom contradicts itself or nature, which is equally necessary, it would have to be surrendered in competition with natural necessity.

But it would be impossible to escape this contradiction if the subject, which seems to himself free, thought of himself in the same sense or in the same relationship when he calls himself free as when he assumes that in the same action he is subject to natural law. Therefore it is an inescapable task of speculative philosophy to show at least that its illusion about the contradiction rests in the fact that we [do not][11] think of man in a different sense and relationship when we call him free from that in which we consider him as a part of nature and subject to its laws. It must

11. [Following the suggestion of R. F. A. Hoernlé, *Mind*, XLV (new ser., 1936), 127–28.]

show not only that they can very well coexist but also that they must be thought of as necessarily united in one and the same subject; for otherwise no ground could be given why we should burden reason with an idea which, though it may without contradiction be united with another that is sufficiently established, nevertheless involves us in a perplexity which sorely embarrasses reason in its speculative use. This duty is imposed only on speculative philosophy, so that it may clear the way for practical philosophy. Thus the philosopher has no choice as to whether he will remove the apparent contradiction or leave it untouched, for in the latter case the theory of it would be *bonum vacans*, into the possession of which the fatalist can rightly enter and drive all morality from its alleged property as occupying it without title.

Yet we cannot say here that we have reached the beginnings of practical philosophy. For the settlement of the controversy does not belong to practical philosophy, as the latter only demands from speculative reason that it put an end to the discord in which it entangles itself in theoretical questions, so that practical reason may have rest and security from outer attacks which could dispute it the ground on which it desires to erect its edifice.

The title to freedom of the will claimed by common reason is based on the consciousness and the conceded presupposition of the independence of reason from merely subjectively determining causes which together constitute what belongs only to sensation, being comprehended under the general name of sensibility. Man, who in this way regards himself as intelligence, puts himself in a different order of things and in a relationship to determining grounds of an altogether different kind when he thinks of himself as intelligence with a will and thus as endowed with causality, compared with that other order of things and that other set of determining grounds which become relevant when he perceives himself as a phenomenon in the world of sense (as he really is also) and submits his causality to external determination according to natural laws. Now he soon realizes that both can subsist together—indeed, that they must. For there is not the least contradiction between a thing in appearance (as belonging to the world of sense) being subject to certain laws from which it is independent as a thing or a being in itself. That it must think of itself in this twofold manner rests, with regard to the first, on the consciousness of itself as an object affected through the senses, and, with regard to what is required by the second, on the consciousness of itself as intelligence, i.e., as independent from sensuous impressions in the use of reason and thus as belonging to the intelligible world.

This is why man claims to possess a will which does not let him become accountable for what belongs merely to his desires and inclinations, but thinks of actions, which can be done only by disregarding all desires and sensuous attractions, as possible and indeed necessary for him. The causality of these actions lies in him as an intelligence and in effects and actions in accordance with principles of an intelligible world, of which he knows only that reason alone and indeed pure reason independent of sensibility gives the law in it. Moreover, since it is only as intelligence that he is his proper self (being as man only appearance of himself), he knows that those laws apply to him directly and categorically, so that that to which inclinations and impulses and hence the entire nature of the world of sense incite him cannot in the least impair the laws of his volition as an intelligence. He does not even hold himself responsible for these inclinations and impulses or attribute them to his proper self, i.e., his will, though he does ascribe to his will the indulgence which he may grant to them when he permits them an influence on his maxims to the detriment of the rational laws of his will.

When practical reason thinks itself into an intelligible world, it does in no way transcend its limits. It would do so, however, if it tried to intuit or feel itself into it. The intelligible world is only a negative thought with respect to the world of sense, which does not give reason any laws for determining the will. It is positive only in the single point that freedom as negative determination is at the same time connected with a positive faculty and even a causality of reason. This causality we call a will to act so that the principle of actions will accord with the essential characteristic of a rational cause, i.e., with the condition of universal validity of a maxim as a law. But if it were to borrow an object of the will, i.e., a motive, from the intelligible world, it would overstep its boundaries and pretend to be acquainted with something of which it knows nothing. The concept of a world of understanding is therefore only a standpoint which reason sees itself forced to take outside appearances, in order to think of itself as practical. If the influences of sensibility were determining for man, this would not be possible; but it is necessary unless he is to be denied the consciousness of himself as an intelligence, and thus as a rational and rationally active cause, i.e., a cause acting in freedom. This thought certainly implies the idea of an order and legislation different from that of natural mechanism which applies to the world of sense; and it makes necessary the concept of an intelligible world, the whole of rational beings as things-in-themselves. But it does not give us the least occasion to think of it other than according to its formal condition only, i.e., the universality of the maxim of the will as law and thus the autonomy of the will, which alone is consistent with freedom. All laws, on the other hand, which are directed to an object make for heteronomy, which only belongs to natural laws and which can apply only to the world of sense.

But reason would overstep all its bounds if it undertook to explain how pure reason can be practical, which is the same problem as explaining how freedom is possible.

For we can explain nothing but what we can reduce to laws whose object can be given in some possible experience. But freedom is a mere idea, the objective reality of which can in no way be shown according to natural laws or in any possible experience. Since no example in accordance with any analogy can support it, it can never be comprehended or even imagined. It holds only as the necessary presupposition of reason in a being that believes itself conscious of a will, i.e., of a faculty different from the mere faculty of desire, or a faculty of determining itself to act as intelligence and thus according to laws of reason independently of natural instincts. But where determination according to natural laws comes to an end, there too all explanation ceases, and nothing remains but defense, i.e., refutation of the objections of those who pretend to have seen deeper into the essence of things and therefore boldly declare freedom to be impossible. We can only show them that the supposed contradiction they have discovered lies nowhere else than in their necessarily regarding man as appearance in order to make natural law valid with respect to human actions. And now when we require them to think of him *qua* intelligence as a thing-in-itself, they still persist in considering him as appearance. Obviously, then, the separation of his causality (his will) from all natural laws of the world of sense in one and the same subject is a contradiction, but this disappears when they reconsider and confess, as is reasonable, that behind the appearances things-in-themselves must stand as their hidden ground and that we cannot expect the laws of the activity of these grounds to be the same as those under which their appearances stand.

The subjective impossibility of explaining the freedom of the will is the same as the impossibility of discovering and explaining an interest* which man can take in moral laws. Nevertheless, he does actually take an interest in them, and the foundation in us of this interest we call the moral feeling. This moral feeling has been erroneously construed by some as the standard for our moral judgment, whereas it must rather be regarded as the subjective effect which the law has upon the will to which reason alone gives objective grounds.

In order to will that which reason alone prescribes to the sensuously affected rational being as that which he ought to will, certainly there is required a power of reason to instil a feeling of pleasure or satisfaction in the fulfilment of duty, and hence there must be a causality of reason to determine the sensibility in accordance with its own principles. But it is wholly impossible to discern, i.e., to make a priori conceivable, how a mere thought containing nothing sensuous is to produce a sensation of pleasure or displeasure. For that is a particular kind of causality of which, as of all causality, we cannot determine anything a priori but must consult experience only. But since experience can exemplify the relation of cause to effect only as subsisting between two objects of experience, while here pure reason by mere ideas (which furnish no object for experience) is to be the cause of an effect which does lie in experience, an explanation of how and why the universality of the maxim as law (and hence morality) interests us is completely impossible for us men. Only this much is certain: that it is valid for us not because it interests us (for that is heteronomy and dependence of practical reason on sensibility, i.e., on a basic feeling, and thus it could never be morally legislative) but that it interests us because it is valid for us as men, inasmuch as it has arisen from our will as intelligence and hence from our proper self; but what belongs to mere ap-

---

* Interest is that by which reason becomes practical, i.e., a cause determining the will. We therefore say only of a rational being that he takes an interest in something; irrational creatures feel only sensuous impulses. A direct interest in the action is taken by reason only if the universal validity of its maxim is a sufficient determining ground of the will. Only such an interest is pure. But if reason can determine the will only by means of another object of desire or under the presupposition of a particular feeling of the subject, reason takes merely an indirect interest in the action, and since reason for itself alone without experience can discover neither objects of the will nor a particular feeling which lies at its root, that indirect interest would be only empirical and not a pure interest of reason. The logical interest of reason in advancing its insights is never direct but rather presupposes purposes for which they are to be used.

pearance is necessarily subordinated by reason to the nature of the thing-in-itself.

Thus the question, "How is a categorical imperative possible?" can be answered to this extent: We can cite the only presupposition under which it is alone possible. This is the idea of freedom, and we can discern the necessity of this presupposition which is sufficient to the practical use of reason, i.e., to the conviction of the validity of this imperative and hence also of the moral law. But how this presupposition itself is possible can never be discerned by any human reason. However, on the presupposition of freedom of the will of an intelligence, its autonomy as the formal condition under which alone it can be determined is a necessary consequence. To presuppose the freedom of the will is not only quite possible, as speculative philosophy itself can prove, for it does not involve itself in a contradiction with the principle of natural necessity in the interconnection of appearances in the world of sense. But, it is also unconditionally necessary that a rational being conscious of his causality through reason and thus conscious of a will different from desires should practically presuppose it, i.e., presuppose it in the idea as the fundamental condition of all his voluntary actions. Yet how pure reason, without any other incentives, wherever they may be derived, can by itself be practical, i.e., how the mere principle of the universal validity of all its maxims as laws (which would certainly be the form of a pure practical reason), without any material (object) of the will in which we might in advance take some interest, can itself furnish an incentive and produce an interest which would be called purely moral; or, in other words, how pure reason can be practical—to explain this, all human reason is wholly incompetent, and all the pains and work of seeking an explanation of it are wasted.

It is just the same as if I sought to find out how freedom itself as causality of a will is possible; for, in so doing, I would leave the philosophical basis of explanation behind, and I have no other. Certainly I could revel in the intelligible world, the world of intelligences, which still remains to me; but although I have a well-founded idea of it, still I do not have the least knowledge of it, nor can I ever attain to it by all the exertions of my natural capacity of reason. This intelligible world signifies only a something which remains when I have excluded from the determining grounds of my will everything belonging to the world of sense in order to withhold the principle of motives from the field of sensibility. I do so by limiting it and showing that it does not contain absolutely everything in itself but that outside it there is still more; but this more I do not further know. After banishing all material, i.e., knowledge of objects, from pure reason which formulates this ideal, there remain to me only the form, the practical law of universal validity of maxims, and, in conformity with this, reason in relation to a pure intelligible world as a possible effective cause, i.e., as determining the will. An incentive must here be totally absent unless this idea of an intelligible world itself be the incentive or that in which reason primarily takes an interest. But to make this conceivable is precisely the problem we cannot solve.

Here is, then, the supreme limit of all moral inquiry. To define it is very important, both in order that reason may not seek around, on the one hand, in the world of sense, in a way harmful to morals, for the supreme motive and for a comprehensible but empirical interest; and so that it will not, on the other hand, impotently flap its wings in the space (for it, an empty space) of transcendent concepts which we call the intelligible world, without being able to move from its starting-point and losing itself amid phantoms. Furthermore, the idea of a pure intelligible world as a whole of all intelligences to which we ourselves belong as rational beings (though on the other side we are at the same time members of the world of sense) is always a useful and permissible idea for the purpose of a rational faith. This is so even though all knowledge terminates at its boundary, for through the glorious ideal of a universal realm of ends-in-themselves (rational beings) a lively interest in the moral law can be awakened in us. To that realm we can belong as members only when we carefully conduct ourselves according to maxims of freedom as if they were laws of nature.

CONCLUDING REMARK

The speculative use of reason with respect to nature leads to the absolute necessity of some supreme cause of the world. The practical use of reason with respect to freedom leads also to an absolute necessity, but to the necessity only of laws of actions of a rational being as such. Now it is an essential principle of all use of reason to push its knowledge to a consciousness of its necessity, for otherwise it would not be rational knowledge. But it is also an equally essential restriction of this very same reason that it cannot discern the necessity of what is or what occurs or what ought to be done, unless a condition under which it is or occurs or ought to be done is presupposed. In this way, however, the satisfaction of reason is only further and further postponed by the constant inquiry after the condition. Therefore, reason restlessly seeks the unconditionally necessary and sees itself compelled to assume it, though it has no means by which to make it comprehensible and is happy enough if it can only discover the concept which is consistent with this presupposition. It is therefore no objection to our deduction of the supreme principle of morality, but a reproach which we must make to human reason generally, that it cannot render comprehensible the absolute necessity of an unconditional practical law (such as the categorical imperative must be). Reason cannot be blamed for being unwilling to explain it by a condition, i.e., by making some interest its basis, for the law would then cease to be moral, i.e., a supreme law of freedom. And so we do not indeed comprehend the practical unconditional necessity of the moral imperative; yet we do comprehend its incomprehensibility, which is all that can be fairly demanded of a philosophy which in its principles strives to reach the limit of human reason.

II

CRITIQUE OF PRACTICAL REASON

PREFACE

WHY this critique is called simply *Critique of Practical Reason* and not *Critique of Pure Practical Reason*, though the parallelism between it and the critique of speculative reason seems to demand the latter title, will be sufficiently shown in the treatise itself. Its task is merely to show that there is a pure practical reason, and, in order to do this, it critically examines reason's entire practical faculty. If it succeeds in this task, there is no need to examine the pure faculty itself to see whether it, like speculative reason, presumptuously overreaches itself. For if pure reason is actually practical, it will show its reality and that of its concepts in actions, and all disputations which aim to prove its impossibility will be in vain.

With the pure practical faculty of reason, the reality of transcendental freedom is also confirmed. Indeed, it is substantiated in the absolute sense needed by speculative reason in its use of the concept of causality, for this freedom is required if reason is to rescue itself from the antinomy in which it is inevitably entangled when attempting to think the unconditioned in a causal series. For speculative reason, the concept of freedom was problematic but not impossible; that is to say, speculative reason could think of freedom without contradiction, but it could not assure any objective reality to it. Reason showed freedom to be conceivable only in order that its supposed impossibility might not endanger reason's very being and plunge it into an abyss of skepticism.

The concept of freedom, in so far as its reality is proved by an apodictic law of practical reason, is the keystone of the whole architecture of the system of pure reason and even of speculative reason. All other concepts (those of God and immortality) which, as mere ideas, are unsupported by anything in speculative reason now attach themselves to the concept of freedom and gain, with it and through it, stability and objective reality. That is, their possibility is proved by the fact that there really is freedom, for this idea is revealed by the moral law.

Freedom, however, among all the ideas of speculative reason is the only one whose possibility we know a priori. We do not understand it, but we know it as the condition* of the moral law which we do know. The ideas of God and immortality are, on the contrary, not conditions of the moral law, but only conditions of the necessary object of a will which is determined by this law, this will being merely the practical use of our pure reason. Hence we cannot say that we know or understand either the reality or even the possibility of these ideas. Nevertheless, they are the conditions of applying the morally determined will to the object which is given to it a priori (the highest good). Consequently, the possibility of these conditions can and must be assumed in this practical context without our knowing or understanding them in a theoretical sense. To serve their practical function, it suffices that they not contain any internal impossibility (contradiction). Here we have a ground of assent which, in comparison to the speculative reason, is only subjective, but which is just as valid objectively to a practical reason which is equally pure. Thus, through the concept of freedom, the ideas of God and immortality gain objective reality and legitimacy and indeed subjective necessity (as a need of pure reason). Reason is not hereby extended, however, in its theoretical knowledge; the only thing which is different is that the possibility, which was heretofore a problem, now becomes an assertion, and the practical use of reason is thus connected with the elements of theoretical reason. This need is not just a hypothetical one for some *arbitrary* speculative purpose, of the kind that one must assume if he *wishes* to complete the use of reason in speculation; it is rather a need, *with the status of a law*, to assume that without which an aim cannot be achieved which one *ought* to set before himself invariably in all his actions.

It would certainly be more satisfying to our speculative reason

---

* To avoid having anyone imagine that there is an inconsistency when I say that freedom is the condition of the moral law and later assert that the moral law is the only condition under which freedom can be known, I will only remind the reader that, though freedom is certainly the *ratio essendi* of the moral law, the latter is the *ratio cognoscendi* of freedom. For had not the moral law already been distinctly thought in our reason, we would never have been justified in assuming anything like freedom, even though it is not self-contradictory. But if there were no freedom, the moral law would never have been encountered in us.

if those problems could be solved just by themselves without such a detour and if insight into them could be put up for practical use; but our speculative faculty is not so conveniently disposed. Those who boast of such elevated knowledge should not hold it back but present it for public testing and acclaim. They wish to *prove;* very well, let them prove, and the critical philosophy will lay down its weapons before them as victors. *Quid statis? Nolint. Atqui licet esse beatis.*[1] Since they do not actually wish to prove, presumably because they cannot, we must again take up these weapons and seek, in the practical use of reason, sufficient grounds for the concepts of God, freedom, and immortality. These concepts are founded upon the moral use of reason, while speculation could not find sufficient guarantee even of their possibility.

Now is explained the enigma of the critical philosophy, which lies in the fact that we must renounce the objective reality of the supersensible use of the categories in speculation and yet can attribute this reality to them in respect to the objects of pure practical reason. This must have seemed an inconsistency so long as the practical use of reason was known only by name. However, a thorough analysis of the practical use of reason makes it clear that the reality thought of here implies no theoretical determination of the categories and no extension of our knowledge to the supersensible. One then perceives that all that is meant in attributing reality to those concepts is that an object is attributable to them either in so far as they are contained in the necessary determination of the will a priori or because they are indissolubly connected with the object of this determination. The inconsistency vanishes because the use which is now made of these concepts is different from that required by speculative reason.

So far from being incoherent, the highly consistent structure of the *Critique of Pure Reason* is very satisfyingly revealed here. For in that work the objects of experience as such, including even our own subject, were explained as only *appearances*, though as based upon things-in-themselves; consequently, even in that *Critique* it was emphasized that the supersensible was not mere fancy and that its concepts were not empty. Now practical reason itself, without any collusion with the speculative, pro-

1. [" 'Why standing still?' They would refuse. And yet 'tis in their power to be happy" (Horace *Satire* i. i. 19, trans. H. Rushton Fairclough ["Loeb Classical Library" (1936)]).]

vides reality to a supersensible object of the category of causality, i.e., of freedom. This is a practical concept and as such is subject only to practical use; but what in the speculative critique could only be thought is now confirmed by fact. The strange but incontrovertible assertion of the speculative *Critique*, that the thinking subject is only an appearance to itself in inner intuition, now finds its full confirmation in the *Critique of Practical Reason;* the establishment of this thesis is here so cogent that one would be compelled to accept it even if the first had not already proved it.*

In this way I can also understand why the most weighty criticisms of the *Critique* which have come to my attention turn about these two points: first, the reality of the categories as applied to noumena, which is denied in theoretical knowledge but affirmed in practical; and, second, the paradoxical demand to regard one's self, as subject to freedom, as noumenon, and yet from the point of view of nature to think of one's self as a phenomenon in one's own empirical consciousness. So long as one had no definite concept of morality and freedom, no conjecture could be made concerning what the noumenon was which should be posited as the ground of the alleged appearance, and even whether it was possible to form a concept of it, since all the concepts of the pure understanding in their theoretical employment had already been exclusively assigned to mere appearances. Only a detailed *Critique of Practical Reason* can set aside all these misconceptions and put in a clear light the consistency which constitutes its chief merit.

So much for the justification of the fact that the concepts and principles of the pure speculative reason are now and again re-examined in this work, in spite of the fact that they have already been scrutinized in the *Critique of Pure Reason*. This might not seem proper in the systematic construction of a science, since matters which have already been decided should only be referred to and not discussed again. But here it is allowed and even necessary, for these concepts of reason are now seen in transition to an altogether different use from that made of them in the first

---

* The union of causality as freedom with causality as the mechanism of nature, the first being given through the moral law and the latter through natural law, and both as related to the same subject, man, is impossible unless man is conceived by pure consciousness as a being in itself in relation to the former, but by empirical reason as appearance in relation to the latter. Otherwise the self-contradiction of reason is unavoidable.

Critique. Such a transition makes necessary a comparison of their old and new employment, in order to distinguish clearly the new path from the previous one and at the same time to call attention to the connection between them. One must not, therefore, think that such considerations, including those devoted to the concept of freedom in the practical use of pure reason, are only interpolations which serve to fill out gaps in the critical system of speculative reason, for this is complete in its design. They are not like the props and buttresses which usually have to be put behind a hastily erected building, but they are rather true members making the structure of the system plain[2] and letting the concepts, which were previously thought of only in a problematic way, be clearly seen as real.

This reminder pre-eminently concerns the concept of freedom, for it is surprising that so many boast of being able to understand it and to explain its[3] possibility, yet see it only psychologically. But if they had carefully pondered it from a transcendental standpoint, they would have seen its indispensability as a problematic concept in the complete use of speculative reason as well as its complete incomprehensibility; and if they subsequently passed over to the practical use of this concept, they would have been brought to the same description of it in respect to its principles which they are now so unwilling to acknowledge. The concept of freedom is the stumbling block of all empiricists but the key to the most sublime practical principles to critical moralists, who see, through it, that they must necessarily proceed rationally. For this reason, I beg the reader not to run lightly through what is said about this concept at the end of the Analytic.

I leave it to the connoisseur of this kind of work to judge whether such a system into which practical reason has been developed through a critique of this faculty has cost much or little trouble, especially in gaining the right point of view from which the whole can be rightly sketched. It presupposes the *Foundations of the Metaphysics of Morals,* but only in so far as that work gives a preliminary acquaintance with the principle of duty and

2. [Following the reading of Vorländer and Cassirer.]
3. [Kant's first edition has "its" refer to "freedom" and is followed by the Cassirer ed. Kant's second edition makes "its" refer to "concept of freedom."]

justifies a definite formula of it;* otherwise it is an independent work.

The reason the classification of all practical sciences is not completely carried through, as the critique of speculative reason did this for the theoretical sciences, lies in the nature of the practical faculty itself. For the specific definition of duties as human duties, which is necessary to a classification of them, is only possible if the subject of this definition (man) is known in his actual nature, at least in so far as this knowledge is needed in determining his relation to duty in general. Getting this knowledge, however, does not belong in a critique of practical reason as such, which gives an account of the principles of the possibility of duty, of its extent and limits, without particular reference to human nature. Consequently, this classification belongs to the system of science, not to the system of criticism.

I have, I hope, given a sufficient answer, in the second part of the Analytic, to a certain critic,[5] truth-loving and acute and therefore worthy of respect, who made the following objection to the *Foundations of the Metaphysics of Morals:* the concept of the good was not established before the moral principle, as in his opinion was necessary.† I have also paid attention to many other

---

* A critic[4] who wished to say something against that work really did better than he intended when he said that there was no new principle of morality in it but only a new formula. Who would want to introduce a new principle of morality and, as it were, be its inventor, as if the world had hitherto been ignorant of what duty is or had been thoroughly wrong about it? Those who know what a formula means to a mathematician, in determining what is to be done in solving a problem without letting him go astray, will not regard a formula which will do this for all duties as something insignificant and unnecessary.

4. [Gottlob August Tittel, who in his *Über Herrn Kants Moralreform* (1786) asked, "Is the entire Kantian reform of ethics to limit itself just to a new formula?"]

5. [The anonymous author (H. A. Pistorius) of a review of the *Foundations* in *Allgemeine deutsche Bibliothek*, LXVI, Part 2, 447 ff. See Daniel Jentsch's letter to Kant, May 14, 1787, Cassirer ed., IX, 325.]

† One could also raise the objection that I have not previously explained the concept of the faculty of desire or the feeling of pleasure. This reproach would be unfair, however, because this explanation, as given in psychology, could reasonably be presupposed. But then the definition given in psychology might be so framed that the feeling of pleasure would be made basic to the determination of the faculty of desire (as this is commonly done); and, as a result, the supreme principle of practical philosophy would necessarily turn out to be empirical, a conclusion which would have to be proved first and which is, in fact, completely refuted

objections which have come to me from men who show that the discovery of truth lies close to their hearts, and I shall continue to do so; but those who have their old system so much before their eyes that they have already decided what should be approved or disapproved desire no discussion which could stand in the way of their private views.

When it is a question of determining the origin, contents, and limits of a particular faculty of the human mind, the nature of human knowledge makes it impossible to do otherwise than begin with an exact and (as far as is allowed by the knowledge[7] we have already gained) complete delineation of its parts. But still another thing must be attended to which is of a more philosophical and architectonic character. It is to grasp correctly the idea of the whole, and then to see all those parts in their reciprocal interrelations, in the light of their derivation from the concept of the whole, and as united in a pure rational faculty. This examination and the attainment of such a view are obtainable only through a most intimate acquaintance with the system. Those

---

in this *Critique*. Therefore, I shall give this explanation in the way it ought to be given in order to decide properly this controversial question at the beginning.

Life is the faculty of a being by which it acts according to the laws of the faculty of desire. The *faculty of desire* is the faculty such a being has of causing, through its ideas, the reality of the objects of these ideas. *Pleasure* is the idea of the agreement of an object or an action with the *subjective* conditions of life, i.e., with the faculty through which an idea causes the reality of its object (or the direction of the energies of a subject to such an action as will produce the object).

I need no more than this for the purposes of a critique of concepts borrowed from psychology; the rest is supplied by the *Critique* itself. The question as to whether pleasure is always the ground of the faculty of desire or whether under certain conditions it only follows upon a particular modification of this faculty—this question, as is easily seen, remains unanswered by this explanation; for it consists only of terms belonging to the pure understanding, i.e., categories, which contain nothing empirical. Such a precaution against making judgments by venturing definitions before a complete analysis of concepts has been made (usually only far along in a system) is to be recommended throughout philosophy, but it is often neglected. It will be noticed throughout the critiques of both the theoretical and the practical reason that there are many opportunities for supplying inadequacies and correcting errors in the old dogmatic procedure of philosophy which were detected only when concepts, used according to reason,[6] are given a reference to the totality of concepts.

6. [I.e., reason, the faculty of transcendental ideas, as distinguished from understanding, the faculty of empirical knowledge.]

7. [Reading *Erkenntnis* with Vorländer instead of *Elemente*.]

who are loath to engage in the first of these inquiries and who do not consider acquiring this acquaintance worth the trouble will not reach the second stage, the synoptic view, which is a synthetic return to that which was previously given only analytically. It is not to be wondered at if they find inconsistencies everywhere, though the gaps which they presume to find are not in the system itself but in their own incoherent train of thought.

I have no fear, with respect to this treatise, of the reproach that I wish to introduce a new language, since the kind of thinking it deals with is very close to the popular way of thinking. This objection, moreover, could not have been made even to the first *Critique* by anyone who had really thought his way through it instead of merely turning the pages. To make up new words for accepted concepts when the language does not lack expressions for them is a childish effort to distinguish one's self not by new and true concepts but by new patches on old clothes. If any reader of that work can show that he knows more popular expressions which are as adequate to the thoughts as the ones I used seemed to me, or can demonstrate the nullity of the thoughts themselves and therewith of the terms used to express them, he should do so. The first would greatly oblige me, for I only want to be understood; the second would be a service to philosophy itself. But, as long as those thoughts stand, I very much doubt that expressions both more suitable to them and more common can be found.*

---

* More than this kind of unintelligibility, I fear some misinterpretations, here and there, of expressions which I have sought out with the greatest care in order that the concepts which they mean may not be missed. Thus, under the heading "modality," in the table of categories of practical reason the "permitted" and the "forbidden" (objective-practical meanings of the possible and the impossible) have almost the same significance, in popular usage, as the categories which immediately follow them, namely, "duty" and "contrary to duty." Here, however, the former mean that which is in agreement or disagreement with a merely *possible* precept (as, for example, the solution of problems of geometry or mechanics); the latter, however, indicate what is in such a relation to a law actually lying in reason as such. This difference of meaning is not entirely foreign to ordinary language, but it is somewhat unusual. For instance, an orator is not permitted to forge new words or constructions, but this is permitted, to some extent, to a poet. In neither case, though, is there any thought of duty, for if anyone wishes to forfeit his reputation as a speaker, no one can prevent it. Here it is a question of the difference of the imperatives corresponding to the problematic, assertoric, and apodictic ground of

In this manner the a priori principles of two faculties of the mind, cognition and desire, are to be discovered and their scope and limits determined. Thus the firm basis is laid for a systematic philosophy, both theoretical and practical, as a science.

Nothing worse could happen to all these labors, however, than that someone should make the unexpected discovery that there is and can be no a priori knowledge at all. But there is no danger of this. It would be like proving by reason that there is no such thing as reason; for we only say that we know something through reason when we know that we could have known it even if it had not actually come within our experience. Thus knowledge through reason and a priori knowledge are the same thing. It is a clear contradiction to try to extract necessity from an empirical proposition (*ex pumice aquam*),[8] and it is equally contradictory to attempt to procure, along with such necessity, true universality to a judgment (for without it no rational inference is possible, and consequently no inference is possible by analogy either, since the latter has an at least presumed universality and objective necessity and therefore presupposes it). To substitute subjective necessity, i.e., habit, for the objective which pertains only to a priori judgments would be to deny to reason the faculty of

---

determination. Similarly in the note where I compare the moral ideals of practical perfection in the various philosophical schools, I have differentiated between the ideas of wisdom and holiness, although I have shown them to be fundamentally and objectively identical. But I take wisdom, in that note, only in the sense in which man (the Stoic, for example) lays claim to it, and thus as it is thought of subjectively as a human characteristic. (Perhaps the term "virtue," which the Stoic made so much of, would show even better the characteristic of this school.) But the term "postulate of pure practical reason" can occasion the worst misinterpretation if confused with the meaning which postulates have in pure mathematics, where they are of apodictic certainty. The latter, however, postulate the possibility of an action, the object of which one previously knows a priori, theoretically and with complete certainty, to be possible. Those of the pure practical reason, however, postulate the possibility of an object(God and the immortality of the soul) from apodictic practical laws, but therefore only for the use of a practical reason. This certainty of the postulated possibility is not in the least theoretical and consequently also not apodictic, i.e., not a necessity known by reference to an object; it is a necessary assumption, rather, with reference to the subject as conforming to the objective practical laws of reason. Thus it is merely a necessary hypothesis. I could not discover for this subjective yet true and absolute rational necessity a better term than "postulate."

8. ["Water from a pumice stone" (Plautus *Persa* i. i. 14). Cf. our "blood from a turnip."]

judging an object, of knowing it and what belongs to it. It would mean, for example, that what usually or always follows a certain prior condition could not be inferred to follow *from* it, since that would imply objective necessity and an a priori concept of a connection. It would mean only that similar cases may be expected, as animals expect them. It would be to reject the concept of cause as fundamentally false and a mere delusion of thought. As to attempting to remedy this lack of objective and consequently universal validity by arguing that there is no reason not to attribute to other reasonable beings a different type of ideation—well, if this sort of argument should yield a valid inference, then our ignorance would render us greater services in widening our knowledge than all our meditation. Simply because we do not know any reasonable beings other than men, we would have the right only to assume them to be of the same nature as we know ourselves to be, and therefore we would really know them. I need not mention the fact that unversality of assent does not prove the objective validity of a judgment, i.e., its validity as knowledge, but only call attention to the fact that, even if sometimes that which is universally assented to is also correct, this is no proof of its agreement with the object; it is rather the case that only objective validity affords the ground of a necessary universal agreement.

Hume would find himself completely at ease in this system of universal empiricism of principles, for he desired, as is well known, nothing more than that a merely subjectively necessary concept of cause, i.e., habit, be assumed in place of all objective meaning of necessity in the causal concept; he did this in order to deny to reason any judgment concerning God, freedom, and immortality; and he knew very well how to draw conclusions with complete cogency when once the principles were conceded. But even Hume did not make his empiricism so universal as to include mathematics in it. He held its propositions to be analytic, and, if this were correct, they would indeed be apodictic; but this would not give us any right to conclude that there is a faculty of reason which can make apodictic judgments also in philosophy, for in philosophy they would be synthetic, as the law of causality is. But if one assumes a universal empiricism, mathematics will also be involved.

When, however, mathematics comes into conflict with that reason which admits only empirical principles, as this inevitably occurs in the antinomy, since mathematics irrefutably proves the infinite divisibility of space which empiricism cannot allow, there is an obvious contradiction between the highest possible demonstrable evidence and the alleged inferences from empirical principles. One might ask, like Cheselden's[9] blind man, "Which deceives me, sight or touch?" (Empiricism is based on touch, but rationalism on a necessity which can be seen.) Thus universal empiricism is revealed to be genuine skepticism, which has been falsely ascribed to Hume in this unlimited sense,* for he let mathematics stand as a sure touchstone of experience, instead of admitting no touchstone (which can be found only in a priori principles) even though experience consists not only of feelings but also of judgments.

Since in this philosophical and critical age no one can be very much in earnest about such an empiricism, and since it is presumably put forward only as an exercise for judgment and to place the necessity of rational principles in a clearer light by contrast, we can only be grateful to those who trouble themselves with this otherwise uninstructive work.

INTRODUCTION

OF THE IDEA OF A *CRITIQUE OF PRACTICAL REASON*

THE theoretical use of reason is concerned with objects of the merely cognitive faculty, and a critical examination of it with reference to this use deals really only with the pure cognitive faculty, because the latter raised the suspicion, which was subsequently confirmed, that it might easily pass beyond its boundaries and lose itself among unattainable objects or even among contradictory concepts. It is quite different with the practical use of reason. In the latter, reason deals with the grounds determining the will, which is a faculty either of bringing forth objects corresponding to conceptions or of determining itself, i.e., its causality to effect such objects (whether the

---

9. [William Cheselden (1688–1752), an English surgeon, famous for his operation of iridectomy which cured some forms of blindness. Cheselden attended Newton in his last illness.]

* Names which refer to the followers of a sect have always been accompanied by much injustice. It is as if someone said, "N. is an idealist." For although he not only admits, but even emphasizes, that our ideas of external things correspond to real objects, he will still hold that the form of their intuition depends not on them but on the human mind.

physical power is sufficient to this or not). For here reason can at least attain so far as to determine the will, and, in so far as it is a question of volition only, reason does always have objective reality.

This is, then, the first question: Is pure reason sufficient of itself to determine the will, or is it only as empirically conditioned that it can do so? At this point there appears a concept of causality which is justified by the *Critique of Pure Reason*, though subject to no empirical exhibition. That is the concept of freedom, and if we now can discover means to show that freedom does in fact belong to the human will (and thus to the will of all rational beings), then it will have been proved not only that pure reason can be practical but also that it alone, and not the empirically conditioned reason, is unconditionally practical. Consequently, we shall have to make a critical examination, not of the *pure* practical reason, but only of practical reason *as such*.

For pure reason, when it is once demonstrated to exist, is in no need of a critical examination; it is pure reason itself which contains the standard for the critical investigation of its entire use. The critique, therefore, of practical reason as such has the obligation to prevent the empirically conditioned reason from presuming to be the only ground of determination of the will. The use of pure [practical] reason, if it is shown that there is such a reason, is alone immanent; the empirically conditioned use of reason, which presumes to be sovereign, is, on the contrary, transcendent, expressing itself in demands and precepts which go far beyond its own sphere. This is precisely the opposite situation from that of pure reason in its speculative use.

Yet because it is still pure reason, the knowledge of which here underlies its practical use, the organization of the *Critique of Practical Reason* must conform, in its general outline, to that of the critique of speculative reason. We shall therefore have to have a Doctrine of Elements and a Methodology. The former must have as its first part an Analytic as the rule of truth and a Dialectic as an exhibition and resolution of illusion in the judgments of practical reason. Only the order in the subdivision of the Analytic will be the reverse of that in the critique of speculative reason. For in the present work we begin with principles and proceed to concepts, and only then, if possible, go on to the senses, while in the study of speculative reason we had to start with the senses and end with principles. Again the reason for this lies in the fact that here we have to deal with a will and to consider reason not in relation to objects but in relation to this will and its causality. The principles of the empirically unconditioned causality must come first, and afterward the attempt can be made to establish our concepts of the ground of determination of such a will, their application to objects, and finally their application to the subject and its sensuous faculty. The law of causality from freedom, i.e., any pure practical principle, is the unavoidable beginning and determines the objects to which it alone can be applied.

PART I

DOCTRINE OF THE ELEMENTS OF PURE PRACTICAL REASON

BOOK I
ANALYTIC OF PURE PRACTICAL REASON

Chapter I
Principles of Pure Practical Reason

§ 1. *Definition*

PRACTICAL principles are propositions which contain a general determination of the will, having under it several practical rules. They are subjective, or maxims, when the condition is regarded by the subject as valid only for his own will. They are objective, or practical, laws when they are recognized as objective, i.e., as valid for the will of every rational being.

REMARK

Assuming that pure reason can contain a practical ground sufficient to determine the will, then there are practical laws. Otherwise all practical principles are mere maxims. In the will of a rational being affected by feeling,[10] there can be a conflict of maxims with the practical laws recognized by this being. For example, someone can take as his maxim not to tolerate any unavenged offense and yet see at the same time that this is only his own maxim and not a practical law and that, if it is taken as a rule for the will of every rational being, it would be inconsistent with itself.

10. [*Pathologisch affizierter Wille.*]

In natural science the principles of what occurs (e.g., the principle of equivalence of action and reaction in the communication of motion) are at the same time laws of nature, for there the use of reason is theoretical and determined by the nature of the object. In practical philosophy, which has to do only with the grounds of determination of the will, the principles which a man makes for himself are not laws by which he is inexorably bound, because reason, in practice, has to do with a subject and especially with its faculty of desire, the special character of which may occasion variety in the rule. The practical rule is always a product of reason, because it prescribes action as a means to an effect which is its purpose. This rule, however, is an imperative for a being whose reason is not the sole determinant of the will. It is a rule characterized by an "ought," which expresses the objective necessitation of the act and indicates that, if reason completely determined the will, the action would without exception take place according to the rule.

Imperatives, therefore, are valid objectively and are quite distinct from maxims, which are subjective principles. Imperatives determine either the conditions of causality of a rational being as an efficient cause only in respect to its effect and its sufficiency to bring this effect about, or they determine only the will, whether it be adequate to the effect or not. In the former case, imperatives would be hypothetical and would contain only precepts of skill; in the latter, on the contrary, they would be categorical and would alone be practical laws. Maxims are thus indeed principles, but they are not imperatives. Imperatives themselves, however, when they are conditional, i.e., when they determine the will not as such but only in respect to a desired effect, are hypothetical imperatives, which are practical precepts but not laws. Laws must completely determine the will as will, even before I ask whether I am capable of achieving a desired effect or what should be done to realize it. They must thus be categorical; otherwise they would not be laws, for they would lack the necessity which, in order to be practical, must be completely independent of pathological conditions, i.e., conditions only contingently related to the will.

Tell someone, for instance, that in his youth he should work and save in order not to want in his old age—that is a correct and important practical precept of the will. One easily sees, however, that the will is thereby directed to something else which he is assumed to desire; and, as to this desire, we must leave it up to the man himself if he foresees other resources than his own acquisitions, does not even hope to reach old age, or thinks that in case of need he can make out with little. Reason, from which alone a rule involving necessity can be derived, gives necessity to this precept, without which it would not be an imperative; but this necessity is dependent on only subjective conditions, and one cannot assume it in equal measure in all men. But for reason to be legislative, it is required that reason need presuppose only itself, because the rule is objectively and universally valid only when it holds without any contingent subjective conditions which differentiate one rational being from another.

Now tell a man that he should never make a deceitful promise; this is a rule which concerns only his will regardless of whether any purposes he has can be achieved by it or not. Only the volition is to be completely determined a priori by this rule. If, now, it is found that this rule is practically right, it is a law, because it is a categorical imperative. Thus practical laws refer only to the will, irrespective of what is attained by its causality, and one can disregard this causality (as belonging to the sensuous world) in order to have the laws in their purity.

§ 2. *Theorem I*

All practical principles which presuppose an object (material) of the faculty of desire as the determining ground of the will are without exception empirical and can furnish no practical laws.

By the term "material of the faculty of desire," I understand an object whose reality is desired. When the desire for this object precedes the practical rule and is the condition under which the latter becomes a principle, I say, first, that this principle is then always empirical. I say this because the determining ground of choice consists in the conception of an object and its relation to the subject, whereby the faculty of desire is determined to seek its realization. Such a relation to the subject is called pleasure in the reality of an object, and it must be presupposed as the condition of the possibility of the determination of choice. But we cannot know, a priori, of the idea of any object, whatever the nature of this idea, whether it will be associated with pleasure or displeasure or will be merely indifferent. Thus any such determining ground of choice must always be empirical, and the practical material principle which has it as a condition is likewise empirical.

Second, a principle which is based only on the subjective susceptibility to a pleasure or displeasure (which is never known except empirically and cannot be valid in the same form for all rational beings) cannot function as a law even to the subject possessing this susceptibility, because it lacks objective necessity, which must be known a priori. For this reason, such a principle can never furnish a practical law. It can, however, be counted among the maxims of a subject thus susceptible.

§ 3. *Theorem II*

All material practical principles are, as such, of one and the same kind and belong under the general principle of self-love or one's own happiness.

Pleasure from the conception of the existence of a thing, in so far as it is a determining ground of the desire for this thing, is based upon the susceptibility of the subject because it depends upon the actual presence of an object. Thus it belongs to sense (feeling) and not to the understanding, which expresses a relation of a conception to an object by concepts and not the relation of an idea to the subject by feelings. It is only practical in so far as the faculty of desire is determined by the sensation of agreeableness which the subject expects from the actual existence of the object. Now a rational being's consciousness of the agreeableness of life which without interruption accompanies his whole existence is happiness, and to make this the supreme ground for the determination of choice constitutes the principle of self-love. Thus all material principles, which place the determining ground of choice in the pleasure or displeasure to be received from the reality of any object whatsoever, are entirely of one kind. Without exception they belong under the principle of self-love or one's own happiness.

COROLLARY

All material practical rules place the ground of the determination of the will in the lower faculty of desire, and if there were no purely formal laws of the will adequate to determine it, we could not admit [the existence of] any higher faculty of desire.

REMARK I

It is astonishing how otherwise acute men believe they can find a difference between the lower and the higher faculty of desire by noting whether the conceptions which are associated with pleasure have their origin in the senses or in the understanding.

When one inquires into the determining grounds of desire and finds them in an expected agreeableness resulting from something or other, it is not a question of where the conception of this enjoyable object comes from, but merely of how much it can be enjoyed. If a conception, even though it has its origin and status in the understanding, can determine choice only by presupposing a feeling of pleasure in the subject, then its becoming a determining ground of choice is wholly dependent on the nature of the inner sense, i.e., it depends on whether the latter can be agreeably affected by that conception. However dissimilar the conceptions of the objects, be they proper to the understanding or even to the reason instead of to the senses, the feeling of pleasure, by virtue of which they constitute the determining ground of the will (since it is the agreeableness and enjoyment which one expects from the object which impels the activity toward producing it) is always the same. This sameness lies not merely in the fact that all feelings of pleasure can be known only empirically, but even more in the fact that the feeling of pleasure always affects one and the same life-force which is manifested in the faculty of desire, and in this respect one determining ground can differ from any other only in degree. Otherwise how could one make a comparison with respect to magnitude between two determining grounds the ideas of which depend upon different faculties, in order to prefer the one which affects the faculty of desire to the greater extent? A man can return unread an instructive book which he cannot again obtain, in order not to miss the hunt; he can go away in the middle of a fine speech, in order not to be late for a meal; he can leave an intellectual conversation, which he otherwise enjoys, in order to take his place at the gambling table; he can even repulse a poor man whom it is usually a joy to aid, because he has only enough money in his pocket for a ticket to the theater. If the determination of the will rests on the feelings of agreeableness or disagreeableness which he expects from any cause, it is all the same to him through what kind of notion he is affected. The only thing he considers in making a choice is how great, how long lasting, how easily obtained, and how often repeated this agreeableness is. As the man who wants money to spend does not care whether the gold in it was mined in the mountains or washed from the sand, provided it is accepted everywhere as having the same value, so also no man asks, when he is concerned only with the agreeableness of life, whether the ideas are from the sense or the understanding; he asks only how much and how great is the pleasure which they will afford him over the longest time. Only those who would like to deny to pure reason the faculty of determining the will without presupposing any feeling whatsoever could deviate so far from their own exposition as to describe as quite heterogeneous what they have previously brought under one and the same principle. Thus, for instance, a man can find satisfaction in the mere exercise of power, in the consciousness of his spiritual strength in overcoming obstacles in the way of his designs, and in the cultivation of his intellectual talents. We correctly call these the more refined joys and delights, because they are more in our power than others and do not wear out, but, rather, increase our capacity for even more of this kind of enjoyment; they delight and at the same time cultivate. But this is no reason to pass off such pleasures as a mode of determining the will different from that of the senses. For the possibility of these pleasures, too, presupposes, as the first condition of our delight, the existence in us of a corresponding feeling. So to jump to that equation resembles the error of ignorant persons who wish to dabble in metaphysics and who imagine matter as so subtle, so supersubtle, that they almost get dizzy considering it, and then believe that they have conceived of a spiritual but still extended being. If with Epicurus we let virtue determine the will only because of the pleasure it promises, we cannot later blame him for holding that this pleasure is of the same sort as those of the coarsest senses. For we have no reason to charge him with relegating the ideas by which this feeling is excited in us to the bodily senses only. So far as we can tell, he sought the source of many of them in the employment of the higher cognitive faculty. That did not and could not deter him, however, in accordance with the principle stated above, from holding that the pleasure which is given to us by these intellectual ideas and which is the only means by which they can determine the will is of exactly the same kind as that coming from the senses.

Consistency is the highest obligation of a philosopher and yet the most rarely found. The ancient Greek schools afford more examples of it than we find in our syncretistic age, when a certain shallow and dishonest system of coalition between contradictory principles is devised because it is more acceptable to a public which is satisfied to know a little about everything and at bottom nothing, thus playing the jack-of-all-trades. The principle of one's own happiness, however much reason and understanding may be used in it, contains no other determinants for the will than those which belong to the lower faculty of desire. Either, then, no higher faculty of desire exists, or else pure reason alone must of itself be practical, i.e., it must be able to determine the will by the mere form of the practical rule without presupposing any feeling or consequently any idea of the pleasant or the unpleasant as the matter of the faculty of desire and as the empirical condition of its principles. Then only is reason a truly higher faculty of desire, but still only in so far as it determines the will by itself and not in the service of the inclinations. Subordinate to reason as the higher faculty of desire is the pathologically determinable faculty of desire, the latter being really and specifically different from the former, so that even the slightest admixture of its impulses impairs the strength and superiority of reason, just as taking anything empirical as the condition of a mathematical demonstration would degrade and destroy its force and value. Reason determines the will in a practical law directly, not through an intervening feeling of pleasure or displeasure, even if this pleasure is taken in the law itself. Only because, as pure reason, it is practical can it be legislative.

REMARK II

To be happy is necessarily the desire of every rational but finite being, and thus it is an unavoidable determinant of its faculty of desire. Contentment with our existence is not, as it were, an inborn possession or a bliss, which would presuppose a consciousness of our self-sufficiency; it is rather a problem imposed upon us by our own finite nature as a being of needs. These needs are directed to the material of the faculty of desire, i.e., to that which is related to a basic subjective feeling of pleasure or displeasure, determining what we require in order to be satisfied with our condition. But just because this material ground of determination can be known by the subject only empirically, it is impossible to regard this demand for happiness as a law, since the latter must contain exactly the same determining ground for the will of all rational beings and in all cases. Since, though, the concept of happiness always underlies the practical relation of objects to the faculty of desire, it is merely the general name for subjective grounds of determination, and it determines nothing specific concerning what is to be done in a given practical problem; but in a practical problem this is what is alone important, for without some specific determination the problem cannot be solved. Where one places his happiness is a question of the particular feeling of pleasure or displeasure in each man, and even of the differences in needs occasioned by changes of feeling in one and the same man. Thus a subjectively necessary law (as a law of nature) is objectively a very contingent practical principle which can and must be very different in different men. It therefore cannot yield any law, because in the desire for happiness it is not the form (accordance with law) but only the material which is decisive; it is a question only of whether I may expect pleasure from obedience to this law, and, if so, how much. Principles of self-love can indeed contain universal rules of skill (how to find means to some end), but they are only theoretical principles,* as, for example, how someone who wants bread should construct a mill. But practical precepts based on them can never be universal, for the determinant of the faculty of desire is based on the feeling of pleasure and displeasure, which can never be assumed to be universally directed to the same objects.

But suppose that finite rational beings were unanimous in the kind of objects their feelings of pleasure and pain had, and even in the means of obtaining the former and preventing the latter. Even then they could not set up the principle of self-love as a practical law, for the unanimity itself would be merely contingent. The determining ground would still be only subjectively valid and empirical, and it would not have the necessity which is conceived in every law, an objective necessity arising from a priori grounds, unless we hold this necessity to be not at all practical but only physical, maintaining that our action is as inevitably forced upon us by our inclination as yawning is by seeing others yawn. It would be better to maintain that there are no practical laws but merely counsels for the service of our desires than to elevate merely subjective principles to the rank of practical laws, which must have an objective and not just subjective necessity and which must be known a priori by reason instead of by experience no matter how empirically universal. Even the rules of uniform phenomena are denominated natural laws (for example, mechanical laws) only if we really can understand them a priori or at least (as in the case of those of chem-

---

* Propositions called "practical" in mathematics or natural science should properly be called "technical" for in these fields it is not a question of determining the will; they only indicate the manifold of a possible action which is adequate to bring about a certain effect, and are therefore just as theoretical as any proposition which asserts a connection between cause and effect. Whoever chooses the latter must also choose the former.

istry) suppose that they could be known in this way if our insight went deeper. Only in the case of subjective practical principles is it expressly made a condition that not objective but subjective conditions of choice must underlie them, and hence that they must be represented always as mere maxims and never as practical laws.

This remark may appear at first blush to be mere hairsplitting; actually, it defines the most important distinction which can be considered in practical investigations.

§ 4. *Theorem III*

If a rational being can think of its maxims as practical universal laws, he can do so only by considering them as principles which contain the determining grounds of the will formally and not materially.

The material of a practical principle is the object of the will. This object either is the determining ground of the will or it is not. If it is, the rule of the will is subject to an empirical condition (to the relation of the determining notion to feelings of pleasure or displeasure), and therefore it is not a practical law. If all material of a law, i.e., every object of the will considered as a ground of its determination, is abstracted from it, nothing remains except the mere form of a universal legislation. Therefore, a rational being either cannot think of his subjectively practical principles (maxims) as universal laws, or he must suppose that their mere form, through which they are fitted for giving universal laws, is alone that which makes them a practical law.

REMARK

What form of a maxim makes it suitable for universal law-giving and what form does not do so can be distinguished without instruction by the most common understanding. I have, for example, made it my maxim to increase my property by every safe means. Now I have in my possession a deposit, the owner of which has died without leaving any record of it. Naturally, this case falls under my maxim. Now I want to know whether this maxim can hold as a universal practical law. I apply it, therefore, to the present case and ask if it could take the form of a law, and consequently whether I could, by my maxim, make the law that every man is allowed to deny that a deposit has been made when no one can prove the contrary. I immediately realize that taking such a principle as a law would annihilate itself, because its result would be that no one would make a deposit. A practical law, which I acknowledge as such, must qualify for being universal law; this is an identical and therefore a self-evident proposition. Now, if I say that my will is subject to a practical law, I cannot put forward my inclination (in this case, my avarice) as fit to be a determining ground of a universal practical law. It is so far from being worthy of universal legislation that in the form of a universal law it must destroy itself.

It is therefore astonishing how intelligent men have thought of proclaiming as a universal practical law the desire for happiness, and therewith to make this desire the determining ground of the will merely because this desire is universal. Though elsewhere natural laws make everything harmonious, if one here attributed the universality of law to this maxim, there would be the extreme opposite of harmony, the most arrant conflict, and the complete annihilation of the maxim itself and its purpose. For the wills of all do not have one and the same object, but each person has his own (his own welfare), which, to be sure, can accidentally agree with the purposes of others who are pursuing their own, though this agreement is far from sufficing for a law because the occasional exceptions which one is permitted to make are endless and cannot be definitely comprehended in a universal rule. In this way a harmony may result resembling that depicted in a certain satirical poem as existing between a married couple bent on going to ruin, "Oh, marvelous harmony, what he wants is what she wants";[11] or like the pledge which is said to have been given by Francis I to the Emperor Charles V, "What my brother wants (Milan), that I want too." Empirical grounds of determination are not fit for any universal external legislation, and they are just as little suited to an internal, for each man makes his own subject the foundation of his inclination, and in each person it is now one and now another which has preponderance. To discover a law which would govern them all by bringing them into unison is absolutely impossible.

§ 5. Problem I

Granted that the mere legislative form of maxims is the sole sufficient determining ground of a will, find the character of the will which is determinable by it alone.

---

11. [Cf. Kant's earlier epigram: "In marriage, union without unity" (*Fragmente aus dem Nachlass* [Kirchmann ed.], p. 306).]

Since the mere form of a law can be thought only by reason and is consequently not an object of the senses and therefore does not belong among appearances, the conception of this form as the determining ground of the will is distinct from all determining grounds of events in nature according to the law of causality, for these grounds must themselves be appearances. Now as no determining ground of the will except the universal legislative form can serve as a law for it, such a will must be conceived as wholly independent of the natural law of appearances in their mutual relations,[12] i.e., the law of causality. Such independence is called *freedom* in the strictest, i.e., transcendental, sense. Therefore, a will to which only the legislative form of the maxim can serve as a law is a free will.

§ 6. Problem II

Granted that a will is free, find the law which alone is competent to determine it necessarily.

Since the material of the practical law, i.e., an object of the maxim, cannot be given except empirically, and since a free will must be independent of all empirical conditions (i.e., those belonging to the world of sense) and yet be determinable, a free will must find its ground of determination in the law, but independently of the material of the law. But besides the latter there is nothing in a law except the legislative form. Therefore, the legislative form, in so far as it is contained in the maxim, is the only thing which can constitute a determining ground of the free[13] will.

REMARK

Thus freedom and unconditional practical law reciprocally imply each other. I do not here ask whether they are actually different, instead of an unconditional law being merely the self-consciousness of a pure practical reason, and thus identical with the positive concept of freedom.[14] The question now is whether our *knowledge* of the unconditionally practical takes its inception from freedom or from the practical law. It cannot start from freedom, for this we can neither know immediately, since our

---

12. [Following the word order suggested by Adickes.]
13. [*Free* is inserted by Hartenstein. The Cassirer ed. regards it as unnecessary, since the free will is the presupposition of the argument. To avoid a very easy misconception, however, we follow Hartenstein here.]
14. [Reading *dieses*, with Paton, instead of *diese*.]

first concept of it is negative, nor infer from experience, since experience reveals us only the law of appearances and consequently the mechanism of nature, the direct opposite of freedom. It is therefore the moral law, of which we become immediately conscious as soon as we construct maxims for the will, which first presents itself to us; and, since reason exhibits it as a ground of determination which is completely independent of and not to be outweighed by any sensuous condition, it is the moral law which leads directly to the concept of freedom.

But how is the consciousness of that moral law possible? We can come to know pure practical laws in the same way we know pure theoretical principles, by attending to the necessity with which reason prescribes them to us and to the elimination from them of all empirical conditions, which reason directs. The concept of a pure will arises from the former, as the consciousness of a pure understanding from the latter. That this is the correct organization of our concepts, and that morality first reveals the concept of freedom to us while practical reason deeply perplexes the speculative with this concept which poses the most insoluble of problems, is shown by the following considerations. First, nothing in appearances is explained by the concept of freedom, but there the mechanism of nature must be the only clue. Second, there is the antinomy of pure reason which arises when reason aspires to the unconditioned in a causal series and which involves it in inconceivabilities on both sides, since at least mechanism has a use in the explanation of appearances, while no one would dare introduce freedom into science had not the moral law and, with it, practical reason come to the concept and forced it upon us.

Experience also confirms this order of concepts in us. Suppose that someone says his lust is irresistible when the desired object and opportunity are present. Ask him whether he would not control his passion if, in front of the house where he has this opportunity, a gallows were erected on which he would be hanged immediately after gratifying his lust. We do not have to guess very long what his answer would be. But ask him whether he thinks it would be possible for him to overcome his love of life, however great it may be, if his sovereign threatened him with the same sudden death unless he made a false deposition against an honorable man whom the ruler wished to destroy under a plausible pretext. Whether he would or not he perhaps will not venture to say; but that it would be possible for him he would certainly admit without hesitation. He judges, therefore, that he can do something because he knows that he ought, and he recognizes that he is free—a fact which, without the moral law, would have remained unknown to him.

§ 7. *Fundamental Law of Pure Practical Reason*

So act that the maxim of your will could always hold at the same time as the principle of a universal legislation.

REMARK

Pure geometry has postulates as practical propositions, which, however, contain nothing more than the presupposition that one *can* do something and that, when some result is needed, one *should* do it; these are the only propositions of pure geometry which apply to an existing thing. They are thus practical rules under a problematic condition of the will. Here, however, the rule says: One ought absolutely to act in a certain way. The practical rule is therefore unconditional and thus is thought of a priori as a categorically practical proposition. The practical rule, which is thus here a law, absolutely and directly determines the will objectively, for pure reason, practical in itself, is here directly legislative. The will is thought of as independent of empirical conditions and consequently as pure will, determined by the mere form of the law, and this ground of determination is regarded as the supreme condition of all maxims.

The thing is strange enough and has no parallel in the remainder of practical knowledge. For the a priori thought of the possibility of giving universal law, which is thus merely problematic, is unconditionally commanded as a law without borrowing anything from experience or from any external will. It is, however, not a prescription according to which an act should occur in order to make a desired effect possible, for such a rule is always physically conditioned; it is, on the contrary, a rule which determines the will a priori only with respect to the form of its maxims. Therefore, it is at least not impossible to conceive of a law which merely serves the purpose of the *subjective* form of principles and yet is a ground of determination by virtue of the *objective* form of a law in general. The consciousness of this fundamental principle may be called a fact of reason, since one cannot ferret it out from antecedent data of reason, such as the consciousness of freedom (for this is not antecedently given), and since it forces itself upon us as a synthetic proposition a priori based on no pure or empirical intuition. It would be analytic if the freedom of the will were presupposed, but for this, as a positive concept, an intellectual intuition would be needed, and here we cannot assume it. In order to regard this law without any misinterpretation as given, one must note that it is not an empirical fact but the sole fact of pure reason, which by it proclaims itself as originally legislative (*sic volo, sic iubeo*).[15]

COROLLARY

Pure reason is practical of itself alone, and it gives (to man) a universal law, which we call the *moral law*.

REMARK

The fact just mentioned is undeniable. One need only analyze the sentence which men pass upon the lawfulness of their actions to see in every case that their reason, incorruptible and self-constrained, in every action confronts the maxim of the will with the pure will, i.e., with itself regarded as a priori practical; and this it does regardless of what inclination may say to the contrary. Now this principle of morality, on account of the universality of its legislation which makes it the formal supreme determining ground of the will regardless of any subjective differences among men, is declared by reason to be a law for all rational beings in so far as they have a will, i.e., faculty of determining their causality through the conception of a rule, and consequently in so far as they are competent to determine their actions according to principles and thus to act according to practical a priori principles, which alone have the necessity which reason demands in a principle. It is thus not limited to human beings but extends to all finite beings having reason and will; indeed, it includes the Infinite Being as the supreme intelligence. In the former case, however, the law has the form of an imperative. For though we can suppose that men, as rational beings, have a pure will, since they are affected by wants and sensuous motives, we cannot suppose them to have a holy will, a will incapable of any maxims which conflict with the moral law. The moral law for them, therefore, is an imperative, commanding categorically because it is unconditioned. The relation of such a will to this law is one of dependence under the name of *obligation*. This term implies a constraint to an action, though this constraint is only that of reason

15. [An allusion to Juvenal *Satire* vi: "This is my will and my command: let my will be the voucher for the deed" (trans. G. G. Ramsay ["Loeb Classical Library" (1918)]).]

and its objective law. Such an action is called *duty*, because a pathologically affected (though not pathologically determined—and thus still free) choice involves a wish arising from subjective causes, and consequently such a choice often opposes pure objective grounds of determination. Such a will is therefore in need of the moral constraint of the resistance offered by the practical reason, which may be called an inner but intellectual compulsion. In the supremely self-sufficing intelligence choice is correctly thought of as incapable of any maxim which could not at the same time be objectively a law, and the concept of holiness, which is applied to it for this reason, elevates it not indeed above all practical laws but above all practically restrictive laws, and thus above obligation and duty. This holiness of will is, however, a practical ideal which must necessarily serve as a model which all finite rational beings must strive toward even though they cannot reach it. The pure moral law, which is itself for this reason called holy, constantly and rightly holds it before their eyes. The utmost that finite practical reason can accomplish is to make sure of the indefinite progress of its maxims toward this model and of their immutability in achieving constant progress. This is virtue, and, as a naturally acquired faculty, it can never be perfect, because assurance in such a case never becomes apodictic certainty, and as a mere persuasion it is very dangerous.

§ 8. *Theorem IV*

The *autonomy* of the will is the sole principle of all moral laws and of the duties conforming to them; *heteronomy* of choice, on the other hand, not only does not establish any obligation but is opposed to the principle of duty and to the morality of the will.

The sole principle of morality consists in independence from all material of the law (i.e., a desired object) and in the accompanying determination of choice by the mere universal legislating form which a maxim must be capable of having. That independence, however, is freedom in the negative sense, while this intrinsic legislation of pure and thus practical reason is freedom in the positive sense. Therefore, the moral law expresses nothing else than the autonomy of the pure practical reason, i.e., freedom.[16] This autonomy or freedom is itself the formal condition of all maxims, under which alone they can all agree with the su-

---

16. [With Natorp, reading *die Freiheit*, instead of *der Freiheit*, inasmuch as autonomy of pure practical reason is equivalent to freedom.]

preme practical law. If, therefore, the material of volition, which cannot be other than an object of a desire which is connected to the law, comes into the practical law as a condition of its possibility, there results heteronomy of choice, or dependence on natural laws in following some impulse or inclination; it is heteronomy because the will does not give itself the law but only directions for a reasonable obedience to pathological laws. The maxim, however, which for this reason can never contain universally legislative form, not only produces no obligation but is itself opposed to the principle of a pure practical reason and thus also to the moral disposition, even when the action which comes from it conforms to the law.

REMARK I

Thus a practical precept which contains a material and therefore empirical condition must never be reckoned a practical law. For the law of pure will, which is free, puts the will in a sphere entirely different from the empirical, and the necessity which it expresses, not being a natural necessity, can consist only in the formal conditions of the possibility of a law in general. All the material of practical rules rests only on subjective conditions, which can afford the rules[17] no universality for rational beings (except a merely conditioned one as in the case where I desire this or that, and then there is something which I must do in order to make it real). Without exception, they all revolve about the principle of one's own happiness. Now it is certainly undeniable that every volition must have an object and therefore a material; but the material cannot be supposed for this reason to be the determining ground and condition of the maxim. If it were, the maxim could not be presented as giving universal law, because then the expectation of the existence of the object would be the determining cause of the choice, the dependence of the faculty of desire on the existence of some thing would have to be made basic to volition, and this dependence would have to be sought out in empirical conditions and therefore never could be a foundation of a necessary and universal rule. Thus the happiness of others may be the object of the will of a rational being, but if it were the determining ground of the maxim, not only would one have to presuppose that we find in the welfare of others a natural satisfaction but also one would have to find a want such

17. [With Natorp, reading *ihnen*. Kant and the Cassirer ed. read *ihr* (= the material of the rules).]

as that which is occasioned in some men by a sympathetic disposition. This want, however, I cannot presuppose in every rational being, certainly not in God. The material of the maxim can indeed remain but cannot be its condition, for then it would not be fit for a law. The mere form of a law, which limits its material, must be a condition for introducing this material into the will but not for presupposing it as the condition of the will. Let the material content be, for example, my own happiness. If I attribute this to everyone, as in fact I may attribute it to all finite beings, it can become an objective practical law only if I include within it the happiness of others. Therefore, the law that we should further the happiness of others arises not from the presupposition that this law is an object of everyone's choice but from the fact that the form of universality, which reason requires as condition for giving to the maxim of self-love the objective validity of law, is itself the determining ground of the will. Therefore not the object, i.e., the happiness of others, was the determining ground of the pure will but rather it was the lawful form alone. Through it I restricted my maxim, founded on inclination, by giving it the universality of a law, thus making it conformable to the pure practical reason. From this limitation alone, and not from the addition of any external incentive, the concept of obligation arises to extend the maxim of self-love also to the happiness of others.

REMARK II

When one's own happiness is made the determining ground of the will, the result is the direct opposite of the principle of morality; and I have previously shown that, whenever the determining ground which is to serve as a law is located elsewhere than in the legislative form of the maxim, we have to reckon with this result. This conflict is not, however, merely logical, as is that between empirically conditioned rules which someone might nevertheless wish to erect into necessary principles of knowledge; it is rather a practical conflict, and, were the voice of reason with respect to the will not so distinct, so irrepressible, and so clearly audible to even the commonest man, it would drive morality to ruin. But it can only maintain itself in the perplexing speculations of the schools which are audacious enough to close their ears to that heavenly voice in order to uphold a theory that costs no brainwork.

Suppose that an acquaintance whom you otherwise liked

were to attempt to justify himself before you for having borne false witness by appealing to what he regarded as the holy duty of consulting his own happiness and, then, by recounting all the advantages he had gained thereby, pointing out the prudence he had shown in securing himself against detection, even by yourself, to whom alone he now reveals the secret only in order that he may be able at any time to deny it. And suppose that he then affirmed, in all seriousness, that he had thereby fulfilled a true human duty—you would either laugh in his face or shrink from him in disgust, even though you would not have the least grounds for objecting to such measures if a man regulated his principles solely with a view to his own advantage. Or suppose someone recommends you a man as steward as one to whom you could blindly trust your affairs and, in order to inspire you with confidence, further extols him as a prudent man who has a masterly understanding of his own interest and is so indefatigably active that he misses no opportunity to further it; furthermore, lest you should be afraid of finding a vulgar selfishness in him, he praises the good taste with which he lives, not seeking his pleasure in making money or in coarse wantonness, but in the increase of his knowledge, in instructive conversation with a select circle, and even in relieving the needy. But, he adds, he is not particular as to the means (which, of course, derive their value only from the end), being as willing to use another's money and property as his own, provided only that he knows he can do so safely and without discovery. You would believe that the person making such a recommendation was either mocking you or had lost his mind. So distinct and sharp are the boundaries between morality and self-love that even the commonest eye cannot fail to distinguish whether a thing belongs to the one or the other. The few remarks which follow may appear superfluous where the truth is so obvious, but they serve at least to furnish somewhat greater distinctness to the judgment of common sense.

The principle of happiness can indeed give maxims, but never maxims which are competent to be laws of the will, even if universal happiness were made the object. For, since the knowledge of this rests on mere data of experience, as each judgment concerning it depends very much on the very changeable opinion of each person, it can give general but never universal rules; that is, the rules it gives will on the average be most often the right ones for this purpose, but they will not be rules which must hold always and necessarily. Consequently, no practical laws can be based on this principle. Since here an object of choice is made the basis of the rule and therefore must precede it, the rule cannot be founded upon or related to anything other than what one approves;[18] and thus it refers to and is based on experience. Hence the variety of judgment must be infinite. This principle, therefore, does not prescribe the same practical rules to all rational beings, even though all the rules go under the same name —that of happiness. The moral law, however, is thought of as objectively necessary only because it holds good for everyone having reason and will.

The maxim of self-love (prudence) merely advises; the law of morality commands. Now there is a great difference between that which we are advised to do and that which we are obligated to do.

What is required in accordance with the principle of autonomy of choice is easily and without hesitation seen by the commonest intelligence; what is to be done under the presupposition of its heteronomy is hard to see and requires knowledge of the world. That is to say, what duty is, is plain of itself to everyone, but what is to bring true lasting advantage to our whole existence is veiled in impenetrable obscurity, and much prudence is required to adapt the practical rule based upon it even tolerably to the ends of life by making suitable exceptions to it. But the moral law commands the most unhesitating obedience from everyone; consequently, the decision as to what is to be done in accordance with it must not be so difficult that even the commonest and most unpracticed understanding without any worldly prudence should go wrong in making it.

It is always in everyone's power to satisfy the commands of the categorical command of morality; this is but seldom possible with respect to the empirically conditioned precept of happiness, and it is far from being possible, even in respect to a single purpose, for everyone. The reason is that in the former it is only a question of the maxim, which must be genuine and pure, but in the latter it is also a question of capacity and physical ability to realize a desired object. A command that everyone should seek to make himself happy would be foolish, for no one commands another to do what he already invariably wishes to do. One must only command—or better, provide—the means to him, since he cannot do everything which he wishes. But to com-

18. [*Empfiehlt*. Hartenstein and Abbott read *empfindet* (= feels).]

mand morality under the name of duty is very reasonable, for its precept will not, for one thing, be willingly obeyed by everyone when it is in conflict with his inclinations. Then, regarding the means of obeying this law, there is no need to teach them, for in this respect whatever he wishes to do he also can do.

He who has lost at play may be vexed at himself and his imprudence; but, when he is conscious of having cheated at play, even though he has won, he must despise himself as soon as he compares himself with the moral law. This must therefore be something else than the principle of one's own happiness. For to have to say to himself, "I am a worthless man, though I've filled my purse," he must have a different criterion of judgment than if he approves of himself and says, "I am a prudent man, for I've enriched my treasure."

Finally, there is something else in the idea of our practical reason which accompanies transgression of a moral law, namely, its culpability. Becoming a partaker in happiness cannot be united with the concept of punishment as such. For even though he who punishes can do so with the benevolent intention of directing this punishment to this end, it must nevertheless be justified as punishment, i.e., as mere harm in itself, so that even the punished person, if it stopped there and he could see no glimpse of kindness behind the harshness, would yet have to admit that justice had been done and that his reward perfectly fitted his behavior. In every punishment as such there must first be justice, and this constitutes the essence of the concept. With it benevolence may, of course, be associated, but the person who deserves punishment has not the least reason to count on it. Punishment is physical harm which, even if not bound as a natural consequence to the morally bad, ought to be bound to it as a consequence according to principles of moral legislation. Now if every crime, without regard to the physical consequences to him who commits it, is punishable, i.e., involves a forfeiture of happiness at least in part, it is obviously absurd to say that the crime consists just in the fact that one has brought punishment upon himself and thus has injured his own happiness (which, according to the principle of self-love, must be the correct concept of all crime). In this way, the punishment would be the reason for calling anything a crime, and justice would consist in withholding all punishment and even hindering natural punishment, for there would be no longer any evil in an action, since the harm which would otherwise follow upon it and because of which alone the action was called bad would now be omitted. To look upon all punishment and reward as machinery in the hand of a higher power, which by this means sets rational beings in action toward their final purpose (happiness), so obviously reduces the will to a mechanism destructive of freedom that it need not detain us.

More refined, but equally untrue, is the pretense of those who assume a certain particular moral sense which, instead of reason, determines the moral law, and in accordance with which the consciousness of virtue is directly associated with satisfaction and enjoyment, while consciousness of vice is associated with mental restlessness and pain. Thus everything is reduced to the desire for one's own happiness. Without repeating what has already been said, I will only indicate the fallacy they fall into. In order to imagine the vicious person as tormented with mortification by the consciousness of his transgressions, they must presuppose that he is, in the core of his character, at least to a certain degree morally good, just as they have to think of the person who is delighted by the consciousness of doing dutiful acts as already virtuous. Therefore, the concept of morality and duty must precede all reference to this satisfaction and cannot be derived from it. One must already value the importance of what we call duty, the respect for the moral law, and the immediate worth which a person obtains in his own eyes through obedience to it, in order to feel satisfaction in the consciousness of his conformity to law or the bitter remorse which accompanies his awareness that he has transgressed it. Therefore, this satisfaction or spiritual unrest cannot be felt prior to the knowledge of obligation, nor can it be made the basis of the latter. One must be at least halfway honest even to be able to have an idea of these feelings. For the rest, as the human will by virtue of its freedom is directly determined by the moral law, I am far from denying that frequent practice in accordance with this determining ground can itself finally cause a subjective feeling of satisfaction. Indeed, it is a duty to establish and cultivate this feeling, which alone deserves to be called the moral feeling. But the concept of duty cannot be derived from it, for we would have to presuppose a feeling for law as such and regard as an object of sensation what can only be thought by reason. If this did not end up in the flattest contradiction, it would destroy every concept of duty and fill its place with a merely mechanical play of refined inclinations, sometimes contending with the coarser.

If we now compare our supreme formal principle of pure practical reason, that of the autonomy of will, with all previous material principles of morality, we can exhibit them in a table which exhausts all possible cases except the one formal principle; thus we can show visually that it is futile to look around for another principle than the one presented here. All possible determining grounds of the will are either merely subjective and therefore empirical or objective and rational; in either case they may be external or internal.

Practical material determining grounds in the principle of morality are:

SUBJECTIVE

External:
  Education (Montaigne)
  Civil Constitution (Mandeville)

Internal:
  Physical Feeling (Epicurus)
  Moral Feeling (Hutcheson)

OBJECTIVE

Internal:
  Perfection (Wolff and the Stoics)

External:
  Will of God (Crusius and other theological moralists)

Those in the first group are without exception empirical and are obviously unfit for being the supreme principle of morality. Those in the second, however, are based on reason, for perfection, as a character of things, and the highest perfection thought of in substance, i.e., God, can be thought of only through concepts of reason. The first concept, perfection, can be taken in either a theoretical or a practical sense. In the former, it means nothing more than the perfection of anything in its own kind (transcendental perfection) or the perfection of a thing merely as a thing generally (metaphysical perfection); and we need not discuss these here. The concept of perfection in its practical meaning, however, is the fitness or sufficiency of a thing to any kind of ends. This perfection, as a characteristic of man and thus as internal, is nothing else than talent, or skill, which strengthens or completes talent. The supreme perfection in substance, i.e., God (hence external), when regarded practically, is the sufficiency of this Being to all ends in general. Only if ends are already given can the concept of perfection in relation to them (either internal perfection in ourselves or external perfection of God) be the determining ground of the will. An end, however, as an object which precedes and contains the ground of determination of the will by a practical rule—that is, an end as the material of the will—is, if taken as a determining ground of the will, only empirical; it could thus serve for the Epicurean principle in the happiness theory but never as a pure rational principle of ethics and duty. Thus talents and their cultivation, because they contribute to the advantages of life, or the will of God, if agreement with it (without any practical principle independent of this idea) be taken as an object of the will, can be motives only by reason of the happiness expected from them.

From these considerations, it follows, first, that all the principles exhibited here are material, and, second, that they include all possible material principles. Finally, since it was shown that all material principles were wholly unfit to be the supreme moral law, it follows that the formal practical principle of pure reason, according to which the mere form of a universal legislation possible through our maxims must constitute the supreme and direct determining ground of the will, is the only principle which can possibly furnish categorical imperatives, i.e., practical laws which enjoin actions as dutiful. Only a so defined principle can serve as a principle of morality, whether in judging conduct or in application to the human will in determining it.

I. OF THE DEDUCTION OF THE PRINCIPLES OF PURE PRACTICAL REASON

This Analytic proves that pure reason can be practical, i.e., that of itself and independently of everything empirical it can determine the will. This it does through a fact, wherein pure reason shows itself actually to be practical. This fact is autonomy in the principle of morality by which reason determines the will to action.

At the same time it shows this fact to be inextricably bound up with the consciousness of freedom of the will, and actually to be identical with it. By this freedom the will of a rational being, as belonging to the sensuous world, recognizes itself to be, like all other efficient causes, necessarily subject to the laws of causality, while in practical matters, in its other aspect as a being in itself, it is conscious of its existence as determinable in an intelligible order of things. It is conscious of this not by virtue of a particular intuition of itself but because of certain dynamic laws which determine its causality in the world of sense, for it has been sufficiently proved in another place that if freedom is attributed to us, it transfers us into an intelligible order of things.

Now if we compare the analytical part of the critique of the pure speculative reason with this Analytic, a noteworthy contrast between them appears. In that other critique, not principles but pure sensuous intuition (space and time) was the first datum which made a priori knowledge possible, though only of objects of the senses. Synthetical principles could not be derived from mere concepts without intuition; rather, these principles could exist only in relation to sensuous intuition and thus only in relation to objects of possible experience, since it is only the concepts of the understanding united with this intuition which can make that knowledge possible which we call experience. Beyond objects of experience, i.e., concerning things as noumena, all positive knowledge was correctly denied to the speculative reason. This reason, however, was successful to the extent that it established with certainty the concept of noumena, i.e., it established the possibility—indeed, the necessity—of thinking of them. For example, it showed against all objections that the assumption of freedom, negatively considered, was entirely compatible with those principles and limitations of pure theoretical reason. But it could not give us anything definite to enlarge our knowledge of such objects, but rather it cut off any such prospect altogether.

On the other hand, the moral law, although it gives no such prospect, does provide a fact absolutely inexplicable from any data of the world of sense or from the whole compass of the theoretical use of reason, and this fact points to a pure intelligible world—indeed, it defines it positively and enables us to know something of it, namely, a law.

This law gives to the sensible world, as sensuous nature (as this concerns rational beings), the form of an intelligible world, i.e., the form of supersensuous nature, without interfering with the mechanism of the former. Nature, in the widest sense of the word, is the existence of things under laws. The sensuous nature of rational beings in general is their existence under empirically conditioned laws, and therefore it is, from the point of view of reason, heteronomy. The supersensuous nature of the same beings, on the other hand, is their existence according to laws which are independent of all empirical conditions and which therefore belong to the autonomy of pure reason. And since the laws, according to which the existence of things depends on cognition, are practical, supersensuous nature, so far as we can form a concept of it, is nothing else than nature under the autonomy of the pure practical reason. The law of this autonomy is the moral law, and it, therefore, is the fundamental law of supersensuous nature and of a pure world of the understanding, whose counterpart must exist in the world of sense without interfering with the laws of the latter. The former could be called the archetypal world (*natura archetypa*) which we know only by reason; the latter, on the other hand, could be called the ectypal world (*natura ectypa*), because it contains the possible effect of the idea of the former as the determining ground of the will. For, in fact, the moral law ideally transfers us into a nature in which reason would bring forth the highest good were it accompanied by sufficient physical capacities; and it determines our will to impart to the sensuous world the form of a system of rational beings. The least attention to ourself shows that this idea really stands as a model for the determination of our will.

When the maxim according to which I intend to give testimony is tested by practical reason, I always inquire into what it would be if it were to hold as a universal law of nature. It is obvious that, in this way of looking at it, it would oblige everyone to truthfulness. For it cannot hold as a universal law of nature that an assertion should have the force of proof and yet be intentionally false. Also the maxim which I adopt in respect to freely disposing of my life is at once determined when I inquire what it would have to be in order that a system of nature could maintain itself in accordance with such a law. Obviously in such a system of nature no one could arbitrarily end his life, for such an arrangement could not constitute a permanent natural order. And so in all other cases.

Now, however, in actual nature as an object of experience, the free will is not of itself determined to such maxims as could of themselves establish a nature based on universal laws, or even to such maxims as would fit into a system of nature so constituted; rather, they are private inclinations, which form a natural whole according to pathological (physical) laws but not a system of nature which is possible only through our will acting according to pure practical laws. However, through reason we are conscious of a law to which all our maxims are subject as though through our will a natural order must arise. Therefore, this law must be the idea of a supersensuous nature, a nature not empirically given yet possible through freedom; to this nature we give objective reality, at least in a practical context, because we regard it as the object of our will as pure rational beings.

The difference, therefore, between the laws of a system of

nature to which the will is subject and of a system of nature which is subject to a will (as far as the relation of the will to its free actions is concerned) rests on this: in the former, the objects must be the causes of the conceptions which determine the will, and in the latter the will is the cause of the objects. Consequently, in the latter the causality of the objects has its determining ground solely in the pure faculty of reason, which therefore may be called pure practical reason.

There are, therefore, two very different problems. The first is: How can pure reason know objects a priori? The second is: How can pure reason be a directly determining ground of the will, i.e., of the causality of a rational being with respect to the reality of the objects merely through the thought of the universal validity of its own maxims as a law?

The first of these questions belongs to the critical examination of pure speculative reason; it requires that we first show how intuitions, without which no object can be given and therefore none can be known synthetically, are possible a priori. Its answer lies in the fact that intuitions are without exception sensuous, and therefore no speculative knowledge is possible which reaches further than possible experience; consequently, all principles of pure speculative reason avail only to make possible experience of objects which are actually given or of objects which though they may be given *ad infinitum* are never completely given.

The second question belongs to the *Critique of Practical Reason*. It requires no explanation of how objects of the faculty of desire are possible, for that, as a task of the theoretical knowledge of nature, is left to the critique of speculative reason. It asks only how reason can determine the maxim of the will, whether this occurs only by means of empirical conceptions as determining grounds, or whether pure reason is also practical and a law of a possible order of nature which is empirically unknowable. The possibility of such a supersensuous nature, the concept of which can be the ground of its reality through our free will, requires no a priori intuition of an intelligible world, which even in this case would be impossible to us, since it is supersensuous. For it is only a question of the determining ground of volition in its own maxims: Is the determining ground empirical, or is it a concept of pure reason (a concept of its lawfulness in general)? And how can it be the latter? The decision as to whether the causality of the will is sufficient to the reality of the objects is left up to the theoretical principles of reason, involving as it does an investigation of the possibility of objects of volition, the intuition of which is of no importance in the practical problem. The only concern here is with the determination of the will and with the determining ground of its maxims as a free will, not with its result. For if the will be only in accord with the law of pure reason, the will's power in execution may be what it may; and a system of nature may or may not actually arise according to these maxims of the legislation of a possible nature—all this does not trouble us in this *Critique*. This *Critique* concerns itself only with whether and how reason can be practical, i.e., how it can directly determine the will.

In this inquiry no objection can be raised that the *Critique* begins with pure practical laws and their reality. Instead of intuition, it makes the concept of their existence in the intelligible world, i.e., freedom, its foundation. For this concept has no other meaning, and these laws are possible only in relation to the freedom of the will; but, if the will is presupposed as free, then they are necessary. Conversely, freedom is necessary because those laws are necessary, being practical postulates. How this consciousness of the moral laws or—what amounts to the same thing—how this consciousness of freedom is possible cannot be further explained; its permissibility, however, is established in the theoretical *Critique*.

The exposition of the supreme principle of practical reason is now finished. It has shown, first, what it contains, and that it is of itself entirely a priori and independent of empirical principles; and then it has shown how it differs from all other practical principles. With the deduction, i.e., the justification of its objective and universal validity and the discernment of the possibility of such a synthetic a priori proposition, one cannot hope to have everything as easy as it was with the principles of pure theoretical understanding. For the latter referred to objects of possible experience, i.e., appearances, and it could be proved that they could be known as objects of experience and, consequently, that all possible experience must be conformable to these laws, only because these appearances, in accordance with these laws, could be brought under the categories. Such a procedure, however, I cannot follow in the deduction of the moral law. For it does not concern knowledge of the properties of objects, which may be given to reason from some other source; rather, it concerns knowledge in so far as it can itself become the ground of the existence of objects, and in so far as reason, by virtue of this same knowledge, has causality in a rational being. Our deduction is concerned with pure reason, regarded as a faculty directly determining the will.

But human insight is at an end as soon as we arrive at fundamental powers or faculties, for their possibility can in no way be understood and should not be just arbitrarily imagined or assumed. Therefore, in the theoretical use of reason only experience could justify their assumption. Such empirical proof, as a substitute for deduction from sources of knowledge a priori, is, however, denied to us with respect to the pure practical faculty of reason. For whatever needs to draw the evidence of its reality from experience must depend for the grounds of its possibility on principles of experience; by its very notion, however, pure yet practical reason cannot be held to be dependent in this way. Moreover, the moral law is given, as an apodictically certain fact, as it were, of pure reason, a fact of which we are a priori conscious, even if it be granted that no example could be found in which it has been followed exactly. Thus the objective reality of the moral law can be proved through no deduction, through no exertion of the theoretical, speculative, or empirically supported reason; and, even if one were willing to renounce its apodictic certainty, it could not[19] be confirmed by any experience and thus proved a posteriori. Nevertheless, it is firmly established of itself.

Instead of this vainly sought deduction of the moral principle, however, something entirely different and unexpected appears: The moral principle itself serves as a principle of the deduction of an inscrutable faculty which no experience can prove but which speculative reason had to assume as at least possible (in order not to contradict itself in finding among its cosmological ideas something unconditional in its causality). This is the faculty of freedom, which the moral law, itself needing no justifying grounds, shows to be not only possible but actual in beings which acknowledge the law as binding upon them. The moral law is, in fact, a law of causality through freedom and thus a law of the possibility of a supersensuous nature, just as the metaphysical law of events in the world of sense was a law of the causality of sensuous nature; the moral law thus defines that which speculative philosophy had to leave undefined. That is, it defines the law for a causality the concept of which was only negative in speculative philosophy, and for the first time it gives objective reality to this concept.

19. [*Not* inserted by Grillo and Vorländer; omitted in the Cassirer ed.]

This kind of credential for the moral law, namely, that it is itself demonstrated to be the principle of the deduction of freedom as a causality of pure reason, is a sufficient substitute for any a priori justification, since theoretical reason had to assume at least the possibility of freedom in order to fill one of its own needs. For the moral law sufficiently proves its reality even for the critique of speculative reason by giving a positive definition to a causality thought merely negatively, the possibility of which was incomprehensible to speculative reason though this reason was compelled to assume it. The moral law adds to the negative concept a positive definition, that of a reason which determines the will directly through the condition of a universal lawful form of the maxims of the will. Thus reason, which with its ideas always became transcendent when proceeding in a speculative manner, can be given for the first time an objective although still only practical reality; its transcendent use is changed into an immanent use, whereby reason becomes, in the field of experience, an efficient cause[20] through ideas.

The determination of the causality of beings in the world of sense as such can never be unconditioned, and yet for every series of conditions there must be something unconditioned, and consequently a causality which is entirely self-determining. Therefore, the idea of freedom as a faculty of absolute spontaneity was not just a desideratum but, as far as its possibility was concerned, an analytical principle of pure speculation. But because it is absolutely impossible to give an example of it from experience, since no absolutely unconditioned determination of causality can be found among the causes of things as appearances, we could defend the supposition of a freely acting cause when applied to a being in the world of sense only in so far as the being was regarded also as noumenon. This defense was made by showing that it was not self-contradictory to regard all its actions as physically conditioned so far as they are appearances, and yet at the same time to regard their causality as physically unconditioned so far as the acting being is regarded as a being of the understanding. Thus the concept of freedom is made the regulative principle of reason. I thereby do not indeed learn what the object may be to which this kind of causality is attributed. I do, however, remove the difficulty, since, on the one hand, in the

20. [Reading *cause* with Hartenstein; the Cassirer ed. follows the original and reads *causes*, admitting, however, the plausibility of the singular, since it refers to *reason*.]

explanation of natural occurrences, including the actions of rational beings, I leave to the mechanism of natural necessity the right to ascend from conditioned to condition *ad infinitum*, while, on the other hand, I hold open for speculative reason the place which for it is vacant, i.e., the intelligible, in order to transfer the unconditioned to it. I could not, however, give content to this supposition, i.e., convert it into knowledge even of the possibility of a being acting in this way. Pure practical reason now fills this vacant place with a definite law of causality in an intelligible world (causality through freedom). This is the moral law. Speculative reason does not herewith grow in insight but only in respect to the certitude of its problematic concept of freedom, to which objective though only practical reality is now indubitably given. Even the concept of causality, having its application and hence significance only in relation to appearances which it connects into experiences (as shown in the *Critique of Pure Reason*), is not enlarged by this reality so as to extend its employment beyond these limits. For if reason sought to go beyond them, it would have to show how the logical relation of ground and consequence could be synthetically used with another kind of intuition than the sensuous, i.e., how a *causa noumenon* is possible. This reason cannot do, but as practical reason it does not concern itself with this demand, since it only posits the determining ground of the causality of man as a sensuous being (this causality being given) in pure reason (which is therefore called practical); it does so not in order to know objects but only to define causality in respect to objects in general. It can altogether abstract the concept of cause itself from that application to objects which has theoretical knowledge as its purpose, since this concept can always be found a priori in the understanding, independently of any intuition. Thus reason uses this concept only for a practical purpose, transferring the determining ground of the will to the intelligible order of things, at the same time readily confessing that it does not understand how the concept of cause can be a condition of the knowledge of these things. Causality with respect to the actions of the will in the world of sense must, of course, be known by reason in a definite way, for otherwise practical reason could produce no act. But the concept which reason makes of its own causality as noumenon is significant even though it cannot be defined theoretically for the purpose of knowing its supersensuous existence. Regardless of this, it acquires significance through the moral law, although only for practical use. Even regarded theoretically, the concept remains always a pure concept of the understanding, given a priori, and applicable to objects whether sensuously given or not. If they are not sensuously given, however, the concept has no definite theoretical significance and application but is only the understanding's formal but nevertheless essential thought of an object in general. The significance which reason gives to it through the moral law is exclusively practical, since the idea of the law of a causality (of the will) has causality itself or is its determining ground.

II. OF THE RIGHT OF PURE REASON TO AN EXTENSION IN ITS PRACTICAL USE WHICH IS NOT POSSIBLE TO IT IN ITS SPECULATIVE USE

In the moral principle as we have presented it there is a law of causality which puts the determining ground of causality above all conditions of the world of sense. We have thought of the will as determinable inasmuch as it belongs to an intelligible world and of the subject of this will (man) as belonging to a pure intelligible world, though in this relation man is unknown to us. (How this relation can be thought and yet be unknowable has been shown in the critique of the pure speculative reason.) We have, I say, *thought* of man and his will in this way, but, furthermore, we have *defined* the will with respect to its causality by means of a law which cannot be counted among the natural laws of the world of sense; finally, we have thereby *widened* our knowledge beyond the limits of the world of sense. But this is a presumption which the *Critique of Pure Reason* declared to be void in all speculation. How, then, is the practical use of pure reason to be reconciled with its theoretical use in respect to determining the boundaries of their competence?

David Hume, who can be said to have begun the assault on the claims of pure reason which made a thorough examination of them necessary, argued as follows. The concept of cause is one which involves the necessity of a connection between different existing things, in so far as they are different. Thus, when A is granted, I recognize that B, something entirely different from it, must necessarily exist also. Necessity, however, can be attributed to a connection only so far as it is known a priori, for experience of a connection would only give knowledge that it existed, not that it necessarily existed. Now it is impossible, he says, to know a priori and as necessary the connection which holds between one thing and another (or between one property and another entirely different from it) if this connection is not given in perception. Therefore, the concept of a cause is itself fraudulent and deceptive. To speak in the mildest way, it is an illusion which is excusable only since the custom (a subjective necessity) of frequently perceiving certain things or their properties along with or in succession to one another is insensibly taken for an objective necessity of placing such a connection in the objects themselves. Thus the concept of cause has been acquired surreptitiously and illegitimately—nay, it can never be acquired or certified, because it demands a connection in itself void, chimerical, and untenable before reason, a connection to which no object could ever correspond.

So first with reference to all knowledge which concerned the existence of things (thus excepting mathematics), empiricism was introduced as the exclusive source of principles; with it, however, came the most unyielding skepticism with respect to the whole science of nature (as philosophy). For on such principles we can never infer a consequence from the given properties of things as existing, for to such an inference there is needed a concept of cause, a concept implying necessity in such a connection; we can only expect, by the rule of imagination, similar cases, though this expectation is never certain no matter how often it is fulfilled. Indeed, of no occurrence could one say: something *must* have preceded it on which it *necessarily* followed, i.e., that it must have had a *cause*. Thus, even if one knew of such frequent cases in which this antecedent was present that a rule could be derived from them, we could still not assume that it happens this way always and necessarily. Thus the sway of blind chance, with which all use of reason ceases, must be admitted; this firmly and irrefutably establishes skepticism toward all inferences from effects to causes.

Mathematics at first escaped lightly because Hume thought that its propositions were analytical, i.e., proceeded from one property to another by virtue of identity and consequently according to the law of contradiction. This, however, is false; they are all synthetical. And though geometry, for example, has nothing to do with the existence of things but only with their a priori properties in a possible intuition, it nevertheless proceeds just as in the case of the causal concept, going from one property A to another entirely different property B necessarily connected with it. But even this science, so highly esteemed for its apodictic certainty, must finally succumb to empiricism with regard to its principles for the same reason that Hume substituted custom for objective necessity in the concept of cause. In spite of all its pride, it will have to acquiesce to this skepticism by lowering its bold claims demanding a priori assent, expecting approval of the universal validity of its theorems only because of the kindness of observers who, as witnesses, would not hesitate to admit that what the geometer propounds as axioms they had always perceived as facts, and that consequently they could be expected to be true in the future even though there was no necessity in them. In this way, Hume's empiricism leads inevitably to skepticism, even with respect to mathematics and consequently in the entire theoretical scientific employment of reason (for this is either philosophy or mathematics). In view of the terrible overthrow of these chief branches of knowledge, whether ordinary reason will come through any better I leave to the judgment of each. It may be that it will rather become inextricably entangled in the same destruction of all knowledge, with the consequence that from the same principles there will result a universal skepticism, even though it concern only the learned.

My own labors in the *Critique of Pure Reason* were occasioned by Hume's skeptical teaching, but they went much further and covered the entire field of pure theoretical reason in its synthetic use, including what is generally called metaphysics. I proceeded as follows with reference to the doubts raised by the Scottish philosopher concerning the concept of causality. I granted that, when Hume took the objects of experience as things-in-themselves (as is almost always done), he was entirely correct in declaring the concept of cause to be deceptive and an illusion; for it cannot be understood, with reference to things-in-themselves and their properties as such, why, if A is given, something else, B, must also necessarily be given. Thus he could not admit such an a priori knowledge of things-in-themselves. This acute man could even less admit an empirical origin of the concept, for this would directly contradict the necessity of the connection which constitutes the essence of the concept of causality. Consequently, the concept was proscribed, and into its place stepped custom in observing the course of perceptions.

From my investigations, however, it resulted that the objects with which we have to do in experience are by no means things-in-themselves but only appearances. Furthermore, if we assume that they are things-in-themselves, it is impossible to see how, if *A* is granted, it would be contradictory not to grant *B*, which is altogether different from *A*. That is, it is impossible to see how it would be contradictory not to grant the necessity of the connection of *A* as cause with *B* as effect; but it is very understandable that *A* and *B* as appearances in one experience must necessarily be connected in a certain manner (e.g., with reference to their temporal relations) and that they cannot be separated without contradicting that connection by means of which experience is possible, in which experience they become objects and alone knowable to us. This was actually the case, so that I could not only prove the objective reality of the concept of cause with reference to objects of experience but also deduce it as an a priori concept because of the necessity of the connection it implies. That is, I could show its possibility from pure understanding without any empirical sources. So, after banishing empiricism from its origin, I was able to overthrow its inevitable consequence, skepticism, first in natural science and then in mathematics, both of which sciences have reference to objects of possible experience, and in both of which skepticism has the same grounds. Thus I removed the radical doubt of whatever theoretical reason professes to discern.

But how lies it with reference to the application of this category of causality (and similarly of all the others, for without them there can be no knowledge of existing things) to things which are not objects of possible experience but lie beyond its boundaries? For it must be remembered that I could deduce the objective reality of these concepts only with reference to objects of possible experience. But the very fact that I have saved them only in this case and that I have shown that by virtue of them objects may be thought without being a priori defined—this fact gives them a place in the pure understanding from which they are referred to objects in general, whether sensuous or not. If anything is lacking, it is the conditions for the application of these categories, and especially that of causality, to objects. This condition is intuition, and, when it is lacking, this application for the purpose of theoretical *knowledge* of the object as noumenon is rendered impossible. This knowledge is absolutely forbidden (even in the *Critique of Pure Reason*) to anyone who ventures upon it. Still, the objective reality of the concept remains and can even be used with reference to noumena, though it is not in the least theoretically defined, and no knowledge can be effected with it. That this concept, even in relation to a [supersensuous] object, contains nothing impossible was proved by the fact that in all its application to objects of the senses its seat in the pure understanding remained assured. And even if, when subsequently applied to things-in-themselves which cannot be objects of experience, it cannot be defined so as to represent a definite object for the purposes of a theoretical cognition, it could nevertheless be defined for an application for some other purpose, such as the practical. This would not be so if, as Hume asserted, the concept of causality contained something inconceivable.

In order to discover the condition for applying the concept in question to noumena, we need only to refer back to the reason why we are not satisfied with its application to objects of experience but wish also to apply it to things-in-themselves. It soon appears that it is not a theoretical but a practical purpose which makes it a necessity for us. In speculation, even if we were successful [in this new application], we should still have made no true gain in the knowledge of nature or of any given objects; but we should have taken a long step from the sensuously conditioned (in which we have already enough to do to remain and industriously to follow the chain of causes) to the supersensuous, in order to complete our knowledge of its foundations and to fix its boundaries. But there always remains an infinite unfilled chasm between that limit and what we know, and [in taking such a step] we should have hearkened to a vain curiosity instead of acting from a sober desire for knowledge.

But besides the relationship which the understanding has to objects in theoretical knowledge, there is also the relationship in which it stands to the faculty of desire, which is therefore called the will, or the pure will in so far as the pure understanding (which in such a case is called reason) is practical through the mere conception of a law. The objective reality of a pure will or of a pure practical reason (they being the same) is given in the moral law a priori, as it were by a fact, for the latter term can be applied to a determination of the will which is inevitable even though it does not rest on any empirical principles. In the concept of a will, however, the concept of causality is already contained; thus in that of a pure will there is the concept of causality with freedom, i.e., of a causality not determinable according to natural laws and consequently not susceptible to any empirical intuition as proof [of the reality of the free will]. Nevertheless, it completely justifies its objective reality in the pure practical law a priori, though it is easily seen that it is not for the purpose of the theoretical but for that of the merely practical use of reason. Now the concept of a being which has a free will is that of a *causa noumenon;* and we are assured that this concept does not contradict itself, because the concept of a cause originates exclusively in pure understanding, and also because its objective reality with reference to objects in general is guaranteed by the Deduction. As independent in origin from all sensuous conditions, it is in itself not to be restricted to phenomena, so that, unless a definite theoretical[21] use of it is to be made, it could certainly be applied to things as pure beings of the understanding. But because no intuition, which could only be sensuous, can support this application, *causa noumenon* is, for the theoretical use of reason, an empty concept, although a possible and thinkable one. Through it I do not strive to know theoretically the characteristic of a being in so far as it has a pure will; it is enough for me to denote it as such by means of this concept and thus to couple the concept of causality with that of freedom (and with what is inseparable from it, i.e., the moral law as its determining ground). I have this right by virtue of the pure nonempirical origin of the concept of cause, since I make no other use of the concept than in relation to the moral law which determines its reality; that is, I hold that I am justified only in making a practical use of it.

Had I, with Hume, denied objective reality in the theoretical[22] use to the concept of causality, not only in its reference to things-in-themselves (the supersensuous) but also in reference to objects of the senses, this concept would have lost all meaning, and as a theoretically impossible concept it would have been declared entirely worthless; and since that which is nothing lends itself to no use, the practical use of a theoretically null concept would have been absurd. The concept of an empirically unconditioned causality is indeed theoretically empty, since it has no appropriate intuition even though it is still possible and refers to an indeterminate object; in compensation for this, the concept gains significance [not from a given object but] in the moral law and consequently in a practical relation. Even though I have no intuition which would determine its objective theoretical reality, it nevertheless has a real application exhibited *in concreto*

21. [Inverting, with Vorländer, *theoretical definite.*]
22. [Reading *theoretical* with Schöndorffer and Vorländer instead of *practical.*]

in intentions or maxims; that is, its practical reality can be pointed out. All this is sufficient to justify the concept even with reference to noumena.

This objective reality of a pure concept of the understanding in the field of the supersensuous, once ushered in, gives objective reality to all the other categories, though only in so far as they stand in a necessary connection with the determining ground of the pure will (the moral law). This objective reality, however, is one of only practical application, since it has not the slightest effect in enlarging theoretical knowledge of these objects as insight into their nature by pure reason. As we shall find in the sequel, they have always reference only to beings as intelligences, and in them only to the relation of the reason to the will, and consequently only to the practical; further than that they pretend to no knowledge of them. Other characteristics belonging to the theoretical mode of conceiving of such supersensuous beings, and brought forward in connection with these categories, are not to be counted as knowledge but only as a right (for practical purposes, however, a necessity) to assume and presuppose them. This must be done even where one assumes a supersensuous being (e.g., God) by analogy, i.e., by a purely rational relation which we make practical use of with reference to what is sensuous. Thus the application of the categories to the supersensuous, which occurs only from a practical point of view, gives to pure theoretical reason not the least encouragement to run riot into the transcendent.

Chapter II

The Concept of an Object of Pure Practical Reason

BY A concept of an object[23] of practical reason I understand the idea of an object as an effect possible through freedom. To be an object of practical knowledge as such signifies, therefore, only the relation of the will to the action whereby it or its opposite is brought into being. To decide whether or not something is an object of the pure practical reason is only to discern the possibility or impossibility of willing the action by which a certain object would be made real, provided we had the ability to bring it about (the latter being a matter which experience must decide). If the object is taken as the determining ground of our faculty of desire, its physical possibility through the free use

23. [*Of an object* inserted by Vorländer.]

of our strength must precede the decision as to whether it is or is not an object of the practical reason. But if, on the other hand, the a priori law can be regarded as the determining ground of action, which is consequently seen as determined by the pure practical reason, then the judgment as to whether or not something is an object of the pure practical reason is wholly independent of any question of our physical ability; the only question is whether we should will an action directed to the existence of an object if it were within our power. Consequently, the moral possibility of the action takes precedence, for in this case it is not the object but the law of the will which is its ground of determination.

The sole objects of a practical reason are thus those of the good and the evil. By the former one understands a necessary object of the faculty of desire, and by the latter a necessary object of aversion, both according to a principle of reason.

If the concept of the good is not derived from a practical law but rather serves as the ground of the latter, it can only be the concept of something whose existence promises pleasure and thus determines the causality of the subject (the faculty of desire) to produce it. Now, because it is impossible to see a priori which idea will be accompanied with pleasure and which with pain, it would be solely a matter of experience to discern what is immediately good or evil. The property of the subject, by virtue of which such experience could be had, is the feeling of pleasure or displeasure as a receptivity belonging to the inner sense; thus the concept of that which is immediately good would only refer to that with which the sensation of pleasure is immediately associated, and the concept of the absolutely evil would have to be related only to that which directly excites pain.

Even the usage of language is opposed to this, however, since it distinguishes the pleasant from the good and the unpleasant from the evil, and demands that good and evil be judged by reason and thus through concepts which alone can be universally communicated, and not by mere sensation which is limited to the individual subjects and their susceptibility. For this reason, and also because pleasure or displeasure cannot be immediately associated with an idea of an object a priori, the philosopher who felt obliged to make a feeling of pleasure basic to his practical judgment would have to denominate "good" that which is a means to the pleasant and "evil" that which is the cause of unpleasantness and pain, for the judgment of the relation of means to end certainly belongs to reason. Although reason alone is capable of discerning the connection of means and purposes (so that the will could be defined as the faculty of ends, since they are always determining grounds of the faculty of desire according to principles), the practical maxims which follow merely as means from the concept of the good never contain anything good in itself as the object of the will but only something good *for* something else. In this way the good would be only the useful and that for which it is useful must always lie outside the will, in sensation. If the latter, as pleasant sensation, had to be distinguished from the concept of the good, there would be nothing immediately good, and the good would have to be sought in the means to something else, i.e., some pleasantness.

There is an old formula of the schools: *Nihil appetimus, nisi sub ratione boni; nihil aversamur, nisi sub ratione mali.* It is often used correctly, but often in a manner very injurious to philosophy, since the expressions *boni* and *mali* contain an ambiguity due to the poverty of the language. These words are capable of a double meaning and therefore inevitably bring practical laws into a precarious position; and philosophy, in using these expressions, becomes aware of the divergence of concepts associated with the same word even though it can find no special expressions for them, and is forced to subtle distinctions about which later agreement cannot be obtained, since the difference cannot be directly stated by any suitable expression.*

The German language has the good fortune to possess expressions which do not permit this difference to be overlooked. It has two very different concepts and equally different expressions for what the Latins named with the single word *bonum*. For *bonum*, it has *das Gute* [the good] and *das Wohl* [well-being]; for *malum, das Böse* [evil, wicked] and *das Übel* [bad, ill] or *das Weh* [woe]. Thus there are two very different judgments if in an action we have regard to its goodness or wickedness or to our

* Moreover, the expression *sub ratione boni* is also ambiguous. For it can mean: we represent something to ourselves as good, if and because we desire (will) it. Or it can mean: we desire something, because we represent it to ourselves as good. Thus either the desire is the determining ground of the concept of the object as a good or the concept of the good is the determining ground of desire (will). In the first case, *sub ratione boni* would mean: we will something under the idea of the good; and in the second: we will something in consequence of this idea, which must precede volition as its determining ground.

weal or woe (ill). It follows just from this that the aforementioned psychological proposition is at least very doubtful if it is translated: "We desire nothing except with a view to our weal or woe." On the other hand, it is indubitably certain and at the same time clearly expressed when rendered: "We desire nothing, under the direction of reason, except in so far as we hold it to be good or bad."

Well-being or woe indicates only a relation to our condition of pleasantness or unpleasantness, of enjoyment or pain; if for that reason we desire or avoid an object, we do so only in so far as it is related to our sensibility and to the feeling of pleasure or displeasure which it produces. But the *good* or *evil* always indicates a relation to the will so far as it is determined by the law of reason to make something its object, for the will is never determined directly by the object and our conception of it. Rather, the will is a faculty which makes a rule of reason the efficient cause of an action which can make an object real. Thus good or evil are properly referred to actions and not to the sensory state of the person. If something is to be, or is held to be, absolutely good or evil in all respects and without qualification, it could not be a thing but only the manner of acting, i.e., it could be only the maxim of the will, and consequently the acting person himself as a good or evil man.

Though one may laugh at the Stoic who in the worst paroxysm of gout cried out, "Pain, however thou tormentest me, I will never admit that thou art anything bad (κακόν, *malum*)!" he was nevertheless right. He felt it was an evil, and he betrayed that in his cry; but that anything [morally] evil attached to him he had no reason to concede, for the pain did not in the least diminish the worth of his person but only the worth of his condition. A single lie of which he was conscious would have struck down his pride, but pain served only as an occasion for raising it when he was conscious that he had not made himself liable to it by an unrighteous action and thus culpable.

What we call good must be, in the judgment of every reasonable man, an object of the faculty of desire, and the evil must be, in everyone's eyes, an object of aversion. Thus, in addition to sense, this judgment requires reason. So it is with truthfulness as opposed to a lie, with justice in contrast to violence, etc. But we can call something an ill, however, which everyone at the same time must acknowledge as good, either directly or indirectly.

Whoever submits to a surgical operation feels it without doubt as an ill, but by reason he and everyone else will describe it as good. When, however, someone who delights in annoying and vexing peace-loving folk receives at last a right good beating, it is certainly an ill, but everyone approves of it and considers it as good in itself even if nothing further results from it; nay, even he who gets the beating must acknowledge, in his reason, that justice has been done to him, because he sees the proportion between welfare and well-doing, which reason inevitably holds before him, here put into practice.

Certainly our weal and woe are very important in the estimation of our practical reason; and, as far as our nature as sensible beings is concerned, our happiness is the only thing of importance, provided this is judged, as reason especially requires, not according to transitory sensation but according to the influence which this contingency has on our whole existence and our satisfaction with it. But still not everything depends upon that. Man is a being of needs, so far as he belongs to the world of sense, and to this extent his reason certainly has an inescapable responsibility from the side of his sensuous nature to attend to its interest and to form practical maxims with a view to the happiness of this and, where possible, of a future life. But still he is not so completely an animal as to be indifferent to everything which reason says on its own and to use it merely as a tool for satisfying his needs as a sensuous being. That he has reason does not in the least raise him in worth above mere animality if reason only serves the purposes which, among animals, are taken care of by instinct; if this were so, reason would be only a specific way nature had made use of to equip man for the same purposes for which animals are qualified, without fitting him for any higher purpose. No doubt, as a result of this unique arrangement, he needs reason, to consider at all times his weal and woe. But he has reason for a yet higher purpose, namely, to consider also what is in itself good or evil, which pure and sensuously distinterested reason alone can judge, and furthermore, to distinguish this estimation from a sensuous estimation and to make the former the supreme condition of the good and evil.[24]

24. [Natorp: *of the latter* (i.e., of the sensuous estimation). The Cassirer ed., following Kant's two editions in this reading, gives the following paraphrase: "The pure form of judgment of good and evil is the supreme condition of good and evil *materialiter*."]

In this estimation of the difference between the good and evil as such and that which can be so called only with respect to well-being or ill, it is a question of the following points. Either a principle of reason is thought of as already the determining ground of the will without reference to possible objects of the faculty of desire (and thus as a determining ground only through the lawful form of the maxim); then that principle is a practical law a priori, and pure reason is assumed to be in itself practical; the law directly determines the will; action in accordance with it is in itself good; and a will whose maxims always accord with this law is absolutely and in every respect good and the supreme condition of all good. Or a determining ground of the faculty of desire precedes the maxim of the will, and this determining ground presupposes an object of pleasure or displeasure and consequently something that pleases or pains; in this case the maxim of reason, to pursue the former and to avoid the latter, determines actions which are good only with reference to our inclination and consequently only mediately good, being a means to a further purpose; and such maxims can never be called laws but only reasonable practical precepts. In the latter case, the end itself, the enjoyment we seek, is not a good but only well-being, not a concept of reason but an empirical concept of an object of sensation. Only the use of the means to it, i.e., action, is called good (because reasonable deliberation is required for it). But, even so, the action is not absolutely good but good only in relation to our sensibility and its feeling of pleasure or displeasure. The will whose maxims are affected by it is not a pure will, for the latter concerns itself only with that by which pure reason can of itself be practical.

This is the place for an explanation of the paradox of method in a critical examination of practical reason. The paradox is that the concept of the good and evil is not defined prior to the moral law, to which, it would seem, the former would have to serve as foundation; rather the concept of the good and evil must be defined after and by means of the law. Even if we did not know that the principle of morality was a pure law determining the will a priori, we would nevertheless at the beginning have to leave it undecided whether the will has merely empirical or also pure determining grounds a priori in order not to assume principles quite arbitrarily, since it is against all the basic rules of a philosophical method to assume as already decided that which is the point in question. Assuming that we wished to begin with the concept of the good in order to derive the laws of the will from it, this concept of an object (as a good object)[25] would designate this object as the sole determining ground of the will. But because this concept had no practical law a priori as its standard, the criterion of good or evil could be placed only in the agreement of the object with our feeling of pleasure or displeasure, and the use of the reason could only consist in part in determining this pleasure or displeasure in connection with all the sensations of our existence and in part in determining the means of providing ourselves with the object of these feelings. Now, since only through experience can we find out what is in accordance with the feeling of pleasure, and since by hypothesis the practical law is to be based on it, the possibility of practical laws a priori is excluded because it was thought necessary first of all to find an object for the will the concept of which, as a good object, would have to constitute the universal though empirical determining ground of the will. It was, however, necessary first to investigate whether there was not also an a priori determining ground of the will which could have been found nowhere except in a pure practical law (and indeed in this only in so far as its mere lawful form prescribed maxims without reference to an object). But because an object, according to concepts of good and evil, had been made the basis of every practical law, and because the former, in the absence of any prior law, could be thought only according to empirical concepts, the possibility was already removed even of conceiving a pure practical law. Had one previously analyzed the practical law, he would have found, on the contrary, not that the concept of the good as an object of the moral law determines the latter and makes it possible but rather the reverse, i.e., that the moral law is that which first defines the concept of the good—so far as it absolutely deserves this name—and makes it possible.

This remark, which refers only to the method of the deepest moral investigations, is important. It explains once and for all the reasons which occasion all the confusions of philosophers concerning the supreme principle of morals. For they sought an object of the will in order to make it into the material and the foundation of a law (which would then be not the directly determining ground of the will, but only by means of that object referred to the feeling of pleasure or displeasure); instead, they should have looked for a law which directly determined the will a priori

25. [The Cassirer ed. suggests (*as a good*).]

and only then sought the object suitable to it. Whether they placed this object of pleasure, which was to deliver the supreme concept of the good, in happiness, or in perfection, in moral feeling,[26] or in the will of God—their fundamental principle was always heteronomy, and they came inevitably to empirical conditions for a moral law. This was because they could call their object, as the direct determining ground of the will, good or bad only according to its exclusively empirical relation to feeling. Only a formal law, i.e., one which prescribes to reason nothing more than the form of its universal legislation as the supreme condition of maxims, can be a priori a determining ground of practical reason. The ancients openly revealed this error by devoting their ethical investigation entirely to the definition of the concept of the highest good and thus posited an object which they intended subsequently to make the determining ground of the will in the moral law. But only much later, when the moral law has been established by itself and justified as the direct determining ground of the will, can this object be presented to the will whose form now is determined a priori. This we shall undertake in the Dialectic of Pure Practical Reason. The moderns, among whom the concept of the highest good has fallen into disuse or at least seems to have become something secondary, hide the error (as they do many others) behind vague expressions; but one can nevertheless see it shine through their systems since it always reveals heteronomy of practical reason, from which an a priori universally commanding moral law can never issue.

Now since the concepts of the good and evil, as consequences of the a priori determination of the will, presuppose also a pure practical principle and thus a causality of pure reason, they do not (as determinations of the synthetic unity of the manifold of given intuitions in one consciousness) refer originally to objects as do the pure concepts of the understanding or categories of the theoretically employed reason. Rather, they presuppose these objects as given, and they are without exception modes of a single category, that of causality, so far as its determining ground consists in reason's idea of a law of causality which, as the law of freedom, reason gives itself, thereby showing itself a priori to be practical. On the one side the actions are under a law which is a law of freedom instead of a natural law and thus belong to the

26. [Reading "feeling" with Hartenstein instead of "law" with Kant and the Cassirer ed. Either is perhaps acceptable, for a law dictated by pleasure would be heteronomous.]

conduct of intelligible beings, and on the other side as events in the world of sense they belong to appearances; so that the rules of a practical reason are possible only with respect to the latter and consequently in accordance with the categories of the understanding. These rules, however, contribute nothing to the theoretical use of the understanding in bringing the manifold of (sensuous) intuitions under one consciousness a priori, but only to the a priori subjection of the manifold of desires to the unity of consciousness of a practical reason commanding in the moral law, i.e., of a pure will.

These categories of freedom—for we wish to call them this in contrast to the theoretical concepts which are categories of nature—have a manifest advantage over the latter. The latter categories are only forms of thought which, through universal concepts, designate in an indefinite manner objects in general for every intuition possible to us. The categories of freedom, on the contrary, are elementary practical concepts which determine the free faculty of choice; though no intuition perfectly corresponding to the latter can be given, it yet has as its foundation a pure practical law a priori, and this cannot be said for any of the concepts of the theoretical use of our cognitive faculty. Instead of having as its given basis the form of intuition (space and time), which does not lie in reason itself but which rather has to be taken over from sensibility, the elementary practical concepts have as their foundation the form of a pure will given in reason and thus in the faculty of thought itself [and do not have to borrow their form from another faculty]. Since in all precepts of the pure will it is only a question of the determination of the will and not of the natural conditions (of practical ability) for achieving its purpose, it thereby happens that the practical concepts a priori in relation to the supreme principle of freedom immediately become cognitions, not needing to wait upon intuitions in order to acquire a meaning. This occurs for the noteworthy reason that they themselves produce the reality of that to which they refer (the intention of the will)—an achievement which is in no way the business of theoretical concepts. One must carefully observe, however, that these categories concern only practical reason in general, and so they proceed in order from those which are as yet morally undetermined and sensuously conditioned to those which, being sensuously unconditioned, are determined merely by the moral law.

TABLE OF CATEGORIES OF FREEDOM WITH REFERENCE TO THE CONCEPTS OF GOOD AND EVIL

1. Categories of Quantity
    Subjective, according to maxims (intentions of the individual's will)
    Objective, according to principles (precepts)
    A priori principles of freedom, both subjective and objective (laws)
2. Categories of Quality
    Practical rules of commission (*praeceptivae*)
    Practical rules of omission (*prohibitivae*)
    Practical rules of exceptions (*exceptivae*)
3. Categories of Relation
    Relation to personality
    Relation to the condition of the person
    Reciprocally, relation of one person to the condition of another
4. Categories of Modality[27]
    The permitted and the forbidden
    Duty and that which is contrary to duty
    Perfect and imperfect duty

One quickly perceives that in this table freedom is regarded as a kind of causality (not subject to empirical grounds of determination) with reference to actions possible through it, which are appearances in the world of sense, and that consequently it is referred to the categories of their possibility in nature, while, however, each category is taken so universally that the determining ground of the causality can be placed beyond the world of sense in freedom as the property of an intelligible being. Finally, the categories of modality initiate the transition, though only in a *problematical* way, from practical principles in general to those of morality; and only later will it be possible to establish the principles of morality in a *dogmatic* form through the moral law.

I add nothing here to elucidate the table, for it is sufficiently understandable in itself. Such a division based on principles is very useful in any science, for the sake of both thoroughness and

27. [See note, p. 125. "The *modality* of judgments is a quite peculiar function. Its distinguishing characteristic is that it contributes nothing to the content of the judgment ... but concerns only the value of the copula in relation to thought in general" (*Critique of Pure Reason*, A 74 = B 99-100 [Smith trans.]).]

intelligibility. One knows immediately, for example, from the table and its first division where one must begin in practical considerations: from the maxims which each person bases on his inclinations, from the precepts which hold for a species of rational beings in so far as they agree in certain inclinations, and finally from the law, which holds for all irrespective of their inclinations. And so on. In such a manner one surveys the whole plan of what has to be done, every question of practical philosophy which has to be answered, and also the order to be followed.

OF THE TYPIC OF PURE PRACTICAL REASON

It is the concepts of the good and evil which first determine an object for the will. They themselves, however, stand under a practical rule of reason which, if the reason is pure, determines the will a priori in relation to its object. To decide whether an action which is possible for us in the sensuous world is or is not a case under the rule requires practical judgment, which applies what is asserted universally in the rule (*in abstracto*) to an action *in concreto*. A practical rule of pure reason, as *practical*, concerns the existence of an object, and, as a practical *rule* of pure reason, implies necessity with reference to the occurence of an action; hence it is a practical law, not a natural law because of empirical determining grounds but a law of freedom by which the will is determinable independently of everything empirical and merely through the conception of a law in general and its form. Because of this, and since all instances of possible actions are only empirical and can belong only to experience and nature, it seems absurd to wish to find a case in the world of sense, and thus standing under the law of nature, which admits the application of a law of freedom to it, and to which we could apply the supersensuous ideal of the morally good, so that the latter could be exhibited *in concreto*.

The judgment of pure practical reason, therefore, is subject to the same difficulties as that of the pure theoretical, though the latter had a means of escape. It could escape because in its theoretical use everything depended upon intuitions to which pure concepts of the understanding could be applied, and such intuitions (though only of objects of the senses), as a priori and hence concerning the connection of the manifold in intuitions, could be given a priori in conformity to the concepts of the understanding, i.e., as schemata. The morally good, on the contrary, is something which, by its object, is supersensuous; nothing corresponding to it can be found in sensuous intuition; consequently, judgment under laws of the pure practical reason seems to be subject to special difficulties, which result from the fact that a law of freedom is to be applied to actions which are events occurring in the world of sense and thus, to this extent, belonging to nature.

But here again a favorable prospect for the pure practical judgment opens up. The subsumption under a pure practical law of an action which is possible to me in the world of sense does not concern the possibility of the action as an event of the world of sense. This possibility is a matter to be decided by the theoretical use of reason according to the law of causality, a pure concept of the understanding for which reason has a schema in sensuous intuition. The physical causality or the condition under which it occurs belongs among the concepts of nature, whose schema is sketched by the transcendental imagination. Here, however, we are concerned not with the schema of a case occurring according to laws but with the schema (if this word is suitable here) of a law itself, because the determination of the will through law alone and without any other determining ground (and not the action with reference to its consequences) connects the concept of causality to conditions altogether different from those which constitute natural connection.

A schema is a universal procedure of the imagination in presenting a priori to the senses a pure concept of the understanding which is determined by the law; and a schema must correspond to natural laws as laws to which objects of sensuous intuition as such are subject. But to the law of freedom (which is a causality not sensuously conditioned), and consequently to the concept of the absolutely good, no intuition and hence no schema can be supplied for the purpose of applying it *in concreto*. Thus the moral law has no other cognitive faculty to mediate its application to objects of nature than the understanding (not the imagination); and the understanding can supply to an idea of reason not a schema of sensibility but a law. This law, as one which can be exhibited *in concreto* in objects of the senses, is a natural law. But this natural law can be used only in its formal aspect, for the purpose of judgment, and it may, therefore, be called the *type* of the moral law.

The rule of judgment under laws of pure practical reason is: Ask yourself whether, if the action which you propose should take place by a law of nature of which you yourself were a part, you could regard it as possible through your will. Everyone does, in fact, decide by this rule whether actions are morally good or bad. Thus people ask: If one belonged to such an order of things that anyone would allow himself to deceive when he thought it to his advantage, or felt justified in shortening his life as soon as he was thoroughly weary of it, or looked with complete indifference on the need of others, would he assent of his own will to being a member of such an order of things? Now everyone knows very well that if he secretly permits himself to deceive, it does not follow that everyone else will do so, or that if, unnoticed by others, he is lacking in compassion, it does not mean that everyone else will immediately take the same attitude toward him. This comparison of the maxims of his actions with a universal natural law, therefore, is not the determining ground of his will. But such a law is still a type for[28] the estimation of maxims according to moral principles. If the maxim of action is not so constituted as to stand the test of being made the form of a natural law in general, it is morally impossible [though it may still be possible in nature.] Even common sense judges in this way, for its most ordinary judgments, even those of experience, are always based on natural law. Thus it is always at hand, but in cases where the causality from freedom is to be judged, natural law serves only as the *type* of a law of freedom, for if common sense did not have something to use in actual experience as an example, it could make no use of the law of pure practical reason in applying it to that experience.

We are therefore allowed to use the nature of the sensuous world as the type of an intelligible nature, so long as we do not carry over to the latter intuitions and what depends on them but only apply to it the form of lawfulness in general (the concept of which occurs in the most ordinary use of reason, though it cannot be known definitely a priori except with reference to the pure practical use of reason. For laws as such are all equivalent, regardless of where they derive their determining grounds.

Furthermore, since of all the intelligible objects absolutely nothing [is known] except freedom (through the moral law), and even this only in so far as it is a presupposition inseparable from the moral law; and since, moreover, all intelligible objects

28. [The original has *of*.]

to which reason might eventually lead us under the guidance of the law can have no reality for us except for the purpose of this law and of the use of pure practical reason; and, finally, since reason has a right, and is even compelled, to use nature (in its pure intelligible form) as the type of judgment—for all these reasons the present remark should serve to guard against counting among the concepts themselves what merely belongs to the typic of the concepts. This, as the typic of judgment, guards against the empiricism of practical reason, which bases the practical concepts of good and evil merely on empirical consequences (on so-called happiness). Happiness and the infinite useful consequences of a will determined only by [the maxim of] helping itself could, if this will made itself into a universal law, certainly serve as a very adequate type for the morally good but still not be identical with it. The same typic guards also against the mysticism of practical reason, which makes into a schema that which should serve only as a symbol, i.e., proposes to supply real yet nonsensuous intuitions (of an invisible kingdom of God) for the application of the moral law, and thus plunges into the transcendent. Only rationalism of judgments is suitable to the use of moral laws, for rationalism takes no more from sensuous nature than that which pure reason can also think for itself, i.e., lawfulness, and conversely transfers into the supersensuous nothing more than can be actually exhibited by actions in the world of sense according to a formal rule of natural law in general. Thus the protest against empiricism of practical reason is much more important and commendable, because mysticism is compatible with the purity and sublimity of the moral law; and as it is not natural to ordinary ways of thinking to stretch its imagination to supersensuous intuitions, the danger from this side is not so general. On the other hand, empiricism uproots the morality of intentions, while the highest worth which human beings can and should procure for themselves lies in intentions and not in actions only. It substitutes for duty something entirely different, namely, an empirical interest, with which inclinations generally are secretly in league. For this reason empiricism is allied with the inclinations, which, no matter what style they wear, always degrade mankind when they are raised to the dignity of a supreme practical principle. But these inclinations are so favorable to everyone's feelings that empiricism is far more dangerous than all mystical enthusiasm, which can never be a lasting condition for any great number of persons.

Chapter III
The Incentives of Pure Practical Reason

WHAT is essential in the moral worth of actions is that the moral law should directly determine the will. If the determination of the will occurs in accordance with the moral law but only by means of a feeling of any kind whatsoever, which must be presupposed in order that the law may become a determining ground of the will, and if the action thus occurs not for the sake of the law, it has legality but not morality. Now, if by an incentive (*elater animi*) we understand a subjective determining ground of a will whose reason does not by its nature necessarily conform to the objective law, it follows, first, that absolutely no incentives can be attributed to the Divine will; and, second, that the [moral][29] incentive of the human will (and that of every created rational being) can never be anything other than the moral law; and, third, that the objective determining ground must at the same time be the exclusive and subjectively sufficient determining ground of action if the latter is to fulfil not merely the letter of the law but also its spirit.*

Any further motives which would make it possible for us to dispense with that of moral law must not be sought, for they would only produce hypocrisy without any substance. Even to let other motives (such as those toward certain advantages) co-operate with the moral law is risky. Therefore, for the purpose of giving the moral law influence on the will, nothing remains but to determine carefully in what way the moral law becomes an incentive and, since the moral law is such an incentive, to see what happens to the human faculty of desire as a consequence of this determining ground. For how a law in itself can be the direct determining ground of the will (which is the essence of morality) is an insoluble problem for the human reason. It is identical with the problem of how a free will is possible. Therefore, we shall not have to show a priori why the moral law supplies an incentive but rather what it effects (or better, must effect) in the mind, so far as it is an incentive.

29. [See p. 86. The distinction between incentive and motive is difficult to preserve when it becomes a question of how the law can itself be practical.]

* Of every action which conforms to the law but does not occur for the sake of the law, one may say that it is morally good in letter but not in spirit (in intention).

The essential point in all determination of the will through the moral law is this: as a free will, and thus not only without co-operating with sensuous impulses but even rejecting all of them and checking all inclinations so far as they could be antagonistic to the law, it is determined merely by the law. Thus far, the effect of the moral law as an incentive is only negative, and as such this incentive can be known a priori. For all inclination and every sensuous impulse is based on feeling, and the negative effect on feeling (through the check on the inclinations) is itself feeling. Consequently, we can see a priori that the moral law as a ground of determination of the will, by thwarting all our inclinations, must produce a feeling which can be called pain. Here we have the first and perhaps the only case wherein we can determine from a priori concepts the relation of a cognition (here a cognition of pure practical reason) to the feeling of pleasure or displeasure. All inclinations taken together (which can be brought into a fairly tolerable system, whereupon their satisfaction is called happiness) constitute self-regard (*solipsismus*). This consists either of self-love, which is a predominant benevolence toward one's self (*philautia*) or of self-satisfaction (*arrogantia*). The former is called, more particularly, selfishness; the latter, self-conceit. Pure practical reason merely checks selfishness, for selfishness, as natural and active in us even prior to the moral law, is restricted by the moral law to agreement with the law; when this is done, selfishness is called rational self-love. But it strikes self-conceit down, since all claims of self-esteem which precede conformity to the moral law are null and void. For the certainty of a disposition which agrees with this law is the first condition of any worth of the person (as will soon be made clear), and any presumption [to worth] prior to this is false and opposed to the law. Now the propensity to self-esteem, so long as it rests only on the sensibility, is one of the inclinations which the moral law checks. Therefore, the moral law strikes down self-conceit.

Since this law, however, is in itself positive, being the form of an intellectual causality, i.e., the form of freedom, it is at the same time an object of respect, since, in conflict with its subjective antagonists (our inclinations), it weakens self-conceit. And as striking down, i.e., humiliating, self-conceit, it is an object of the greatest respect and thus the ground of a positive feeling which is not of empirical origin. This feeling, then, is one which can be known a priori. Respect for the moral law, therefore, is a feeling produced by an intellectual cause, and this feeling is the only one which we can know completely a priori and the necessity of which we can discern.

In the preceding chapter we have seen that anything which presents itself as the object of the will prior to the moral law is excluded from the determining grounds of the will (which are called the unconditionally good) by the law itself as the supreme condition of practical reason. We have also seen that the mere practical form, which consists in the competency of the maxims to give universal laws, first determines what is of itself and absolutely good and is the ground of the maxims of a pure will, which alone is good in every respect. We find now, however, our nature as sensuous beings so characterized that the material of the faculty of desire (objects of the inclination, whether of hope or fear) first presses upon us; and we find our pathologically determined self, although by its maxims it is wholly incapable of giving universal laws, striving to give its pretensions priority and to make them acceptable as the first and original claims, just as if it were our entire self. This propensity to make the subjective determining grounds of one's choice into an objective determining ground of the will in general can be called self-love; when it makes itself legislative and an unconditional practical principle, it can be called self-conceit. The moral law, which alone is truly, i.e., in every respect, objective, completely excludes the influence of self-love from the highest practical principle and forever checks self-conceit, which decrees the subjective conditions of self-love as laws. If anything checks our self-conceit in our own judgment, it humiliates. Therefore, the moral law inevitably humbles every man when he compares the sensuous propensity of his nature with the law. Now if the idea of something as the determining ground of the will humiliates us in our self-consciousness, it awakens respect for itself so far as it is positive and the ground of determination. The moral law, therefore, is even subjectively a cause of respect.

Now everything in self-love belongs to inclination, and all inclination rests on feelings; therefore, whatever checks all inclinations in self-love necessarily has, by that fact, an influence on feeling. Thus we conceive how it is possible to understand a priori that the moral law can exercise an effect on feeling, since it blocks the inclinations and the propensity to make them the supreme practical condition (i.e., self-love) from all participation in supreme legislation. This effect is on the one side merely negative; but on the other, in respect to the restrictive practical ground of pure practical reason, it is positive. And to the latter, no kind of feeling, [even] under the name of a practical or moral feeling, may be assumed as prior to the moral law and as its basis.

The negative effect on feeling (unpleasantness) is, like all influences on feeling and every feeling itself, pathological. As the effect of the consciousness of the moral law, and consequently in relation to an intelligible cause, i.e., to the subject of the pure practical reason as the supreme legislator, this feeling of a rational subject affected with inclinations is called humiliation (intellectual contempt). But in relation to its positive ground, the law, it is at the same time respect for the law; for this law there is no feeling, but, as it removes a resistance, this dislodgment of an obstacle is, in the judgment of reason, equally esteemed as a positive assistance to its causality. Therefore, this feeling can also be called a feeling of respect for the moral law; on both grounds, however, it can be called a moral feeling.

Thus the moral law, as a formal determining ground of action through practical pure reason, and moreover as a material though purely objective determining ground of the objects of action (under the name of good and evil), is also a subjective ground of determination. That is, it is the incentive to this action, since it has an influence on the sensibility of the subject and effects a feeling which promotes the influence of the law on the will. In the subject there is no antecedent feeling tending to morality; that is impossible, because all feeling is sensuous, and the incentives of the moral disposition must be free from every sensuous condition. Rather, sensuous feeling, which is the basis of all our inclinations, is the condition of the particular feeling we call respect, but the cause that determines this feeling lies in the pure practical reason; because of its origin, therefore, this particular feeling cannot be said to be pathologically effected; rather, it is practically effected. Since the idea of the moral law deprives self-love of its influence and self-conceit of its delusion, it lessens the obstacle to pure practical reason and produces the idea of the superiority of its objective law to the impulses of sensibility; it increases the weight of the moral law by removing, in the judgment of reason, the counterweight to the moral law which bears on a will affected by the sensibility. Thus respect for the law is not the incentive to morality; it is morality itself, regarded subjectively as an incentive, inasmuch as pure practical reason, by rejecting all the rival claims of self-love, gives authority and absolute sovereignty to the law. It should be noticed that, as respect is an effect on feeling and thus on the sensibility of a rational being, it presupposes the sensuousness and hence the finitude of such beings on whom respect for the moral law is imposed; thus respect for the law cannot be attributed to a supreme being or even to one free from all sensibility, since to such a being there could be no obstacle to practical reason.

This feeling, under the name of moral feeling, is therefore produced solely by reason. It does not serve for an estimation of actions or as a basis of the objective moral law itself but only as an incentive to make this law itself a maxim. By what name better than moral feeling could we call this singular feeling, which cannot be compared with any pathological feeling? It is of such a peculiar kind that it seems to be at the disposal only of reason, and indeed only of the pure practical reason.

Respect always applies to persons only, never to things. The latter can awaken inclinations, and even love if they are animals (horses, dogs, etc.), or fear, as do the sea, a volcano, or a beast of prey; but they never arouse respect. Something which approaches this feeling is admiration, and this, as an affect (astonishment) can refer also to things, e.g., lofty mountains, the magnitude, number, and distance of the heavenly bodies, the strength and swiftness of many animals, etc. All of this, however, is not respect. A man can also be an object of love, fear, or admiration even to astonishment, and yet not be an object of respect. His jocular humor, his courage and strength, and his power resulting from his rank among others may inspire me with such feelings, though inner respect for him is still lacking. Fontanelle[30] says, "I bow to a great man, but my mind does not bow." I can add: to a humble plain man, in whom I perceive righteousness in a higher degree than I am conscious of in myself, *my mind bows* whether I choose or not, and however high I carry my head that he may not forget my superior position. Why? His example holds a law before me which strikes down my self-conceit when I compare my own conduct with it; that it is a law which can be obeyed, and consequently is one that can actually be put into practice, is proved before my eyes by the act. I may even be conscious of a like degree of righteousness in myself, and yet respect remains. In men all good is defective, but the law made visible in an example always humbles my pride, since the man

---

30. [Bernard Le Bovier de Fontanelle (1657–1757), a French satirist and popular philosopher.]

whom I see before me provides me with a standard, by clearly appearing to me in a more favorable light regardless of his imperfections, which, though perhaps always with him, are not so well known to me as are my own. Respect is a tribute we cannot refuse to pay to merit whether we will or not; we can indeed outwardly withhold it, but we cannot help feeling it inwardly.

Respect is so far from being a feeling of pleasure that one only reluctantly gives way to it as regards a man. We seek to discover something that will lighten the burden of it for us, some fault to compensate us for the humiliation which we suffer from such an example. The dead themselves are not immune from this criticism, especially when their example appears inimitable. Even the moral law itself in its solemn majesty is exposed to this endeavor to keep one's self from yielding respect to it. Can it be thought that there is any reason why we like to degrade it to the level of our familiar inclination and why we take so much trouble to make it the chosen precept of our well-understood interest, other than the fact that we want to be free of the awesome respect which so severely shows us our own unworthiness? Nevertheless, there is on the other hand so little displeasure in it that, when once we renounce our self-conceit and respect has established its practical influence, we cannot ever satisfy ourselves in contemplating the majesty of this law, and the soul believes itself to be elevated in proportion as it sees the holy law as elevated over it and its frail nature. Certainly, great talents and activity proportionate to them can occasion respect or an analogous feeling, and it is proper to accord it to them; then it seems that admiration is the same as this feeling [of respect]. But if one looks more closely it is noticed that it is always uncertain how great a part of the ability must be ascribed to innate talent and how much to cultivation through one's own diligence. Presumably reason represents it to us as a fruit of cultivation, and therefore as merit which perceptibly diminishes our self-conceit and therefore either reproaches us or else imposes it upon us as an example to be followed in a suitable manner. This respect which we have for a person (really for the law, which his example holds before us) is, therefore, not mere admiration. This is also confirmed by the way the common run of men give up their respect for a man (e.g., Voltaire) when they think they have in some manner found the badness of his character, while the true scholar still feels this respect at least for his talents, since he is himself involved in a business and a vocation which makes imitation of him to some extent a law.

Respect for the moral law is therefore the sole and undoubted moral incentive, so far as this feeling is directed to no object except on this basis. First, the moral law determines the will directly and objectively in the judgment of reason. Freedom, the causality of which is determinable merely through the law, consists, however, only in the fact that it limits all inclinations, including self-esteem, to the condition of obedience to its pure law. This limitation exerts an effect on feeling and produces the sensation of displeasure, which can be known a priori from the moral law. Since, however, it is so far a merely negative effect, originating from the influence of pure practical reason, it checks the activity of the subject to the extent that inclinations are its grounds of determination, and consequently it checks also the opinion of his personal worth, which is nothing without accordance with the moral law. Thus the effect of this law on feeling is merely humiliation, which we thus see a priori, though we cannot know the force of the pure practical law as incentive but only the resistance to the incentives of sensibility. The same law, however, is objectively, i.e., in the conception of pure reason, a direct determining ground of the will. Hence this humiliation occurs proportionately to the purity of the law; for that reason the lowering of the pretensions of moral self-esteem (humiliation) on the sensuous side is an elevation of the moral, i.e., practical, esteem for the law on the intellectual side. In a word, respect for the law is thus by virtue of its intellectual cause a positive feeling that can be known a priori. For any diminution of obstacles to an activity furthers this activity itself. The acknowledgment of the moral law is the consciousness of an activtity of practical reason on objective grounds, and it fails to express its effect in actions simply because subjective (pathological) causes hinder it. Therefore, respect for the moral law must be regarded also as a positive but indirect effect of the law on feeling, in so far as this feeling [of respect] weakens the hindering influence of the inclinations through humiliating self-conceit; consequently, we must see it as a subjective ground of activity, as an incentive for obedience to the law and as the ground of maxims of a course of life conformable to it. From the concept of an incentive there comes that of an interest which can never be attributed to a being which does not have reason; it indicates an incentive of the will so far as it is presented by reason. Since the law itself must be the incentive in a morally good will, the moral interest must be a pure nonsensuous interest of the practical reason alone. Now on the concept of an interest rests that of a maxim. The latter is thus morally genuine only when it rests on the mere interest that one takes in obedience to the law. All three concepts—of incentive, interest, and maxim—can, however, be applied only to finite beings. For without exception they presuppose a limitation of the nature of the being, in that the subjective character of its choice does not of itself agree with the objective law of a practical reason; they presuppose that the being must be impelled in some manner to action, since an internal obstacle stands against it. They cannot, therefore, be applied to the divine will.

In the boundless esteem for the pure moral law, removed from all advantage, as practical reason presents it to us for obedience, whose voice makes even the boldest sinner tremble and forces him to hide himself from it, there is something so singular that we cannot wonder at finding this influence of a merely intellectual idea on feeling to be inexplicable to speculative reason, and at having to be satisfied with being able to see a priori that such a feeling is inseparably bound with the idea of the moral law in every finite rational being. If this feeling of respect were pathological and thus a feeling of pleasure grounded on the inner sense, it would be futile to try to discover a relation of the feeling to any idea a priori. But it is a feeling which is concerned only with the practical, and with the idea of a law simply as to its form and not on account of any object of the law; thus it cannot be reckoned either as enjoyment or as pain, yet it produces an interest in obedience to the law, and this we call the moral interest. And the capacity of taking such an interest in the law (or of having respect for the moral law itself) is really moral feeling.

The consciousness of a free submission of the will to the law, combined with an inevitable constraint imposed only by our own reason on all inclinations, is respect for the law. The law which commands and inspires this respect is, as we see, no other than the moral law, for no other law precludes all inclinations from having a direct influence on the will. The action which is objectively practical according to this law, and excluding inclination from its determining grounds, is called duty; and, because of this exclusion, in the concept of duty there is that of practical constraint,[31] i.e., determination to actions however reluctantly they may be done. The feeling which arises from the conscious-

31. [*Nötigung.* Abbott reads "obligation."]

ness of this constraint is not pathological, as are those caused by objects of the senses, but practical, i.e., possible through a prior (objective) determination of the will and the causality of reason. As submission to a law, i.e., as a command (which constrains the sensuously affected subject), it contains, therefore, no pleasure but rather displeasure proportionate to this constraint. On the other hand, since this constraint is exercised only through the legislation of one's own reason, it also contains something elevating, and the subjective effect on feeling, in so far as pure practical reason is its sole cause, can also be called self-approbation with reference to pure practical reason, for one knows himself to be determined thereto solely by the law and without any interest; he becomes conscious of an altogether different interest which is subjectively produced by the law and which is purely practical and free. Our taking this interest in an action of duty is not suggested by an inclination, but the practical law absolutely commands it and also actually produces it. Consequently, it has a very special name, viz., respect.

The concept of duty thus requires of action that it objectively agree with the law, while of the maxim of the action it demands subjective respect for the law as the sole mode of determining the will through itself. And thereon rests the distinction between consciousness of having acted *according to duty* and *from duty*, i.e., from respect for the law. The former, legality, is possible even if inclinations alone are the determining grounds of the will, but the latter, morality or moral worth, can be conceded only where the action occurs from duty, i.e., merely for the sake of the law.*

It is of the utmost importance in all moral judging to pay strictest attention to the subjective principle of every maxim, so that all the morality of actions may be placed in their necessity from duty and from respect for the law, and not from love for or leaning toward that which the action is to produce. For men and all rational creatures, the moral necessity is a constraint, an obligation. Every action based on it is to be considered as duty, and

---

* If one examines more accurately the concept of respect for persons, as this has been previously presented, one will perceive that it always rests on the consciousness of a duty which an example holds before us and that consequently respect can never have other than a moral ground. It is also seen to be very good and, from the psychological point of view, very useful to our understanding of human nature, that wherever we use the term to pay attention to the mysterious and wonderful, but frequent, regard which human judgment does have for the moral law.

not as a manner of acting which we naturally favor or which we sometime might so favor. This would be tantamount to believing we could finally bring it about that, without respect for the law (which is always connected with fear or at least apprehension that we might transgress it) we, like the independent deity, might come into possession of holiness of will through irrefragable agreement of the will with the pure moral law becoming, as it were, our very nature. This pure law, if we could never be tempted to be untrue to it, would finally cease altogether to be a command for us.

The moral law is, in fact, for the will of a perfect being a law of holiness. For the will of any finite rational being, however, it is a law of duty, of moral constraint, and of the determination of his actions through respect for the law and reverence for its duty. No other subjective principle must be assumed as incentive, for though it might happen that the action occurs as the law prescribes, and thus in accord with duty but not from duty, the intention to do the action would not be moral, and it is the intention which is precisely in question in this legislation.

It is a very beautiful thing to do good to men because of love and a sympathetic good will or to do justice because of a love of order. But this is not the genuine moral maxim of our conduct, the maxim which is suitable to our position among rational beings as men, when we presume, like volunteers, to flout with proud conceit the thought of duty and, as independent of command, merely to will of our own good pleasure to do something to which we think we need no command. We stand under a discipline of reason, and in all our maxims we must not forget our subjection to it, or withdraw anything from it, or by an egotistical illusion detract from the authority of the law (even though it is given by our own reason) so that we could place the determining ground of our will (even though it is in accordance with the law) elsewhere than in the law itself and in respect for it. Duty and obligation are the only names which we must give to our relation to the moral law. We are indeed legislative members of a moral realm which is possible through freedom and which is presented to us as an object of respect by practical reason; yet we are at the same time subjects in it, not sovereigns, and to mistake our inferior position as creatures and to deny, from self-conceit, respect to the holy law is, in spirit, a defection from it even if its letter be fulfilled.

The possibility of such a command as, "Love God above all

and thy neighbor as thyself,"* agrees very well with this. For, as a command, it requires respect for a law which orders love and does not leave it to arbitrary choice to make love the principle. But love to God as inclination (pathological love) is impossible, for He is not an object of the senses. The latter is indeed possible toward men, but it cannot be commanded, for it is not possible for man to love someone merely on command. It is, therefore, only practical love which can be understood in that kernel of all laws. To love God means in this sense to like to do His commandments, and to love one's neighbor means to like to practice all duties toward him. The command which makes this a rule cannot require that we have this disposition but only that we endeavor after it. To command that one do something gladly is self-contradictory. For a law would not be needed if we already knew of ourselves what we ought to do and moreover were conscious of liking to do it; and if we did it without liking but only out of respect for the law, a command which makes just this respect the incentive of the maxim would counteract the disposition it commands. That law of all laws, like every moral prescription of the Gospel, thus presents the moral disposition in its complete perfection, and though as an ideal of holiness it is unattainable by any creature, it is yet an archetype which we should strive to approach and to imitate in an uninterrupted infinite progress. If a rational creature could ever reach the stage of thoroughly liking to do all moral laws, it would mean that there was no possibility of there being in him a desire which could tempt him to deviate from them, for overcoming such a desire always costs the subject some sacrifice and requires self-compulsion, i.e., an inner constraint to do that which one does not quite like to do. To such a level of moral disposition no creature can ever attain. For since he is a creature, and consequently is always dependent with respect to what he needs for complete satisfaction with his condition, he can never be wholly free from desires and inclinations which, because they rest on physical causes, do not of themselves agree with the moral law, which has an entirely different source. Consequently, it is with reference to these desires always necessary to base the intention of the creature's maxims on moral constraint and not on ready willingness, i.e., to base it on respect

* The principle of one's own happiness, which some wish to make the supreme principle of morality, is in striking contrast to this law. This principle would read: "Love thyself above all, but God and thy neighbor for thine own sake."

which demands obedience to the law even though the creature does not like to do it, and not on love, which apprehends no inward reluctance to the law by the will. This would be true even if the mere love for the law (which would in this case cease to be a command, and morality, subjectively passing over into holiness, would cease to be virtue) were made the constant but unattainable goal of its striving. For in the case of what we esteem and yet dread because of our consciousness of our weaknesses, the most reverential awe would be changed into inclination, and respect into love, because of the greater ease in satisfying the latter. At least this would be the perfection of a disposition dedicated to the law, if it were ever possible for a creature to attain it.

This reflection is not intended so much to clarify by exact concepts the evangelical command just cited in order to prevent religious fanaticism with reference to the love of God as to define accurately the moral intention directly with regard to our duties to others and to control and, if possible, to prevent a narrowly moral fanaticism, which infects many persons. The stage of morality on which man (and, so far as we know, every rational creature) stands is respect for the moral law. The disposition which obliges him to obey it is: to obey it from duty and not from a spontaneous inclination or from an endeavor unbidden but gladly undertaken. The moral condition which he can always be in is virtue, i.e., moral disposition in conflict, and not holiness in the supposed possession of perfect purity of the intentions of the will. The mind is disposed to nothing but blatant moral fanaticism and exaggerated self-conceit by exhortation to actions as noble, sublime, and magnanimous. By it people are led to the illusion that the determining ground of their actions is not duty, i.e., respect for the law whose yoke must be borne whether liked or not (though it is a mild yoke, as imposed by reason). This law always humbles them when they follow (obey) it, but by this kind of exhortation they come to think that those actions are expected of them not because of duty but only because of their own bare merit. For not only do they not fulfil the spirit of the law when they imitate such acts on the basis of such a principle, since the spirit of the law lies in the submissive disposition and not in the merely lawful character of the act, leaving the principle to be what it may; and not only do they in this manner make the incentives pathological (locating them in sympathy or self-love) and not moral (located in the law). But they produce in this way a shallow, high-flown, fantastic way of thinking, flattering themselves with a spontaneous goodness of heart, needing neither spur nor bridle nor even command, and thereby forgetting their obligation, which they ought to think of rather than their merit. Certainly actions of others which have been done with great sacrifice and merely for the sake of duty may be praised as noble and sublime deeds, yet only in so far as there are clues which suggest that they were done wholly out of respect for duty and not from aroused feelings. But if anyone wishes to put them forward as examples for imitation, the incentive to be employed must be only the respect for duty, the sole genuine moral feeling, this earnest holy precept which does not leave it to our vain self-love to dally with pathological impulses (as far as they are analogous to morality) and to pride ourselves on our meritorious worth. For all actions which are praiseworthy, if we only search we shall find a law of duty which commands and does not leave us to choose what may be agreeable to our propensity. That is the only way of representing [morality] which morally educates the soul, because it is the only one which is capable of constant and accurately defined principles.

If fanaticism in its most general sense is a deliberate overstepping of the limits of human reason, moral fanaticism is this overstepping of limits which practical pure reason sets to mankind. Pure practical reason thereby forbids us to place the subjective determining ground of dutiful actions, i.e., their moral incentive, anywhere else than in the law itself, and to place the disposition which is thereby brought into the maxims elsewhere than in the respect for this law; it commands that we make the thought of duty, which strikes down all arrogance as well as vain self-love, the supreme life-principle of all human morality.

If this is so, then not only novelists and sentimental educators (even though they may be zealously opposed to sentimentalism) but also philosophers and indeed the strictest of them, the Stoics, have instituted moral fanaticism instead of a sober but wise moral discipline, though the fanaticism of the latter was more heroic, while that of the former is of a more shallow and pliable nature. And we may, without hypocrisy, truly say of the moral teaching of the Gospel that, through the purity of its moral principle and at the same time through the suitability of its principle to the limitations of finite beings, it first brought all good conduct of man under the discipline of a duty clearly set before him, which does not permit him to indulge in fancies of moral perfections;

and that it set bounds of humility (i.e., self-knowledge) to self-conceit as well as to self-love, both of which readily mistake their limits.

Duty! Thou sublime and mighty name that dost embrace nothing charming or insinuating but requirest submission and yet seekest not to move the will by threatening aught that would arouse natural aversion or terror but only holdest forth a law which of itself finds entrance into the mind and yet gains reluctant reverence (though not always obedience)—a law before which all inclinations are dumb even though they secretly work against it: what origin is there worthy of thee, and where is to be found the root of thy noble descent which proudly rejects all kinship with the inclinations and from which to be descended is the indispensable condition of the only worth which men can give themselves?

It cannot be less than something which elevates man above himself as a part of the world of sense, something which connects him with an order of things which only the understanding can think and which has under it the entire world of sense, including the empirically determinable existence of man in time, and the whole system of all ends which is alone suitable to such unconditional practical laws as the moral. It is nothing else than personality, i.e., the freedom and independence from the mechanism of nature regarded as a capacity of a being which is subject to special laws (pure practical laws given by its own reason), so that the person as belonging to the world of sense is subject to his own personality so far as he belongs to the intelligible world. For it is then not to be wondered at that man, as belonging to two worlds, must regard his own being in relation to his second and higher vocation with reverence and the laws of this vocation with the deepest respect.

Many expressions which indicate the worth of objects according to moral ideas are based on this origin. The moral law is holy (inviolable). Man is certainly unholy enough, but humanity in his person must be holy to him. Everything in creation which he wishes and over which he has power can be used merely as a means; only man, and, with him, every rational creature, is an end in itself. He is the subject of the moral law which is holy, because of the autonomy of his freedom. Because of the latter, every will, even the private will of each person directed to himself, is restricted to the condition of agreement with the autonomy of the rational being, namely, that it be subjected to no purpose which is not possible by a law which could arise from the will of the passive subject itself. This condition thus requires that the person never be used as a means except when it is at the same time an end. We may rightly attribute this condition even to the divine will with respect to the rational beings in the world as its creatures, since the condition rests on the personality of these beings, whereby alone they are ends in themselves.

This idea of personality awakens respect; it places before our eyes the sublimity of our own nature (in its [higher] vocation), while it shows us at the same time the unsuitability of our conduct to it, thus striking down our self-conceit. This is naturally and easily observed by the most common human reason. Has not every even fairly honest man sometimes found that he desists from an otherwise harmless lie which would extricate him from a vexing affair or which would even be useful to a beloved and deserving friend simply in order not to have to contemn himself secretly in his own eyes? In the greatest misfortunes of his life which he could have avoided if he could have disregarded duty, does not a righteous man hold up his head thanks to the consciousness that he has honored and preserved humanity in his own person and in its dignity, so that he does not have to shame himself in his own eyes or have reason to fear the inner scrutiny of self-examination? This comfort is not happiness, not even the smallest part of happiness; for no one would wish to have occasion for it, not even once in his life, or perhaps even would desire life itself in such circumstances. But he lives and cannot tolerate seeing himself as unworthy of life. This inner satisfaction is therefore merely negative with reference to everything which might make life pleasant; it is the defense against the danger of sinking in personal worth after the value of his circumstances has been completely lost. It is the effect of a respect for something entirely different from life, in comparison and contrast to which life and its enjoyment have absolutely no worth. He yet lives only because it is his duty, not because he has the least taste for living.

Such is the nature of the genuine incentive of pure practical reason. It is nothing else than the pure moral law itself, so far as it lets us perceive the sublimity of our own supersensuous existence and subjectively effects respect for their higher vocation in men who are conscious of their sensuous existence and of the accompanying dependence on their pathologically affected nature. Now let there be associated with this incentive so many charms and pleasures of life that even for their sake alone the most skilful choice of a reasonable Epicurean, considering the highest welfare of life, would declare himself for moral conduct (and it may even be advisable to connect this prospect of a merry enjoyment of life with that supreme determining motive which is sufficient of itself); but this is only in order to hold a balance against the attractions which vice on the other side does not fail to offer and not in order to place in these prospects even the smallest part of the real moving force when duty is what we are concerned with. For the latter would be simply to destroy the purity of the moral disposition at its source. The majesty of duty has nothing to do with the enjoyment of life; it has its own law, even its own tribunal, and however much one wishes to mix them together, in order to offer the mixture to the sick as though it were a medicine, they nevertheless soon separate of themselves; but, if they do not separate, the moral ingredient has no effect at all, and even if the physical life gained some strength in this way, the moral life would waste away beyond rescue.

CRITICAL EXAMINATION OF THE ANALYTIC OF PURE PRACTICAL REASON

By a critical examination of a science, or of one of its portions which is a system by itself, I understand the investigation and justification of the fact that it must have precisely the systematic form which it does have and no other when compared with another system which has as its basis a similar cognitive faculty. Now practical reason has the same cognitive faculty for its foundation as the speculative, so far as they are both pure reason. Thus the difference in their systematic form must be determined by a comparison between them, and the ground of this difference be given.

The Analytic of pure theoretical reason deals with knowledge of objects which may be given to the understanding. It therefore had to begin from intuition and consequently (since intuition is always sensuous) from sensibility; only then could it progress to concepts (of objects of this intuition); it could end with principles only after these two had been dealt with. On the other hand, practical reason is concerned not with objects in order to know them but with its own capacity to make them real (according to knowledge of them), i.e., it has to do with a will which is a causality so far as reason contains its determining ground. Consequently, it does not have to furnish an object of intuition, but as practical reason it has only to give a law [for objects] of intuition, because the concept of causality always contains a relation to a law which determines the existence of the many in their relation to one another. Thus a critical examination of the Analytic of reason, if it is to be practical reason (which is the real problem), must begin from the possibility of practical fundamental principles a priori. Only from these can it proceed to concepts of objects of a practical reason, i.e., to the concepts of the absolutely good and evil in order first to assign them in accordance with those principles, for prior to these principles there is no cognitive faculty by which they could be given as [concepts of the] good and evil. Only then could the last chapter, dealing with the relation of pure practical reason to sensibility and with its necessary influence on it, i.e., the moral feeling which is known a priori, close this part of the work. Thus the Analytic of practical pure reason distinguishes among the conditions of its use in a way analogous to that of the theoretical reason but in reverse order.[32] The Analytic of theoretical pure reason was divided into Transcendental Aesthetic and Transcendental Logic; that of the practical reason is divided, conversely, into logic and aesthetic of pure practical reason, if I may be allowed to use, on the basis of analogy, these terms which are not entirely suitable. The Logic in turn was there divided into Analytic of Concepts and Analytic of Principles; here it is divided into that of principles and concepts. The Aesthetic had there two parts, because of the dual nature of sensuous intuition; here the sensibility is regarded not as a faculty of intuition but merely as feeling (which can be a subjective ground of desire), and in this respect pure practical reason allows no further subdivision.

The reason this division into two parts together with their

32. [The analogy drawn is erroneous. The *Critique of Pure Reason* is actually divided as follows:

Doctrine of Elements	Aesthetic	
	Logic — Analytic	of concepts
		of principles
	Dialectic	
Doctrine of Method		

For a simpler statement of the relationship between the organization of the two *Critiques*, see above, p. 129.]

subdivision is not actually carried out is easily seen, even though in the beginning an attempt to do this might have been tempting because of the example of the first *Critique*. For since it is pure reason, which is here seen in its practical use and thus as commencing from a priori principles and not from empirical grounds of determination, the division of the Analytic of Pure Practical Reason must turn out to be similar to that of a syllogism, i.e., proceeding from the universal in the major premise (the moral principle), through a minor premise containing a subsumption of possible actions (as good or bad) under the major, to the conclusion, viz., the subjective determination of the will (an interest in the practically possible good and the maxim based on it). Whoever has been able to convince himself of the truth of the propositions in the Analytic will get a certain enjoyment out of such comparisons, for they correctly occasion the expectation of bringing some day into one view the unity of the entire pure rational faculty (both theoretical and practical) and of being able to derive everything from one principle. The latter is an unavoidable need of human reason, as it finds complete satisfaction only in a perfectly systematic unity of its cognitions.

But if we regard also the content of the knowledge which we can have of and through a pure practical reason, as the Analytic presents this content, there is to be found, besides a remarkable analogy between it and the content of the theoretical knowledge, no less remarkable differences. With reference to the theoretical, the faculty of a pure rational a priori knowledge could be easily and obviously proved through examples from the sciences (in which one does not need so much to fear a secret admixture of empirical grounds of cognition as in ordinary knowledge, since they put their principles to the test in so many ways by methodical use). But that pure reason is of itself alone practical, without any admixture of any kind of empirical grounds of determination—one had to show this from the commonest practical use of reason by producing evidence that the highest practical principle is a principle recognized by every natural human reason as the supreme law of its will, as a law completely a priori and independent of any sensuous data. It was necessary first to establish and justify it, by proof of the purity of its origin, in the judgment of this common reason, before science could take it in hand to make use of it, so to speak, as a fact which precedes all disputation about its possibility and all consequences which may be drawn from it. But this circumstance is easily explained from what has previously been said: it is because practical pure reason necessarily must begin with fundamental principles, which thus, as the original data, must be made the basis of the whole science and not regarded as first originating from it. On this account, the justification of moral principles as principles of a pure reason could be made with sufficient certainty through merely appealing to the judgment of common sense, since everything empirical which might insinuate itself into our maxims as a determining ground of the will immediately reveals itself through the feeling of enjoyment or pain which necessarily attaches to it in so far as it arouses desire, and pure practical reason immediately refuses to take it as a condition into its principle. The dissimilarity of rational and empirical grounds of determination is made recognizable through the resistance of a practically legislating reason to all interfering inclinations, which is shown in a peculiar kind of feeling which does not precede the legislation of practical reason but which is, on the contrary, first effected by it, as a compulsion. That is, it is revealed through the feeling of respect of a kind that no man has for any inclinations whatever, but which he may feel for the law alone. It is shown so saliently and prominently that no one, not even the commonest mind, can fail in a moment to discover in an example that, though he can be urged by empirical grounds of volition to follow their attractions, he can be expected to *obey* nothing but the pure practical law of reason.

In the doctrine of happiness empirical principles constitute the entire foundation, but in the doctrine of morality they do not form even the smallest part of it. The differentiation between these two is the first and most important task charged to the Analytic of Pure Practical Reason, and in it we must proceed as exactly and as punctiliously as ever a geometer went about his job. But the philosopher here (as everywhere else in rational knowledge, having to use mere concepts without any constructions for them) must struggle with greater difficulties than the geometer,[33] because he can take no intuition as a foundation (of[34] a pure noumenon). He has the advantage, however, that, almost like the chemist, he can at any time arrange an experiment with the practical reason of any man, in order to distinguish the moral (pure) determining ground from the empirical; he does so when he adds the moral law (as a ground of determination) to the

---

33. [Cf. the argument of the *Inquiry*, below, pp. 264 ff.]
34. [Inserting *vom* (following Adickes).]

empirically affected will (e.g., to the will of a person who would like to tell a lie so that he could thereby gain something). When the analyst adds alkali to a solution of lime in muriatic acid, the acid breaks away from the lime and combines with the alkali, and the lime precipitates. Just in the same way, if a man who is otherwise honest (or who this one time puts himself only in thought in the place of an honest man) is confronted with the moral law, by which he recognizes the worthlessness of the liar, his practical reason, in its judgment of what ought to be done, immediately forsakes the advantage, combines with that which maintains in him his respect for his own person (truthfulness), and the advantage is easily weighed by anyone after it is separated and washed of every particle of reason (which is wholly on the side of duty). Thus it can enter into combination with reason in still other cases, though not in any case where it could be opposed to the moral law, for reason never forsakes this but rather combines most closely with it.

But this distinction of the principle of happiness from that of morality is not for this reason an opposition between them, and pure practical reason does not require that we should renounce the claims to happiness; it requires only that we take no account of them whenever duty is in question. It can even be a duty in certain respects to provide for one's happiness, in part because (since it includes skill, health, and riches) it contains means to the fulfilment of one's duty and in part because the lack of it (e.g., poverty) contains temptations to transgress against duty. But to further one's happiness can never be a direct duty, and even less can it be a principle of all duty. Since all determining grounds of the will (except the one and only pure practical law of reason, i.e., the moral law) are empirical and as such belong to the principle of happiness, they must be separated from the supreme practical principle and never be incorporated with it as a condition, for this would destroy all moral worth just as surely as any admixture of anything empirical to geometrical axioms would destroy all mathematical certainty, which is, according to Plato's judgment, the highest excellence mathematics has, surpassing even its utility.

But instead of the deduction of the supreme principle of pure practical reason, i.e., the explanation of the possibility of such a knowledge a priori, nothing more could be done than to show that, if we saw the possibility of freedom of an efficient cause, we would see not only the possibility but also the necessity of the moral law as the supreme practical law of rational beings, to whom freedom of the causality of their will is ascribed. This is because the two concepts are so inextricably bound together that practical freedom could be defined through the will's independence of everything except the moral law. But the possibility of freedom of an efficient cause cannot be comprehended, especially in the world of sense; we are indeed fortunate if we can be sufficiently assured that no proof of its impossibility can be given and that we are compelled (and thus authorized) to assume it by the moral law, which postulates it.

But there are many who believe they can explain this freedom with empirical principles, just as they can explain other natural abilities. They regard it as a psychological property, the explanation of which turns solely upon a more exact investigation of the nature of the soul and of the incentives of the will and not as the transcendental predicate of the causality of a being which belongs to the world of sense; but it is this latter which is what really counts. Thus they deprive us of the great revelation which we experience through pure practical reason by means of the moral law—the revelation of an intelligible world through realization of the otherwise transcendent concept of freedom; they deprive us of moral law itself, which assumes absolutely no empirical ground of determination. Therefore, it will be necessary to add something here as a protection against this delusion and to expose empiricism in its naked superficiality.

The concept of causality as natural necessity, unlike the concept of causality as freedom, concerns only the existence of things so far as it is determinable in time, and consequently as appearances in contrast to their causality as things-in-themselves. If one takes the attributes of the existence of things in time for attributes of things-in-themselves, which is the usual way of thinking, the necessity in the causal relation can in no way be united with freedom. They are contradictory to each other, for the former implies that every event, and consequently every action, which occurs at a certain point of time is necessary under the condition of what preceded it. Since the past is no longer in my power, every action which I perform is necessary because of determining grounds which are not in my power. That means that at the time I act I am never free. Indeed, if I assumed my entire existence was independent of any external cause (e.g., God), so that the determining grounds of my causality and even of my whole existence were not outside me, this would not in the least convert that natural necessity into freedom. For at every point of time I still stand under the necessity of being determined to act by what is not in my power, and the *a parte priori* infinite series of events which I can continue only by an already predetermined order would never commence of itself. It would be a continuous natural chain, and thus my causality would never be freedom.

Therefore, if one attributes freedom to a being whose existence is determined in time, it cannot be excepted from the law of natural necessity of all events in its existence, including also its actions. Making such an exception would be equivalent to delivering this being to blind chance. Since this law inevitably concerns all causality of things so far as their existence is determinable in time, freedom would have to be rejected as a void and impossible concept if this were the way in which we thought of the existence of these things as they are in themselves. Consequently, if we wish still to save it, no other course remains than to ascribe the existence of a thing so far as it is determinable in time, and accordingly its causality under the law of natural necessity, merely to appearance, and to attribute freedom to the same being as a thing-in-itself. This is absolutely unavoidable if one wishes to maintain both these mutually incompatible concepts; but in applying them, when one wishes to explain them as united in one and the same action and thus explain this union itself, great difficulties turn up, which seem to make such a unification unfeasable.

Suppose I say of a man who has committed a theft that this act, by the natural law of causality, is a necessary result of the determining grounds existing in the preceding time and that it was therefore impossible that it could have not been done. How then can judgment according to the moral law make any change in it? And how can it be supposed that it still could have been left undone because the law says that it should have been left undone? That is, how can he be called free at this point of time with reference to this action, when in this moment and in this action he stands under inexorable natural necessity? It is a wretched subterfuge to seek an escape in the supposition that the *kind* of determining grounds of his causality according to natural law agrees with a comparative concept of freedom. According to this concept, what is sometimes called "free effect" is that of which the determining natural cause is internal to the acting thing. For example, that which a projectile performs when it is in free motion is called by the name "freedom" because it is not pushed by anything external while it is in flight. Or, another example: we call the motion of a clock "free movement" because it moves the hands itself, which need not be pushed by an external force. So one might call the actions of man "free" because they are actions caused by ideas we have produced by our own powers, whereby desires are evoked on occasion of circumstances and thus because they are actions brought about at our own pleasure; in this sense they are called free even though they are necessary because their determining grounds have preceded them in time. With this manner of argument many allow themselves to be put off and believe that with a little quibbling they have found the solution to the difficult problem which centuries have sought in vain and which could hardly be expected to be found so completely on the surface. In the question of freedom which lies at the foundation of all moral laws and accountability to them, it is really not at all a question of whether the causality determined by a natural law is necessary through determining grounds lying within or without the subject, or whether, if they lie within him, they are in instinct or in grounds of determination thought by reason. If these determining conceptions themselves have the ground of their existence in time and, more particularly, in the antecedent state and these again in a preceding state, and so on (as these men themselves admit); and if they are without exception internal; and if they do not have mechanical causality but a psychological causality through conceptions instead of through bodily movements: they are nonetheless determining grounds of the causality of a being so far as its existence is determinable in time. As such, this being is under necessitating conditions of past time which are no longer in his power when he acts. Thus these conceptions do indeed imply psychological freedom (if one wishes to use this word for a merely internal concatenation of ideas of the mind), but nonetheless they also imply natural necessity, leaving no room for transcendental freedom which must be thought of as independence from everything empirical and hence from nature generally, whether regarded as an object of the inner sense merely in time or also as an object of the outer sense in both space and time. Without transcendental freedom, which is its proper meaning, and which is alone a priori practical, no moral law and no accountability to it are possible. For this reason, all necessity of events in time according to natural law can be called the "mechanism of nature," even though it is not supposed that things which are subject to it must really be material machines. Here reference is made only to the necessity of the connection of events in a temporal series as they develop according to natural law, whether the subject in which this evolution occurs be called *automaton materiale* when the machinery is impelled by matter, or, with Leibniz, *automaton spirituale* when it is impelled by ideas. And if the freedom of our will were nothing else than the latter, i.e., psychological and comparative and not at the same time also transcendental or absolute, it would in essence be no better than the freedom of a turnspit, which when once wound up also carries out its motions of itself.

Now in order to remove the apparent contradiction between the mechanism of nature and freedom in the case under discussion, we must remember what was said in the *Critique of Pure Reason* or what it implies, viz., that natural necessity, which cannot coexist with the freedom of the subject, attaches merely to the determinations of a thing which stands under the conditions of time, and consequently applies only to the acting subject as appearance. As a consequence, [it pertains to the subject] only so far as the determining grounds of any action of the subject lie in what belongs to the past and is no longer in his power; in this must be counted also his already performed acts and his character as a phenomenon as this is determined for him in his own eyes by those acts. But the same subject, which, on the other hand, is conscious also of his own existence as a thing-in-itself, also views his existence so far as it does not stand under temporal conditions, and to himself as determinable only by laws which he gives to himself through reason. In this existence nothing is antecedent to the determination of his will; every action and, in general, every changing determination of his existence according to the inner sense, even the entire history of his existence as a sensuous being, is seen in the consciousness of his intelligible existence as only a consequence, not as a determining ground of his causality as a noumenon. From this point of view, a rational being can rightly say of any unlawful action which he has done that he could have left it undone, even if as an appearance it was sufficiently determined in the past and thus far was inescapably necessary. For this action and everything in the past which determined it belong to a single phenomenon of his character, which he himself creates, and according to which he imputes to himself as a cause independent of all sensibility the causality of that appearance.

The judicial sentences of that marvelous faculty in us called conscience are in complete agreement with this. A man may dissemble as much as he will in order to paint his unlawful behavior, which he remembers, as an unintentional error, as mere oversight, which can never be entirely avoided, and consequently as something to which he was carried along by the stream of natural necessity, and in this way to make himself out as innocent. But he finds that the advocate who speaks in his behalf cannot silence the accuser in him when he is conscious that at the time when he committed the wrong he was in his senses, i.e., he was in possession of his freedom. Nevertheless, he explains his misdeed by some bad habits which he has grown into by gradual neglect of attention to such a degree that he can regard the act as a natural consequence of them, but this cannot protect him from the blame and the reproach he casts upon himself. On this is based the repentance for an action long past every time he remembers it. It is a painful feeling caused by the moral disposition, empty in a practical sense since it cannot undo that which has been done. Priestley, as a true and consistent fatalist, even declares it to be absurd, and he deserves more applause for his candor than those who, asserting the mechanism of the will in acts but affirming its freedom in words, wish to have it thought that they include it in their syncretistic system, though they cannot render the possibility of such an imputation comprehensible. But as a pain, repentance is entirely legitimate, because reason, when it is a question of the law of our intelligible existence (the moral law), acknowledges no temporal distinctions and only asks whether the event belongs to me as my act, and then morally connects with it the same feeling, whether the event occurs now or is long since past. For the sensuous life is but a single phenomenon in the view of an intelligible consciousness of its existence (the consciousness of freedom), and this phenomenon, so far as it contains merely manifestations of the disposition which is of concern to the moral law (i.e., appearances of character), must be judged not according to natural necessity which pertains to it as appearance but according to the absolute spontaneity of freedom.

It may be admitted that if it were possible for us to have so deep an insight into a man's character as shown both in inner and in outer actions, that every, even the least, incentive to these actions and all external occasions which affect them were so known to us that his future conduct could be predicted with as great a certainty as the occurrence of a solar or lunar eclipse, we could nevertheless still assert that the man is free. For if we were capable of another view (which, however, is certainly not given us, but in place of which we have only the concept of reason), i.e., if we were capable of an intellectual intuition of the same subject, we would then discover that the entire chain of appearances, with reference to that which concerns only the moral law, depends upon the spontaneity of the subject as a thing-in-itself, for the determination of which no physical explanation can be given. Lacking this intuition, the moral law assures us of this difference between the relation of our actions as appearances to our sensuous being and the relation by which this sensuous being is itself connected to the intelligible substrate in us.

From this point of view, which is natural although inexplicable to our reason, judgments may be justified which, though made in all conscientiousness, seem at first glance to conflict with equity. There are cases in which men, even with an education which was profitable to others, have shown from childhood such depravity, which continues to increase during their adult years, that they are held to be born villains and incapable of any improvement of character; yet they are judged by their acts, they are reproached as guilty of their crimes; and, indeed, they themselves find these reproaches as well grounded as if they, regardless of the hopeless quality ascribed to their minds, were just as responsible as any other men. This could not happen if we did not suppose that whatever arises from man's choice (as every intentional act undoubtedly does) has a free causality as its ground, which from early youth expresses its character in its appearances (its actions). These actions, by the uniformity of conduct, exhibit a natural connection. But the latter does not render the vicious quality of the will necessary, for this quality is rather the consequence of the freely assumed evil and unchangeable principles. This fact makes it only the more objectionable and culpable.

But there is still another difficulty in the way of freedom so far as it is to be united with the mechanism of nature in a being belonging to the world of sense. Even after all the foregoing has been agreed to, it is a difficulty which threatens freedom with its complete downfall. But in this danger, one circumstance gives hope for a successful outcome to the asseveration of freedom, namely, that the same difficulty presses even stronger (and in fact, as we shall soon see, only) on the system in which the existence which is determinable in time and space is held to be the existence of things-in-themselves. Therefore, this difficulty does not compel us to give up our principal presupposition of the ideality of time as a mere form of sensuous intuition and thus as only a mode of representation proper to the subject as belonging to the world of sense. It only demands, on the contrary, that this presupposition be united with the idea of freedom.

[This difficulty[35] is as follows.] If it be conceded that the intelligible subject can be free with reference to a given action, even though as a subject belonging to the world of sense it is mechanically determined in this action, it nevertheless appears that as soon as it is assumed that God as the Universal Primordial Being is the cause also of the existence of substance (and this assumption can never be given up without surrendering the concept of God as the Being of all Beings and thus His all-sufficiency, on which everything in theology is based), one must also grant that the actions of a man have their determining ground in something completely beyond his own power, i.e., in the causality of a Highest Being which is different from him and upon which his existence and the entire determination of his causality absolutely depend. Actually, if the actions of man, as they pertain to his determinations in time, were not merely properties of his being as appearance but also of his being as a thing in himself, freedom could not be saved. Man would be a marionette or an automaton like Vaucanson's,[36] fabricated and wound up by the Supreme Artist; self-consciousness would indeed make him a thinking automaton, but the consciousness of his spontaneity, if this is held to be freedom, would be a mere illusion. It would deserve to be called so only comparatively, as the proximate determining causes of its movement and a long series of their determining causes would be internal, while the ultimate and highest would lie wholly in a foreign hand. Therefore, I cannot conceive how those who persist in seeing space and time as attributes belonging to the existence of things-in-themselves can avoid fatalism of actions. Or, when they (like the otherwise so acute Mendelssohn)[37] concede both as necessarily

---

35. [The difficulty referred to, of course, is implicit in Leibniz's monadology. Leibniz's metaphor is that of a clock instead of a marionette.]
36. [A. von Vaucanson demonstrated automatic figures in Paris in 1738.]
37. [*Morgenstunden.*]

belonging to the existence of finite and derived beings but not that of the infinite First Being, I do not see how they justify themselves or where they get the right to make such a distinction. I do not even see how they can evade the contradiction into which they fall when they regard existence in time as an attribute necessary to finite things-in-themselves. This contradiction is as follows. God is the cause of this existence, and yet He cannot be the cause of time (or space) itself (because, as the necessary condition a priori for the existence of things, it must be presupposed [by this hypothesis]); consequently, God's causation of the existence of these things would have to be conditioned—in fact, temporally conditioned. Thereby everything which contradicts the concept of His infinity and independence would be unavoidably brought in.

It is very easy for us, on the other hand, to differentiate between the attribute of divine existence as independent of all temporal conditions and that of a being in the world of sense, as this distinction is precisely that between the existence of a thing-in-itself and that of a thing in appearance. Therefore, if the ideality of time and space is not assumed, only Spinozism remains, which holds space and time to be essential attributes to the First Being itself and the things dependent upon it (ourselves included) not to be substances but merely accidents inhering in it. For if these things exist only as its effects in time, which would then be the condition of their existence itself, the actions of these beings would have to be merely *its* actions, which it performs anywhere and at any time. Spinozism, therefore, in spite of the absurdity of its basic idea, argues far more cogently than the creation theory can when it sees beings which have been presumed to be substances existing in themselves in time as effects of a supreme cause, yet not as belonging to it and to its action but as substances in themselves.

The difficulty mentioned above is resolved briefly and clearly as follows. If existence in time is merely a sensuous mode of presentation belonging to thinking beings in the world, and consequently does not concern the things-in-themselves, the creation of these beings is a creation of the things-in-themselves, because the concept of creation does not belong to the sensuous mode of conceiving of existence or to causality but can be referred only to noumena. Consequently, if I say of beings in the world of sense that they are created, I regard them only as noumena. Just as it would therefore be contradictory to say God is the creator of appearances, it is also a contradiction to say that He, as the Creator, is the cause of actions in the world of sense, as these are appearances; yet at the same time He is the cause of the existence of the acting beings (as noumena). Now, assuming existence in time to hold only of appearances and not of things-in-themselves, if it is possible to affirm freedom without detriment to the natural mechanism of actions as appearances, then the circumstance that the acting beings are creatures cannot make the least difference to the argument, because creation concerns their intelligible but not their sensuous existence, and therefore creation cannot be regarded as the determining ground of appearances. It would turn out very differently if the beings in the world existed as things-in-themselves in time, since the Creator of substance would then be also the author of the entire mechanism of this substance.

Such is the importance of the separation of time (as well as space) from the existence of things-in-themselves, as this was effected in the critique of the pure speculative reason.

The solution which is given here to the difficulty will be said to have so much difficulty in it, however, that it is hardly susceptible of a lucid presentation. But is any other solution, which anyone has attempted or may attempt, any easier or more comprehensible? Rather might we say that the dogmatic teachers of metaphysics have shown more shrewdness than frankness in removing this difficult point as far as possible from view in the hope that, if they did not speak of it, no one would be likely to think of it. But, if a science is to be advanced, all difficulties must be exposed, and those which lie hidden in its way must even be sought out, for each of them calls forth a remedy without which means cannot be found to advance the science, whether in scope or in accuracy. In this way even obstacles will be means for furthering the thoroughness of the science. But, if, on the contrary, difficulties are intentionally hidden or merely removed with palliatives, sooner or later they break out in incurable evils, which bring the science to ruin in complete skepticism.

Since it is, properly speaking, only the concept of freedom, among all the ideas of pure speculative reason, which brings [knowledge] such a great extension in the field of the supersensuous, though it is only practical knowledge which is enlarged, I ask myself: Why does it alone have such great fruitful-ness, the others merely indicating the empty place for merely possible beings of the understanding without being able in any way to define the concept of them? I soon see that, since I cannot think without a category, I must first seek out the category in reason's idea of freedom. This is the category of causality. I also see that, although no corresponding intuition can be made the basis of reason's concept of freedom, inasmuch as it is a transcendent concept, a sensuous intuition must previously be given to the understanding's concept of causality (for the synthesis of which the reason's concept of freedom requires the unconditioned), and only by this intuition is it assured objective reality.

Now all categories are divided in two classes: the mathematical, which deal with the unity of synthesis in the conception of objects, and the dynamical, which concern the synthetic unity in the conception of the existence of objects. The former (the categories of quantity and quality) always contain a synthesis of the homogeneous, in which the unconditioned for the sensuously conditioned cannot be found, since the unconditioned would itself be in space and time and thus would itself still be conditioned. Therefore, in the Dialectic of pure theoretical reason, the contrasted ways of finding the unconditioned and the totality of conditions for it were both false. The categories of the second class (those of causality and of the necessity of a thing) did in no way require this homogeneity of the conditioned and the condition in synthesis, because here it was not a question of how intuition is synthesized from a manifold within it but only of how existence of the conditioned object corresponding to the intuition is added to the existence of the condition (added in the understanding as connected with it). In these categories it was permitted to add to the completely conditioned in the world of sense (to the causality and the contingent existence of things) the unconditioned in the intelligible world and to make the synthesis transcendent; this was permissible, even though the unconditioned was not further defined. Therefore in the Dialectic of pure speculative reason it was found that the two apparently incompatible modes of finding the unconditioned for the conditioned (e.g., in the synthesis of causality, to find a causality which has no sensuous condition for the conditioned in the series of causes and effects in the world of sense) do not in fact contradict each other and that the same act, which as belonging to the world of sense is always sensuously conditioned, i.e., mechanically necessary, can at the same time, as belonging to the causality of the acting being in so far as it belongs to the intelligible world, have a sensuously unconditioned causality as its foundation. That is, it can be thought of as free.

Then it was only a question of whether this "can be" could be changed to an "is"; it was a question of whether in an actual case and, as it were, by a fact, one could prove that certain actions presupposed such an intellectual, sensuously unconditioned, causality, regardless of whether they are actual or only commanded, i.e., objectively and practically necessary. In actions actually given in experience as events in the world of sense we could not hope to meet with this connection, since causality through freedom must always be sought outside the world of sense in the intelligible. But things which are not sensuous are not given to our perception and observation. Thus nothing remained but that perhaps an incontrovertible, objective principle of causality could be found which excluded every sensuous condition from its determination, i.e., a principle in which reason does not call upon anything else as the determining ground of the causality but rather by that principle itself contains it, thus being, as pure reason, practical of itself. This principle, however, needs no search and no invention, having long been in the reason of all men and embodied in their being. It is the principle of morality. Therefore, that unconditioned causality and its faculty, freedom, and therewith a being (myself) which belongs to the world of sense and at the same time to the intelligible world, are no longer thought merely indeterminately and problematically (which even speculative reason could detect as possible) but with respect to the law of its causality are determinately and assertorically known; thus is the reality of the intelligible world definitely established from a practical point of view, and this determinateness, which would be transcendent (extravagant) for theoretical purposes, is for practical purposes immanent.

We could not, however, take this step with the second dynamical idea, i.e., that of a necessary being. Without the mediation of the first dynamical idea we could not rise to it from the world of sense. For if we wish to try it, we should have to make the venture of leaving everything which is given to us and to plunge into that of which nothing is given to us by which we could mediate the connection of such an intelligible being with the world of sense (because the necessary being would be known as given *outside* us). Nevertheless, with respect to our own subject so far as it knows itself, on the one hand, as an intelligible being determined because of its freedom by the moral law, and, on the other, as acting according to this determination in the world of sense, it is obvious that all this is quite possible. Only the concept of freedom enables us to find the unconditioned for the conditioned and the intelligible for the sensuous without going outside ourselves. For it is our reason itself which through the supreme and unconditioned practical law recognizes itself, and the being which knows this law (our own person) as belonging to the pure world of the understanding and indeed defines the way in which it can be active as such a being. Thus it can be seen why in the entire faculty of reason only the practical can lift us above the world of sense and furnish cognitions of a supersensuous order and connection, though these cognitions can be extended only as far as is needed for pure practical purposes.

Here I wish to call attention, if I may, to one thing, namely, that every step which one takes with pure reason, even in the practical field where one does not take subtle speculation into account, so neatly and naturally dovetails with all parts of the critique of theoretical reason that it is as if each step had been carefully thought out merely to establish this confirmation. This agreement was by no means sought after. It is rather (as one can convince himself if he only follows moral considerations back to their principles) a self-evident agreement between the most important propositions of practical reason with the often seemingly too subtle and unnecessary remarks of the critique of speculative reason—an accord that occasions surprise and astonishment, strengthening the maxim, already known and recommended by others, that in every scientific investigation we should unswervingly pursue our course with all possible accuracy and candor without attending to any extraneous difficulties it might involve, carrying out as far as we can our investigation by itself honestly and completely. Frequent observation has convinced me that once one has seen through such business, that which, when half-finished, appeared very dubious in view of extraneous theories is at last found to be in an unexpected way completely harmonious with that which had been discovered separately without the least regard for them, provided this dubiousness is left out of sight for a while and only the business at hand is attended to until it is finished. Writers would save themselves many errors and much labor lost (because spent on delusions) if they could only resolve to go to work with a little more unaffectedness.

BOOK II
DIALECTIC OF PURE PRACTICAL REASON

Chapter I
A Dialectic of Pure Practical Reason in General

IN BOTH its speculative and its practical employment, pure reason always has its dialectic, for it demands the absolute totality of conditions for a given conditioned thing, and this can be attained only in things-in-themselves. Since, however, all concepts of things must be referred to intuitions which for us human beings can never be other than sensuous, and which thus let the objects be known not as things-in-themselves but only as appearances, which are a series of the conditioned and their conditions in which the unconditioned can never be found, it follows that an unavoidable illusion arises from the application of the rational idea of the totality of conditions (and thus of the unconditioned) to appearances as if they were things-in-themselves (for this is the way in which they are considered in default of a warning critique). But the illusion would never be noticed as deceptive if it were not betrayed by a conflict of reason with itself in applying to appearances its principle of presupposing the unconditioned for every conditioned thing. Reason is thus forced to investigate this illusion, to find out how it arises and how it can be removed. This can be done only through a complete critical examination of the entire pure faculty of reason; the antinomy of pure reason, which becomes obvious in its dialectic, is, in fact, the most fortunate perplexity in which human reason could ever have become involved, since it finally compels us to seek the key to escape from this labyrinth. This key, when once found, discovers that which we did not seek and yet need, namely, a view into a higher immutable order of things in which we already are, and in which, to continue our existence in accordance with the supreme decree of reason, we may now, after this discovery, be directed by definite precepts.

How to solve that natural dialectic and to avoid the error arising from an otherwise natural illusion in the speculative use of pure reason can be found in detail in the critical examination of that faculty. But reason in its practical use is not a bit better off. As pure practical reason it likewise seeks the unconditioned for the practically conditioned (which rests on inclinations and natural need); and this unconditioned is not only sought as the determining ground of the will but, even when this is given (in the moral law), is also sought as the unconditioned totality of the object of the pure practical reason, under the name of the *highest good.*

To define this idea practically, i.e., sufficiently for the maxims of our rational conduct, is [the task of] the doctrine of wisdom, which, as a science, is philosophy in the sense in which the ancients understood this word, for whom it meant instruction in the concept wherein the highest good was to be placed and in the conduct by which it was to be obtained. It would be well if we left this word with its old meaning, as a doctrine of the highest good so far as reason strives to bring it to [the level of] science. For, on the one hand, the qualifying condition would be suitable to the Greek expression (which means love of *wisdom*), and yet entirely adequate to comprehend under the name of philosophy the love of *science,* and thus of all speculative rational knowledge, so far as it is serviceable to reason [in defining] that concept and the practical determining ground; and [it could do all this] without letting us lose sight of the chief goal for the sake of which alone it is called a doctrine of wisdom. On the other hand, it would also do no harm to deter the self-conceit of whoever presumed to the title of philosopher, if one merely held before him the definition as the standard for his self-estimation, as this would lower his pretensions very much. For to be a teacher of wisdom would mean something more than to be a scholar, who has not yet progressed far enough to conduct himself, and even less anyone else, to so high an end; it would mean to be a master of the knowledge of wisdom, which says more than a modest man would himself presume to claim. Philosophy as well as wisdom itself would always remain an ideal, which objectively is represented completely only in reason and which subjectively is only the goal for the person's unceasing endeavors. No one would be justified in professing to be in possession of it, under the assumed name of philosopher, unless he could show its infallible effect (in self-mastery and the unquestioned interest which he pre-eminently takes in the general good) on his own person as an example. This the ancients required as a condition for deserving that honorable title.

We have to make only one more preliminary remark with respect to the dialectic of pure practical reason in its definition of the concept of the highest good; and, if the solution of this dialectic is attained, we may expect a result just as useful as that accruing from the dialectic of theoretical reason, since the self-contradictions of pure practical reason, if properly exposed and not concealed, impel us to an exhaustive critical examination of its capacities.

The moral law is the sole determining ground of the pure will. Since it is merely formal, requiring only that the form of the maxim be universally legislative, as a determining ground it abstracts from all material and thus from every object of volition. Consequently, though the highest good may be the entire *object* of a pure practical reason, i.e., of a pure will, it is still not to be taken as the *determining ground* of the pure will; the moral law alone must be seen as the ground for making the highest good and its realization or promotion the object of the pure will. This reminder is of importance in a case as delicate as that of the definition of moral principles, where even the slightest mistake perverts the character. For one sees from the Analytic that when we assume any object, under the name of good, as the determining ground of the will prior to the moral law, and then derive the supreme practical principle from it, this always produces heteronomy and rules out the moral principle.

But it is self-evident not merely that, if the moral law is included as the supreme condition in the concept of the highest good, the highest good is then the object, but also that the concept of it and the idea of its existence as possible through our practical reason are likewise the determining ground of the pure will. This is because the moral law, included in this concept, and no other object, determines the will as required by the principle of autonomy. This order of concepts of the determination of the will should not be lost sight of, for otherwise we misunderstand ourselves and believe we are contradicting ourselves when everything really stands in the most perfect harmony.

Chapter II

The Dialectic of Pure Reason in Defining the Concept of the Highest Good

THE concept of the "highest" contains an ambiguity which, if not attended to, can occasion unnecessary disputes. The "highest" can mean the "supreme" (*supremum*) or the "perfect" (*consummatum*). The former is the unconditional condition, i.e., the condition which is subordinate to no other (*origina-*

rium); the latter is that whole which is no part of a yet larger whole of the same kind (*perfectissimum*). That virtue (as the worthiness to be happy) is the supreme condition of whatever appears to us to be desirable and thus of all our pursuit of happiness and consequently that it is the supreme good have been proven in the Analytic. But these truths do not imply that it is the entire and perfect good as the object of the faculty of desire of rational finite beings. In order to be this, happiness is also required, and indeed not merely in the partial eyes of a person who makes himself his end but even in the judgment of an impartial reason, which in general regards persons in the world as ends-in-themselves. For to be in need of happiness and also worthy of it and yet not to partake of it could not be in accordance with the complete volition of an omnipotent rational being, if we assume such only for the sake of the argument. Inasmuch as virtue and happiness together constitute the possession of the highest good for one person, and happiness in exact proportion to morality (as the worth of a person and his worthiness to be happy) constitutes that of a possible world, the highest good means the whole, the perfect good, wherein virtue is always the supreme good, being the condition having no condition superior to it, while happiness, though something always pleasant to him who possesses it, is not of itself absolutely good in every respect but always presupposes conduct in accordance with the moral law as its condition.

Two terms necessarily combined in one concept must be related as ground and consequence, and this unity must be regarded either as analytic (logical connection) according to the law of identity or as synthetic (real connection) according to the law of causality. The connection of virtue with happiness can, therefore, be understood in one of two ways. Either the endeavor to be virtuous and the rational pursuit of happiness are not two different actions but absolutely identical; in this case no maxim is needed as a ground of the former other than that needed for the latter. Or that connection is predicated upon virtue producing happiness as something different from the consciousness of virtue, as a cause produces an effect.

Of the ancient Greek schools, there were only two opposing each other on this issue. But so far as the definition of the concept of the highest good is concerned, they followed one and the same method, since neither held virtue and happiness to be two different elements of the highest good, both seeking the unity of principle under the rule of identity. But again they differed in that each selected a different principle as the fundamental one. The Epicurean said: To be conscious of one's maxims as leading to happiness is virtue. The Stoic said: To be conscious of one's virtue is happiness. To the former, prudence amounted to morality; to the latter, who chose a higher term for virtue, morality alone was true wisdom.

We cannot but regret that these men (whom we must nevertheless admire since they so early attempted all the conceivable ways of extending philosophy's conquest) unfortunately applied their acuteness to digging up an identity between such extremely heterogeneous concepts as those of happiness and virtue. But it fit the dialectical spirit of their times (and still sometimes leads subtle minds astray) to overcome essential differences in principle, which can never be united, by seeking to translate them into a conflict of words and thus to devise an apparent unity of concepts with other terms. This commonly occurs in cases where the unification of heterogeneous principles lies either so high or so deep, or would require so thorough a revolution of doctrines otherwise accepted in a philosophical system, that men fear to go deeply into the real difference and prefer to treat it as a mere diversity in formulas.

While both schools tried to ferret out the sameness of the practical principles of virtue and happiness, they were not for that reason agreed as to the way in which to force out this identity; rather they became widely separated from each other, as the one sought its principle on the sensuous[38] and the other on the logical side, one putting it in the consciousness of sensuous need and the other in the independence of practical reason from all sensuous grounds of determination. The concept of virtue, according to the Epicurean, lay already in the maxim of furthering one's own happiness; the feeling of happiness, for the Stoic, was, on the contrary, already contained in the consciousness of his virtue. Whatever is contained in another concept, however, is the same as one of its parts but not the same as the whole, and two wholes can, moreover, be specifically different from each other though they consist of the same content, that is, if their parts are combined in different ways. The Stoic asserted virtue to be the entire highest good, and happiness was only the consciousness of this possession as belonging to the state of the subject. The Epicurean stated that happiness was the entire

38. [*Aesthetischen.*]

highest good and that virtue was only the form of the maxim by which it could be procured through the rational use of means to it.

But it is clear from the Analytic that the maxims of virtue and those of one's own happiness are wholly heterogeneous and far removed from being at one in respect to their supreme practical principle; and even though they belong to a highest good, which they jointly make possible, they strongly limit and check each other in the same subject. Thus the question, "How is the highest good practically possible?" remains an unsolved problem in spite of all previous attempts at conciliation. That which makes it so difficult a problem is shown in the Analytic: happiness and morality are two specifically different elements of the highest good and therefore their combination cannot be known analytically (as if a person who sought his happiness found himself virtuous merely through solving his problem, or one who followed virtue found himself *ipso facto* happy in the consciousness of this conduct). The highest good is a *synthesis* of concepts. Since, however, this combination is known as a priori and thus as practically necessary, and not derivable from experience, and since the possibility of the highest good therefore rests on no empirical principles, the deduction of this concept must be transcendental. It is a priori (morally) necessary to bring forth the highest good through the freedom of the will; the condition of its possibility, therefore, must rest solely on a priori grounds of knowledge.

I. THE ANTINOMY OF PRACTICAL REASON

In the highest good which is practical for us, i.e., one which is to be made real by our will, virtue and happiness are thought of as necessarily combined, so that the one cannot be assumed by a practical reason without the other belonging to it. Now this combination is, like every other, either analytic or synthetic. Since it cannot be analytic, as has been shown, it must be thought synthetically and, more particularly, as the connection of cause and effect, for it concerns a practical good, i.e., one that is possible through action. Therefore, the desire for happiness must be the motive to maxims of virtue, or the maxim of virtue must be the efficient cause of happiness. The first is absolutely impossible, because (as has been proved in the Analytic) maxims which put the determining ground of the will in the desire for one's happiness are not moral at all and can serve as ground for no virtue. The second is, however, also impossible, since every practical connection of causes and effects in the world, as a result of the determination of the will, is dependent not on the moral intentions of the will but on knowledge of natural laws and the physical capacity of using them to its purposes; consequently, no necessary connection, sufficient to the highest good, between happiness and virtue in the world can be expected from the most meticulous observance of the moral law. Since, now, the furthering of the highest good, which contains this connection in its concept, is an a priori necessary object of our will and is inseparably related to the moral law, the impossibility of the former must prove the falsity of the latter also. If, therefore, the highest good is impossible according to practical rules, then the moral law which commands that it be furthered must be fantastic, directed to empty imaginary ends, and consequently inherently false.

II. CRITICAL RESOLUTION OF THE ANTINOMY OF PRACTICAL REASON

In the antinomy of pure speculative reason there is a similar conflict between natural necessity and freedom in the causality of events in the world. It was resolved by showing that there is no true conflict if the events and even the world in which they occur are regarded as only appearances (as they should be). This is because one and the same acting being as appearance (even to his own inner sense) has a causality in the sensuous world always in accord with the mechanism of nature; while with respect to the same event, so far as the acting person regards himself as noumenon (as pure intelligence, existing without temporal determination), he can contain a determining ground of that causality according to natural laws, and this determining ground of natural causality itself is free from every natural law.

It is just the same with the present antinomy of pure practical reason. The first of the two propositions, viz., that striving for happiness produces a ground for the virtuous disposition, is absolutely false; the second, viz., that a virtuous disposition necessarily produces happiness, is not, however, *absolutely* false but false only in so far as this disposition is regarded as the form of causality in the world of sense. Consequently, it is false only if I assume existence in this world to be the only mode of existence of a rational being, and therefore it is only *conditionally* false. But not only since I am justified in thinking of my existence as that of a noumenon in an intelligible world but also since I have in the moral law a pure intellectual determining ground of my causality (in the sensuous world), it is not impossible that the morality of intention should have a necessary relation as cause to happiness as an effect in the sensuous world; but this relation is indirect, mediated by an intelligible Author of nature. This combination, however, can occur only contingently in a system of nature which is merely the object of the senses and as such is not sufficient to the highest good.

Thus, in spite of this apparent conflict of a practical reason with itself, the highest good is the necessary highest end of a morally determined will and a true object thereof; for it is practically possible, and the maxims of this will, which refer to it by their material, have objective reality. At first this objective reality was called in question by the antinomy in the combination of morality with happiness according to a general law; but this difficulty arose only from a misconception, because the relationship between appearances was held to be a relationship of things-in-themselves to these appearances.

When we see ourselves obliged to seek at such distance—namely, in the context of an intelligible world—the possibility of the highest good which reason presents to all rational beings as the goal of all their moral wishes, it must appear strange that philosophers of both ancient and modern times have been able to find happiness in very just proportion to virtue in *this* life (in the world of sense) or at least have been able to convince themselves of it. For Epicurus as well as the Stoics extolled happiness springing from the consciousness of virtuous living above everything else, and the former was not so base in his practical precepts as one might conclude from the principles of his theory, which he used for explanation and not for action, or from the principles as interpreted by many who were mislead by his use of the term "pleasure" for "contentment." He, on the contrary, reckoned the most disinterested practice of the good among the ways of experiencing the most intimate joy; and moderation and control of the inclinations, as these might have been required by the strictest moral philosopher, belonged in his scheme for enjoyment, whereby he understood constant cheerfulness. He diverged from the Stoics chiefly by placing the *motive* in this enjoyment, which the Stoics correctly refused to do. For the virtuous Epicurus, like even now many morally well-meaning persons who do not give deep enough consideration to their principles, fell into the error of presupposing the virtuous disposition to be already in the persons to whom he wished to provide incentives to virtue. It is true that the upright man cannot be happy if he is not already conscious of his righteousness, since with such a character the moral self-condemnation to which his own way of thinking would force him in case of any transgression would rob him of all enjoyment of the pleasantness which his condition might otherwise entail. But the only question is, "How is such a character and turn of mind in estimating the worth of his existence even possible?" For prior to this no feeling for any moral worth can be found in a subject. A man, if he is virtuous, will certainly not enjoy life without being conscious of his righteousness in each action, however favorable fortune may be to him in the physical circumstances of life; but can one make him virtuous before he has so high an estimation of the moral worth of his existence merely by commending to him the contentment of spirit which will arise from the consciousness of righteousness for which he as yet has no sense?[39]

But, on the other hand, there is always here an occasion for a subreption (*vitium subreptionis*) and, as it were, for an optical illusion in the self-consciousness of what one does in contradistinction to what one feels, which even the most experienced person cannot entirely avoid. The moral disposition is necessarily connected with a consciousness of the determination of the will directly by a law. Now the consciousness of a determination of the faculty of desire is always a ground for satisfaction in the resulting action; but this pleasure, this satisfaction with one's self, is not the determining ground of the action; on the contrary, the determination of the will directly by reason alone is the ground of the feeling of pleasure, and this remains a pure practical determination of the faculty of desire, not a sensuous one. Since this determination produces the same inward effect, i.e., an impulse to activity, as does a feeling of agreeableness which is expected from the desired action, we see that what we ourselves do may

---

39. [Hutcheson himself anticipates Kant in this argument. To the theory that virtue is pursued because of concomitant pleasure, he says: "To which we may answer, first by observing, that this plainly supposes a sense of virtue antecedent to ideas of advantage, upon which this advantage is founded; and that from the very frame of our nature we are determined to perceive pleasure in the practice of virtue, and to approve it when practiced by ourselves or others" (*Concerning Goods and Evils*, sec. ii, in Selby Bigge, *British Moralists*, I, 92 [spelling and punctuation modernized]).]

easily be looked upon as something which we merely passively feel, the moral motive being held to be a sensuous impulse, as it always occurs in so-called illusions of the senses (and here we have such an illusion of the inner sense). It is a very sublime[40] thing in human nature to be determined to actions directly by a pure law of reason, and even the illusion wherein the subjective element of this intellectual determinability of the will is held to be sensuous and an effect of a particular sensuous feeling (an "intellectual feeling" being self-contradictory) partakes of this sublimity. It is of great importance to point out this quality of our personality and to cultivate so far as possible the effect of reason on this feeling. But we must, nevertheless, be on guard against degrading and deforming the real and authentic incentive, the law itself, by awarding spurious praise to the moral ground of determination as incentive as though it were based on feelings of particular joys, thus setting it, as it were, against a false foil; for these joys are only its consequences. Respect, in contrast to the enjoyment or gratification of happiness, is something for which there can be no feeling basic and prior to reason, for such a feeling would always be sensuous and pathological. Respect as the consciousness of the direct constraint of the will through law is hardly analogous to the feeling of pleasure, although in relation to the faculty of desire it produces exactly the same effect, but from different sources. But only through this mode of conception can one achieve what is sought, namely, that actions be done not merely according to duty (as a consequence of pleasant feelings) but from duty, which must be the true goal of all moral cultivation.

Do we not have a word to denote a satisfaction with existence, an analogue of happiness which necessarily accompanies the consciousness of virtue, and which does not indicate a gratification, as "happiness" does? We do, and this word is "self-contentment," which in its real meaning refers only to negative satisfaction with existence in which one is conscious of needing nothing. Freedom and the consciousness of freedom, as a capacity for following the moral law with an unyielding disposition, is inde-

---

40. [Cf. *Observations on the Feeling of the Sublime and the Beautiful, passim,* but especially the Cassirer ed., II, 255: "Accordingly, true virtue can be grafted only on principles which are nobler and more sublime the more universal they are. These principles are not speculative rules but the consciousness of a feeling that lives in every human breast and that extends far wider than if based on particular motives of sympathy and amiability."]

pendence from inclinations, at least as motives determining (though not as affecting) our desiring; and, so far as I am conscious of freedom in obeying my moral maxims, it is the exclusive source of an unchanging contentment necessarily connected with it and resting on no particular feeling. This may be called intellectual contentment. Sensuous contentment (improperly so called) which rests on the satisfaction of inclinations, however refined they may be, can never be adequate to that which is conceived under contentment. For inclinations vary; they grow with the indulgence we allow them, and they leave behind a greater void than the one we intended to fill. They are consequently always burdensome to a rational being, and, though he cannot put them aside, they nevertheless elicit from him the wish to be free of them. Even an inclination to do that which accords with duty (e.g., to do beneficent acts) can at most facilitate the effectiveness of moral maxims but not produce any such maxims. For in such maxims, everything must be directed to the thought of the law as the determining ground if the action is not to contain mere legality but also morality. Inclination, be it good-natured or otherwise, is blind and slavish; reason, when it is a question of morality, must not play the part of mere guardian of the inclinations, but, without regard to them, as pure practical reason it must care for its own interest to the exclusion of all else. Even the feeling of sympathy and of warmhearted fellow-feeling, when preceding the consideration of what is duty and serving as a determining ground, is burdensome even to right-thinking persons, confusing their considered maxims and creating the wish to be free from them and subject only to law-giving reason.

Thus we can understand how the consciousness of this capacity of a pure practical reason through a deed (virtue) can produce a consciousness of mastery over inclinations and thus of independence from them and from the discontentment which always accompanies them, bringing forth a negative satisfaction with one's condition, i.e., contentment, whose source is contentment with one's own person. Freedom itself thus becomes in this indirect way capable of an enjoyment. This cannot be called happiness, since it does not depend upon a positive participation of feeling; nor can it be called bliss, because it does not include complete independence from inclinations and desires. It does nevertheless resemble the latter so far at least as the determination of the will which it involves can be held to be free from their influence, and thus, at least in its origin, it is analogous to the self-sufficiency which can be ascribed only to the Supreme Being.

From this solution of the antinomy of practical pure reason, it follows that in practical principles a natural and necessary connection between the consciousness of morality and the expectation of proportionate happiness as its consequence may be thought at least possible, though it is by no means known or understood. On the other hand, it is seen that principles for the pursuit of happiness cannot possibly produce morality and that therefore the supreme good (as the first condition of the highest good) is morality; and that happiness, though it indeed constitutes the second element of the highest good, does so only as the morally conditioned but necessary consequence of the former. Only with this subordination is the highest good the entire object of pure practical reason, which pure practical reason must necessarily think as possible because reason commands us to contribute everything possible to its realization. But the possibility of such a connection of the conditioned with its condition belongs wholly to the supersensuous relations of things and cannot be given under the laws of the world of sense, even though the practical consequence of this idea, i.e., the actions which are devoted to realizing the highest good, do belong to this world. Therefore, we shall seek to establish the grounds of that possibility primarily with respect to what is immediately in our power, and secondarily in that which is beyond our power but which reason holds out to us as the supplement to our impotence to [realize] the possibility of the highest good, which is necessary according to practical principles.

III. ON THE PRIMACY OF THE PURE PRACTICAL REASON IN ITS ASSOCIATION WITH SPECULATIVE REASON

By primacy between two or more things connected by reason, I understand the prerogative of one by virtue of which it is the prime ground of determination of the combination with all the others. In a narrower practical sense it refers to the prerogative of the interest of one so far as the interest of the others is subordinated to it and it is not itself inferior to any other. To every faculty of the mind an interest can be ascribed, i.e., a principle which contains the condition under which alone its exercise is advanced. Reason, as the faculty of principles, determines the interest of all the powers of the mind and its own. The interest of its speculative use consists in the knowledge of objects up to the highest a priori principles; that of its practical employment lies in the determination of the will with respect to the final and perfect end. That which is needed in general for the possibility of any employment of reason, i.e., that its principles and assertions not contradict one another, is not a part of its interest but is rather the condition of having any reason at all; only its extension, and not the mere agreement with itself, is reckoned as its interest.

If practical reason may not assume and think as given anything further than what speculative reason affords from its own insight, the latter has primacy. But suppose that the former has of itself original a priori principles with which certain theoretical positions are inseparably bound but which are beyond any possible insight of the speculative reason (although not contradictory to it). Then the question is: Which interest is superior? It is not a question of which must yield, for one does not necessarily conflict with the other. It is a question of whether speculative reason, which knows nothing of all that which the practical reason offers for its acceptance, must take up these principles and seek to integrate them, even though they transcend it, with its own concepts as a foreign possession handed over to it; or whether it is justified in stubbornly following its own isolated interest, rejecting, according to the canon of Epicurus, everything as an empty sophism which does not certify its objective reality by manifest examples from experience, doing so however much it is interwoven with the interest of the practical (pure) use of reason and however far removed from contradicting the theoretical, merely because it infringes upon the interest of the speculative reason by removing the bounds which the latter has set itself, opening it to every nonsense and delusion of the imagination.

In fact, so long as practical reason is pathologically conditioned, i.e., as merely regulating the interest of the inclinations by the sensuous principle of happiness, this demand [that theoretical reason should yield primacy to practical reason] could not be made on the speculative reason. Mohammed's paradise or the fusion with the deity of the theosophists and mystics, according to the taste of each, would press their monstrosities on reason, and it would be as well to have no reason at all as to surrender it in such a manner to all sorts of dreams. But if pure reason of itself can be and really is practical, as the consciousness of the moral law shows it to be, it is only one and the same reason which judges a priori by principles, whether for theoretical or for practical purposes. Then it is clear that, if its capacity in the former is not sufficient to establish certain propositions positively (which however do not contradict it), it must assume these propositions just as soon as they are sufficiently certified as belonging imprescriptibly to the practical interest of pure reason. It must assume them indeed as something offered from the outside and not grown in its own soil and seek to compare and connect them with everything which it has in its power as speculative reason. It must remember that they are not its own insights but extensions of its use in some other respect, viz., the practical; and that this is not in the least opposed to its interest, which lies in the restriction of speculative folly.

Thus in the combination of pure speculative with pure practical reason in one cognition, the latter has the primacy, provided that this combination is not contingent and arbitrary but a priori and based on reason itself and is thus necessary. Without this subordination, a conflict of reason with itself would arise, since if the speculative and the practical reason were arranged merely side by side (co-ordinated), the first would close its borders and admit into its domain nothing from the latter, while the latter would extend its boundaries over everything and, when its needs required, would seek to comprehend the former within them. Nor could we reverse the order and expect practical reason to submit to speculative reason, because every interest is ultimately practical, even that of speculative reason being only conditional and reaching perfection only in practical use.

IV. THE IMMORTALITY OF THE SOUL AS A POSTULATE OF PURE PRACTICAL REASON

The achievement of the highest good in the world is the necessary object of a will determinable by the moral law. In such a will, however, the complete fitness of intentions to the moral law is the supreme condition of the highest good. This aptness, therefore, must be just as possible as its object, because it is contained in the command that requires us to promote the latter. But complete fitness of the will to the moral law is holiness, which is a perfection of which no rational being in the world of sense is at any time capable. But since it is required as practically necessary, it can be found only in an endless progress to that complete fitness; on principles of pure practical reason, it is necessary to assume such a practical progress as the real object of our will.

This infinite progress is possible, however, only under the presupposition of an infinitely enduring existence and personality of the same rational being; this is called the immortality of the soul. Thus the highest good is practically possible only on the supposition of the immortality of the soul, and the latter, as inseparably bound to the moral law, is a postulate of pure practical reason. By a postulate of pure practical reason I understand a theoretical proposition which is not as such demonstrable, but which is an inseparable corollary of an a priori unconditionally valid practical law.

The thesis of the moral destiny of our nature, viz., that it is able only in an infinite progress to attain complete fitness to the moral law, is of great use, not merely for the present purpose of supplementing the impotence of speculative reason, but also with respect to religion. Without it, either the moral law is completely degraded from its holiness, by being made out as lenient (indulgent) and thus compliant to our convenience, or our notions of our vocation and our expectation are strained to an unattainable destination, i.e., a hoped-for complete attainment of holiness of will, thus losing themselves in fanatical theosophical dreams which completely contradict our knowledge of ourselves. In either case, we are only hindered in the unceasing striving toward the precise and persistent obedience to a command of reason which is stern, unindulgent, truly commanding, really and not just ideally possible. Only endless progress from lower to higher stages of moral perfection is possible to a rational but finite being. The Infinite Being, to whom the temporal condition is nothing, sees in this series, which is for us without end, a whole conformable to the moral law; holiness, which His law inexorably commands in order to be true to His justice in the share He assigns to each in the highest good, is to be found in a single intellectual intuition of the existence of rational beings. All that can be granted to a creature with respect to hope for this share is consciousness of his tried character. And on the basis of his previous progress from the worse to the morally better, and of the immutability of intention which thus becomes known to him, he may hope for a further uninterrupted continuation of this progress, however long his existence may last, even beyond this life.* But he cannot hope here or at

---

* The conviction of the immutability of character in progress toward the good may appear to be impossible for a creature. For this reason, Christian doctrine lets it derive from the same Spirit which works sanctification,

any foreseeable point of his future existence to be fully adequate to God's will, without indulgence or remission which would not harmonize with justice. This he can do only in the infinity of his duration which God alone can survey.

V. THE EXISTENCE OF GOD AS A POSTULATE OF PURE PRACTICAL REASON

The moral law led, in the foregoing analysis, to a practical problem which is assigned solely by pure reason and without any concurrence of sensuous incentives. It is the problem of the completeness of the first and principal part of the highest good, viz., morality; since this problem can be solved only in eternity, it led to the postulate of immortality. The same law must also lead us to affirm the possibility of the second element of the highest good, i.e., happiness proportional to that morality; it must do so just as disinterestedly as heretofore, by a purely impartial reason. This it can do on the supposition of the existence of a cause adequate to this effect, i.e., it must postulate the existence of God as necessarily belonging to the possibility of the highest good (the object of our will which is necessarily connected with the moral legislation of pure reason). We proceed to exhibit this connection in a convincing manner.

Happiness is the condition of a rational being in the world, in whose whole existence everything goes according to wish and will. It thus rests on the harmony of nature with his entire end and with the essential determining ground of his will. But the moral law commands, as a law of freedom, by grounds of determination which are wholly independent of nature and its harmony with our faculty of desire (as incentives). Still, the

---

i.e., this firm intention and therewith the consciousness of steadfastness in moral progress. But naturally one who is conscious of having persisted, from legitimate moral motives, to the end of a long life in a progress to the better may very well have the comforting hope, though not the certainty, that he will be steadfast in these principles in an existence continuing beyond this life. Though he can never be justified in his own eyes either here or in the hoped-for increase of natural perfection together with an increase of his duties, nevertheless in this progress toward a goal infinitely remote (a progress which in God's sight is regarded as equivalent to possession) he can have prospect of a blessed future. For "blessed" is the word which reason uses to designate a perfect well-being independent of all contingent causes in the world. Like holiness, it is an idea which can be contained only in an infinite progress and its totality and thus is never fully reached by any creature.

acting rational being in the world is not at the same time the cause of the world and of nature itself. Hence there is not the slightest ground in the moral law for a necessary connection between the morality and proportionate happiness of a being which belongs to the world as one of its parts and as thus dependent on it. Not being nature's cause, his will cannot by its own strength bring nature, as it touches on his happiness, into complete harmony with his practical principles. Nevertheless, in the practical task of pure reason, i.e., in the necessary endeavor[41] after the highest good, such a connection is postulated as necessary: we *should* seek to further the highest good (which therefore must be at least possible). Therefore also the existence is postulated of a cause of the whole of nature, itself distinct from nature, which contains the ground of the exact coincidence of happiness with morality. This supreme cause, however, must contain the ground of the agreement of nature not merely with a law of the will of rational beings but with the idea of this law so far as they make it the supreme ground of determination of the will. Thus it contains the ground of the agreement of nature not merely with actions moral in their form but also with their morality as the motive to such actions, i.e., with their moral intention. Therefore, the highest good is possible in the world only on the supposition of a supreme cause of nature which has a causality corresponding to the moral intention. Now a being which is capable of actions by the idea of laws is an intelligence (a rational being), and the causality of such a being according to this idea of laws is his will. Therefore, the supreme cause of nature, in so far as it must be presupposed for the highest good, is a being which is the cause (and consequently the author) of nature through understanding and will, i.e., God. As a consequence, the postulate of the possibility of a highest derived good (the best world) is at the same time the postulate of the reality of a highest original good, namely, the existence of God. Now it was our duty to promote the highest good; and it is not merely our privilege but a necessity connected with duty as a requisite to presuppose the possibility of this highest good. This presupposition is made only under the condition of the existence of God, and this condition inseparably connects this supposition with duty. Therefore, it is morally necessary to assume the existence of God.

It is well to notice here that this moral necessity is subjective,

41. [*Bearbeitung.*]

i.e., a need, and not objective, i.e., duty itself. For there cannot be any duty to assume the existence of a thing, because such a supposition concerns only the theoretical use of reason. It is also not to be understood that the assumption of the existence of God is necessary as a ground of all obligation in general (for this rests, as has been fully shown, solely on the autonomy of reason itself). All that here belongs to duty is the endeavor to produce and to further the highest good in the world, the existence of which may thus be postulated though our reason cannot conceive it except by presupposing a highest intelligence. To assume its existence is thus connected with the consciousness of our duty, though this assumption itself belongs to the realm of theoretical reason. Considered only in reference to the latter, it is a hypothesis, i.e., a ground of explanation. But in reference to the comprehensibility of an object (the highest good) placed before us by the moral law, and thus as a practical need, it can be called *faith* and even pure *rational faith*, because pure reason alone (by its theoretical as well as practical employment) is the source from which it springs.

From this deduction it now becomes clear why the Greek schools could never succeed in solving their problem of the practical possibility of the highest good. It was because they made the rule of the use which the human will makes of its freedom the sole and self-sufficient ground of its possibility, thinking that they had no need of the existence of God for this purpose. They were certainly correct in establishing the principle of morals by itself, independently of this postulate and merely from the relation of reason to the will, thus making the principle of morality the *supreme* practical condition of the highest good; but this principle was not the *entire* condition of its possibility. The Epicureans had indeed raised a wholly false principle of morality, i.e., that of happiness, into the supreme one, and for law had substituted a maxim of arbitrary choice of each according to his inclination. But they proceeded consistently enough, in that they degraded their highest good in proportion to the baseness of their principle and expected no greater happiness than that which could be attained through human prudence (wherein both temperance and the moderation of inclinations belong), though everyone knows prudence to be scarce enough and to produce diverse results according to circumstances, not to mention the exceptions which their maxims continually had to admit and which made them worthless as laws. The Stoics, on the other hand, had chosen their supreme practical principle, virtue, quite correctly as the condition of the highest good. But as they imagined the degree of virtue which is required for its pure law as completely attainable in this life, they not only exaggerated the moral capacity of man, under the name of "sage," beyond all the limits of his nature, making it into something which is contradicted by all our knowledge of men; they also refused to accept the second component of the highest good, i.e., happiness, as a special object of human desire. Rather, they made their sage, like a god in the consciousness of the excellence of his person, wholly independent of nature (as regards his own contentment), exposing him to the evils of life but not subjecting him to them. (They also represented him as free from everything morally evil.) Thus they really left out of the highest good the second element (personal happiness), since they placed the highest good only in acting and in contentment with one's own personal worth, including it in the consciousness of moral character. But the voice of their own nature could have sufficiently refuted this.

The doctrine of Christianity,* even when not regarded as a

* The view is commonly held that the Christian precept of morals has no advantage over the moral concept of the Stoics in respect to its purity; but the difference between them is nevertheless obvious. The Stoic system makes the consciousness of strength of mind the pivot around which all moral intentions should turn; and, if the followers of this system spoke of duties and even defined them accurately, they nevertheless placed the incentives and the real determining ground of the will in an elevation of character above the base incentives of the senses which have their power only through weakness of the mind. Virtue was, therefore, for them a certain heroism of the sage who, raising himself above the animal nature of man, was sufficient to himself, subject to no temptation to transgress the moral law, and elevated above duties though he propounded duties to others. But all this they could not have done had they conceived this law in the same purity and rigor as does the precept of the Gospel. If I understand by "idea" a perfection to which the senses can give nothing adequate, the moral ideas are not transcendent, i.e., of such a kind that we cannot even sufficiently define the concept or of which we are uncertain whether there is a corresponding object (as are the ideas of speculative reason); rather, they serve as models of practical perfection, as an indispensable rule of moral conduct, and as a standard for comparison. If I now regard Christian morals from their philosophical side, it appears in comparison with the ideas of the Greek schools as follows: the ideas of the Cynics, Epicureans, Stoics, and Christians are, respectively, the simplicity of nature, prudence, wisdom, and holiness. In respect to the way they achieve them, the Greek schools differ in that the Cynics found common sense sufficient, while the others found it in the path of science, and thus all held it

religious doctrine, gives at this point a concept of the highest good (the Kingdom of God) which is alone sufficient to the strictest demand of practical reason. The moral law is holy (unyielding) and demands holiness of morals, although all moral perfection to which man can attain is only virtue, i.e., a law-abiding disposition resulting from respect for the law and thus implying consciousness of a continuous propensity to transgress it or at least to a defilement, i.e., to an admixture of many spurious (not moral) motives to obedience to the law; consequently, man can achieve only a self-esteem combined with humility. And thus with respect to the holiness required by the Christian law, nothing remains to the creature but endless progress, though for the same reason hope of endless duration is justified. The worth of a character completely accordant with the moral law is infinite, because all possible happiness in the judgment of a wise and omnipotent dispenser of happiness has no other limitation than the lack of fitness of rational beings to their duty. But the moral law does not of itself promise happiness, for the latter is not, according to concepts of any order of nature, necessarily connected with obedience to the law. Christian ethics supplies this defect of the second indispensable component of the highest good by presenting a world wherein reasonable beings single-mindedly devote themselves to the moral law; this is the Kingdom of God, in which nature and morality come into a harmony, which is foreign to each as such, through a holy Author of the world, who makes possible the derived highest good. The holiness of morals is prescribed to them even in this life as a guide to conduct, but the well-being proportionate to this, which is bliss, is thought of as attainable only in eternity. This is due to the fact that the former must always be the pattern of their conduct in every state, and progressing toward it is even in this life possible and necessary, whereas the latter, under the name of happiness, cannot (as far as our own capacity is concerned) be reached in this life and therefore is made only an object of hope. Nevertheless, the Christian principle of morality

---

to lie in the mere use of man's natural powers. Christian ethics, because it formulated its precept as pure and uncompromising (as befits a moral precept), destroyed man's confidence of being wholly adequate to it, at least in this life; but it re-established it by enabling us to hope that, if we act as well as lies in our power, what is not in our power will come to our aid from another source, whether we know in what way or not. Aristotle and Plato differed only as to the origin of our moral concepts.

is not theological and thus heteronomous, being rather the autonomy of pure practical reason itself, because it does not make the knowledge of God and His will the basis of these laws but makes such knowledge the basis only of succeeding to the highest good on condition of obedience to these laws; it places the real incentive to obedience to the laws not in the desired consequences of obedience but in the conception of duty alone, in true observance of which the worthiness to attain the latter alone consists.

In this manner, through the concept of the highest good as the object and final end of pure practical reason, the moral law leads to religion. Religion is the recognition of all duties as divine commands, not as sanctions, i.e., arbitrary and contingent ordinances of a foreign will, but as essential laws of any free will as such. Even as such, they must be regarded as commands of the Supreme Being because we can hope for the highest good (to strive for which is made our duty by the moral law) only from a morally perfect (holy and beneficent) and omnipotent will; and, therefore, we can hope to attain it only through harmony with this will. But here again everything remains disinterested and based only on duty, without the basis being placed in fear or hope as incentives, which, if they became principles, would destroy the entire moral worth of the actions. The moral law commands us to make the highest possible good in a world the final object of all our conduct. This I cannot hope to effect except through the agreement of my will with that of a holy and beneficent Author of the world. And although my own happiness is included in the concept of the highest good as a whole wherein the greatest happiness is thought of as connected in exact proportion to the greatest degree of moral perfection possible to creatures, still it is not happiness but the moral law (which, in fact, sternly places restricting conditions upon my boundless longing for happiness) which is proved to be the ground determining the will to further the highest good.

Therefore, morals is not really the doctrine of how to make ourselves happy but of how we are to be *worthy* of happiness. Only if religion is added to it can the hope arise of someday participating in happiness in proportion as we endeavored not to be unworthy of it.

One is worthy of possessing a thing or a state when his possession is harmonious with the highest good. We can easily see now that all worthiness is a matter of moral conduct, because this constitutes the condition of everything else (which belongs to one's state [not his action]) in the concept of the highest good, i.e., participation in happiness. From this there follows that one must never consider morals itself as a doctrine of happiness, i.e., as an instruction in how to acquire happiness. For morals has to do only with the rational condition (*conditio sine qua non*) of happiness and not with means of achieving it. But when morals (which imposes only duties instead of providing rules for selfish wishes) is completely expounded, and a moral wish has been awakened to promote the highest good (to bring the Kingdom of God to us), which is a wish based on law and one to which no selfish mind could have aspired, and when for the sake of this wish the step to religion has been taken—then only can ethics be called a doctrine of happiness, because the *hope* for it first arises with religion.

From this it can also be seen that, if we inquire into God's final end in creating the world, we must name not the happiness of rational beings in the world but the highest good, which adds a further condition to the wish of rational beings to be happy, viz., the condition of being worthy of happiness, which is the morality of these beings, for this alone contains the standard by which they can hope to participate in happiness at the hand of a *wise* creator. For since wisdom, theoretically regarded, means the knowledge of the highest good and, practically, the suitability of the will to the highest good, one cannot ascribe to a supreme independent wisdom an end based merely on benevolence. For we cannot conceive the action of this benevolence (with respect to the happiness of rational beings) except as conformable to the restrictive conditions of harmony with the holiness* of His will as the highest original good. Then perhaps those who have placed the end of creation in the glory of God,

---

* Incidentally, and in order to make the peculiarity of this concept clear, I make the following remark. Since we ascribe various attributes to God, whose quality we find suitable also to creatures (e.g., power, knowledge, presence, goodness, etc.), though in God they are present in a higher degree under such names as omnipotence, omniscience, omnipresence, and perfect goodness, etc., there are three which exclusively and without qualification of magnitude are ascribed to God, and they are all moral. He is the only holy, the only blessed, and the only wise being, because these concepts of themselves imply unlimitedness. By the arrangement of these He is thus the holy lawgiver (and creator), the beneficent ruler (and sustainer),

provided this is not thought of anthropomorphically as an inclination to be esteemed, have found the best term. For nothing glorifies God more than what is the most estimable thing in the world, namely, respect for His command, the observance of sacred duty which His law imposes on us, when there is added to this His glorious plan of crowning such an excellent order with corresponding happiness. If the latter, to speak in human terms, makes Him worthy of love, by the former He is an object of adoration. Human beings can win love by doing good, but by this alone even they never win respect; the greatest well-doing does them honor only by being exercised according to worthiness.

It follows of itself that, in the order of ends, man (and every rational being) is an end-in-himself, i.e., he is never to be used merely as a means for someone (even for God) without at the same time being himself an end, and that thus the humanity in our person must itself be holy to us, because man is subject to the moral law and therefore subject to that which is of itself holy, and it is only on account of this and in agreement with this that anything can be called holy. For this moral law is founded on the autonomy of his will as a free will, which by its universal laws must necessarily be able to agree with that to which it subjects itself.

VI. ON THE POSTULATES OF PURE PRACTICAL REASON IN GENERAL

The postulates of pure practical reason all proceed from the principle of morality, which is not a postulate but a law by which reason directly determines the will. This will, by the fact that it is so determined, as a pure will requires these necessary conditions for obedience to its precept. These postulates are not theoretical dogmas but presuppositions of necessarily practical import; thus, while they do not extend speculative knowledge, they give objective reality to the ideas of speculative reason in general (by means of their relation to the practical sphere), and they justify it in holding to concepts the possibility of which it could not otherwise even venture to affirm.

---

and the just judge. These three attributes contain everything whereby God is the object of religion, and in conformity to them the metaphysical perfections of themselves arise in reason.

These postulates are those of immortality, of freedom affirmatively regarded (as the causality of a being so far as he belongs to the intelligible world), and of the existence of God. The first derives from the practically necessary condition of a duration adequate to the perfect fulfilment of the moral law. The second comes from the necessary presupposition of independence from the world of sense and of the capacity of determining man's will by the law of an intelligible world, i.e., the law of freedom itself; the third arises from the necessary condition of such an intelligible world by which it may be the highest good, through the presupposition of the highest independent good, i.e., the existence of God.

The prospect of the highest good, necessary through respect for the moral law and the consequent supposition of its objective reality, thus leads through postulates of practical reason to concepts which the speculative reason only exhibited as problems which it could not solve. It leads first to the problem of immortality, in the solution of which speculative reason could only commit paralogisms, because the marks of permanence, by which the psychological concept of an ultimate subject necessarily ascribed to the soul in self-consciousness, were lacking though they were needed to complete the real conception of a substance. Practical reason, through the postulate of fitness to the moral law in the highest good as the whole end of practical reason, consigns to this subject the requisite duration. Secondly, it leads to the concept which speculative reason contained only as an antinomy, and the solution of which it could base only on a problematical, though thinkable, concept whose objective reality was not provable or determinable by speculative reason. This is the cosmological idea of an intelligible world and the consciousness of our existence in it. It leads to this by means of the postulate of freedom (the reality of which practical reason exhibits in the moral law, at the same time exhibiting the law of an intelligible world, which the speculative reason could only indicate but whose concept it could not define). Thirdly, it gives significance to what speculative reason could indeed think but had to leave indeterminate as a mere transcendental ideal, i.e., to the theological concept of a First Being. This significance is given in a practical point of view, i.e., as a condition of the possibility of the object of a will determined by that law. It is that of a supreme principle of the highest good in an intelligible world having sovereign power in it by means of a moral legislation.

Is our knowledge really widened in such a way by pure practical reason, and is that which was transcendent for speculative reason immanent in practical reason? Certainly, but only from a practical point of view. For we thereby know neither the nature of our soul nor the intelligible world nor the Supreme Being as they are in themselves but have only united the concepts of them in a practical concept of the highest good as the object of our will and have done so entirely a priori through pure reason. We have so united them only by means of the moral law and merely in relation to it, with respect to the object which it commands. But how freedom is possible, and how we should think theoretically and positively of this type of causality, is not thereby discovered. All that is comprehended is that such a causality is postulated through the moral law and for its sake. It is the same with the remaining ideas, whose possibility cannot be fathomed by human understanding, though no sophistry will ever wrest from the conviction of even the most ordinary man an admission that they are not true.

VII. HOW IS IT POSSIBLE TO CONCEIVE OF EXTENDING PURE REASON IN A PRACTICAL RESPECT WITHOUT THEREBY EXTENDING ITS KNOWLEDGE AS SPECULATIVE?

In order not to be too abstract, we shall answer this question by direct application to the present case. In order to extend pure knowledge practically, an a priori purpose must be given, i.e., an end as an object (of the will) which, independently of all theoretical principles, is thought of as practically necessary through a categorical imperative directly determining the will. In this case, the object is the highest good; but it is not possible unless three theoretical concepts are presupposed: freedom, immortality, and God. Since they are pure concepts of reason, however, no corresponding intuition can be given and consequently no objective reality for them can be found in a theoretical way. Therefore, through the practical law, which requires the existence of the highest good possible in the world, there is postulated the possibility of those objects of pure speculative reason, whose objective reality could not be assured by speculative reason. By this, then, the theoretical knowledge of pure reason does obtain an accession, but it consists only in this—that those concepts which for it are otherwise problematical (merely thinkable) are now described assertorically as actually having objects, because practical reason inexorably requires the existence of these objects for the possibility of its practically and absolutely necessary object, the highest good. Theoretical reason is, therefore, justified in assuming them.

This extension of the theoretical reason, however, is not an extension of the speculative. That is, a positive use cannot be made of those objects for theoretical purposes. For nothing more has here been accomplished by practical reason than to show that those concepts are real and actually have (possible) objects, but no intuitions of them are thereby given (and indeed none can be demanded), and thus no synthetic proposition is made possible by conceding their reality. Consequently, this disclosure does not in the least help us in a speculative respect, but it does aid us with reference to the practical use of pure reason in extending our knowledge in this field. The three aforementioned ideas of speculative reason are not themselves cognitions; they are, nevertheless, transcendent thoughts in which there is nothing impossible. Now through an apodictic practical law, they, as necessary conditions of the possibility of that which this law requires to be made an object, acquire objective reality. That is to say, they show by this that they have objects, but we cannot indicate how their concept refers to an object; this, too, is not yet knowledge of these objects, for we can thereby neither make synthetic judgments about them nor theoretically determine their application. Consequently, we can make no theoretical rational use of them, and it is in this that all speculative knowledge of reason actually consists. Nevertheless, theoretical knowledge not of these objects but of reason in general was extended so far that, by the practical postulates, objects were given to those ideas, and a merely problematical thought thereby obtained objective reality. It was therefore no extension of knowledge of given supersensuous objects, but still an extension of theoretical reason and of its knowledge with respect to the supersensuous in general, inasmuch as knowledge is compelled to concede that there are such objects without more exactly defining them, and thus without being able to extend this knowledge of objects given to it only on practical grounds and only for practical use. For this accession, pure theoretical reason has thus to thank its pure practical faculty, for all these ideas are to it transcendent and without objects. Here they become immanent and constitutive, since they are the grounds of the possibility of realizing the necessary object of pure practical reason (the highest good); for otherwise they are transcendent and merely regulative principles of speculative reason, which is charged with the task not of assuming a new object beyond experience but only of approaching perfection in its employment within experience. Once in possession of this accession, for the security of its practical employment it will set to work as speculative reason with these ideas in a negative manner, i.e., not broadening but purifying, in order to ward off anthropomorphism as the source of superstition (apparent extension of those concepts through alleged experience) and fanaticism which promises such an extension through supersensuous intuition or feelings. Both of these are obstacles to the practical use of pure reason, and the safeguard against them certainly belongs in the extension of our knowledge in a practical direction, without contradicting the admission that reason has not gained anything at all in a speculative direction.

To each employment of reason with respect to objects, pure concepts of the understanding (categories) are required, for without them no object can be thought. These can be applied to the theoretical employment of reason, i.e., to that kind of knowledge only in case intuition (which is always sensuous) is supplied as their basis in order that through it an object of possible experience may be presented. Ideas of reason, which cannot be given in any experience, are that which I would have to think here through categories in order to know the object. But here we have not to do with theoretical knowledge of objects of these ideas but only with whether they do have objects or not. This reality is supplied by pure practical reason, and in relation to them theoretical reason has nothing further to do than merely to think those objects by means of categories. This occurs very well, as we have elsewhere clearly shown, without need of intuition (either sensuous or supersensuous), because the categories have their seat and origin in pure understanding as the sole faculty of thinking independent of and prior to any intuition; and they always signify only an object in general, in whatever way it may be given to us. Now no object in intuition can be given to the categories so far as they are applied to these ideas; but that such an object really exists and that here the category as a mere form of thought is not empty but has significance—this is sufficiently demonstrated by an object which practical reason indubitably presents in the concept of the highest good, namely, by the reality of the concepts which are required for the possibility of the highest good. But even the least extension of our knowledge by theoretical principles is not effected by this accession.

When these ideas of God, an intelligible world (the Kingdom of God), and immortality are further defined with predicates derived from our own nature, such definition cannot be regarded as making pure rational ideas sensuous (which is equivalent to anthropomorphism) or as being a transcendent knowledge of supersensuous objects. For these predicates are nothing else than understanding and will, in their contrasting relationship to one another, as they must be thought in the moral law, i.e., as they must be thought only in so far as a pure practical use is made of them. Everything else which pertains psychologically to these concepts, i.e., everything known only as we empirically observe these faculties of ours in their exercise, is therefore abstracted from them. For example, it is disregarded that human understanding is discursive, that its presentations are thoughts and not intuitions, that intuitions succeed each other in time, that the human will is always dependent for its contentment upon the existence of its object, etc., none of which can be the case with the highest being. Thus there remains nothing more in the concepts by which we think a pure rational being than what is directly required for thinking a moral law. There remains, then, a knowledge of God, but only in a practical context. And if we essay to extend it to a theoretical context, we get a divine understanding which does not think but intuits and a will which is directed to objects on the existence of which its contentment does not in the least depend. (I need not even mention the transcendental predicates, e.g., of magnitude of existence, duration, which is not in time even though this is the only means by which we can think of the magnitude of existence.) All of them are just qualities of which we can form no concept which is adequate to knowledge of objects. We learn in this way that they can never be used in a *theory* of supersensuous beings and that therefore from the theoretical aspect they can never support speculative knowledge, their use being restricted solely to the practice of the moral law.

The latter is so obvious and can be so clearly proved by fact that one can confidently challenge all alleged natural theologians (a curious name)* to cite one single definitive attribute (beyond the merely ontological predicates) of their object (say, of the understanding or the will), of which one could not irrefutably show that, when everything anthropomorphic is removed, only the word remains, without there being any possibility of connecting the least concept with it by which an extension of theoretical knowledge might be expected. But as to the practical, there still remains to us, of the attributes of an understanding and a will, the concept of a relation which is given objective reality by the practical law, which a priori determines precisely this relation of the understanding to the will. If this is once done, reality is given to the concept of the object of a morally determined will (i.e., to the highest good), and therewith the conditions of its possibility, the ideas of God, freedom, and immortality. But this reality is still given only with reference to the practice of the moral law and not for any speculative use.

After this reminder it is easy to find the answer to the important question: Is the concept of God a concept belonging to physics (and thus also to metaphysics, as this only contains the pure a priori principles of physics in their universal import) or a concept belonging to morals? To have recourse to God, as the Author of all things, in explaining the arrangements of nature and their changes is at any rate not a physical explanation but a complete confession that one has come to the end of his philosophy, since he is compelled to assume something of which in itself he otherwise has no concept in order to conceive of the possibility of something he sees before his very eyes. It is impossible by means of metaphysics to progress from knowledge of this world to concepts of God and a proof of his existence through cogent inferences, because we should have to know *this* world as the most perfect possible whole, and to this end

---

* "Learning" is a word properly applied only to the historical sciences. Consequently, only the teacher of revealed theology can be called a theologian.[42] But if one wishes to call someone who is in possession of the rational sciences (mathematics and philosophy) a "learned" man, even though this would contradict the meaning of the word (which attributes to learning only that which must be *taught* and thus what one cannot of himself discover by reason), the philosopher with his knowledge of God as a positive science would certainly cut too poor a figure to deserve the name of a "learned" man.

42. [*Gottesgelehrter*, lit., "God-learned."]

we should have to know all possible worlds in order to compare it to them—in short, we should have to be omniscient—in order to say that it is only possible through a God, however we understand this concept. To know completely the existence of this Being from mere concepts is absolutely impossible, for any existential proposition which asserts the existence of a being of which I have a concept is a synthetic proposition; that is, it is such that I must go beyond the concept and assert more than was thought in it, namely, that outside the understanding there is an object corresponding to the concept within the understanding. This assertion obviously cannot be reached by any inference.

Thus there remains to reason only one single procedure by which it can arrive at this knowledge: as pure reason it must determine its object by starting from the supreme principle of its pure *practical* use (since this is directed in every case only to the *existence* of something as a consequence of reason). In the unavoidable task of directing the will to the highest good, there is not only shown the necessity of assuming such a First Being in relation to the possibility of this good in the world but—which is more remarkable—there is also shown an exactly defined concept of this being, something completely lacking in the progress of reason in the path of nature. Since we know only a small part of this world and even less can compare it with all possible worlds, we can very well infer from its order, design, and magnitude to a wise, beneficent, and powerful Author of it, but not that He is all-knowing, all-good, and all-powerful. It may even be conceded that one is privileged to supplement this unavoidable lack by a permissible and wholly reasonable hypothesis to the effect that since wisdom, beneficence, etc., are displayed in all the parts offered to our more exact knowledge, it will be the same with all the rest, and that therefore it is reasonable to ascribe every possible perfection to the Author of the world. But these are not inferences in which we can pride ourselves on our insight; they are only liberties which may be allowed but which need further recommendation before they can be used. On the path of empirical inquiry (physics), the concept of God always remains a concept of the perfection of the First Being which is not accurately enough defined to be held suitable to the concept of Deity. (And with metaphysics in its transcendental part nothing at all can be accomplished.)

When I now try to test this concept by reference to the object of practical reason, I find that the moral principle admits this concept as possible only under the presupposition of an Author of the world having the highest perfection. This Being must be omniscient, in order to be able to know my conduct even to the most intimate parts of my intention in all possible cases and in the entire future. In order to allot fitting consequences to it, He must be omnipotent; and similarly for omnipresence, eternity, etc. Thus the moral law, by the concept of the highest good as the object of a pure practical reason, defines the concept of the First Being as that of a Supreme Being. This cannot be accomplished by the physical (and its higher development, the metaphysical) or, consequently, by any speculative procedure of reason. Therefore, the concept of God is one which belongs originally not to physics, i.e., to speculative reason, but to morals. The same may be said of the other concepts of reason which we have previously treated as postulates of reason in its practical use.

In the history of Greek philosophy before Anaxagoras there is no definite trace of a pure rational theology. The reason for this is not that the earlier philosophers lacked the understanding and insight to raise themselves to it by way of speculation, at least with the aid of a very reasonable hypothesis. For what could be easier than the thought which of itself occurs to everyone, to assume a single rational world cause possessing every perfection instead of several different causes or indeterminate degrees of perfection? But the evils in the world appeared to them to be too important an objection for them to hold such a hypothesis to be justified. Thus they showed their understanding and insight precisely in that they did not permit themselves this hypothesis but rather sought among natural causes to see whether they could find among them the character and competence required for the primordial beings. But when this acute people had progressed far enough in their inquiries to deal philosophically even with moral subjects, about which other peoples had never done more than talk, they found for the first time a new need, a practical need which gave them the definite concept of the First Being. In this speculative reason was only a spectator, or at best it had the merit of embellishing a concept which did not grow on its own ground and of promoting it with a series of confirmations drawn from the observation of nature (which now for the first time came into play). It did not have to strengthen the authority of this concept (which was already established) but only to make a show with an alleged theoretical insight of reason.

By this reminder, the reader of the Critique of pure speculative reason will be convinced how much that laborious deduction of the categories was needed for theology and morals and how fruitful it was for them. For if we place them in the pure understanding, it is only by this deduction that we are prevented from holding them, with Plato, to be inborn and from erecting on them transcendent presumptions and theories of the supersensuous end to which we can see, making theology merely a magic lantern of phantoms. And if, on the other hand, they are held to be acquired, this deduction prevents us from limiting their use, with Epicurus, to sensuous objects and grounds of determination even when their use is practical. But the critique showed in that deduction, first, that they are not of empirical origin but have their source and place a priori in pure understanding; and, second, that since they are related to objects in general independently of an intuition of them, they produce theoretical knowledge only by application to empirical objects. Yet it showed, furthermore, that they enable us to have definite thoughts about the supersensuous when applied to an object given by pure practical reason, but only so far as this is defined by predicates which necessarily belong to a pure practical purpose and its possibility, as given a priori. Speculative restriction and practical extension of pure reason bring pure reason into that relation of equivalence, wherein reason as such can be suitably used; and this example proves better than any other that the path to wisdom, if it is assured and not made impassable or misleading, must for us men unavoidably pass through science. But we can be sure that it leads to that goal only after the completion of science.

VIII. ON ASSENT ARISING FROM A NEED OF PURE REASON

A need of pure reason in its speculative use leads only to hypotheses; that of pure practical reason, to postulates. For, in the first case, I may ascend from the result as far as I wish in the series of conditions, and I shall need an ultimate ground not in order to give objective reality to the result (e.g., the causal connection of things and changes in the world) but only in order completely to satisfy my inquiring reason with respect to them. Thus before me I see order and design in nature, and I do not need to go over to speculation in order to assure myself of their reality, though in order to explain them I need to presuppose a Deity as their cause; but since an inference from an effect to a definite cause, especially to one so exactly and perfectly defined as we have to think God to be, is always uncertain and fallible, such a presupposition cannot be brought to a higher degree of certainty than the acknowledgment that it is the most reasonable opinion for us men.*

A need of pure practical reason, on the other hand, is based on a duty to make something (the highest good) the object of my will so as to promote it with all my strength. In doing so, I must presuppose its possibility and also its conditions, which are God, freedom, and immortality; for these conditions I am not in a position to prove by my speculative reason, though I cannot disprove them either. This duty is based on an apodictic law, the moral law, which is independent of these presuppositions, and thus in need of no further support from theoretical opinions on the inner character of things, on the secret final end of the world order, or on a ruler presiding over it in order to bind us completely to actions unconditionally conformable to the law. But the subjective effect of this law, i.e., the intention which is suitable to this law and which is necessary because of it, the intention to promote the practically possible highest good, at least presupposes that the latter is possible. Otherwise it would be practically impossible to strive for the object of a concept, which, at bottom, would be empty and without an object. Now the aforementioned postulates concern only the physical or metaphysical conditions (that is, those lying in the nature of things) of the possibility of the highest good, though not for the sake of some arbitrary speculative design but only for the sake of a practically necessary end of the pure rational will which does not here choose but rather obeys an inexorable command of reason. This command of reason has its ground objectively in the character of things as they must be universally judged by pure reason and is not based on inclination, which would by no means justify us in assuming the means to be possible or the object to be real for the sake of that which we wish on merely

---

* But even here we could not allege a need of reason if there were not before us a problematical but inevitable concept of reason, that of an absolutely necessary being. This concept requires to be defined, and, when the tendency to extend [the competence of reason] is added, it is the objective ground of a need of speculative reason, which is the need to define more accurately the concept of a necessary being which will serve as the ultimate ground of others and thus to characterize this necessary being by a distinctive mark. Without such prior necessary problems there are no needs, at least none of pure reason, the others being needs of inclination.

subjective grounds. This is, therefore, an absolutely necessary need and justifies its presupposition not merely as an allowable hypothesis but as a practical postulate. Granted that the pure moral law inexorably binds every man as a command (not as a rule of prudence), the righteous man may say: I will that there be a God, that my existence in this world be also an existence in a pure world of the understanding outside the system of natural connections, and finally that my duration be endless. I stand by this and will not give up this belief, for this is the only case where my interest inevitably determines my judgment because I will not yield anything of this interest; I do so without any attention to sophistries, however little I may be able to answer them or oppose them with others more plausible.*

In order to avoid all misinterpretations of the use of such an unusual concept as that of pure practical faith, I may add one more remark. It might almost seem as if this rational faith is here decreed as a command to assume as possible the highest good. But faith that is commanded is an absurdity. If one remembers from the preceding analysis what is needed to be presupposed in the concept of the highest good, one will realize that to assume this possibility cannot be commanded, and that no practical disposition to grant it can be demanded, but that speculative reason

* In the *Deutsches Museum* for February, 1787, there is a dissertation by a very subtle and clearheaded man, the late Wizenmann,[43] whose early death is to be lamented. In this he disputes the right to argue from a need to the objective reality of the object of the need, and he illustrates his point by the example of a man in love, who has fooled himself with an idea of beauty which is merely a chimera of his own brain and who now tries to argue that such an object really exists somewhere. I concede that he is right in all cases where the need is based on inclination, which cannot postulate the existence of its object even for him who is beset by it, and which even less contains a demand valid for everyone, and which is therefore a merely subjective ground of wishes. Here we have to do, however, with a need of reason arising from an objective determining ground of the will, i.e., the moral law, which is necessarily binding on every rational being; this, therefore, justifies a priori the presupposition of suitable conditions in nature and makes them inseparable from the complete practical use of reason. It is a duty to realize the highest good as far as it lies within our power to do so; therefore, it must be possible to do so. Consequently, it is unavoidable for every rational being in the world to assume whatever is necessary to its objective possibility. The assumption is as necessary as the moral law, in relation to which alone it is valid.

43. [See below, p. 294, n. 3.]

must admit it without being asked; for no one can affirm that it is impossible of itself that rational beings in the world should at the same time be worthy of happiness in conformity to the moral law and be in possession of happiness proportionate to this worthiness. Now with respect to the first component of the highest good, viz., morality, the moral law gives merely a command, and to doubt the possibility of that ingredient would be the same as to call the moral law itself into question. But with respect to the second component of that object, viz., happiness perfectly proportionate to that worthiness, the assumption of its possibility is not at all in need of a command, for theoretical reason has nothing to say against it. It is only in the way in which we are to think of this harmony of natural laws with laws of freedom that there is anything about which we have a choice, because here theoretical reason does not decide with apodictic certainty, and in this respect there can be a moral interest which turns the scale.

I have said above that in the mere course of nature happiness exactly proportionte to moral worth is not to be expected and is indeed impossible and that therefore the possibility of the highest good from this side cannot be granted except under the presupposition of a moral Author of the world. I intentionally postponed restricting this judgment to the subjective conditions of our reason in order to make use of this restriction only when the manner of the assent had been more precisely defined. In fact, the impossibility mentioned is merely subjective, i.e., our reason finds it impossible to conceive, in the mere course of nature, a connection so exactly proportioned and so thoroughly adapted to an end between natural events which occur according to laws so heterogeneous. But, as with every other purposive thing in nature, it still cannot prove that it is impossible according to universal laws of nature [only], i.e., show this by objectively sufficient reasons.

But now a determining factor of another kind comes into play to turn the scale in this indecision of speculative reason. The command to further the highest good is objectively grounded (in practical reason), and its possibility itself is likewise objectively grounded (in theoretical reason, which has nothing to say against it). But as to the manner in which this possibility is to be thought, reason cannot objectively decide whether it is by universal laws of nature without a wise Author presiding over nature or whether only on the assumption of such an Author.

Now a subjective condition of reason enters, which is the only way in which it is theoretically possible for it to conceive of the exact harmony of the realm of nature with the realm of morals as the condition of the possibility of the highest good; and it is the only way which is conducive to morality (which is under an objective law of reason). Since the promotion of the highest good and thus the presupposition of its possibility are objectively necessary (though only as a consequence of practical reason); and since the manner in which we are to think of it as possible is subject to our own choice, in which a free interest of pure practical reason is decisive for the assumption of a wise Author of the world, it follows that the principle which here determines our judgment, while subjectively a need, is the ground of a maxim of moral assent, as a means to promoting that which is objectively (practically) necessary; that is, it is a faith of pure practical reason.[44] As a voluntary decision of our judgment to assume that existence and to make it the foundation of further employment of reason, conducing to the moral (commanded) purpose and agreeing moreover with the theoretical need of reason, it is itself not commanded. It rather springs from the moral disposition itself. It can therefore often waver even in the well disposed but can never fall into unbelief.

IX. OF THE WISE ADAPTATION OF MAN'S COGNITIVE FACULTIES TO HIS PRACTICAL VOCATION

If human nature is called upon to strive for the highest good, the measure of its cognitive faculties and especially their relation to one another must be assumed to be suitable to this end. But the critique of pure speculative reason demonstrates the utter insufficiency of speculative reason to solve the most weighty problems which are presented to it in a way satisfactory to its end; but that critique did not ignore the natural and unmistakable hints of the same reason or the great steps that it can take in approaching this great goal which is set before it but which it can never of itself reach even with the aid of the greatest knowledge of nature. Thus nature here seems to have provided us only in a stepmotherly fashion with a faculty needed for our end.

Now assuming that it had here indulged our wish and had provided us with that power of insight or enlightenment which

44. [*Vernunftglaube.*]

we would like to possess or which some erroneously believe they do possess, what would be the consequence so far as we can discern it? In so far as our whole nature was not changed at the same time, the inclinations (which under any condition have the first word) would first strive for their satisfaction and, conjoined with reasonable consideration, for the greatest possible and most lasting satisfaction under the name of happiness. The moral law would afterward speak in order to hold them within their proper limits and even to subject them all to a higher end which has no regard to inclination. But instead of the conflict which now the moral disposition has to wage with inclinations and in which, after some defeats, the moral strength of mind may be gradually won, God and eternity in their awful majesty would stand unceasingly before our eyes (for that which we can completely prove is as certain as that which we can ascertain by sight). Transgression of the law would indeed be shunned, and the commanded would be performed. But because the disposition from which actions should be done cannot be instilled by any command, and because the spur to action would in this case be always present and external, reason would have no need to endeavor to gather its strength to resist the inclinations by a vivid idea of the dignity of the law. Thus most actions conforming to the law would be done from fear, few would be done from hope, none from duty. The moral worth of actions, on which alone the worth of the person and even of the world depends in the eyes of supreme wisdom, would not exist at all. The conduct of man, so long as his nature remained as it now is, would be changed into mere mechanism, where, as in a puppet show, everything would gesticulate well but no life would be found in the figures.

But it is quite otherwise with us. With all the exertion of our reason we have only a very obscure and ambiguous view into the future; the Governor of the world allows us only to conjecture His existence and majesty, not to behold or clearly prove them; the moral law in us, without promising or threatening us with anything certain, demands of us a disinterested respect; finally, only when this respect has become active and dominating, it allows us a view into the realm of the supersensuous, though only a glimpse. Thus only can there be a truly moral character dedicated directly to the law and the rational creature become worthy of participating in the highest good corresponding to the moral worth of his person and not merely to his actions. Thus what the study of nature and of man has sufficiently shown elsewhere may well be true here, viz., that the inscrutable wisdom through which we exist is not less worthy of veneration in respect to what it denies us than in what it has granted.

PART II

METHODOLOGY OF PURE PRACTICAL REASON

BY THE methodology of pure practical reason we are not to understand the manner of study or exposition which proceeds with pure practical principles for the purpose of a scientific knowledge of them, even though this procedure is the only one which is properly called "method" in theoretical reason. Popular knowledge requires a "manner," while science stands in need of a method, i.e., a procedure according to principles of reason, through which alone the manifold of knowledge can become a system. Here, on the contrary, we understand by methodology the way in which we can secure to the laws of pure practical reason access to the human mind and an influence on its maxims. That is to say, it is the way we can make the objectively practical reason also subjectively practical.

Now it is clear that those grounds of determination of the will, the direct thought of the law and objective obedience to it as duty, which alone make the maxims really moral and give them a moral worth, must be thought of as the real incentives of actions, for otherwise legality of actions but not morality of intentions would result. But it is not so clear—in fact, it must appear highly improbable at first glance—that even subjectively the exhibition of pure virtue can have more power over the human mind, giving a far stronger incentive to effectuate even that legality and to bring forward more powerful resolves to prefer the law to everything else merely out of respect for it, than all allurements arising from enjoyment and everything which may be counted as happiness or from all threats of pain and harm. But it is really so, and if human nature were not so constituted, no way of presenting the law by circumlocutions and indirect recommendations could ever produce morality of intentions. Everything would be mere cant; the law would be hated or even perhaps despised, though nevertheless followed for the sake of one's own advantage. The letter of the law (legality) would be met with in our actions, but the spirit of the law (morality) would not be found in our intentions. Since with all our efforts we cannot completely free ourselves from reason in judging, we would inevitably appear in our own eyes as worthless and depraved men, even if we sought to compensate ourselves for this mortification before the inner tribunal by indulging in all the enjoyments which a supposed natural or divine law might be thought, in our delusion, to have connected with legality by means of a kind of police machinery regulating its operations by that which we do without troubling itself about our motives for doing it.

Certainly it cannot be denied that in order to bring either an as yet uneducated or a degraded mind into the path of the morally good, some preparatory guidance is needed to attract it by a view to its own advantage or to frighten it by fear of harm. As soon as this machinery, these leading strings, have had some effect, the pure moral motive must be brought to mind. This is not only because it is the sole ground of character (a consistent practical habit of mind according to unchangeable maxims) but also because, in teaching a man to feel his own worth, it gives his mind a power, unexpected even by himself, to pull himself loose from all sensuous attachments (so far as they would fain dominate him) and, in the independence of his intelligible nature and in the greatness of soul to which he sees himself called, to find himself richly compensated for the sacrifice he makes. We should prove, by observations which anyone can make, that this property of our minds, this receptivity to a pure moral interest and the moving force in the pure thought of virtue when properly commended to the human heart, is the strongest incentive to the good and indeed the only one when it is a question of continual and meticulous obedience to moral maxims. It must be remembered, however, that if these observations show only the reality of such a feeling but no moral improvement resulting from it, that is no argument against the only method by which the objectively practical laws of pure reason can be made subjectively practical through the mere thought of duty, nor does it show it to be an empty fantasy. For since this method has never yet been widely used, experience can tell us nothing of its results; one can ask only for proofs of the receptivity to such motives, which I shall briefly present and then in few words outline the method of founding and cultivating genuine moral dispositions.

If we attend to the course of conversation in mixed companies consisting not merely of scholars and subtle reasoners but also of business people or women, we notice that besides storytelling and jesting they have another entertainment, namely, arguing; for storytelling, if it is to have novelty and interest, soon exhausts itself, while jesting easily becomes insipid. Now of all arguments there are none which excite more ready participation by those who are otherwise soon bored with all subtle thinking, or which are more likely to bring a certain liveliness into the company, than one about the moral worth of this or that action from which the character of some person is to be made out. Those who otherwise find everything which is subtle and punctilious in theoretical questions dry and vexing soon take part when it is a question of the moral import of a good or bad act that is recounted; and they are exacting, meticulous, and subtle in excogitating everything which lessens or even casts suspicion on the purity of purpose and thus on the degree of virtue to an extent we do not expect of them on any other subject of speculation. One can often see the character of the person who judges others revealed in his judgments. Some of them appear to be chiefly inclined, as they exercise their judicial office especially upon the dead, to defend the good that is related of this or that deed against all injurious charges of insincerity, finally protecting the entire moral worth of the person against the reproach of dissimulation and secret wickedness. Others, on the contrary, incline more to attacking this worth by accusations and fault-finding. But we cannot always ascribe to the latter the wish to argue away virtue from all human examples in order to reduce it to an empty name; often it is only a well-meaning strictness in the definition of genuine moral import according to an uncompromising law, in comparison with which (in contrast to comparison with examples) self-conceit in moral matters is very much reduced, and humility is not merely taught but is also felt by each in a penetrating self-examination. Nevertheless, we can often see, in the defenders of purity of purpose in given examples, that where there is a presumption of righteousness they would gladly remove the least spot; and they do so lest, if all examples be disputed and all human virtue be denied its purity, the latter be held to be a mere phantom and all effort to attain it be deprecated as vain affectation and delusory conceit.

I do not know why the educators of youth have not long since made use of this propensity of reason to enter with pleasure upon the most subtle examination of practical questions put to them, and why, after laying the foundation in a purely moral catechism, they have not searched through biographies of ancient and modern times with the purpose of having examples at hand of the duties they lay down, so that, by comparing similar actions under various circumstances, they could begin to exercise the moral judgment of their pupils in marking the greater or less moral significance of the actions. They would find that even very young people, who are not yet ready for speculation of other kinds, would soon become very acute and not a little interested, since they would feel the progress of their power of judgment; what is most important, they could confidently hope that frequent practice of knowing and approving of good conduct in all its purity, and of noting even the least deviation from it with sorrow or contempt, would leave a lasting impression of esteem for the one and disgust for the other, even though this practice is pursued only as a game of judgment in which children could compete with one another. By the mere habit of frequently looking upon actions as praiseworthy or blameworthy, a good foundation would be laid for righteousness in the future course of life. But I wish they would spare them examples of so-called noble (super-meritorious) actions, which so fill our sentimental writings, and would refer everything to duty only and the worth which a man can and must give himself in his own eyes through the consciousness of not having transgressed his duty, since whatever runs up into empty wishes and longings for unattainable perfection produces mere heroes of romance, who, while priding themselves on their feeling of transcendent greatness, release themselves from observing the common and everyday responsibility, as petty and insignificant.*

If one asks, however, what pure morality really is, by which, as the touchstone, the moral import of each action must be tested, I must confess that only philosophers can put the decision on

---

* It is entirely proper to extol actions which display a great, unselfish, and sympathetic disposition and humanity. But in them we must attend not so much to the elevation of soul, which is very fleeting and ephemeral, as to the subjection of the heart to duty, from which a more lasting impression can be expected as it entails principles and not just ebullitions as the former does. One need only to reflect a little to find an indebtedness which the vaunted hero has in some way incurred to the human race (even if it be only that, by the inequality of men under the civil constitution, he enjoys advantages on account of which others must be lacking to just that extent), which will prevent the thought of duty from being repressed by the self-complacent imagination of merit.

this question in doubt. For by common sense it is long since decided, not by abstract general formulas but rather by habitual use, like the difference between the right and the left hand. We will therefore first show the distinctive mark of pure virtue in an example and, imagining that we have put it before, say, a ten-year-old boy for his judgment, see whether he must necessarily judge so by himself without being guided by the teacher.

Tell him the story of an honest man whom someone wishes to induce to join the calumniators of an innocent but powerless person (say, Anne Boleyn accused by Henry VIII of England). He is offered advantages, e.g., great gifts or high rank; he rejects them. This will cause only applause and approval in the mind of the hearer, because they represent mere gain. Now come threats of loss. Among the slanderers there are his best friends who now renounce his friendship; near-relatives who threaten him (who is without fortune) with disinheritance; powerful persons who can persecute and harass him in all places and in every circumstance; a prince who threatens him with loss of freedom and even of life itself. But that the measure of his suffering may be full, so that he may feel the pain which only the morally good heart can very deeply feel, let his family, which is threatened with extreme need and want, entreat him to yield; think of the man himself, who, though righteous, has feelings which are not insensible or hardened to either sympathy or his own needs, at the moment when he wishes never to have lived to see the day which brings him such unutterable pain—think of him without any wavering or even a doubt remaining true to his resolution to be honest. Thus one can lead the young listener step by step from mere approval to admiration, and from admiration to amazement, and finally to the greatest veneration and a lively wish that he himself could be such a man (though certainly not in his circumstances). Yet virtue is here worth so much only because it costs so much, not because it brings any advantage. All the admiration and even the endeavor to resemble this character rest here solely on the purity of the moral principle, which can be clearly shown only by removing from the incentive of the action everything which men might count as a part of happiness. Thus morality must have more power over the human heart the more purely it is presented. From this it follows that, if the law of morals and the image of holiness and virtue are to exert any influence at all on our minds, they can do so only in so far as they are laid to heart in their purity as incentives unmixed with any view to welfare, because it is in suffering that they most notably show themselves. But a factor whose removal strengthens the effect of a moving force must have been a hindrance; consequently, all admixture of incentives which derive from one's own happiness are a hindrance to the influence of the moral law on the human heart.

I assert further that, if in the admired action the motive from which it was done was esteem for duty, this respect for the law, and not any pretension to inner greatness of mind or noble and meritorious sentiment, is that which has the most power over the mind of the spectator. Consequently, duty, not merit, has not only the most definite influence but, when seen in the true light of its inviolability, also the most penetrating influence on the mind.

In our times, when men hope to have more effect on the mind through yielding, soft-hearted feelings or high-flying, puffed-up pretensions, which wither instead of strengthening the heart, than through the dry and earnest idea of duty which is more fitting to human imperfection and progress in goodness, attention to this method is more needed than ever. One defeats his purpose by setting actions called noble, magnanimous, and meritorious as models for children with the notion of captivating them by infusing an enthusiasm for these actions. For as they are considerably backward in the observance of the commonest duty and even in the correct estimation of it, this amounts to speedily making them fantastic romancers. Even among the instructed and experienced portion of mankind, this supposed incentive has, if not an injurious, at least no genuine moral, effect on the heart, which is what one hoped to produce by its means.

All feelings, and especially those which produce unusual exertions, must produce their effect in the moment when they are at their height and before they subside, else they have no effect at all. This is due to the fact that the heart naturally returns to its natural and moderate behavior and soon falls back into its previous languor because it has been brought into contact with something which stimulated it, not with something that strengthened it. Principles must be erected on concepts; on any other foundation only passing moods can be achieved which give the person no moral worth and not even confidence in himself, without which the consciousness of his moral disposition and character, the highest good in man, cannot arise. These concepts, as they are to become subjectively practical, must not remain objective laws of morality which we merely admire and esteem in relation to mankind in general. Rather we must see the idea of them in relation to man as an individual, for then the law appears in a form which is indeed deserving of high respect though not as pleasing as if it belonged to the element to which he is naturally accustomed; on the contrary, it often compels him to leave this element, not without self-denial, and to give himself over to a higher element in which he can maintain himself only with effort and with unceasing apprehension of falling back into the former. In a word, the moral law demands obedience from duty, not from a predilection which cannot and should not be presupposed at all.

Let us now see in an example whether there is more subjective moving force of an incentive in the thought of an action as noble and magnanimous than when the action is thought of merely as duty in relation to the solemn moral law. The action by which someone with the greatest danger to his own life seeks to save others in a shipwreck and at last loses his own life will indeed be counted, on the one hand, as duty, but, on the other hand, even more as a meritorious action; but [in the latter case] our esteem for it will be weakened very much by the concept of his duty to himself, which here seems to have been infringed. More decisive is the magnanimous sacrifice of his life for the preservation of his country, and yet there still remain some scruples as to whether it is so perfect a duty to devote one's self spontaneously and unbidden to this purpose, and the action itself does not have the full force of a model and impulse to imitation. But if it is an inexorable duty, transgression against which violates of itself the moral law without respect to human welfare and, as it were, tramples on its holiness (the kind of duties which one usually calls duties to God, because we think of Him as the ideal of holiness in a substance), we give our most perfect esteem to pursuing it and sacrifice everything that ever had value for our dearest inclinations; and we find our soul strengthened and elevated by such an example when we convince ourselves, by contemplating it, that human nature is capable of such an elevation above everything that nature can present as an incentive in opposition to it. Juvenal describes such an example in a climax which makes the reader vividly feel the power of the incentive which lies in the pure law of duty as duty: "Be a stout soldier, a faithful guardian, and an incorruptible judge; if summoned to bear witness in some dubious and uncertain cause, though Phalaris himself should bring up his bull and dictate to you a perjury, count it the greatest of all sins to prefer life to honor, and to lose, for the sake of living, all that makes life worth living."[45]

Whenever we bring any flattering thought of merit into our actions, the incentive is already mixed with self-love and thus has some assistance from the side of sensibility. But to put everything else after the holiness of duty and to know that we *can* do it because our own reason acknowledges it as its law and says that we *ought* to do it—that is, as it were, to lift ourselves altogether out of the world of sense; this elevation is inseparably present in the consciousness of the law as an incentive of a faculty which rules over the sensibility, though not always effectively. But frequent concern with this incentive and the at first minor attempts at using it give hope of its effectiveness, so that gradually the greatest but still purely[46] moral interest in it will be produced in us.

The method therefore takes the following course. The first step is to make judging according to moral laws a natural occupation which accompanies our own free actions as well as our observation of those of others, and to make it, as it were, a habit. We must sharpen these judgments by first asking whether the action is objectively in accordance with the moral law, and if so, with which one; by this, heed to the law which merely gives a principle of obligation is distinguished from one which is in fact obligatory (*leges obligandi a legibus obligantibus*). For instance, we distinguish between the law of that which the needs of men require of me from that which their rights demand, the latter prescribing essential duties while the former assigns nonessential duties. This teaches how to distinguish between the different duties which come together in an action. The second point to which attention must be directed is the question as to whether the action also is done (subjectively) for the sake of the moral law, and thus not only is morally correct as a deed but also has moral worth as a disposition because of the maxim from which it was done. Now there is no doubt that this exercise and the consciousness of cultivation of our reason which judges concerning the practical must gradually produce a certain interest even in its own law and thus in morally good actions. For we ultimately

---

45. [Juvenal *Satire* viii. 79–84, trans. G. G. Ramsey ("Loeb Classical Library"). Phalaris was tyrant of Agrigentum who had Perillus construct a brass ox in which criminals were burned to death.]

46. [Reading *rein* with Natorp.]

take a liking to that the observation of which makes us feel that our powers of knowledge are extended, and this extension is especially furthered by that wherein we find moral correctness, since reason, with its faculty of determining according to a priori principles what should occur, can find satisfaction only in such an order of things. Even an observer of nature finally likes objects which first offend his senses when he discovers in them the great design of their organization, so that his reason finds nourishment in observing them; Leibniz spared an insect which he had carefully examined under the microscope, and replaced it on its leaf, because he had been instructed by viewing it and, as it were, had received a benefit from it.

But this occupation of the faculty of judgment, which makes us feel our own powers of knowledge, is not yet interest in actions and their morality itself. It only enables one to entertain himself with such judging and gives virtue or a turn of mind based on moral laws a form of beauty which is admired but not yet sought ("[Honesty] is praised and starves").[47] It is the same with everything whose contemplation produces subjectively a consciousness of the harmony of our powers of representation by which we feel our entire cognitive faculty (understanding and imagination) strengthened; it produces a satisfaction that can be communicated to others, but the existence of its object remains indifferent to us, as it is seen only as the occasion for our becoming aware of the store of talents which are elevated above the mere animal level.

Now the second exercise begins its work. It lies in calling to notice the purity of will by a vivid exhibition of the moral disposition in examples. It is presented first only as negative perfection, i.e., indicating that no incentives of inclinations are the determining grounds influencing an action done as a duty. By this, the pupil's attention is held to the consciousness of his freedom; and, although this renunciation excites an initial feeling of pain, at the same time, by relieving him of the constraint even of his true needs it frees him from the manifold discontent in which all these needs involve him and makes his mind receptive to the feeling of contentment from other sources. The heart is freed from a burden which has secretly pressed upon it; it is lightened when in instances of pure moral resolutions there is revealed to man, who previously has not correctly known it, a

---

47. [*Laudatur et alget*, an allusion to Juvenal *Satire* i. 74.]

faculty of inner freedom to release himself from the impetuous importunity of the inclinations, to such an extent that not even the dearest of them has an influence on a resolution for which he now makes use of his reason. In a case where I alone know that injustice lies in what I do, and where an open confession of it and an offer to make restitution is in direct conflict with vanity, selfishness, and an otherwise not illegitimate antipathy to the man whose rights I have impaired, if I can set aside all these considerations, there is a consciousness of an independence from inclinations and circumstances and of the possibility of being sufficient to myself, which is salutary for me in yet other respects. The law of duty, through the positive worth which obedience to it makes us feel, finds easier access through the respect for ourselves in the consciousness of our freedom. If it is well established, so that a man fears nothing more than to find himself on self-examination to be worthless and contemptible in his own eyes, every good moral disposition can be grafted on to this self-respect, for the consciousness of freedom is the best, indeed the only, guard that can keep ignoble and corrupting influences from bursting in upon the mind.

With these remarks I have intended only to point out the most general maxims of the methodology of moral cultivation and exercise. Since the manifold variety of duties requires specific definitions of each kind, and these would constitute a prolix affair, the reader will excuse me if in a work like this, which is only preliminary, I go no further than these outlines.

CONCLUSION

TWO things fill the mind with ever new and increasing admiration and awe, the oftener and more steadily they are reflected on: the starry heavens above me and the moral law within me. I do not merely conjecture them and seek them as though obscured in darkness or in the transcendent region beyond my horizon: I see them before me, and I associate them directly with the consciousness of my own existence. The former begins from the place I occupy in the external world of sense, and it broadens the connection in which I stand into an unbounded magnitude of worlds beyond worlds and systems of systems and into the limitless times of their periodic motion, their beginning and continuance. The latter begins from my invisible self, my personality, and exhibits me in a world which has true infinity but which is comprehensible only to the understanding—a world with which I recognize myself as existing in a universal and necessary (and not only, as in the first case, contingent) connection, and thereby also in connection with all those visible worlds. The former view of a countless multitude of worlds annihilates, as it were, my importance as an animal creature, which must give back to the planet (a mere speck in the universe) the matter from which it came, the matter which is for a little time provided with vital force, we know not how. The latter, on the contrary, infinitely raises my worth as that of an intelligence by my personality, in which the moral law reveals a life independent of all animality and even of the whole world of sense—at least so far as it may be inferred from the purposive destination assigned to my existence by this law, a destination which is not restricted to the conditions and limits of this life but reaches into the infinite.

But though admiration and respect can indeed excite to inquiry, they cannot supply the want of it. What, then, is to be done in order to set the latter on foot in a useful way suitable to the sublimity of its object? Examples may serve for warnings here, but also for imitation. The observation of the world began from the noblest spectacle that was ever placed before the human senses and that our understanding can bear to follow in its vast expanse, and it ended in—astrology. Morals began with the noblest attribute of human nature, the development and cultivation of which promised infinite utility, and it ended in—fanaticism or superstition. So it goes with all crude attempts in which the principal part of the business depends on the use of reason, a use which does not come of itself, like that of the feet, from frequent exercise, especially when it concerns attributes which cannot be so directly exhibited in common experience. Though late, when the maxim did come into vogue of carefully examining every step which reason had to take and not to let it proceed except on the path of a well-considered method, the study of the structure of the world took an entirely different direction and therewith attained an incomparably happier result. The fall of a stone and the motion of a sling, resolved into their elements and the forces manifested in them treated mathematically, finally brought that clear and henceforth unchangeable insight into the structure of the world which, as observations continue, we may hope to broaden but need not fear having to retract.

This example recommends to us the same path in treating of

the moral capacities of our nature and gives hope of a similarly good issue. We have at hand examples of the morally judging reason. We may analyze them into their elementary concepts, adopting, in default of mathematics, a process similar to that of chemistry, i.e., we may, in repeated experiments on common sense, separate the empirical from the rational, exhibit each of them in a pure state, and show what each by itself can accomplish. Thus we shall avoid the error of a crude and unpracticed judgment and (which is far more important) the extravagances of genius, by which, as by the adepts of the philosopher's stone, visionary treasures are promised and real treasures are squandered for lack of a methodical study and knowledge of nature. In a word, science (critically sought and methodically directed) is the narrow gate that leads to the doctrine of wisdom, when by this is understood not merely what one ought to do but what should serve as a guide to teachers in laying out plainly and well the path to wisdom which everyone should follow and in keeping others from going astray. It is a science of which philosophy must always remain the guardian; and though the public takes no interest in its subtle investigations, it may very well take an interest in the doctrines which such considerations first make clear to it.

III

AN INQUIRY INTO THE DISTINCTNESS[1] OF THE PRINCIPLES OF NATURAL THEOLOGY AND MORALS

*Verum animo satis haec vestigia parva sagaci
Sunt, per quae possis cognoscere caetera tute.*[2]

INTRODUCTION

THE proposed question[3] is of such a kind that, if it can be properly answered, higher philosophy as a result must thereby obtain a definite form. Once the method has been established by which the highest possible certainty in this species of knowledge can be attained, and after the nature of this certainty is fully comprehended, the unchanging precept of a method of instruction must unite thinking minds in identical labors. It will replace the perpetual instability of opinions and school factions just as Newton's method in natural science changed the extravagance of physical hypotheses into an unequivocal procedure conform-

---

1. [*Deutlichkeit* = *distinctness* as contrasted with *clearness*, these two characteristics being the marks of truth in rationalistic philosophy. Wolff states: "When we know that which we perceive, or are able to distinguish it from other perceptible things, we have a *clear* perception.... If we distinguish within the perceived thing that which can be separately asserted, the clear perception is called *distinct*" (J. Baumann, *Wolffsche Begriffsbestimmungen* [Leipzig: Meiner, n.d.], pp. 1-2). Kant defines: "*Clearness* is the consciousness of one's conceptions which is sufficient to distinguish one object from another. But the consciousness through which the organization of conceptions becomes clear is *distinctness*. Through the latter alone can a sum of conceptions become knowledge" (*Anthropology*, I, 6; Cassirer ed., VIII, 22). Occasionally, when Kant is speaking nontechnically, *deutlich* has been translated as *clear* when this conforms better to English style.]

2. [But ample these, I ween,
Though but the footsteps of the mighty whole,
To fix thy faith, and guide thee to the rest.
—*De rerum natura* i. 403-4 (trans.
John Mason Good [London, 1890]).]

3. [Cf. Introduction, p. vi.]

ing to experience and geometry. But what kind of exposition should there be in this essay itself, in which metaphysics is to be shown both its true measure of certainty and the way in which this can be reached? If this exposition is itself metaphysics, its conclusion is just as uncertain as is the science which now hopes by this exposition to obtain some degree of consistency and stability; in this event all is lost. I shall, therefore, let certain empirical propositions and immediate inferences from them be the entire content of my essay. I shall trust neither the teachings of philosophers, the uncertainty of which is precisely the occasion of our present task, nor definitions, which often delude. The method I use will be both simple and cautious. Some ideas which may still be found uncertain will be of such a kind as to serve only for elucidation but not for proof.

FIRST REFLECTION

GENERAL COMPARISON OF THE WAY OF ATTAINING CERTAINTY IN MATHEMATICAL KNOWLEDGE WITH THAT IN PHILOSOPHICAL KNOWLEDGE

§ 1. *Mathematics Achieves All Its Definitions Synthetically; Philosophy Achieves Its Analytically*

WE CAN reach a universal concept in two ways, viz., through arbitrary combination of concepts or through setting apart those elements of knowledge which have been made distinct by analysis. Mathematics formulates definitions only in the former way. We arbitrarily think, for example, of four lines inclosing a plane so that the opposite sides are not parallel, and we call this figure a trapezoid. The concept which I define is not given prior to the definition but only arises by means of it. Outside mathematics a cone may mean what it pleases; but in mathematics it arises from the arbitrary conception of a right triangle rotating on one of its legs. The definition obviously arises here and in all other cases through synthesis.

But the situation is entirely different with philosophical definitions. Here the concept of a thing is already given, though confusedly or insufficiently determined. I must analyze it, compare its segregated characteristics with the given concept in all kinds of cases, and make this abstract thought detailed and definite. Everyone has, for example, a concept of time; this is to be defined. I must consider this idea in various kinds of relations in order to discover its characteristics by analysis; I must combine different abstract characteristics in order to see whether they give an adequate concept, whether they are consistent among themselves, and whether or not one of them partially contains the other. If I wished to try to arrive synthetically at a definition of time, what a fortunate accident would have to occur in order for this synthetic concept to be exactly that which fully expresses the idea given to us!

Still, we shall be told, philosophers sometimes define synthetically and mathematicians analytically. For instance, the philosopher arbitrarily thinks of a substance having the faculty of reason and calls it a mind. But I answer that such definitions of the meaning of a word are never philosophical definitions; if they are to be called definitions at all, they are only grammatical definitions. No philosophy at all is required to say what name I will attribute to an arbitrary concept. Leibniz thought of a simple substance which had only unclear ideas, and he called it a sleeping monad. In so doing, he did not explain this monad; rather, he invented it, for the concept of it was not given to him but was created by him. On the other hand, mathematicians have sometimes defined analytically, I admit, but in every case it has been a mistake. Thus Wolff considered similarity in geometry with a philosophical eye in order to comprehend geometrical similarity under the general concept of similarity.[4] But he could better have left that alone, for, when we think of figures in which the angles are equal and the sides proportional, this can in every case be regarded as the definition of the similarity of figures. It is the same with all other spatial similarities. The universal definition of similarity in general is of no concern to the geometer. When, as sometimes happens, the geometer concerns himself with such analytical definitions through a misunderstanding of his responsibility, it is fortunate for mathematics that he actually draws no conclusions from them, or that their immediate consequences constitute a basic mathematical definition. Otherwise this science would be exposed to the same unhappy dissension as philosophy.

4. [*Elementa matheseos universae* (Halle, 1717), I, 96.]

The mathematician deals with concepts—for example, with that of space in general—which in many cases are subject to philosophical definition. But he takes such a concept as given in accordance with the clear and ordinary idea of it. Sometimes (chiefly in applied mathematics) he is given philosophical definitions from other sciences, for instance, the definition of fluidity. But that kind of definition does not arise in mathematics but is only used in it. It is the business of philosophy to analyze concepts which are given as confused, and to make them detailed and definite; but it is the business of mathematics to combine and to compare given concepts of magnitude which are clear and certain in order to see what can be inferred from them.

§ 2. *Mathematics in Its Analyses, Proofs, and Inferences Considers the Universal as Concretely within the Signs; Philosophy Considers the Universal Abstractly by Means of the Signs*

Since we here deal with our theses only as immediate inferences from experience, for the present one I appeal, first, to arithmetic, both to the universal arithmetic of undefined magnitudes and to that which deals with numbers, where the relation of magnitudes to unity is defined. In both, instead of things themselves, their signs are posited together with special indications of their increase or decrease, their ratios, etc. Thereafter we proceed with these signs according to easy and certain rules by substitution, addition, subtraction, and many other kinds of operations, so that the indicated things are completely dropped from sight until the meaning of the symbolic consequence is finally deciphered. Second, for instance in geometry, in order to know the properties of all circles, we draw a circle and then put two lines in it instead of all the possible ones which intersect within it. We show the relationship of these two, and in them we observe *in concreto* the universal rule of the relationship of lines intersecting in any circle.

Compared to this, the procedure in philosophy is quite different. The signs of philosophical observation are always verbal expressions. In their organization they cannot indicate the partial concepts which constitute the complete idea expressed by the word, nor in their connections can they signify the relationships between the philosophical thoughts. In this kind of knowledge, therefore, we must always have the thing itself in view; we must think of the universal *in abstracto* without being able to make use of the important simplification of dealing with single signs instead of general concepts of the things themselves. If a geometer wishes to prove, for example, that space is infinitely divisible, he takes a straight line which stands perpendicular to two parallels, and then from a point on one of these parallel lines he draws others which intersect the perpendicular. In this symbol he recognizes with the greatest certainty that the division must proceed without end. But if a philosopher wishes to prove that every body consists of simple substances, he must first ascertain that a body in general is a whole of substances, that for these substances combination is a contingent state outside of which they could still exist, and thus that all combination in a body could be abolished in thought and yet the substances of which a body is composed exist; and since that which remains of a compounded body, when all combination as such is abolished, must be simple, he concludes that a body must consist of simple substances. In this proof neither figures nor visible signs can express the thoughts or their relations. No substitution of signs by rules can take the place of abstract contemplation so that the philosopher could exchange the conception of the things themselves for the clearer and easier conception of signs; the universal must be considered *in abstracto*.

§ 3. *In Mathematics There Are Few Unanalyzable Concepts and Indemonstrable Propositions, but in Philosophy There Are Many*

The concepts of magnitude as such—unity, quantity, space, etc.—are unanalyzable at least within mathematics; that is, their analysis and definition do not belong to this science. I know very well that some geometers mistake the boundaries between the sciences and sometimes wish to philosophize in mathematics in order to try to define this kind of concept, and this in spite of the fact that in such cases the definition has absolutely no mathematical result. But it is certain that a concept is unanalyzable within a particular discipline if it does not require a definition, at least in this science, and this is true regardless of whether it may be defined elsewhere or not. And I have said that there are few such concepts in mathematics; but I go even further and state that actually none of them can be present in mathematics in the sense that their definition by analysis of concepts belongs to mathematical knowledge, even granting that the definition is possible elsewhere. For mathematics never defines by analyzing a given concept. Only by arbitrary combination can it define an object, the thought of which is first made possible by this combination.

Compare this with philosophy, and what a difference we see! In all its disciplines, especially in metaphysics, we need every analysis that can be made, for the distinctness of knowledge and the possibility of certain inferences depend upon it. But we can see in advance that by analysis we shall inevitably arrive at unanalyzable concepts, whether these concepts are intrinsically unanalyzable or only unanalyzable for us. We also see that there will be a good many of these, since it is impossible that universal cognitions of such great complexity should be compounded from few fundamental concepts. Many concepts, for example, those of a presentation,[5] of contiguity, or of succession, can hardly be defined at all. Others can be defined only in part, as, for example, the concepts of space, time, and of many kinds of feelings of the human mind such as those of the sublime, of the beautiful, of the repulsive, etc. Without more exact knowledge and definition of these feelings, the urges of our nature cannot be adequately recognized; they cannot be fully defined even though a careful observer realizes that a [given] analysis is insufficient. I confess that definitions of pleasure and displeasure, of desire and aversion, and countless others of that kind have never been given by adequate analyses, and I do not wonder at their irresolvability. For distinguishable elementary concepts must be at the basis of concepts of such different kinds. The mistake made by some, who attempt to treat these kinds of cognition as though they could all be broken down into a few simple concepts, is an error like that into which ancient students of nature fell when they taught that all the matter of nature consisted of the so-called four elements—a view which has been superseded by better observation.

5. [*Vorstellung.* When used in a specific and technical sense, as here, this word is translated as *presentation.* Otherwise it is rendered as *conception* or *notion* and occasionally as *impression* or *idea.* It denotes any content of consciousness without specifying the kind.]

Furthermore, at the foundations of mathematics there are only few indemonstrable propositions. Even though they might be proved outside mathematics, within this science they are regarded as immediately certain. "The whole is equal to the sum of its parts." "Only one straight line can be drawn between two points." Mathematicians customarily state such axioms in the beginning to make one aware that only propositions as evident as these are presupposed as true and that all others will be rigorously proved.

If we compare philosophy, and especially metaphysics, with mathematics in this respect, I well might wish to see a table listing the indemonstrable propositions which lie at the foundation of this science in its entire scope. It would take up immeasurable space. The most important occupation of higher philosophy consists only in searching out these indemonstrable basic truths, and discovery of them will never cease so long as knowledge of this kind grows. For, whatever object we take, those characteristics of it which the understanding immediately perceives first are data for just that many indemonstrable propositions, and these then afford the basis on which definitions can be established. Before I even set out to define what space is, I distinctly see that, since this concept is given to me, I must first of all seek out by analysis those characteristics which are immediately thought in this concept. After that I notice that many parts in it are external to each other and that these are not substances (for I do not wish to know objects in space but space itself). Then I notice that space can have only three dimensions, etc. Propositions of this kind can very well be explained; one must see them *in concreto* in order to know them intuitively; but they can never be proved. For how could this be done when we realize that they constitute the first and simplest thoughts I can ever have of the object when I begin to think about it? In mathematics the definitions are the first thought I can have of the defined thing, because my concept of the object arises first from the definition; therefore it is absolutely absurd to consider definitions as demonstrable. In philosophy, where the concept of the thing to be defined is given to me, that which immediately and first of all is perceived in it must serve as an indemonstrable fundamental judgment. For, since I do not yet have the whole distinct concept of the thing but rather seek it, that whole distinct concept is so far from demonstrated by these concepts that it rather serves to generate this distinct knowledge and definition. Thus I must have the first fundamental judgments prior to all philosophical definition of things, and I can fall into the error of considering what is merely a derivative characteristic to be a primordial one. In the following observation there will be remarks that will put this beyond doubt.

§ 4. *The Object of Mathematics Is Easy and Simple; That of Philosophy Is Difficult and Involved*

Since magnitude is the object of mathematics, and since mathematical considerations have regard only to how many times something is posited, it is evident that this knowledge must rest on few and very clear basic theories of general mathematics, which is really universal arithmetic. The increase and decrease of quantities and their resolution into like factors in the theory of roots are easily seen to arise from few and simple basic concepts. A few fundamental concepts of space enable us to apply this general knowledge of quantity to geometry. To convince ourselves of this, we need only, for example, compare the ease in comprehending an arithmetic object which contains a tremendous multiplicity with the very great difficulty in comprehending a philosophical idea through which we try to know but little. The relation of a trillion to unity is very distinctly understood, while philosophers have not yet been able to make the concept of freedom intelligible from its unities, i.e., its simple and familiar concepts. That is, the qualities which make up the proper object of philosophy are infinitely many, and to distinguish between them is extraordinarily demanding; moreover, it is far more difficult to resolve complicated cognitions by analysis than to combine given simple cognitions by synthesis and to reach conclusions in this way. There are many, I know, who find philosophy very easy in comparison with higher mathematics; but they call everything philosophy which is found in books bearing this title. The success shows the difference. Philosophical cognitions often have the fate of opinions and are like meteors whose brilliance holds no promise of duration; they disappear, while mathematics remains. Metaphysics is without doubt the most difficult of all human insights—but a metaphysics has never been written. The question which the Academy proposes shows that we have reason to reconnoiter the path by which we expect, first of all, to seek it.

SECOND REFLECTION

THE SOLE METHOD OF ACHIEVING THE GREATEST POSSIBLE CERTAINTY IN METAPHYSICS

METAPHYSICS is nothing else than a philosophy of the ultimate grounds of our knowledge; what has been shown in the preceding observation to be true of mathematical knowledge in comparison with philosophy will hold also with reference to metaphysics. We have seen noteworthy and essential differences between knowledge in the two sciences, and with reference to them we can say, with Bishop Warburton,[6] that nothing has been more harmful to philosophy than mathematics; or better, there is nothing more harmful than the idea of imitating mathematics as a method of thinking where it cannot possibly be used; for, as concerns the application of mathematics in those parts of philosophy where knowledge of quantities occurs, it is a different matter, and there the usefulness of mathematics is immeasurable.

In mathematics I begin with the definition of my object, such as a triangle or a circle. In metaphysics I can never so begin, and here the definition is so far from being the first thing I know of an object that it is rather almost invariably the last. In mathematics I have no concept whatever of my object before the definition gives rise to it; in metaphysics I have a concept which is already given, though confusedly, and I am to search out the distinct, detailed, and definite concept of the object. How can I then begin? Augustine said, "I know what time is, but when someone asks me, I do not know it."[7] Many stages in the development of obscure ideas by means of comparison, subsumption, and limitation must precede definition, and I dare say that, although many acute and true things have been said about time, the real definition of time has never been given. With regard to nominal definitions, they help little or not at all, for even with-

---

6. [William Warburton (1698–1779), bishop of Gloucester, in his *Julian; or, A Discourse concerning the Earthquake and Fiery Eruption Which Defeated That Emperor's Attempt To Rebuild the Temple at Jerusalem* (London, 1753; German trans., Gotha, 1755), *Works* (London, 1811), VIII, xiv.]

7. [Cf. *The Confessions*, Book ii.]

out them we understand the word well enough not to misuse it. If we only had as many correct definitions as appear under this name in books, with what certainty could we infer and what conclusions could we derive from them! But experience teaches the contrary.

In philosophy and especially in metaphysics we can often distinctly and with certainty know very much about an object and derive sure consequences from it before we are in possession of its definition and even when we do not undertake to give one. Various predicates of anything can be immediately certain, although I do not yet know enough to state the definite itemized concept of the thing, i.e., its definition. Though I might never define what desire is, I would yet be able to say with certainty that every desire presupposes an idea of that which is desired, that this idea is an anticipation of something in the future, that it is associated with the idea of pleasure, etc. All this is constantly perceived by each person in the immediate consciousness of desire. From comparing observations of this kind with each other, we could perhaps eventually arrive at the definition of desire. But so long as we can infer what we seek from some immediately certain characteristics of the desire, even without a definition of it, it is unnecessary to venture on an undertaking which is so precarious. In mathematics it is, as we know, entirely different.

In mathematics the meaning of the signs is certain, because we can easily know what meaning they were intended to have. In philosophy in general, and in metaphysics in particular, verbal expressions have their meaning through customary usage, except where their meaning has been more accurately defined by logical limitation. But because the same expression is frequently used for very similar concepts which nevertheless contain a fair amount of hidden difference, we must, in every application of the concept and even when its designation appears from usage to be entirely fitting, carefully note whether it is really an identical concept which is associated with one and the same sign. We say that a man distinguishes gold from brass when he knows, for instance, that they have different densities. We say, moreover, that cattle distinguish one feed from another when they eat one and let the other alone. Here in two cases the word "distinguish" is used, although in the first case it means "to recognize difference," and this can never occur without making a judgment; but in the second it only indicates that, when there are different impressions, the actions are different also, even when a judgment need not occur. Thus, in the case of cattle, we know only that they are driven to different actions by different sensations, and this is quite possible without their needing to judge about agreement or difference.

The rules of the only method by which the greatest possible metaphysical certainty can be achieved flow quite naturally from the preceding considerations. They are very different from those which have been previously followed, and, if applied, they promise an issue more favorable than anyone has been able to expect on any other path. The first and chief rule is that one should not begin from definitions, for then only verbal definitions would be sought—for example, "That is necessary, the opposite of which is impossible." But, even with these, there are only few cases where one can so confidently establish a distinctly defined concept at the very beginning. Rather one should carefully seek in one's object that of which one is immediately certain, even before one has a definition of it. One should draw inferences from it and seek to obtain only true and perfectly certain judgments on the object. Nor should one parade a hoped-for definition, or even risk it until it offers itself manifestly in the most evident judgments and thus must finally be conceded.

The second rule is that one should particularly note immediate judgments of the object with respect to that which is first found with certainty in it; and, after one is certain that one such judgment is not included in the others, they should, like the axioms of geometry, be made the basis of all inferences. From this it follows that in metaphysical considerations one should particularly indicate whatever is known with certainty, even though it be little. Though one can make experiments with uncertain cognitions in order to see if they might not lead to clues to certain knowledge, this should be done in such a way that it is not confused with the former. I do not cite the other rules which this method has in common with every other rational method but proceed to make them clear by examples.

The genuine method of metaphysics is, in fundamentals, identical with that which was introduced into natural science by Newton and which had such useful consequences there. It says that, by means of certain experiences and always with the aid of geometry, a search should be conducted for the rules according to which particular appearances of nature occur.

Even though we do not understand the ultimate cause of appearances in bodies, it is nevertheless certain that they occur by this law [which Newton discovered], and we explain complicated natural events when we distinctly show how they are included under these well-proved rules. Similarly in metaphysics: through certain inner experience, i.e., self-evident consciousness, we should search for those characteristics which assuredly lie in the concept of any universal property; and, even though we may not know the entire essence of the thing, we can nevertheless make sure use of such characteristics in order to derive from them many properties of the thing.

EXAMPLE OF THE ONLY SURE METHOD OF METAPHYSICS IN THE KNOWLEDGE OF THE NATURE OF BODIES

For the sake of brevity, I refer to a proof, adduced briefly in the First Reflection at the end of § 2, and so use here as a basis the proposition that every body must consist of simple substances. Without establishing what a body is, I know certainly that it consists of parts which would exist even if they were not compounded together; and, if the concept of a substance is an abstract concept, it is without doubt abstracted from corporeal things in the world. But it is not at all necessary to call them substances; it suffices that from them we can infer with utmost certainty that a body consists of simple parts. The obvious analysis of this is easy but too lengthy for this place. Now by means of infallible proofs of geometry I can show that space does not consist of simple parts; and the arguments for this are sufficiently well known not to need repeating. Accordingly, there are a definite number of parts of any body, each of which is simple, and an equal number of parts of the space occupied by the body, each of which parts is compound. From this it follows that each simple part (element) in a body occupies a space. Now if I ask, "What does occupying a space mean?" I become aware, without troubling myself about the essence of space, that if a space can be penetrated by every body without there being anything to resist it, one could certainly, if he wished, say that something was in this space but not that anything occupied it. From this I know that a space is occupied by something when there is something there which resists a moving body in its attempt to penetrate into it. This resistance, however, is impenetrability. Consequently, bodies occupy space by impenetrability.

Impenetrability, however, is a force, for it exerts resistance, i.e., an action opposing an external force. And the force which belongs to a body must belong to its simple parts. Therefore, the elements of every body fill their space by the force of impenetrability. But I further ask, "Are not the ultimate elements of a body extended, since each one fills a space?" Here for once I can offer an explanation which is immediately certain: that is extended which, taken by itself (*absolute*), fills a space, just as each single body would fill a space even if I imagined that there were nothing except it. But if I consider an absolutely simple element taken alone (without connection with others), it is impossible that there should be in it a plurality of things outside each other or that it should by itself occupy a space. Therefore, it cannot be extended. But since an impenetrable force applied against external things is the cause of the element's occupying a space, it may follow that there is a plurality in its external action but not that there is plurality with respect to its internal parts. Consequently, we cannot say that, simply because an element occupies a space in the body (*in nexu cum aliis*), it is extended.

It will take only a few words to make it evident how superficial are the proofs of metaphysicians when they confidently infer from definitions once placed at the foundation, as is their custom. Their inferences are completely lost if the definitions are deceptive. It is well known that most Newtonians go further than Newton and assert that bodies directly attract each other at a distance (or, as they say, through empty space). I pass over the correctness of this proposition, which indeed has much to be said for it. I merely assert that metaphysics has not refuted it. First, bodies are separated when they are not in contact with each other. This is precisely the meaning of the word. Now if I ask, "What is understood by the word 'contact'?" I become aware, without bothering with the definition, that I judge in each case from the impenetrable resistance of another body that I touch it. For I find that this concept originally arises from feeling, just as by the judgment of sight I only surmise that one material body touches another, whereas through feeling the impenetrability of resistance I finally come to know it with certainty. Thus if I say, "A body affects a distant body directly," this means the same as, "It affects it immediately but not by means of impenetrability." But it is not at all obvious why this should be impossible; to prove this, it would have to be shown that impenetrability is either the only force of a body or at least that one body could not be causally related to another except by virtue of their impenetrability. Since this, however, has never been demonstrated and would presumably be hard to prove, metaphysics at least has no good reason to rebel against direct attraction at a distance.

However, let the arguments of the metaphysicians come forward. First there appears the definition: "Immediate reciprocal presence of two bodies is contact." From this it follows that, when two bodies have direct effects on each other, they are in contact. Things in contact are not separated. Consequently, two separated bodies never affect each other directly. And so forth. The definition is surreptitious. Not every immediate presence is contact, but only that which comes through impenetrability. The rest is built on air.

I proceed with my disquisition. It is clear from the examples given that we can say much with certainty about an object, in metaphysics as well as in other sciences, without having defined it. For here neither body nor space has been defined, and yet of both we have trustworthy propositions. The main point I am aiming at is that in metaphysics we must proceed analytically throughout, for its business is in fact to resolve confused cognitions. If we compare with this the actual procedure of philosophers, as it is the fashion in all schools, how perverted we shall find it! The most highly abstract concepts, to which the understanding naturally proceeds only at the end, constitute their starting-point, because the itinerary of the mathematician is in their heads, and him they wish to imitate under all circumstances. But there is a peculiar difference between metaphysics and every other science. In geometry and other fields of mathematics we begin with the easier things and gradually ascend to more difficult exercises. In metaphysics the start is taken from what is most difficult, from possibility and existence in general, necessity and contingency, etc. These concepts demand much abstraction and attention, especially since in being applied their signs suffer many imperceptible modifications, and the differences between these must not be overlooked. Instead we are told the procedure must by all means be synthetic. Accordingly, one defines at the outset and confidently draws conclusions. Philosophers of this taste congratulate each other on having learned from the geometer the secret of thorough thinking; they do not notice that geometers obtain concepts by synthesis which philosophers can attain only by analysis and that this completely changes the method of thinking.

On the other hand, as soon as philosophers strike out on the natural path of sound reason, seeking first that which they assuredly know about the abstract concept of an object (e.g., space or time) without making any claim to definitions; when they infer only from these sure data; when they inquire at each changed application of a concept whether the concept itself has not changed even though its sign remains the same—then perhaps they will not have so many insights for sale, but those which they do offer will be of definite value. I will give one more illustration of the latter mistake. Most philosophers use as an example of obscure concepts those which we may have in deep sleep. Obscure notions are those of which we are not conscious. Now some experiences show that in deep sleep we do have ideas, and, since we are not conscious of them, they must have been obscure. Here *consciousness* has two meanings. Either one is not conscious of having an idea, or one is not conscious that one has had it. The former signifies the obscurity of the idea as it is in the mind; the latter shows no more than that he does not remember it. Now the given example shows only that there can be ideas which one does not remember when awake. But it does not follow that in sleep they could not have been clear to consciousness, as in Sauvage's[8] example of a cataleptic person or in the ordinary actions of a somnambulist. By not giving, through attention to every particular case, the definite meaning to the concept, and by jumping too quickly at a conclusion, a presumably great secret of nature is overlooked, namely, that in deepest sleep perhaps the greatest perfection of the mind might be exercised in rational thought. For we have no reason for asserting the opposite except that we do not remember the idea when awake. This reason, however, proves nothing.

It is far from the time for proceeding synthetically in metaphysics; only when analysis will have helped us to distinct concepts understood in their details will synthesis be able to subsume compounded cognitions under the simplest cognitions, as in mathematics.

---

8. [François Bossier de Sauvage de la Croix (1706–67), a physician, in his "Betrachtungen über die Seele in der Erstarrung und Schlafwanderung," *Hamburger Magazin*, VII, 489–512.]

THIRD REFLECTION
OF THE NATURE OF METAPHYSICAL CERTAINTY

§ 1. *Philosophical Certainty Is of an Altogether Different Nature from Mathematical Certainty*

ONE is certain in so far as he knows that a cognition cannot possibly be false. The degree of this certainty, when taken objectively, is a matter of the sufficiency of the characteristics of the necessity of a truth. But so far as it is considered subjectively, it is higher the more intuition there is in the cognition of this necessity. In either case, mathematical certainty is of a different kind from philosophical. I shall show this with the greatest plainness.

Human understanding, like any other force of nature, is bound by certain rules. We do not err because the understanding connects concepts without any rule but because we deny to a thing a characteristic we do not perceive, and we judge that of which we are not conscious in a thing does not exist. Now mathematics first arrives at its concepts synthetically, and it can say with certainty that what it did not intend to represent in its object by definition is not included in it. For the concept of the defined arises first from the definition, and it has no meaning at all other than that which the definition gives it. If we compare philosophy and especially metaphysics with mathematics in this respect, they are far more uncertain in their definitions when they do venture to give them, for the concept of that which is to be defined is already given. If we do not note one or another characteristic even though it belongs to the adequate discrimination of the object, and then judge that this characteristic is lacking in the full concept, the definition becomes false and deceptive. We could bring that kind of error to light through countless examples, but I refer only to the already given example of contact.

Secondly, mathematics in its inferences and proofs considers its universal knowledge as concretely in its signs, while philosophy considers its as continuing abstractly alongside its signs. This makes a noteworthy difference in the way each attains certainty, for, since the signs of mathematics are sensuous instruments of knowledge, we can, with the same assurance we have in that which we see, also know that we have left no concept out of sight, that each individual comparison is made according to simple rules, etc. Attention herein is greatly facilitated by not having to consider the things in their universal sense but rather signs in the individual cognition we have of them. On the other hand, the verbal expressions, as the signs of philosophical knowledge, help in nothing but remembering the signified universal concepts. We must always keep their meaning directly before us. Pure understanding must be kept in a state of exertion, for how imperceptibly a characteristic of an abstract concept may slip away, since nothing sensuous can reveal its omission! Then, however, different things are held to be the same, and we bring forth erroneous cognitions.

It has now been shown that the grounds from which we can conclude the impossibility of having erred in a particular philosophical cognition are never equal to those we have in mathematics. Moreover, the intuition of this cognition is greater regarding its correctness in mathematics than in philosophy, since in the former the object is considered concretely in the sensuous sign, while in the latter it is only considered in universal abstract concepts, the clear impression of which cannot be nearly so great as that of the former. In geometry, where the signs have in addition a similarity to the designated things, the evidence is even greater, though in calculations with letters the certainty is just as dependable.

§ 2. *Metaphysics Is Capable of a Certainty Which Is Sufficient for Conviction*

Certainty in metaphysics is of the same kind as that in any other philosophical knowledge, as the latter can only be certain in so far as it conforms to the universal principles which metaphysics furnishes. We know from experience that on rational grounds even outside mathematics we can in many cases achieve certainty to the point of conviction. Metaphysics is only philosophy applied to more universal rational insights, and it cannot be otherwise with it.

Errors do not arise simply because we do not know some particular thing but because we undertake to judge even though we do not know everything requisite. A large number of falsities —indeed, almost all of them—owe their origin to such rashness. You know some predicates of a thing with certainty? Very well, make these the basis of your inferences, and you will not err.

But you wish to make a definition with them, although you are not certain that you know everything requisite for a definition? If in spite of this you risk a definition, you fall into error. It is therefore possible to avoid errors if we seek certain and distinct cognitions without presuming to give definitions so readily. Further, you can infer a considerable part of a certain conclusion with assurance, but do not permit yourself to infer to the complete conclusion, however trivial the difference may seem to be. I concede that we have a good proof that the soul is not matter. But take care not to conclude that the soul is not of a material nature, for by this everyone understands not merely that the soul is not matter but also that it is not a simple substance such as an element of matter could be. This requires a special proof, namely, that this thinking being cannot be like a corporeal element in space and that, because of impenetrability, it could, with other corporeal elements, constitute an extended being or a mass. But actually no proof has yet been given of this; and the proof, when discovered, would show the inconceivable manner in which a mind is present in space.

§ 3. *The Certainty of the Ultimate Fundamental Truths in Metaphysics Is of No Other Kind than That in Every Other Rational Knowledge, with the Exception of Mathematics*

In our time the philosophy of Crusius*⁹ has undertaken to give metaphysics an altogether different form, because he does not concede to the law of contradiction the prerogative of being the universal and supreme principle of all knowledge; rather he has

---

* I have not found it necessary to discuss here the method of this new philosophy. It has quickly become so famous and has so much merit in respect to the better clarification of many views that it would be an essential lack, when metaphysics itself is discussed, to pass over it in silence. But what I am here dealing with is only the proper method of metaphysics; the difference in single propositions is not sufficient to indicate an essential difference between one philosophy and another.

9. [Christian August Crusius (1715–75), an influential anti-Wolffian generally held in high regard by Kant. From the principle Kant quotes, Crusius attempted to derive the law of contradiction and the principles of inseparability (what cannot be thought as separate cannot exist as separate) and of incompatibility (things which cannot be thought together cannot exist together). He thus attempted to bring together what was kept independent in the rationalistic laws of contradiction and of sufficient reason.]

introduced many other immediately certain and indemonstrable principles and asserted that their correctness is grasped by the nature of our understanding according to the rule, "That which I cannot think except as true is true." He counts as such principles the following propositions, among others: what I cannot think of as existing has never existed, everything that exists must be somewhere at some time, and the like. In a few words I shall show the true property of the ultimate truths of metaphysics and also the true import of Crusius' method, which does not depart so far from the manner of philosophical thinking about these matters as one might think. From this one will be able to deduce the degree of certainty possible in metaphysics.

All true judgments must be either affirmative or negative. As the form of any affirmation consists in something being thought as a characteristic of a thing, i.e., as identical with the thing's characteristic, any affirmative judgment is true when the predicate is identical with the subject. And since the form of any negation consists in thinking something as conflicting with a thing, a negative judgment is true when the predicate contradicts the subject. The proposition expressing the essence of any affirmation and thus containing the supreme formula of all affirmative judgments, therefore, reads as follows: "For every subject there is a predicate which is identical with it." This is the law of identity. And the proposition which expresses the essence of all negation is: "No subject has a predicate which contradicts it." This is the law of contradiction, and hence this law is the basic formula of all negative judgments. Both together constitute the supreme and universal principles, in a formal sense, of the entire human reason. And here most philosophers have erred in conceding to the law of contradiction a rank with respect to all truths which it actually has only in respect to negative truths. Every proposition is indemonstrable which is immediately thought under one of these supreme principles but which cannot be thought otherwise; that is, when either identity or contradiction lies directly in the concepts and cannot be seen by analysis or needs to be discerned by means of some intermediate characteristic. All other propositions are demonstrable. That a body is divisible is a demonstrable proposition, since we can show the identity of the predicate with the subject by analysis and hence indirectly. (A body is compound, and what is compound is divisible; therefore a body is divisible. The intermediate characteristic here is "compound.") Now in philosophy there are many indemonstrable propositions, as I have said. All of them stand under these formal ultimate principles, though indirectly; but, so far as they also contain grounds of other cognitions, they are the ultimate material principles of human reason. For instance, that a body is compound is an indemonstrable proposition, in so far as the predicate can only be thought as an immediate and primary characteristic in the concept of a body. Such material principles constitute, as Crusius correctly says, the foundation and stability of human reason, for, as we have said, they are the content to be defined and the data from which sure inferences can be drawn even when we have no definition.

Crusius is right in reproaching other schools of philosophers for having passed over these material principles and for having restricted themselves merely to the formal principles. For from the latter alone nothing at all can be proved, because propositions are required which contain the mediating concept by which the logical relation of other concepts are to be recognized in a syllogism, and among these propositions there must be some which are fundamental. But we can never attribute the status of material supreme principles to any propositions if they are not evident to every human understanding. But I hold that several of the principles Crusius adduces even permit of considerable doubt.

But with respect to the supreme rule of all certainty which this celebrated man proposes to set before all knowledge and hence also before metaphysical knowledge—"What I cannot think except as true is true," etc.—it is easy to see that this proposition can never be a basis of the truth of any cognition. For if one admits that no other ground of truth can be given than that it would be impossible to regard it otherwise than as true, this is to admit that no further ground of truth can be given, and hence that the cognition is indemonstrable. Now there certainly are many indemonstrable cognitions, but the feeling of conviction with reference to them is an avowal that they are true but not a basis of proof of it.

Metaphysics, therefore, has no formal or material basis of certainty of any other kind than geometry. In both the formal element of judgment occurs in accordance with the laws of identity and contradiction. In both there are indemonstrable propositions which are the foundations of inferences. But since the definitions in mathematics are the primary indemonstrable concepts of the defined things, in their stead various indemonstrable propositions in metaphysics must furnish the primary data. They can be just as certain, however, and they afford either the content for definition or the basis of sure implications. There is a certainty needed for conviction, and metaphysics is capable of it just as mathematics is, though mathematics is easier and partakes of a greater degree of intuition.

FOURTH REFLECTION

OF THE DISTINCTNESS AND CERTAINTY OF WHICH THE PRIMARY GROUNDS OF NATURAL THEOLOGY AND MORALS ARE CAPABLE

§ 1. *The Primary Grounds of Natural Theology Are Capable of the Greatest Philosophical Evidence*

A THING can be most easily and distinctly differentiated from all others when it is the only possible thing of its kind. The object of natural religion is the only first cause; its attributes are so constituted that they cannot easily be mistaken for those of another. The greatest conviction is possible where it is absolutely necessary that precisely these and no other predicates apply to a thing; for with accidental attributes is is often difficult to discover the variable conditions of the predicates of a thing. The absolutely necessary being is therefore an object of such a kind that, as soon as one obtains a true clue to its concept, it seems to promise more certainty than most other philosophical cognitions. Concerning this part of the problem I cannot do more than direct attention to the possible philosophical cognition of God in general, for it would take us too far afield to examine the actual theories of philosophers on this subject.

The chief concept which offers itself to the metaphysician in this field is that of the absolutely necessary existence of a being. In order to arrive at this concept, he could first ask whether it be possible that nothing at all existed. When he becomes aware that then neither existence is given, nor anything that might be thought, and that no possibility takes place, he may investigate only the concept of the existence of that which must be the foundation of all possibility. This thought will broaden itself, and it will establish the definite concept of the absolutely necessary being. Without going particularly into this procedure, it is clear that as soon as the existence of the one and only most perfect and necessary being is known, the concepts of its other attributes will become much more precise, because they are without exception the greatest and most perfect, and they are much more certain since only those can be admitted which are necessary to the being. I wish, for example, to define the concept of divine omnipresence. I easily recognize that the being on which everything else depends, while being itself independent, will determine by its presence the location of everything else in the world but that it itself cannot have a location among them, for then it would belong, with them, to the world. Therefore, God is, properly speaking, in no place, but He is present to all things in all places where they are. Similarly I see that, since the successive things of the world are in His power, He does not take up a particular point in this series; thus I see that with respect to Him nothing is future or past. If I thus say that God foresees the future, that does not mean that He sees what is future with respect to Himself but what is future with respect to certain things in the world, that is, what follows on a condition in which they are. From this it is seen that knowledge of the future, past, and present with respect to the actions of the divine understanding is identical and that God sees them all as real things in the universe. Thus we can conceive of this prevision much more definitely and distinctly as belonging to God than as belonging to a thing which is a part of the world-whole.

In all cases where an analogy to contingency is not present, therefore, metaphysical knowledge of God can be very certain. But judgments[10] of His free actions, of providence, of the ways of His justice and benevolence, even in the concepts which we have of these attributes in ourselves, are far less developed; in this science they can have either certainty only by approximation or certainty which is moral.

§ 2. *The Primary Grounds of Morals Are, in Their Present State, Not Yet Capable of All Requisite Evidence*

In order to make this clear, I wish only to show how little even the primary concept of obligation is known, and how far removed we must therefore be in practical philosophy from proffering the distinctness and certainty of fundamental concepts and principles which are required for evidence. One ought to do

10. [*Urteil*, but a plural verb is used.]

this or that and leave something else undone; this is the formula under which every obligation is enunciated. Now that "ought" expresses a necessity of action and is capable of two meanings. That is, either I ought to do something (as a means) if I wish something else (as an end), or I ought directly to do something else and make it real (as an end). The former we can call the necessity of means (*necessitatem problematicam*), and the latter the necessity of ends (*necessitatem legalem*). No obligation is present in necessity of the first kind; it only prescribes the solution of a problem, saying what are the means I must use if I wish to reach a particular end. When anyone prescribes to another the actions which he should do or refrain from doing if he wishes to promote his happiness, perhaps all the teachings of morals could be brought under the precepts; but they are then no longer obligations but only like what might be called an obligation to make two arcs if I wish to bisect a line. That is, they are not obligations at all but only counsels to suitable actions if one wishes to attain a particular end. Since the use of means has no other necessity than that which pertains to the end, it follows that all actions which morals prescribes under the condition of particular ends are contingent and cannot be called obligations so long as they are not subordinated to an end necessary in itself. I ought, for example, to promote the greatest total perfection, or I ought to act according to the will of God; to whichever of these propositions all practical philosophy were subordinated, that proposition, if it is to be a rule and principle of obligation, must command the action as directly necessary, not commanding it merely under the condition of some particular end. And here we find that such an immediate supreme rule of all obligation would have to be absolutely indemonstrable. For from no consideration of a thing or concept, whatever it be, is it possible to know and infer what we should do, unless what is presupposed is an end and the action a means. But this it must not be, because it would then be a formula not of obligation but only of problematic skill.

Now I can briefly suggest, after long consideration of this subject, that I am convinced that the rule, *Do the most perfect thing that can be done by you* is the primary formal principle of all obligation of commission, and the proposition *Refrain from that whereby the greatest perfection possible through you is hindered* is the primary formal principle with respect to the duty of omission. And just as nothing follows from the primary formal principles of our judgments of truth except when primary material grounds are given, so also no particular definite obligation follows from these two rules except when indemonstrable material principles of practical knowledge are connected with them.

In these times we have first begun to realize that the faculty of conceiving of truth is intellection, while that of sensing the good is feeling, and that they must not be interchanged. Just as there are unanalyzable concepts of the true, that is, what is met with in the objects of intellection considered by themselves, there is also an unanalyzable feeling for the good. (The good is never found in a thing by itself but always with relation to a feeling being.) It is a task of the understanding to resolve the compounded and confused concept of the good and to make it distinct by showing how it arises from simpler sensations of the good. But if the sensation of the good[11] is simple, the judgment, "This is good," is completely indemonstrable and a direct effect of the consciousness of the feeling of pleasure associated with the conception of the object. And since many simple sensations of the good are certainly in us, there are many simple unanalyzable conceptions of the good. Consequently, if an action is directly thought of as good without surreptitiously containing another particular good which can be found in it by analysis, and because of which it is called perfect, it follows that the necessity of this action is an indemonstrable material principle of obligation. For instance, "Love him who loves you" is a practical proposition which certainly and directly stands under the supreme formal and affirmative rule of obligation. For since it cannot be shown by further analysis why a particular perfection inheres in mutual love, this rule is not proved practically, i.e., by tracing it back to the necessity of another perfect action. Rather, it is directly subsumed under the universal rule of good actions. It may be that my example does not distinctly and convincingly prove my point; but the limits of an essay like the present one—which I have perhaps already exceeded—do not allow me the completeness which I would wish. There is an immediate deformity in the action which conflicts with the will of that Being from Whom our existence and everything good is derived. This deformity is clear even if no attention is given to the disadvantages which can accompany such conduct as its consequence. Therefore, the proposition that we should do that which conforms to the will

11. [Reading, with Vorländer, "the sensation of the good."]

of God becomes a material principle of morals standing formally, but directly, under the already mentioned supreme and universal formula. Just as in theoretical philosophy, so also in the practical we should not so readily consider something indemonstrable when it is not. Nevertheless, these principles cannot be dispensed with, for as postulates they contain the foundations of the rest of the other practical propositions. In this respect, under the name of the "moral feeling," Hutcheson and others have provided a start toward some excellent observations.

From this it can be seen that, although it must be possible to achieve the highest degree of philosophical evidence in the primary bases of morality, the supreme principles of obligation must first be defined with more certainty. In this respect the task is greater in practical than in speculative philosophy, since it is still to be settled whether it is simply the cognitive faculty or whether it is feeling (the primary inner ground of the appetitive faculty) which decides the basic principles of practical philosophy.

POSTSCRIPT

THESE are the thoughts which I submit to the judgment of the Royal Academy of Sciences. I venture to hope that the principles I have expounded are of some significance for the desired clarification of the subject. I have preferred to be neglectful with respect to carefulness, proportion, and neatness of execution so that I should not, by attending to them, be hindered from transmitting these thoughts for examination within the allowed time, especially since this lack can easily be made up in the event that the essay is favorably received.

IV

WHAT IS ENLIGHTENMENT?

ENLIGHTENMENT is man's release from his self-incurred tutelage. Tutelage is man's inability to make use of his understanding without direction from another. Self-incurred is this tutelage when its cause lies not in lack of reason but in lack of resolution and courage to use it without direction from another. *Sapere aude!*[1] "Have courage to use your own reason!"—that is the motto of enlightenment.

Laziness and cowardice are the reasons why so great a portion of mankind, after nature has long since discharged them from external direction (*naturaliter maiorennes*), nevertheless remains under lifelong tutelage, and why it is so easy for others to set themselves up as their guardians. It is so easy not to be of age. If I have a book which understands for me, a pastor who has a conscience for me, a physician who decides my diet, and so forth, I need not trouble myself. I need not think, if I can only pay—others will readily undertake the irksome work for me.

That the step to competence is held to be very dangerous by the far greater portion of mankind (and by the entire fair sex)—quite apart from its being arduous—is seen to by those guardians who have so kindly assumed superintendence over them. After the guardians have first made their domestic cattle dumb and have made sure that these placid creatures will not dare take a single step without the harness of the cart to which they are confined, the guardians then show them the danger which threatens if they try to go alone. Actually, however, this danger is not so great, for by falling a few times they would finally learn to walk alone. But an example of this failure makes them timid and ordinarily frightens them away from all further trials.

For any single individual to work himself out of the life under tutelage which has become almost his nature is very difficult. He has come to be fond of this state, and he is for the present really incapable of making use of his reason, for no one

---

1. ["Dare to know!" (Horace, *Ars poetica*).]

has ever let him try it out. Statutes and formulas, those mechanical tools of the rational employment or rather misemployment of his natural gifts, are the fetters of an everlasting tutelage. Whoever throws them off makes only an uncertain leap over the narrowest ditch because he is not accustomed to that kind of free motion. Therefore, there are only few who have succeeded by their own exercise of mind both in freeing themselves from incompetence and in achieving a steady pace.

But that the public should enlighten itself is more possible; indeed, if only freedom is granted, enlightenment is almost sure to follow. For there will always be some independent thinkers, even among the established guardians of the great masses, who, after throwing off the yoke of tutelage from their own shoulders, will disseminate the spirit of the rational appreciation of both their own worth and every man's vocation for thinking for himself. But be it noted that the public, which has first been brought under this yoke by their guardians, forces the guardians themselves to remain bound when it is incited to do so by some of the guardians who are themselves capable of some enlightenment—so harmful is it to implant prejudices, for they later take vengeance on their cultivators or on their descendants. Thus the public can only slowly attain enlightenment. Perhaps a fall of personal despotism or of avaricious or tyrannical oppression may be accomplished by revolution, but never a true reform in ways of thinking. Rather, new prejudices will serve as well as old ones to harness the great unthinking masses.

For this enlightenment, however, nothing is required but freedom, and indeed the most harmless freedom of all, which alone should be called by this name. It is the freedom to make public use of one's reason at every point.[2] But I hear on all sides, "Do not argue!" The officer says: "Do not argue but drill!" The tax-collector: "Do not argue but pay!" The cleric: "Do not argue but believe!" Only one prince in the world says, "Argue as much as you will, and about what you will, but obey!" Everywhere there is restriction on freedom.

Which restriction is an obstacle to enlightenment, and which is not an obstacle but a promoter of it? I answer: The public use of one's reason must always be free, and it alone can bring about enlightenment among men. The private use of reason, on the

---

2. [It is this freedom Kant claimed later in his conflict with the censor, deferring to the censor in the "private" use of reason, i.e., in his lectures.]

other hand, may often be very narrowly restricted without particularly hindering the progress of enlightenment. By the public use of one's reason I understand the use which a person makes of it as a scholar before the reading public. Private use I call that which one may make of it in a particular civil post or office which is intrusted to him. Many affairs which are conducted in the interest of the community require a certain mechanism through which some members of the community must passively conduct themselves with an artificial unanimity, so that the government may direct them to public ends, or at least prevent them from destroying those ends. Here argument is certainly not allowed—one must obey. But so far as a part of the mechanism regards himself at the same time as a member of the whole community or of a society of world citizens, and thus in the role of a scholar who addresses the public (in the proper sense of the word) through his writings, he certainly can argue without hurting the affairs for which he is in part responsible as a passive member. Thus it would be ruinous for an officer in service to debate about the suitability or utility of a command given to him by his superior; he must obey. But the right to make remarks on errors in the military service and to lay them before the public for judgment cannot equitably be refused him as a scholar. The citizen cannot refuse to pay the taxes imposed on him; indeed, an impudent complaint at those levied on him can be punished as a scandal (as it could occasion general refractoriness). But the same person nevertheless does not act contrary to his duty as a citizen when, as a scholar, he publicly expresses his thoughts on the inappropriateness or even the injustice of these levies. Similarly a clergyman is obligated to make his sermon to his pupils in catechism and his congregation conform to the symbol of the church which he serves, for he has been accepted on this condition. But as a scholar he has complete freedom, even the calling, to communicate to the public all his carefully tested and well-meaning thoughts on that which is erroneous in the symbol and to make suggestions for the better organization of the religious body and church. In doing this, there is nothing that could be laid as a burden on his conscience. For what he teaches as a consequence of his office as a representative of the church, this he considers something about which he has no freedom to teach according to his own lights; it is something which he is appointed to propound at the dictation of and in the name of another. He will say, "Our church teaches this or that; those are the proofs which it adduces." He thus extracts all practical uses for his congregation from statutes to which he himself would not subscribe with full conviction but to the enunciation of which he can very well pledge himself because it is not impossible that truth lies hidden in them, and, in any case, there is at least nothing in them contradictory to inner religion. For if he believed he had found such in them, he could not conscientiously discharge the duties of his office; he would have to give it up. The use, therefore, which an appointed teacher makes of his reason before his congregation is merely private, because this congregation is only a domestic one (even if it be a large gathering); with respect to it, as a priest, he is not free, nor can he be free, because he carries out the orders of another. But as a scholar, whose writings speak to his public, the world, the clergyman in the public use of his reason enjoys an unlimited freedom to use his own reason and to speak in his own person. That the guardians of the people (in spiritual things) should themselves be incompetent is an absurdity which amounts to the eternalization of absurdities.

But would not a society of clergymen, perhaps a church conference or a venerable classis (as they call themselves among the Dutch), be justified in obligating itself by oath to a certain unchangeable symbol in order to enjoy an unceasing guardianship over each of its members and thereby over the people as a whole, and even to make it eternal? I answer that this is altogether impossible. Such a contract, made to shut off all further enlightenment from the human race, is absolutely null and void even if confirmed by the supreme power, by parliaments, and by the most ceremonious of peace treaties. An age cannot bind itself and ordain to put the succeeding one into such a condition that it cannot extend its (at best very occasional) knowledge, purify itself of errors, and progress in general enlightenment. That would be a crime against human nature, the proper destination of which lies precisely in this progress; and the descendants would be fully justified in rejecting those decrees as having been made in an unwarranted and malicious manner.

The touchstone of everything that can be concluded as a law for a people lies in the question whether the people could have imposed such a law on itself. Now such a religious compact might be possible for a short and definitely limited time, as it were, in expectation of a better. One might let every citizen, and especially the clergyman, in the role of scholar, make his comments freely and publicly, i.e., through writing, on the erroneous aspects of the present institution. The newly introduced order might last until insight into the nature of these things had become so general and widely approved that through uniting their voices (even if not unanimously) they could bring a proposal to the throne to take those congregations under protection which had united into a changed religious organization according to their better ideas, without, however, hindering others who wish to remain in the order. But to unite in a permanent religious institution which is not to be subject to doubt before the public even in the lifetime of one man, and thereby to make a period of time fruitless in the progress of mankind toward improvement, thus working to the disadvantage of posterity—that is absolutely forbidden. For himself (and only for a short time) a man can postpone enlightenment in what he ought to know, but to renounce it for himself and even more to renounce it for posterity is to injure and trample on the rights of mankind.

And what a people may not decree for itself can even less be decreed for them by a monarch, for his lawgiving authority rests on his uniting the general public will in his own. If he only sees to it that all true or alleged improvement stands together with civil order, he can leave it to his subjects to do what they find necessary for their spiritual welfare. This is not his concern, though it is incumbent on him to prevent one of them from violently hindering another in determining and promoting this welfare to the best of his ability. To meddle in these matters lowers his own majesty, since by the writings in which his subjects seek to present their views he may evaluate his own governance. He can do this when, with deepest understanding, he lays upon himself the reproach, *Caesar non est supra grammaticos*. Far more does he injure his own majesty when he degrades his supreme power by supporting the ecclesiastical despotism of some tyrants in his state over his other subjects.

If we are asked, "Do we now live in an *enlightened age?*" the answer is, "No," but we do live in an *age of enlightenment*.[3] As things now stand, much is lacking which prevents men from being, or easily becoming, capable of correctly using their own reason in religious matters with assurance and free from outside direction. But, on the other hand, we have clear indications that the field has now been opened wherein men may freely deal with

3. ["Our age is, in especial degree, the age of criticism, and to criticism everything must submit" (*Critique of Pure Reason*, Preface to first ed. [Smith trans.]).]

these things and that the obstacles to general enlightenment or the release from self-imposed tutelage are gradually being reduced. In this respect, this is the age of enlightenment, or the century of Frederick.

A prince who does not find it unworthy of himself to say that he holds it to be his duty to prescribe nothing to men in religious matters but to give them complete freedom while renouncing the haughty name of *tolerance*, is himself enlightened and deserves to be esteemed by the grateful world and posterity as the first, at least from the side of government, who divested the human race of its tutelage and left each man free to make use of his reason in matters of conscience. Under him venerable ecclesiastics are allowed, in the role of scholars, and without infringing on their official duties, freely to submit for public testing their judgments and views which here and there diverge from the established symbol. And an even greater freedom is enjoyed by those who are restricted by no official duties. This spirit of freedom spreads beyond this land, even to those in which it must struggle with external obstacles erected by a government which misunderstands its own interest. For an example gives evidence to such a government that in freedom there is not the least cause for concern about public peace and the stability of the community. Men work themselves gradually out of barbarity if only intentional artifices are not made to hold them in it.

I have placed the main point of enlightenment—the escape of men from their self-incurred tutelage—chiefly in matters of religion because our rulers have no interest in playing the guardian with respect to the arts and sciences and also because religious incompetence is not only the most harmful but also the most degrading of all. But the manner of thinking of the head of a state who favors religious enlightenment goes further, and he sees that there is no danger to his lawgiving in allowing his subjects to make public use of their reason and to publish their thoughts on a better formulation of his legislation and even their open-minded criticisms of the laws already made. Of this we have a shining example wherein no monarch is superior to him whom we honor.

But only one who is himself enlightened, is not afraid of shadows, and has a numerous and well-disciplined army to assure public peace can say: "Argue as much as you will, and about what you will, only obey!" A republic could not dare say such a thing. Here is shown a strange and unexpected trend in human affairs in which almost everything, looked at in the large, is paradoxical. A greater degree of civil freedom appears advantageous to the freedom of mind of the people, and yet it places inescapable limitations upon it; a lower degree of civil freedom, on the contrary, provides the mind with room for each man to extend himself to his full capacity. As nature has uncovered from under this hard shell the seed for which she most tenderly cares —the propensity and vocation to free thinking—this gradually works back upon the character of the people, who thereby gradually become capable of managing freedom; finally, it affects the principles of government, which finds it to its advantage to treat men, who are now more than machines, in accordance with their dignity.*

I. KANT

KÖNIGSBERG, PRUSSIA
September 30, 1784

* Today I read in the *Büschingsche Wöchentliche Nachrichten* for September 13 an announcement of the *Berlinische Monatsschrift* for this month, which cites the answer to the same question by Herr Mendelssohn.[4] But this issue has not yet come to me; if it had, I would have held back the present essay, which is now put forth only in order to see how much agreement in thought can be brought about by chance.

4. [Mendelssohn's answer was that enlightenment lay in intellectual cultivation, which he distinguished from the practical. Kant, quite in line with his later essay on theory and practice, refuses to make this distinction fundamental.]

V

WHAT IS ORIENTATION IN THINKING?

HOWEVER high we aim our concepts and however much we thereby abstract them from sensuousness, imaginal notions[1] are always appended to them. Their proper function is to fit the concepts not otherwise derived from experience for empirical use. For how could we give any sense and significance to our concepts if they were not supported by some intuition, which must always be, in the final analysis, an example from some possible experience? If we subsequently omit from the concrete operation of the understanding all admixture of the image, first of the contingent perception by the senses and then pure sensuous intuition in general, there remains the pure concept of the understanding, whose scope now is broadened and contains a rule of thinking in general. In such a way general logic itself came into being. Many heuristic methods of thinking may still lie concealed in the empirical use of understanding and reason, and, if we understood how to extract them carefully from experience, they could enrich philosophy, even in its abstract thinking, with many useful maxims.

Such is the principle which the late Mendelssohn explicitly acknowledged, so far as I know, only in his last works (the *Morgenstunden*, pp. 165–66 and the *Letter to Lessing's Friends*,[2] pp. 33 and 67). That is the maxim that, in the speculative use of reason (which he otherwise trusted very much with respect to knowledge of supersensuous objects, even to the point of evident demonstration), it is necessary to orient one's self by means of a certain guide which he variously called common sense (*Morgenstunden*), sound reason, and mere human understanding (*Letter to Lessing's Friends*). Who would have thought that not only would this avowal have destroyed his high opinion of the power

---

1. [*Bildliche Vorstellung*. Kant is here referring to the schema, the "representation of a universal procedure of imagination in providing an image (*Bild*) for a concept" (*Critique of Pure Reason* A 140 = B 179–80).]

2. [*Brief an die Freunde Lessings; ein Anhang zu Herrn Jacobis Briefwechsel über die Lehre des Spinoza* (Berlin, 1786).]

of speculative reason in matters of theology (which was in fact inevitable) but that common sound reason, through the ambiguity thus permitted in the exercise of its faculty as distinguished from speculation, would become involved in the danger of serving as the basis of fanaticism and of the complete overthrow of reason? Yet this is what happened in the polemic between Mendelssohn and Jacobi, chiefly through the not insignificant inferences of the acute author of the *Resultate.**[3] I will not attribute to either the intention of establishing such a ruinous way of thought but will regard the undertaking of the latter rather as an *argumentum ad hominem* which one is justified in using merely in defense, in order to take advantage of the weakness shown by one's opponent. On the other hand, I shall show that in fact reason alone is required for orientation and not some alleged secret truth-sense, nor a transcendent intuition dubbed faith upon which tradition or revelation could be grafted without the agreement of reason. I shall show, as Mendelssohn asserted with firmness and justified zeal, that it is only pure human reason by which he found it necessary and commendable to obtain orientation. But at the same time it will be shown that the high pretension of the speculative faculty of reason, and especially the authority given to it by demonstration alone, is void and that nothing is left to reason, so far as it is speculative, except the business of purging the common concepts of reason from contradictions and of defense against its own sophistical attacks on the maxims of sound reason.

The broadened and more exactly defined concept of orientation can help us in clearly exhibiting the maxim of sound reason in its efforts toward knowledge of supersensuous objects.

To orient one's self in the strict sense of the word means to find, from one given direction in the world (one of the four into which we divide the horizon), the others, especially the east. If I see the sun in the sky and know that it is now noon, I know

* Jacobi, *Briefe über die Lehre des Spinoza*[4] (Breslau, 1785); *Wider Mendelssohns Beschuldigung betreffend die Briefe über die Lehre des Spinoza* (Leipzig, 1786); *Die Resultate der Jacobischen und Mendelssohnschen Philosophie kritisch untersucht von einem Freiwilligen* (Leipzig, 1786).

3. [Thomas Wizenmann (1759–87). Wizenmann answered Kant in his "An dem Herrn Professor Kant von dem Verfasser der Resultate...," *Deutches Museum*, I (1787), 116–56.]

4. [Correct title: *Über die Lehre des Spinoza, in Briefen an Herrn Moses Mendelssohn.*]

how to find south, west, north, and east. But for this I certainly need the feeling of a distinction in my own person, that between my right and left hand. I call it a feeling, because the two sides in intuition show no externally noticeable difference. Without the capacity to distinguish between motion from left to right and that in the opposite direction in describing a circle, in spite of the absence of any difference in the objects, I would be unable to determine a priori any difference in the position of objects; I would not know whether to put west to the left or right of the south point of the horizon so as to know how to complete the circle from north through east to the south. Thus I orient myself geographically by all the objective data of the sky only by virtue of a subjective ground of distinction; and if someday a miracle occurred whereby the direction of all the stars changed from east to west but preserved the same pattern and position, on the next starry night no human eye would notice the slightest change, and even the astronomer, if he attended to what he merely saw and not what he at the same time felt, would be inevitably disoriented. But the ability to distinguish by feeling between the right and the left hand, which is implanted by nature and made familiar by frequent use, would come naturally to his help, and if he once viewed the pole star, he not only would notice the change but would orient himself regardless of it.

This geographical concept of the procedure of orientation can be broadened to purely mathematical orientation so as to include orientation in any given space. In the dark I orient myself in a familiar room when I can seize on a single object whose position I remember. Here obviously nothing helps me except the capacity of determining positions by a subjective ground of distinction. For I do not see the objects whose position I should find, and if someone had played a joke on me by putting on the left what was previously on the right while still preserving their relationships to each other, I could not find my way in a room with otherwise indistinguishably equal walls. But I soon orient myself through the mere feeling of a difference between my right and left sides. This happens at night when I walk and make the proper turns in a street which I know but in which I cannot distinguish any houses.

Finally I can broaden this concept even more, since it consists in the ability to orient myself not merely in space (i.e., mathematically) but in thought as such (i.e., logically). One can easily guess by analogy that this kind of orientation will be the business of pure reason in directing its use when, starting from known objects of experience, it tries to extend itself beyond all boundaries of experience, finding no object of intuition but merely space for it. For it is then no longer capable of bringing its judgments, in the determination of its own faculty of judgment, under a definite maxim according to objective grounds of knowledge; it can do so only by a subjective ground of distinction.* This subjective means which remains is nothing else than the feeling of a need belonging to reason. One can be assured against all error by not undertaking to judge where he does not know as much as is required for definitive judgment. Thus ignorance is itself the cause of the limitations but not of the errors in our knowledge. But where it is not just an arbitrary matter whether one will judge definitively or not, i.e., where a real need associated with reason itself makes judging necessary even if ignorance with respect to the details required for judging limits us, a maxim is necessary by which we can form a judgment, for reason insists on satisfaction. If then it has been demonstrated that there can be here neither intuition of objects nor anything similar to such intuitions by which we could exhibit appropriate objects to our broadened concepts and thus make sure of their real possibility, nothing remains for us except first to test the concept with which we venture beyond all possible experience to see if it is free of contradictions, and then to bring at least the *relation* of this object to objects of experience under pure concepts of reason. By this we do not make the object sensuous. We only fit something supersensuous to thought in the empirical use of our reason, for without this precaution we could make no use of such a concept and would rave instead of think.

Yet through the mere concept nothing is decided with respect to the existence of this object and its real connection with the world (the sum total of all objects of possible experience). Now, however, the right of a need of reason enters as the right of a subjective ground to presuppose and assume something which it may not pretend to know on objective grounds. Thus there is the right to orient one's self by reason's own need in thinking in the space of the supersensuous, which is for us immeasurable and as if filled with impenetrable darkness.

* To orient one's self in thinking as such therefore means to determine one's assent according to a subjective principle of reason because of the inadequacy of its objective principles.

Many supersensuous things may be thought (for objects of the senses do not exhaust the whole field of possibility) even though reason feels no need to extend itself to them and even less need to assume their existence. Reason finds sufficient occupation with those causes in the world which reveal themselves to the senses (or at least with causes of the same kind). It does not need the influence of pure spiritual natural beings to further this concern, and indeed their assumption would be disadvantageous to it. For since we know nothing of the laws by which such beings might act, while we do know, or may hope to learn, much about the objects of the senses, such a presupposition would not extend but check the use of reason. To search after them or to play with that kind of fantasies is not a need but only meddlesome curiosity which ends in nothing except dreaming. But it is entirely different with the concept of a First Being as the supreme intelligence and highest good. For not only does our reason feel a need to make the concept of the unlimited the basis of limited things and thus of all other things;* this need also

---

* Since reason needs to presuppose reality as given to the possibility of all things and regards only as limitations the differences between things which lie in the negations connected with them, it sees itself compelled to make one sole possibility, that of the unlimited being, the original ground and to regard all others as derivative. Since the complete possibility of each thing must be found in the whole of existence, or at least the principle of complete determination enables our reason to distinguish the possible from the real only in this way, we find a subjective ground for the necessity of making the existence of a most real (highest) being basic to all possibility, and this subjective ground is a need of our reason itself. Thus arises the Cartesian proof of the existence of God, in which subjective grounds for presupposing something for the use of reason (which basically remains only an empirical use) are held to be objective and thus a *need for insight*. So it is with this and with all proofs which the worthy Mendelssohn has made use of in his *Morgenstunden*. They do not serve at all for demonstration. But it does not follow that they are of no use. For it need not be mentioned that these acute developments of the subjective conditions of the use of our reason give excellent opportunities for complete knowledge of this faculty of ours; they are lasting examples for this purpose. Moreover, assent arising from the subjective needs of the use of reason is very important when we have to judge even if objective grounds are lacking. But we must not allow an exacted *presupposition* to masquerade as a *free insight*, else we would unnecessarily expose to our opponent, with whom we would then be dogmatizing, a weakness which he could use to our disadvantage. Mendelssohn perhaps did not realize that dogmatizing with pure reason in the field of the supersensuous was a direct path to philosophical fanaticism and that only critical examination of this rational faculty could remedy this evil in any

applies to the presupposition of the existence of a First Being, without which reason can adduce no satisfying ground for the contingency of the existence of things in the world, least of all for the design and order which is met with everywhere to such a wonderful degree (in the small because it is near us even more than in the large). Without assuming an intelligent author, no comprehensible ground for the design and order can be stated without falling into patent absurdities. Although we cannot prove the impossibility of such design without an original intelligent author (for then we would have sufficient objective grounds for this assertion and would not need to appeal to subjective grounds), there yet remains, in spite of this lack of insight, a sufficient subjective ground for assuming such an author. This subjective ground is reason's need to presuppose something comprehensible to it in order to explain this given appearance, and nothing else with which reason can connect a mere concept can fill this need.

This need of reason can be regarded as twofold: first, in reason's theoretical and, second, in its practical use. I have just cited the first need, but it is easily seen that it is only conditional, i.e., that we must assume the existence of God when we wish to judge concerning the first causes of all contingent things, particularly in the organization of ends actually present in the world. But far more important is the need of reason in its practical use, because here the need is unconditional; here we are compelled to presuppose the existence of God not just if we *wish* to judge but because we *must* judge, for the pure practical use of reason consists only in the prescription of moral laws. They all lead to the idea of the highest good that is possible in the world so far as it is possible only through freedom, i.e., morality. And, on the other hand, they lead to something which does not depend merely on freedom but also on nature, namely, the greatest happiness so far as it is proportioned according to morality. Reason needs to assume such an independent highest

---

fundamental way. The discipline of the scholastic method (for example, of Wolff's method, which he recommends for that reason), in which all concepts must be determined by definitions and all steps justified by principles, can certainly hinder this mischief for some time, but it cannot completely prevent it. For with what right will one prevent reason from going still further when, by Mendelssohn's admission, it has been highly successful in the supersensuous field? And where is then the boundary at which it must stop?

good, and for its sake it needs also to assume a supreme intelligence as the highest independent good. It does not make these assumptions in order to derive obligatory respect for moral laws or incentives to their observance from the assumptions, for the laws would have no moral worth if their motive were derived from anything except the law alone, which is apodictically certain in itself. It needs to assume them only in order to give objective reality to the concept of the highest good, i.e., in order to prevent the highest good, and, consequently, all morality, from being regarded as a mere ideal, which would be the case if the highest good, the idea of which inseparably accompanies morality, never existed.

It is not knowledge, therefore, but a felt* need of reason by which Mendelssohn, without realizing it, oriented himself in speculative thought. And since this guidance is not an objective principle of reason, not a fundamental principle affording insight, but only a subjective principle (i.e., a maxim) of the only employment allowed reason by its limitations, it is only a corollary of the need, and by itself it constitutes the entire determining ground of our judgment on the existence of the highest being. But it is only a contingent use of our faculty of judgment to orient one's self in speculative attempts with reference to this being. Here Mendelssohn was completely in error in crediting so much to speculation, regarding it as capable of doing everything by itself through demonstration. The first means [i.e., the felt need] could be seen as necessary only if the insufficiency of the latter [i.e., speculative judgment] were conceded; and this concession is one to which his acuteness would finally have brought him if, with a longer life, there had also been granted him sufficient agility of mind (which is more proper to youth) to revise easily an old and habitual manner of thought because of changes in the state of the sciences. But he had the merit of consistently seeking the ultimate touchstone of admissibility of a judgment solely in reason alone, whether reason is led by insight or by mere need and the maxim of consistency in choosing its theses. In its latter use he called reason "common human

---

* Reason does not feel; it sees its lack and, through the impulse to cognize, it effects the feeling of need. It is similar to the case of moral feeling, which does not cause the moral law, for the moral law arises only from reason. Instead this feeling is caused or effected by moral laws and hence by reason, because the eager but free will requires definite grounds [on which to act].

reason," for its own interest is always before its eyes, and one must already have gone astray if he forgets it and idly meddles around among objective concepts just in order to extend his knowledge regardless of whether it is needed or not.

The expression, "declaration of sound reason," is here ambiguous and can either be taken as a judgment based on the insight of reason, as Mendelssohn misunderstood it, or as a judgment at the prompting of reason, as the author of the *Resultate* seems to have taken it. Therefore, another name should be given to this source of judgment, and none is more suitable than "rational belief." Every belief, even one in historical matters, must indeed be rational, for the touchstone of truth is always reason. But a "rational belief" is one which is based on no other data than those contained in pure reason. Every belief is a subjectively sufficient assent associated with the consciousness that it is an objectively insufficient assent; therefore, it is contrasted with knowledge. But if something is assented to on objective grounds which are known to be insufficient, i.e., only opined, this opinion can finally become knowledge through gradual supplementation by more grounds of the same kind. On the other hand, if the grounds of assent are of such a kind as not to be objectively valid at all, no use of reason can change the belief into knowledge. A historical belief, for example, in the death of a great man which is reported by some letters, can become knowledge when the local authorities report the place of death, the interment, the testament, etc. It is, therefore, entirely consistent that something, e.g., that the city of Rome exists, may be taken as true, i.e., believed, merely on the testimony of witnesses, and yet that one who has never been there can say, "I know that Rome exists," and not merely, "I believe it." But the pure rational belief can never be converted by all the natural data of reason into knowledge, because the ground of assent in this case is merely subjective. It is only a necessary need of reason to presuppose, not to demonstrate, the existence of a highest being, and, so long as we are men, it will remain so. The need of reason for a theoretical use satisfactory to itself would be nothing more than a *hypothesis* of pure reason, i.e., an opinion based on subjective grounds sufficient to assent, because one could not expect any ground besides a subjective one for explaining given effects, and yet reason still needs some ground of explanation. But the rational belief, which rests on the need of reason's use in a practical sense, could be called a *postu-*

late of reason, not as if it were an insight sufficient to all the logical requirements of certainty, but because this assent (when everything in man is morally arranged) is in degree inferior to no cognition* even though in kind it is wholly different.

A pure rational belief is, therefore, the signpost or compass by which the speculative thinker can orient himself in his rational excursions in the field of supersensuous objects. But to the man of ordinary but (morally) sound reason, it can show the way in both a theoretical and a practical sense, in a manner entirely suitable to the end to which he is destined. This rational belief must also be made the basis of every other belief—indeed, of every revelation.

The concept of God and the conviction of His existence can be met with only in reason; they can come from reason alone, not from either inspiration or any tidings, however great their authority. Even if an immediate intuition befalls me of such a kind as nature, as far as I know it, cannot afford, a concept of God must still serve as the rule for deciding whether this appearance conforms to the characteristics of divinity. Although I do not see how it is possible for any appearance to exhibit, even in its quality, that which may be only thought and never intuited, it is at least clear that in order to judge whether that which appears to me and which affects my feeling either externally or internally is God, I would have to test the appearance by comparing it with my rational concept of God. I would do so not in order to see whether it is adequate to the concept but only to see whether it does not in fact contradict it. Likewise, if in everything whereby He immediately discovers Himself to me, nothing is found which contradicts that concept, even then this appearance, intuition, immediate revelation, or what one wishes to call such a manifestation would never prove the existence of a being the concept of which (if not inaccurately defined and therefore subject to admixture of all possible nonsense) demands infinite magnitude to distinguish it from all creatures. To this concept no experience or intuition can be adequate, and therefore experience or intuition can never defi-

---

* To the firmness of belief belongs the consciousness of its unchangeableness. Now I can be entirely certain that no one can refute the proposition, "There is a God." For where could this insight be obtained? Thus the situation with respect to a rational belief is different from that of a historical belief, for in the latter it is always possible that proofs to the contrary may be found, and we must always hold ourself in readiness to change our opinion when our knowledge of the objects is extended.

nitely prove the existence of such a being. Thus no one can be first convinced of the existence of the highest being by any intuition. The belief of reason must precede the conviction, and only then could certain appearances or disclosures give occasion to investigate whether we are justified in regarding as deity that which speaks or exhibits itself to us, and only after this test could they confirm that belief.

If, therefore, reason is denied the right of being the first to speak of things which concern supersensuous objects, such as the existence of God and the future world, a wide gate is opened to fanaticism, superstition, and even atheistic opinions. And yet in the Jacobi-Mendelssohn polemic everything seems to be aimed at this overthrow. I do not know whether it is merely aimed at an overthrow of rational insight and knowledge (through a presumed strength in speculation) or also of rational belief, and thus at the establishment of another belief which each can formulate in his own arbitrary way. One might almost infer the latter when he sees the Spinozistic concept of God set up as the only one conformable to the principles of reason,* even

* It is hard to conceive how supposed scholars could find support for Spinozism in the *Critique of Pure Reason*. That work clips the wings of dogmatism with respect to knowledge of supersensuous objects, and here Spinozism is so dogmatic that it even competes with the mathematician in rigor of proof. The *Critique* proves that the table of the pure concepts of the understanding contains all the materials of pure thinking; Spinozism speaks of thoughts which think themselves and thus of an accident that exists for itself as subject—a concept that is not in human understanding and cannot be brought into it. The *Critique* shows that it by no means suffices to the assertion of the possibility of a thing thought through itself to prove that there is nothing contradictory in its concept (although merely to assume its possibility must then, if necessary, be allowed). Spinozism, however, pretends to understand something which is actually impossible, viz., a being the idea of which consists merely of pure concepts of the understanding, provided only that all conditions of sensibility have been abstracted from it, thus leaving an idea in which no contradiction can ever be found; it is nevertheless utterly unable to support this unlimited presumption. Precisely for that reason Spinozism leads to fanaticism. On the other hand, there is no sure means of uprooting fanaticism except to determine the limits of the pure faculty of reason.

Similarly, another scholar finds skepticism in the *Critique of Pure Reason*, although the *Critique* begins with the establishment of something certain and definite with respect to the scope of our a priori knowledge. Likewise he discovers [arbitrary] dialectic in critical investigations aimed at the solution and final destruction of that inevitable dialectic in which pure reason, when conducted dogmatically, entraps and entangles itself. The Neo-Platonists, who called themselves Eclectics because they knew though it is a worthless concept. For, although it is entirely consistent with rational belief to concede that speculative reason itself is not even capable of discerning the possibility of a being such as we must think God to be, it cannot be compatible with any belief in and any assent to a being that reason could both discern the impossibility of the object and yet know its reality from other sources.

Men of intellectual power and broad minds! I honor your talents and love your feeling for humanity. But have you considered what you do, and where you will end with your attacks on reason? Without doubt you will that freedom to think should be preserved inviolate, for without this your own free flights of genius would soon be at an end. Let us see what must naturally come out of this freedom of thought if such a procedure as you begin comes to prevail.

Freedom to think is first opposed by civil restraint. Certainly one may say, "Freedom to speak or write can be taken from us by a superior power, but never the freedom to think." But how much, and how correctly, would we think if we did not think as it were in common with others, with whom we mutually communicate! Thus one can well say that the external power which wrests from man the freedom publicly to communicate his thoughts also takes away the freedom to think—the sole jewel that remains to us under all civil repression and through which alone counsel against all the evils of that state can be taken.

Secondly, freedom to think will be taken in such a sense that the constraint of conscience is opposed to it, where without any external power some citizens set themselves up as guardians in matters of religion. Instead of arguing, they know how, by prescribed formulas of belief accompanied by scrupulous fear of the danger of private inquisition, to banish all rational examination by making an early impression on the mind.

Thirdly, freedom in thinking means the subjection of reason under no other laws than those it gives itself. Its opposite is the maxim of a lawless use of reason (in order, as genius supposes, to be able to see further without the restriction imposed by laws). The natural consequence is that, if reason will not subject itself

---

how to find their own whims in the earlier authors after they themselves had interpolated them, proceeded in exactly the same way. There is nothing new under the sun.

to the law it gives itself, it will have to bow under the yoke of laws which others impose on it, for without any law whatsoever nothing, not even the greatest nonsense, can play its hand very long. Thus the inevitable consequence of declared lawlessness in thinking (an emancipation from restrictions of reason) is that freedom to think is finally lost. Since not misfortune but arrogance is responsible, it is, in the true sense of the word, squandered.

The course of the matter is approximately this. The genius enjoys himself at first in his daring flight, for he has thrown off the harness with which reason had guided him. By authoritative decrees and great promises he soon enchants others and seems to himself to be seated on a throne which slow plodding reason so poorly adorns, even though he still speaks its language. We ordinary men call the then assumed maxim of invalidity of supremely legislative reason by the name of "fanaticism"; those favorites of kindly nature, however, call it "illumination." Because a confusion of tongues must soon arise among them, and because reason alone can validly command for everyone, each must now follow his own inspiration. So inner inspiration must finally cede to facts fabricated by external evidence, freely chosen traditions to documents of enforced authority, until the complete subjugation of reason under supposed facts, i.e., superstition, ensues. For superstition can at least have a lawful form and thus bring about a state of peace.

Although human reason always strives for freedom, when it once breaks its fetters, its first use of a long unaccustomed freedom degenerates into abuse and a mistaken confidence in its freedom from all limitation, it falls into a persuasion of the exclusive sovereignty of speculative reason, which assumes nothing except what can justify itself on objective grounds and dogmatic convictions, and it boldly denies everything else. The maxim of the independence of reason from its own need (renunciation of rational belief) is now called "disbelief." It is not a historical disbelief, for one cannot think of it as intentional or even as responsible (because everyone must believe a fact which is sufficiently confirmed just as much as a mathematical demonstration, whether he will or not); it is a "rational disbelief," an unfortunate state of the human mind, which first takes from the moral laws all their effect on the heart as incentives, and then destroys all their authority, occasioning a turn of mind called "free-thinking," i.e., the principle of not acknowledging any duty. Here the authorities take a hand, so as to prevent the utmost disorder even in civil affairs; and as the handiest but most energetic means is to them the best, they completely destroy the freedom to think and subject it, like other pursuits, to the government. And so freedom in thought finally destroys itself when it wishes to proceed independently of the laws of reason.

Friends of the human race and of that which is holiest to it! Assume what appears most believable to you after careful and honest testing, whether it be facts or principles of reason; but do not wrest from reason that which makes it the highest good on earth, i.e., the prerogative of being the ultimate touchstone of truth.* Otherwise you will become unworthy of this freedom and certainly lose it, and you will bring this misfortune on the heads of that blameless portion of mankind which was well inclined to make use of its freedom in a lawful manner toward the good of the world.

I. KANT

KÖNIGSBERG

* Thinking for one's self means to seek the supreme touchstone of truth in one's self, i.e., in one's own reason; and the maxim of always thinking for one's self is enlightenment. But there is not as much in it as they imagine who make enlightenment a matter of information, for the latter is rather a negative principle of the use of the cognitive faculty, and often he who is overly rich in information is least enlightened in the use of it. To make use of one's own reason means nothing more than to ask one's self, with regard to everything that is to be assumed, whether he finds it practicable to make the ground of the assumption or the rule which follows from the assumption a universal principle of the use of his reason. This test can be applied to himself by each person; and by this test he will soon see superstition and fanaticism disappear even if he is far from possessing the knowledge requisite to a refutation of either on objective grounds. For he merely makes use of the maxim of the self-preservation of reason. Enlightenment in the individual is easily established by education; but an early beginning must be made so that young minds may accustom themselves to this reflection. But to enlighten an age is a very protracted task, for there are many external obstacles which in part hinder and in part prevent that kind of education.

VI

PERPETUAL PEACE: A PHILOSOPHICAL SKETCH

[INTRODUCTION]

WHETHER this satirical inscription on a Dutch innkeeper's sign upon which a burial ground was painted had for its object mankind in general, or the rulers of states in particular, who are insatiable of war, or merely the philosophers who dream this sweet dream, it is not for us to decide. But one condition the author of this essay wishes to lay down. The practical politician assumes the attitude of looking down with great self-satisfaction on the political theorist as a pedant whose empty ideas in no way threaten the security of the state, inasmuch as the state must proceed on empirical principles; so the theorist is allowed to play his game without interference from the wordly wise statesman. Such being his attitude, the practical politician—and this is my condition—should at least act consistently also in the case of a conflict and not suspect some danger to the state in the political theorist's opinions which are ventured and publicly expressed without any ulterior purpose. By this *clausula salvatoria* the author desires formally and emphatically to deprecate herewith any malevolent interpretation which might be placed on his words.

SECTION I

CONTAINING THE PRELIMINARY ARTICLES FOR PERPETUAL PEACE AMONG STATES

1. *"No Treaty of Peace Shall Be Held Valid in Which There Is Tacitly Reserved Matter for a Future War"*

OTHERWISE a treaty would be only a truce, a suspension of hostilities but not peace, which means the end of all hostilities—so much so that even to attach the word "perpetual" to it is a dubious pleonasm. The causes for making future wars (which are perhaps unknown to the contracting parties) are without exception annihilated by the treaty of peace, even if they should be dug out of dusty documents by acute sleuthing. When one or both parties to a treaty of peace, being too exhausted to continue warring with each other, make a tacit reservation (*reservatio mentalis*) in regard to old claims to be elaborated only at some more favorable opportunity in the future, the treaty is made in bad faith, and we have an artifice worthy of the casuistry of a Jesuit. Considered by itself, it is beneath the dignity of a sovereign, just as the readiness to indulge in this kind of reasoning is unworthy of the dignity of his minister.

But if, in consequence of enlightened concepts of statecraft, the glory of the state is placed in its continual aggrandizement by whatever means, my conclusion will appear merely academic and pedantic.

2. "No Independent States, Large or Small, Shall Come under the Dominion of Another State by Inheritance, Exchange, Purchase, or Donation"

A state is not, like the ground which it occupies, a piece of property (*patrimonium*). It is a society of men whom no one else has any right to command or to dispose except the state itself. It is a trunk with its own roots. But to incorporate it into another state like a graft is to destroy its existence as a moral person, reducing it to a thing; such incorporation thus contradicts the idea of the original contract without which no right over a people can be conceived.* Everyone knows to what dangers Europe, the only part of the world where this manner of acquisition is known, has been brought, even down to the most recent times, by the presumption that states could espouse one another; it is in part a new kind of industry for gaining ascendancy by means of family alliances and without expenditure of forces and in part a way of extending one's domain. Also the hiring-out of troops by one state to another, so that they can be used against an enemy not common to both, is to be counted under this principle; for in this manner the subjects, as though they were things to be manipulated at pleasure, are used and also used up.

* A hereditary kingdom is not a state which can be inherited by another state, but the right to govern it can be inherited by another physical person. The state thereby acquires a ruler, but he, as a ruler (i.e., as one already possessing another realm), does not acquire the state.

3. "*Standing Armies* (miles perpetuus) *Shall in Time Be Totally Abolished*"

For they incessantly menace other states by their readiness to appear at all times prepared for war; they incite them to compete with each other in the number of armed men, and there is no limit to this. For this reason, the cost of peace finally becomes more oppressive than that of a short war, and consequently a standing army is itself a cause of offensive war waged in order to relieve the state of this burden. Add to this that to pay men to kill or to be killed seems to entail using them as mere machines and tools in the hand of another (the state), and this is hardly compatible with the rights of mankind in our own person. But the periodic and voluntary military exercises of citizens who thereby secure themselves and their country against foreign aggression is entirely different.

The accumulation of treasure would have the same effect, for, of the three powers—the power of armies, of alliances, and of money—the third is perhaps the most dependable weapon. Such accumulation of treasure is regarded by other states as a threat of war, and if it were not for the difficulties in learning the amount, it would force the other state to make an early attack.

4. "*National Debts Shall Not Be Contracted with a View to the External Friction of States*"

This expedient of seeking aid within or without the state is above suspicion when the purpose is domestic economy (e.g., the improvement of roads, new settlements, establishment of stores against unfruitful years, etc.). But as an opposing machine in the antagonism of powers, a credit system which grows beyond sight and which is yet a safe debt for the present requirements—because all the creditors do not require payment at one time—constitutes a dangerous money-power. This ingenious invention of a commercial people in this century is dangerous because it is a war treasure which exceeds the treasures of all other states; it cannot be exhausted except by default of taxes which is inevitable, though it can be long delayed by the stimulus to trade which occurs through the reaction of credit on industry and commerce. This facility in making war, together with the inclination to do so on the part of rulers—an inclination which seems inborn in human nature—is thus a great hindrance to perpetual peace. Therefore, to forbid this credit system must all the more be a preliminary article of perpetual peace, because it must eventually entangle many innocent states in the inevitable bankruptcy, and thus openly harm them. They are therefore justified in allying themselves against such a state and its measures.

5. "No State Shall by Force Interfere with the Constitution or Government of Another State"

For what is there to authorize it to do so? The offense perhaps which a state gives to the subjects of another state? Rather the example of the evil into which a state has fallen because of its lawlessness should serve as a warning. Moreover, the bad example which one free person affords another as a *scandulum acceptum* is not an infringement of his rights. But it would be quite different if a state, by internal rebellion, should fall into two parts, each of which pretended to be a separate state making claim to the whole. To lend assistance to one of these cannot be considered an interference in the constitution of the other state (for it is then in a state of anarchy). But so long as the internal dissension has not come to this critical point, such interference by foreign powers would infringe on the rights of an independent people struggling with its internal disease; hence it would itself be an offense and would render the autonomy of all states insecure.

6. "No State Shall, during War, Permit Such Acts of Hostility Which Would Make Mutual Confidence in the Subsequent Peace Impossible: Such Are the Employment of Assassins (percussores), *Poisoners* (venefici), *Breach of Capitulation, and Incitement to Treason* (perduellio) *in the Opposing State*"

These are dishonorable stratagems. For some confidence in the character of the enemy must remain even in the midst of war, as otherwise no peace could be concluded and the hostilities would degenerate into a war of extermination (*bellum internecinum*). War, however, is only the sad recourse in the state of nature (where there is no tribunal which could judge with the force of law) by which each state asserts its right by violence and in which neither party can be adjudged unjust (for that would presuppose a juridical decision); in lieu of such a decision, the issue of the conflict (as if given by a so-called "judgment of God") decides on which side justice lies. But between states no punitive war (*bellum punitivum*) is conceivable, because there is no relation between them of master and servant.

It follows that a war of extermination, in which the destruction of both parties and of all justice can result, would permit perpetual peace only in the vast burial ground of the human race. Therefore, such a war and the use of all means leading to it must be absolutely forbidden. But that the means cited do inevitably lead to it is clear from the fact that these infernal arts, vile in themselves, when once used would not long be confined to the sphere of war. Take, for instance, the use of spies (*uti exploratoribus*). In this, one employs the infamy of others (which can never be entirely eradicated) only to encourage its persistence even into the state of peace, to the undoing of the very spirit of peace.

Although the laws stated are objectively, i.e., in so far as they express the intention of rulers, mere prohibitions (*leges prohibitivae*), some of them are of that strict kind which hold regardless of circumstances (*leges strictae*) and which demand prompt execution. Such are Nos. 1, 5, and 6. Others, like Nos. 2, 3, and 4, while not exceptions from the rule of law, nevertheless are subjectively broader (*leges latae*) in respect to their observation, containing permission to delay their execution without, however, losing sight of the end. This permission does not authorize, under No. 2, for example, delaying until doomsday (or, as Augustus used to say, *ad calendas Graecas*) the reestablishment of the freedom of states which have been deprived of it—i.e., it does not permit us to fail to do it, but it allows a delay to prevent precipitation which might injure the goal striven for. For the prohibition concerns only the manner of acquisition which is no longer permitted, but not the possession, which, though not bearing a requisite title of right, has nevertheless been held lawful in all states by the public opinion of the time (the time of the putative acquisition).*

* It has not without cause hitherto been doubted whether besides the commands (*leges praeceptivae*) and prohibitions (*leges prohibitivae*) there could also be permissive laws (*leges permissivae*) of pure reason. For laws as such contain a principle of objective practical necessity, while permission implies a principle of the practical contingency of certain actions. Hence a law of permission would imply constraint to an action to do that to which no one can be constrained. If the object of the law

SECTION II

CONTAINING THE DEFINITIVE ARTICLES FOR PERPETUAL PEACE AMONG STATES

THE state of peace among men living side by side is not the natural state (*status naturalis*); the natural state is one of war. This does not always mean open hostilities, but at least an unceasing threat of war. A state of peace, therefore, must be

---

has the same meaning in both cases, this is a contradiction. But in permissive law, which is in question here, the prohibition refers only to the future mode of acquisition of a right (e.g., by succession), while the permission annuls this prohibition only with reference to the present possession. This possession, though only putative, may be held to be just (*possessio putativa*) in the transition from the state of nature to a civil state, by virtue of a permissive law included under natural law, even though it is [strictly] illegal. But, as soon as it is recognized as illegal in the state of nature, a similar mode of acquisition in the subsequent civil state (after this transition has occurred) is forbidden, and this right to continuing possession would not hold if such a presumptive acquisition had taken place in the civil state. For in this case it would be an infringement which would have to cease as soon as its illegality was discovered.

I have wished only to call the attention of the teachers of natural law to the concept of a *lex permissiva*, which systematic reason affords, particularly since in civil (statute) law use is often made of it. But in the ordinary use of it, there is this difference: prohibitive law stands alone, while permission is not introduced into it as a limiting condition (as it should be) but counted among the exceptions to it. Then it is said, "This or that is forbidden, except Nos. 1, 2, 3," and so on indefinitely. These exceptions are added to the law only as an afterthought required by our groping around among cases as they arise, and not by any principle. Otherwise the conditions would have had to be introduced into the formula of the prohibition, and in this way it would itself have become a permissive law. It is, therefore, unfortunate that the subtle question proposed by the wise and acute Count von Windischgrätz[1] was never answered and soon consigned to oblivion, because it insisted on the point here discussed. For the possibility of a formula similar to those of mathematics is the only legitimate criterion of a consistent legislation, and without it the so-called *ius certum* must always remain a pious wish. Otherwise we shall have merely general laws (which apply to a great number of cases), but no universal laws (which apply to all cases), as the concept of a law seems to require.

1. [Reichsgraf Josef Niklas Windisch-Graetz (1744–1802) proposed the following question for a prize essay: "How can contracts be drawn which will be susceptible to no divergent interpretation, and by which any suit concerning transfer of property will be impossible, so that no legal process can arise from any document having this proposed form?"]

established, for in order to be secured against hostility it is not sufficient that hostilities simply be not committed; and, unless this security is pledged to each by his neighbor (a thing that can occur only in a civil state), each may treat his neighbor, from whom he demands this security, as an enemy.*

FIRST DEFINITIVE ARTICLE FOR PERPETUAL PEACE

"The Civil Constitution of Every State Should Be Republican"

The only constitution which derives from the idea of the original compact, and on which all juridical legislation of a people must be based, is the republican.† This constitution is

---

* We ordinarily assume that no one may act inimically toward another except when he has been actively injured by the other. This is quite correct if both are under civil law, for, by entering into such a state, they afford each other the requisite security through the sovereign which has power over both. Man (or the people) in the state of nature deprives me of this security and injures me, if he is near me, by this mere status of his even though he does not injure me actively (*facto*); he does so by the lawlessness of his condition (*statu iniusto*) which constantly threatens me. Therefore, I can compel him either to enter with me into a state of civil law or to remove himself from my neighborhood. The postulate which is basic to all the following articles is: All men who can reciprocally influence each other must stand under some civil constitution.

Every juridical constitution which concerns the person who stands under it is one of the following:

(1) The constitution conforming to the civil law of men in a nation (*ius civitatis*).

(2) The constitution conforming to the law of nations in their relation to one another (*ius gentium*).

(3) The constitution conforming to the law of world citizenship, so far as men and states are considered as citizens of a universal state of men, in their external mutual relationships (*ius cosmopoliticum*).

This division is not arbitrary, being necessary in relation to the idea of perpetual peace. For if only one state were related to another by physical influence and were yet in a state of nature, war would necessarily follow, and our purpose here is precisely to free ourselves of war.

† Juridical (and hence) external freedom cannot be defined, as is usual, by the privilege of doing anything one wills so long as he does not injure another. For what is a privilege? It is the possibility of an action so far as one does not injure anyone by it. Then the definition would read: Freedom is the possibility of those actions by which one does no one an injury. One does another no injury (he may do as he pleases) only if he does another no injury—an empty tautology. Rather, my external (juridical) freedom is to be defined as follows: It is the privilege to lend obedience to no external laws except those to which I could have given consent. Similarly,

established, firstly, by principles of the freedom of the members of a society (as men); secondly, by principles of dependence of all upon a single common legislation (as subjects); and, thirdly, by the law of their equality (as citizens). The republican constitution, therefore, is, with respect to law, the one which is the original basis of every form of civil constitution. The only question now is: Is it also the one which can lead to perpetual peace?

The republican constitution, besides the purity of its origin (having sprung from the pure source of the concept of law), also gives a favorable prospect for the desired consequence, i.e.,

---

external (juridical) equality in a state is that relationship among the citizens in which no one can lawfully bind another without at the same time subjecting himself to the law by which he also can be bound. No definition of juridical dependence is needed, as this already lies in the concept of a state's constitution as such.

The validity of these inborn rights, which are inalienable and belong necessarily to humanity, is raised to an even higher level by the principle of the juridical relation of man to higher beings, for, if he believes in them, he regards himself by the same principles as a citizen of a supersensuous world. For in what concerns my freedom, I have no obligation with respect to divine law, which can be acknowledged by my reason alone, except in so far as I could have given my consent to it. Indeed, it is only through the law of freedom of my own reason that I frame a concept of the divine will. With regard to the most sublime reason in the world that I can think of with the exception of God (say, the great Aeon), when I do my duty in my post as he does in his, there is no reason, under the law of equality, why obedience to duty should fall only to me and the right to command only to him. The reason why this principle of equality does not pertain to our relation to God (as the principle of freedom does) is that this Being is the only one to which the concept of duty does not apply.

But with respect to the right of equality of all citizens as subjects, the question of whether a hereditary nobility may be tolerated turns upon the answer to the question as to whether the pre-eminent rank granted by the state to one citizen over another ought to precede merit or follow it. Now it is obvious that, if rank is associated with birth, it is uncertain whether merit (political skill and integrity) will also follow; hence it would be as if a favorite without any merit were given command. The general will of the people would never agree to this in the original contract, which is the principle of all law, for a nobleman is not necessarily a noble man. With regard to the nobility of office (as we might call the rank of the higher magistracy) which one must earn by merit, this rank does not belong to the person as his property; it belongs to his post, and equality is not thereby infringed, because when one quits his office he renounces the rank it confers and re-enters into the class of his fellows.

perpetual peace. The reason is this. If the consent of the citizens is required in order to decide that war should be declared (and in this constitution it cannot but be the case), nothing is more natural than that they would be very cautious in commencing such a poor game, decreeing for themselves all the calamities of war. Among the latter would be: having to fight, having to pay the costs of war from their own resources, having painfully to repair the devastation war leaves behind, and, to fill up the measure of evils, load themselves with a heavy national debt that would embitter peace itself and that can never be liquidated on account of constant wars in the future. But, on the other hand, in a constitution which is not republican, and under which the subjects are not citizens, a declaration of war is the easiest thing in the world to decide upon, because war does not require of the ruler, who is the proprietor and not a member of the state, the least sacrifice of the pleasures of his table, the chase, his country houses, his court functions, and the like. He may, therefore, resolve on war as on a pleasure party for the most trivial reasons and with perfect indifference leave the justification which decency requires to the diplomatic corps who are ever ready to provide it.

In order not to confuse the republican constitution with the democratic (as is commonly done), the following should be noted. The forms of a state (*civitas*) can be divided either according to the persons who possess the sovereign power or according to the mode of administration exercised over the people by the chief, whoever he may be. The first is properly called the form of sovereignty (*forma imperii*), and there are only three possible forms of it: autocracy, in which one, aristocracy, in which some associated together, or democracy, in which all those who constitute society, possess sovereign power. They may be characterized, respectively, as the power of a monarch, of the nobility, or of the people. The second division is that by the form of government (*forma regiminis*) and is based on the way in which the state makes use of its power; this way is based on the constitution, which is the act of the general will through which the many persons become one nation. In this respect government is either republican or despotic. Republicanism is the political principle of the separation of the executive power (the administration) from the legislative; despotism is that of the autonomous execution by the state of laws which it has itself decreed. Thus in a despotism the public will is administered by the ruler as his own will. Of the three forms of the state, that of democracy is, properly speaking, necessarily a despotism, because it establishes an executive power in which "all" decide for or even against one who does not agree; that is, "all," who are not quite all, decide, and this is a contradiction of the general will with itself and with freedom.

Every form of government which is not representative is, properly speaking, without form. The legislator can unite in one and the same person his function as legislative and as executor of his will just as little as the universal of the major premise in a syllogism can also be the subsumption of the particular under the universal in the minor. And even though the other two constitutions are always defective to the extent that they do leave room for this mode of administration, it is at least possible for them to assume a mode of government conforming to the spirit of a representative system (as when Frederick II[2] at least *said* he was merely the first servant of the State).* On the other hand, the democratic mode of government makes this impossible, since everyone wishes to be master. Therefore, we can say: the smaller the personnel of the government (the smaller the number of rulers), the greater is their representation and the more nearly the constitution approaches to the possibility of republicanism; thus the constitution may be expected by gradual reform finally to raise itself to republicanism. For these reasons it is more difficult for an aristocracy than for a monarchy to achieve the one completely juridical constitution, and it is impossible for a democracy to do so except by violent revolution.

---

2. [In his *Antimachiavell*.]

* The lofty epithets of "the Lord's anointed," "the executor of the divine will on earth," and "the vicar of God," which have been lavished on sovereigns, have been frequently censured as crude and intoxicating flatteries. But this seems to me without good reason. Far from inspiring a monarch with pride, they should rather render him humble, providing he possesses some intelligence (which we must assume). They should make him reflect that he has taken an office too great for man, an office which is the holiest God has ordained on earth, to be the trustee of the rights of men, and that he must always stand in dread of having in some way injured this "apple of God's eye."

The mode of government,* however, is incomparably more important to the people than the form of sovereignty, although much depends on the greater or lesser suitability of the latter to the end of [good] government. To conform to the concept of law, however, government must have a representative form, and in this system only a republican mode of government is possible; without it, government is despotic and arbitrary whatever the constitution may be. None of the ancient so-called "republics" knew this system, and they all finally and inevitably degenerated into despotism under the sovereignty of one, which is the most bearable of all forms of despotism.

SECOND DEFINITIVE ARTICLE FOR A PERPETUAL PEACE

"The Law of Nations Shall Be Founded on a Federation of Free States"

Peoples, as states, like individuals, may be judged to injure one another merely by their coexistence in the state of nature (i.e., while independent of external laws). Each of them may and should for the sake of its own security demand that the others enter with it into a constitution similar to the civil constitution, for under such a constitution each can be secure in his right. This would be a league of nations, but it would not have to be a state consisting of nations. That would be contradictory, since a state

---

* Mallet du Pan,[3] in his pompous but empty and hollow language, pretends to have become convinced, after long experience, of the truth of Pope's well-known saying:

"For forms of government let fools contest:
Whate'er is best administered, is best."[4]

If that means that the best administered state is the state that is best administered, he has, to make use of Swift's expression, "cracked a nut to come at a maggot." But if it means that the best administered state also has the best mode of government, i.e., the best constitution, then it is thoroughly wrong, for examples of good governments prove nothing about the form of government. Whoever reigned better than a Titus and a Marcus Aurelius? Yet one was succeeded by a Domitian and the other by a Commodus. This could never have happened under a good constitution, for their unworthiness to this post was known early enough and also the power of the ruler was sufficient to have excluded them.

3. [Jacques Mallet du Pan (1749-1800), in his *Über die französische Revolution und die Ursachen ihrer Dauer* (1794).]
4. [*Essay on Man*, III, 303-4.]

implies the relation of a superior (legislating) to an inferior (obeying), i.e., the people, and many nations in one state would then constitute only one nation. This contradicts the presupposition, for here we have to weigh the rights of nations against each other so far as they are distinct states and not amalgamated into one.

When we see the attachment of savages to their lawless freedom, preferring ceaseless combat to subjection to a lawful constraint which they might establish, and thus preferring senseless freedom to rational freedom, we regard it with deep contempt as barbarity, rudeness, and a brutish degradation of humanity. Accordingly, one would think that civilized peoples (each united in a state) would hasten all the more to escape, the sooner the better, from such a depraved condition. But, instead, each state places its majesty (for it is absurd to speak of the majesty of the people) in being subject to no external juridical restraint, and the splendor of its sovereign consists in the fact that many thousands stand at his command to sacrifice themselves for something that does not concern them and without his needing to place himself in the least danger.* The chief difference between European and American savages lies in the fact that many tribes of the latter have been eaten up by their enemies, while the former know how to make better use of their conquered enemies than to dine off them; they know better how to use them to increase the number of their subjects and thus the quantity of instruments for even more extensive wars.

When we consider the perverseness of human nature which is nakedly revealed in the uncontrolled relations between nations (this perverseness being veiled in the state of civil law by the constraint exercised by government), we may well be astonished that the word "law" has not yet been banished from war politics as pedantic and that no state has yet been bold enough to advocate this point of view. Up to the present Hugo Grotius, Pufendorf, Wattel, and many other importune comforters have been cited in justification of war, though their code, philosophically or diplomatically formulated, has not and cannot have the least legal force, because states as such do not stand under a

* A Bulgarian prince gave the following answer to the Greek emperor who good-naturedly suggested that they settle their difference by a duel: "A smith who has tongs won't pluck the glowing iron from the fire with his bare hands."

common external power. There is no instance on record that a state has ever been moved to desist from its purpose because of arguments backed up by the testimony of such great men. But the homage which each state pays (at least in words) to the concept of law proves that there is slumbering in man an even greater moral disposition to become master of the evil principle in himself (which he cannot disclaim) and to hope for the same from others. Otherwise the word "law" would never be pronounced by states which wish to war upon one another; it would be used only ironically, as a Gallic prince interpreted it when he said, "It is the prerogative which nature has given the stronger that the weaker should obey him."

States do not plead their cause before a tribunal; war alone is their way of bringing suit. But by war and its favorable issue in victory, right is not decided, and though by a treaty of peace this particular war is brought to an end, the state of war, of always finding a new pretext to hostilities, is not terminated. Nor can this be declared wrong, considering the fact that in this state each is the judge of his own case. Notwithstanding, the obligation which men in a lawless condition have under the natural law, and which requires them to abandon the state of nature, does not quite apply to states under the law of nations, for as states they already have an internal juridical constitution and have thus outgrown compulsion from others to submit to a more extended lawful constitution according to their ideas of right. This is true in spite of the fact that reason from its throne of supreme morally legislating authority absolutely condemns war as a legal recourse and makes a state of peace a direct duty, even though peace cannot be established or secured except by a compact among nations.

For these reasons there must be a league of a particular kind, which can be called a league of peace (*foedus pacificum*), and which would be distinguished from a treaty of peace (*pactum pacis*) by the fact that the latter terminates only one war, while the former seeks to make an end to all wars forever. This league does not tend to any dominion over the power of the state but only to the maintenance and security of the freedom of the state itself and of other states in league with it, without there being any need for them to submit to civil laws and their compulsion, as men in a state of nature must submit.

The practicability (objective reality) of this idea of federation, which should gradually spread to all states and thus lead to perpetual peace, can be proved. For if fortune directs that a powerful and enlightened people can make itself a republic, which by its nature must be inclined to perpetual peace, this gives a fulcrum to the federative unification of other states so that they may adhere to it and thus secure freedom under the idea of the law of nations. By more and more such associations, the federation may be gradually extended.

We may readily conceive that a people should say, "There ought to be no war among us, for we want to make ourselves into a state; that is, we want to establish a supreme legislative, executive, and judiciary power which will reconcile our differences peaceably." But when this state says, "There ought to be no war between myself and other states, even though I acknowledge no supreme legislative power by which our rights are mutually guaranteed," it is not at all clear on what I can base my confidence in my own rights unless it is the free federation, the surrogate of the civil social order, which reason necessarily associates with the concept of the law of nations—assuming that something is really meant by the latter.

The concept of a law of nations as a right to make war does not really mean anything, because it is then a law of deciding what is right by unilateral maxims through force and not by universally valid public laws which restrict the freedom of each one. The only conceivable meaning of such a law of nations might be that it serves men right who are so inclined that they should destroy each other and thus find perpetual peace in the vast grave that swallows both the atrocities and their perpetrators. For states in their relation to each other, there cannot be any reasonable way out of the lawless condition which entails only war except that they, like individual men, should give up their savage (lawless) freedom, adjust themselves to the constraints of public law, and thus establish a continuously growing state consisting of various nations (*civitas gentium*), which will ultimately include all the nations of the world. But since, under the idea of the law of nations, they do not wish this, rejecting in practice what is correct in theory, if all is not to be lost, there can be, in place of the positive idea of a world republic, only the negative surrogate of an alliance which averts war, endures, spreads, and holds back the stream of those hostile inclinations which fear the law, though under constant peril of their breaking loose again.* *Furor impius intus ... fremit horridus ore cruento* (Virgil).⁵

THIRD DEFINITIVE ARTICLE FOR A PERPETUAL PEACE

"The Law of World Citizenship Shall Be Limited to Conditions of Universal Hospitality"

Here, as in the preceding articles, it is not a question of philanthropy but of right. Hospitality means the right of a stranger not to be treated as an enemy when he arrives in the land of another. One may refuse to receive him when this can be done without causing his destruction; but, so long as he peacefully occupies his place, one may not treat him with hostility. It is not a question of being received as a guest in one's house, as a particularly benevolent convention would be needed in order to give him a claim to be treated as a guest for a certain length of time. It is rather a right of visit, a right of demanding of others that they admit one to their society. This right all men have by virtue of their common possession of the surface of the earth, where, as on a spherical surface, they cannot infinitely disperse and hence must finally tolerate the presence of each other. Originally no one had more right than another to a particular part of the earth.

Uninhabitable parts of the earth, the sea and the deserts, divide this community of all men, but the ship and the camel (the desert ship) enable them to approach each other across these unruled regions and to establish communication by using the

* It would not ill become a people that has just terminated a war to decree, besides a day of thanksgiving, also a day of fasting in order to ask heaven, in the name of the state, for forgiveness for the great iniquity which the human race still goes on to perpetuate in refusing to submit to a lawful constitution in their relation to other peoples, preferring, from pride in their independence, to make use of the barbarous means of war even though they are not able to attain what is sought, namely, the rights of a single state. The thanksgivings for victory won during the war, the hymns which are sung to the God of Hosts (in good Israelitic manner), stand in equally sharp contrast to the moral idea of the Father of Men. For they not only show a sad enough indifference to the way in which nations seek their rights, but in addition express a joy in having annihilated a multitude of men or their happiness.

5. ["Within, impious Rage, sitting on savage arms, his hands fast bound behind with a hundred brazen knots, shall roar in the ghastliness of blood-stained lips" (*Aeneid* I, 294–96, trans. H. Rushton Fairclough ["Loeb Classical Library"] (London: Heinemann, 1926)]).]

common right to the face of the earth, which belongs to human beings generally. The inhospitality of the inhabitants of coasts (for instance, of the Barbary Coast) in robbing ships in neighboring seas or of enslaving stranded travelers, or the inhospitality of the inhabitants of the deserts (for instance, the Bedouin Arabs) who see approach to nomadic tribes as conferring the right to plunder them, is thus opposed to natural law, even though it extends the right of hospitality, i.e., the privilege of foreign arrivals, no further than to conditions of the possibility of seeking to communicate with the prior inhabitants. In this way distant parts of the world can come into peaceable relations with each other, and these are finally publicly established by law. Thus the human race can gradually be brought closer and closer to a constitution establishing world citizenship.

But to this perfection compare the inhospitable actions of the civilized and especially of the commercial states of our part of the world. The injustice which they show to lands and peoples they visit (which is equivalent to conquering them) is carried by them to terrifying lengths. America, the lands inhabited by the Negro, the Spice Islands, the Cape, etc., were at the time of their discovery considered by these civilized intruders as lands without owners, for they counted the inhabitants as nothing. In East India (Hindustan), under the pretense of establishing economic undertakings they brought in foreign soldiers and used them to oppress the natives, excited widespread wars among the various states, spread famine, rebellion, perfidy, and the whole litany of evils which afflict mankind.

China[6] and Japan (Nippon), who have had experience with such guests, have wisely refused them entry, the former permitting their approach to their shores but not their entry, while the latter permit this approach to only one European people, the Dutch, but treat them like prisoners, not allowing them any communication with the inhabitants. The worst of this (or, to speak with the moralist, the best) is that all these outrages profit them nothing, since all these commercial ventures stand on the verge of collapse, and the Sugar Islands, that place of the most refined and cruel slavery, produce no real revenue except indirectly, only serving a not very praiseworthy purpose of furnishing sailors for war fleets and thus for the conduct of war in

6. [A long footnote on the propriety of this name is here omitted as contributing nothing to the argument. It does show, however, Kant's immense reading in geography, anthropology, and philology.]

Europe. This service is rendered to powers which make a great show of their piety, and, while they drink injustice like water, they regard themselves as the elect in point of orthodoxy.

Since the narrower or wider community of the peoples of the earth has developed so far that a violation of rights in one place is felt throughout the world, the idea of a law of world citizenship is no high-flown or exaggerated notion. It is a supplement to the unwritten code of the civil and international law, indispensable for the maintenance of the public human rights and hence also of perpetual peace. One cannot flatter himself into believing he can approach this peace except under the condition outlined here.

FIRST SUPPLEMENT

OF THE GUARANTEE FOR PERPETUAL PEACE

THE guarantee of perpetual peace is nothing less than that great artist, nature (*natura daedala rerum*). In her mechanical course we see that her aim is to produce a harmony among men, against their will and indeed through their discord. As a necessity working according to laws we do not know, we call it destiny. But, considering its design in world history, we call it providence, inasmuch as we discern in it the profound wisdom of a higher cause which predetermines the course of nature and directs it to the objective final end of the human race.* We do

---

* In the mechanism of nature, to which man belongs as a sensuous being, a form is exhibited which is basic to its existence; we can conceive of this form only as dependent upon the end to which the Author of the world has previously destined it. This predetermination we call "divine providence" generally, and so far as it is exercised at the beginning of the world we call it "founding providence" (*Providentia conditrix; semel iussit, semper parent*—AUGUSTINE).[7] As maintaining nature in its course by universal laws of design, it is called "ruling providence" (*providentia gubernatrix*); as directing nature to ends not foreseen to man and only conjectured from the actual result, is it called "guiding providence" (*providentia directrix*). With respect to single events as divine ends, it is no longer called "providence" but "dispensation" (*directio extraordinaria*). But since "divine dispensation" indicates miracles even if the events themselves are not called such, it is a foolish pretension of man to wish to interpret them as such, since it is absurd to infer from a single event to a particular

7. ["Providence is a founder; once she orders, they always obey." "A sentence like this has not been found in Augustine. It thus seems to be not a citation but only a pointed formulation of the well-known Augustinian thought."—HEINRICH MAIER (editor of the Academy edition of *Perpetual Peace*).]

not observe or infer this providence in the cunning contrivances of nature, but, as in questions of the relation of the form of things to ends in general, we can and must supply it from our own

principle of the efficient cause, namely, that this event is an end and not merely a mechanical corollary of another end wholly unknown to us. However pious and humble such talk may be, it is full of self-conceit. The division of providence, considered not formally but materially, i.e., with respect to objects in the world to which it is directed, into either general or particular providence, is false and self-contradictory. (This division appears, for instance, in the statement that providence cares for the preservation of the species but leaves individuals to chance.) It is contradictory because it is called universal in its purpose, and therefore no single thing can be excluded from it. Presumably, therefore, a formal distinction is intended, according to the way in which providence seeks its ends. This is the distinction between the ordinary and the special ways of providence. (Under the former we may cite the annual dying-out and rebirth of nature with the changes of the season; under the latter, the transport of wood by ocean currents to arctic lands where it cannot grow, yet where it is needed by the inhabitants who could not live without it. Although we can very well explain the physico-mechanical cause of these extraordinary cases (e.g., by reference to the wooded banks of rivers in temperate lands, the falling of trees into the rivers, and then their being carried along by the Gulf Stream), we must not overlook the teleological cause, which intimates the foresight of a wisdom commanding over nature.

The concept of intervention or concurrence (*concursus*) in producing an effect in the world of sense must be given up, though it is quite usual in the schools. For to try to pair the disparate (*gryphes iungere equis*) and to let that which is itself the perfect cause of events in the world supplement its own predetermining providence in the course of the world (which would therefore have to have been inadequate) is self-contradictory. We fall into this self-contradiction, for example, when we say that next to God it was the physician who cured the ill, as if God had been his helper. For *causa solitaria non iuvat;* God is the author of the physician and all his medicines, and if we insist on ascending to the highest but theoretically inconceivable first cause, the effect must be ascribed entirely to Him. Or we can ascribe it entirely to the physician, so far as we consider the occurrence as explicable in a chain of causes under the order of nature.

But, besides being self-contradictory, such a mode of thought brings an end to all definite principles in judging an effect. In a morally practical point of view, however, which is directed exclusively to the supersensuous, the concept of the divine *concursus* is quite suitable and even necessary. We find this, for instance, in the belief that God will compensate for our own lack of justice, provided our intention was genuine, that He will do so by means that are inconceivable to us, and that therefore we should not relent in our endeavor after the good. But it is self-evident that no one should try to explain a good action (as an event in the world) as a result of this *concursus,* for this would be a vain theoretical knowledge of the supersensuous and therefore absurd.

minds in order to conceive of its possibility by analogy to actions of human art. The idea of the relationship and harmony between these actions and the end which reason directly assigns to us is transcendent from a theoretical point of view; from a practical standpoint, with respect, for example, to the ideal[8] of perpetual peace, the concept is dogmatic and its reality is well established, and thus the mechanism of nature may be employed to that end. The use of the word "nature" is more fitting to the limits of human reason and more modest than an expression indicating a providence unknown to us. This is especially true when we are dealing with questions of theory and not of religion, as at present, for human reason in questions of the relation of effects to their causes must remain within the limits of possible experience. On the other hand, the use of the word "providence" here intimates the possession of wings like those of Icarus, conducting us toward the secret of its unfathomable purpose.

Before we more narrowly define the guarantee which nature gives, it is necessary to examine the situation in which she has placed her actors on her vast stage, a situation which finally assures peace among them. Then we shall see how she accomplishes the latter. Her preparatory arrangements are:

1. In every region of the world she has made it possible for men to live.
2. By war she has driven them even into the most inhospitable regions in order to populate them.
3. By the same means, she has forced them into more or less lawful relations with each other.

That in the cold wastes by the Arctic Ocean the moss grows which the reindeer dig from the snow in order to make itself the prey or the conveyence of the Ostyak or Samoyed; or that the saline sandy deserts are inhabited by the camel which appears created as it were in order that they might not go unused—that is already wonderful. Still clearer is the end when we see how besides the furry animals of the Arctic there are also the seal, the walrus, and the whale which afford the inhabitants food from their flesh and warmth from their blubber. But the care of nature excites the greatest wonder when we see how she brings wood (though the inhabitants do not know whence it comes) to these barren climates, without which they would have neither

8. [*Pflichtbegriff*, following the rendition of M. Campbell Smith.]

canoes, weapons, nor huts, and when we see how these natives are so occupied with their war against the animals that they live in peace with each other—but what drove them there was presumably nothing else than war.

The first instrument of war among the animals which man learned to tame and to domesticate was the horse (for the elephant belongs to later times, to the luxury of already established states). The art of cultivating certain types of plants (grain) whose original characteristics we do not know, and the increase and improvement of fruits by transplantation and grafting (in Europe perhaps only the crab apple and the wild pear), could arise only under conditions prevailing in already established states where property was secure. Before this could take place, it was necessary that men who had first subsisted in anarchic freedom by hunting,* fishing, and sheepherding should have been forced into an agricultural life. Then salt and iron were discovered. These were perhaps the first articles of commerce for the various peoples and were sought far and wide; in this way a peaceful traffic among nations was established, and thus understanding, conventions, and peaceable relations were established among the most distant peoples.

As nature saw to it that men *could* live everywhere in the world, she also despotically willed that they *should* do so, even against their inclination and without this *ought* being based on a concept of duty to which they were bound by a moral law. She chose war as the means to this end. So we see peoples whose common language shows that they have a common origin. For instance, the Samoyeds on the Arctic Ocean and a people with a similar language a thousand miles away in the Altaian Mountains are separated by a Mongolian people adept at horsemanship and hence at war; the latter drove the former into the most inhospitable arctic regions where they certainly would not have spread

* Among all modes of life there is undoubtedly none more opposed to a civilized constitution than that of hunting, because families which must dwell separately soon become strangers and, scattered in extensive forests, also enemies, since each needs a great deal of space for obtaining food and clothing. The Noachic ban on blood (Genesis IX, 4-6) (which was imposed by the baptized Jews as a condition on the later Christians who were converted from heathenism, though in a different connection—see The Acts XV, 20; XXI, 25) seems to have been originally nothing more than a prohibition against the hunting life, because here raw flesh must often have been eaten; when the latter was forbidden, so also was the former.

of their own accord.* Again, it is the same with the Finns who in the most northerly part of Europe are called Lapps; Goths and Sarmatians have separated them from the Hungarians to whom they are related in language. What can have driven the Eskimos, a race entirely distinct from all others in America and perhaps descended from primeval European adventurers, so far into the North, or the Pescherais as far south as Tierra del Fuego, if it were not war which nature uses to populate the whole earth? War itself requires no special motive but appears to be engrafted on human nature; it passes even for something noble, to which the love of glory impels men quite apart from any selfish urges. Thus among the American savages just as much as among those of Europe during the age of chivalry, military valor is held to be of great worth in itself, not only during war (which is natural) but in order that there should be war. Often war is waged only in order to show valor; thus an inner dignity is ascribed to war itself, and even some philosophers have praised it as an ennoblement of humanity, forgetting the pronouncement of the Greek who said, "War is an evil inasmuch as it produces more wicked men than it takes away." So much for the measures nature takes to lead the human race, considered as a class of animals, to her own end.

Now we come to the question concerning that which is most essential in the design of perpetual peace: What has nature done with regard to this end which man's own reason makes his duty? That is, what has nature done to favor man's moral purpose, and how has she guaranteed (by compulsion but without prejudice to his freedom), that he shall do that which he ought to but does not do under the laws of freedom? This question refers to all three phases of public law, namely, civil law, the law of nations, and the law of world citizenship. If I say of nature that she wills that this or that occur, I do not mean that she imposes a duty on us to do it, for this can be done only by free practical reason;

* One could ask: If nature willed that these icy coasts should not remain uninhabited, what would become of the inhabitants if nature ever failed (as might be expected) to bring driftwood to them? For it is reasonable to believe that, in the progress of civilization, the occupants of the temperate zones would make better use of the wood along rivers than simply to let it fall into the water and be carried to the sea. I answer: If nature will first have compelled them to peace, the dwellers along the Ob, the Yenisei, or the Lena will bring it to them commercially, exchanging it for animal products in which the sea around the arctic coasts abounds.

rather I mean that she herself does it, whether we will or not (*fata volentem ducunt, nolentem trahunt*).[9]

1. Even if a people were not forced by internal discord to submit to public laws, war would compel them to do so, for we have already seen that nature has placed each people near another which presses upon it, and against this it must form itself into a state in order to defend itself. Now the republican constitution is the only one entirely fitting to the rights of man. But it is the most difficult to establish and even harder to preserve, so that many[10] say a republic would have to be a nation of angels, because men with their selfish inclinations are not capable of a constitution of such sublime form. But precisely with these inclinations nature comes to the aid of the general will established on reason, which is revered even though impotent in practice. Thus it is only a question of a good organization of the state (which does lie in man's power), whereby the powers of each selfish inclination are so arranged in opposition that one moderates or destroys the ruinous effect of the other. The consequence for reason is the same as if none of them existed, and man is forced to be a good citizen even if not a morally good person.

The problem of organizing a state, however hard it may seem, can be solved even for a race of devils, if only they are intelligent. The problem is: "Given a multitude of rational beings requiring universal laws for their preservation, but each of whom is secretly inclined to exempt himself from them, to establish a constitution in such a way that, although their private intentions conflict, they check each other, with the result that their public conduct is the same as if they had no such intentions."

A problem like this must be capable of solution; it does not require that we know how to attain the moral improvement of men but only that we should know the mechanism of nature in order to use it on men, organizing the conflict of the hostile intentions present in a people in such a way that they must compel themselves to submit to coercive laws. Thus a state of peace is established in which laws have force. We can see, even in actual states, which are far from perfectly organized, that in

---

9. ["Fates lead the willing, drive the unwilling" (Seneca *Epist. mor.* xviii. 4).]

10. [E.g., Rousseau, *Social Contract*, Book III, chap. 4.]

their foreign relations they approach that which the idea of right prescribes. This is so in spite of the fact that the intrinsic element of morality is certainly not the cause of it. (A good constitution is not to be expected from morality, but, conversely, a good moral condition of a people is to be expected only under a good constitution.) Instead of genuine morality, the mechanism of nature brings it to pass through selfish inclinations, which naturally conflict outwardly but which can be used by reason as a means for making room for its own end, the sovereignty of law, and, as concerns the state, for promoting and securing internal and external peace.

This, then, is the truth of the matter: Nature inexorably wills that the right should finally triumph. What we neglect to do comes about by itself, though with great inconveniences to us. "If you bend the reed too much, you break it; and he who attempts too much attempts nothing" (Bouterwek).[11]

2. The idea of international law presupposes the separate existence of many independent but neighboring states. Although this condition is itself a state of war (unless a federative union prevents the outbreak of hostilities), this is rationally preferable to the amalgamation of states under one superior power, as this would end in one universal monarchy, and laws always lose in vigor what government gains in extent; hence a soulless despotism falls into anarchy after stifling the seeds of the good. Nevertheless, every state, or its ruler, desires to establish lasting peace in this way, aspiring if possible to rule the whole world. But nature wills otherwise. She employs two means to separate peoples and to prevent them from mixing: differences of language and of religion.* These differences involve a tendency to mutual hatred and pretexts for war, but the progress of civilization and men's gradual approach to greater harmony in their principles finally leads to peaceful agreement. This is not like

---

11. [Friedrich Bouterwek (1766–1828). "I have not been able to locate the verse cited here."—Heinrich Maier].

* Difference of religion—a singular expression! It is precisely as if one spoke of different moralities. There may very well be different kinds of historical faiths attached to different means employed in the promotion of religion, and they belong merely in the field of learned investigation. Similarly there may be different religious texts (Zendavesta, the Vida, the Koran, etc.), but such differences do not exist in religion, there being only one religion valid for all men and in all ages. These can, therefore, be nothing else than the accidental vehicles of religion, thus changing with times and places.

that peace which despotism (in the burial ground of freedom) produces through a weakening of all powers; it is, on the contrary, produced and maintained by their equilibrium in liveliest competition.

3. Just as nature wisely separates nations, which the will of every state, sanctioned by the principles of international law, would gladly unite by artifice or force, nations which could not have secured themselves against violence and war by means of the law of world citizenship unite because of mutual interest. The spirit of commerce, which is incompatible with war, sooner or later gains the upper hand in every state. As the power of money is perhaps the most dependable of all the powers (means) included under the state power, states see themselves forced, without any moral urge, to promote honorable peace and by mediation to prevent war wherever it threatens to break out. They do so exactly as if they stood in perpetual alliances, for great offensive alliances are in the nature of the case rare and even less often successful.

In this manner nature guarantees perpetual peace by the mechanism of human passions. Certainly she does not do so with sufficient certainty for us to predict the future in any theoretical sense, but adequately from a practical point of view, making it our duty to work toward this end, which is not just a chimerical one.

SECOND SUPPLEMENT

SECRET ARTICLE FOR PERPETUAL PEACE

A SECRET article in contracts under public law is objectively, i.e., from the standpoint of its content, a contradiction. Subjectively, however, a secret clause can be present in them, because the persons who dictate it might find it inconvenient to their dignity to declare openly that they are its authors.

The only article of this kind is contained in the statement: "The opinions of philosophers on the conditions of the possibility of public peace shall be consulted by those states armed for war."

But it appears humiliating to the legislative authority of a state, to whom we must naturally attribute the utmost wisdom, to seek instruction from subjects (the philosophers) on principles of conduct toward other states. It is, nevertheless, very advisable to do so. Therefore, the state tacitly and secretly invites them to give their opinions, that is, the state will let them publicly and freely talk about the general maxims of warfare and of the establishment of peace (for they will do that of themselves, provided they are not forbidden to do so). It does not require a particular convention among states to see that this is done, since their agreement on this point lies in an obligation already established by universal human reason which is morally legislative.

I do not mean that the state should give the principles of philosophers any preference over the decisions of lawyers (the representatives of the state power); I only ask that they be given a hearing. The lawyer, who has made not only the scales of right but also the sword of justice his symbol, generally uses the latter not merely to keep back all foreign influences from the former; but if the scale does not sink the way he wishes, he also throws the sword into it (*vae victis*), a practice to which he often has the greatest temptation because he is not also a philosopher, even in morality. His office is only to apply positive laws, not to inquire whether they might not need improvement. The administrative function, which is the lower one in his faculty, he counts as the highest because it is invested with power (as is the case also with the other faculties [of medicine and theology]).[12] The philosophical faculty occupies a very low rank against this allied power. Thus it is said of philosophy, for example, that she is the handmaiden to theology, and the other faculties claim as much. But one does not see distinctly whether she precedes her mistress with a flambeau or follows bearing her train.

That kings should philosophize or philosophers become kings is not to be expected. Nor is it to be wished, since the possession of power inevitably corrupts the untrammeled judgment of reason. But kings or kinglike peoples which rule themselves under laws of equality should not suffer the class of philosophers to disappear or to be silent but should let them speak openly. This is indispensable to the enlightenment of the business of government, and, since the class of philosophers is by nature incapable of plotting and lobbying, it is above suspicion of being made up of propagandists.

12. [Kant is here referring to the rivalry among the four faculties of the German university of his time, viz., philosophy, theology, law, and medicine. Cf. his *Strife of the Faculties*.]

APPENDIX I
ON THE OPPOSITION BETWEEN MORALITY AND POLITICS WITH RESPECT TO PERPETUAL PEACE

TAKEN objectively, morality is in itself practical, being the totality of unconditionally mandatory laws according to which we ought to act. It would obviously be absurd, after granting authority to the concept of duty, to pretend that we cannot do our duty, for in that case this concept would itself drop out of morality (*ultra posse nemo obligatur*). Consequently, there can be no conflict of politics, as a practical doctrine of right, with ethics, as a theoretical doctrine of right. That is to say, there is no conflict of practice with theory, unless by ethics we mean a general doctrine of prudence, which would be the same as a theory of the maxims for choosing the most fitting means to accomplish the purposes of self-interest. But to give this meaning to ethics is equivalent to denying that there is any such thing at all.

Politics says, "Be ye wise as serpents"; morality adds, as a limiting condition, "and guileless as doves." If these two injunctions are incompatible in a single command, then politics and morality are really in conflict; but if these two qualities ought always to be united, the thought of contrariety is absurd, and the question as to how the conflict between morals and politics is to be resolved cannot even be posed as a problem. Although the proposition, "Honesty is the best policy," implies a theory which practice unfortunately often refutes, the equally theoretical, "Honesty is better than any policy," is beyond refutation and is indeed the indispensable condition of policy.

The tutelary divinity of morality yields not to Jupiter, for this tutelary divinity of force still is subject to destiny. That is, reason is not yet sufficiently enlightened to survey the entire series of predetermining causes, and such vision would be necessary for one to be able to foresee with certainty the happy or unhappy effects which follow human actions by the mechanism of nature (though we know enough to have hope that they will accord with our wishes). But what we have to do in order to remain in the path of duty (according to rules of wisdom) reason instructs us by her rules, and her teaching suffices for attaining the ultimate end.

Now the practical man, to whom morality is merely theory even though he concedes that it can and should be followed, ruthlessly renounces our good-natured hope [that it will be followed]. He does so because he pretends to have seen in advance that man, by his nature, will never will what is required for realizing the end which leads him to perpetual peace. Certainly the will of each individual to live under a juridical constitution according to principles of freedom (i.e., the distributive unity of the will of all) is not sufficient to this end. That all together should will this condition (i.e., the collective unity of the united will)—a solution to this troublous problem—is also required. Thus a whole of civil society is formed. But since a uniting cause must supervene upon the variety of particular volitions in order to produce a common will from them, establishing this whole is something that no one individual in the group can perform; hence in the practical execution of this idea we can count on nothing but force to establish the juridical condition, on the compulsion of which public law will later be established. We can scarcely hope to find in the legislator a moral intention sufficient to induce him to commit to the general will the establishment of a legal constitution after he has formed the nation from a horde of savages; therefore, we cannot but expect (in practice) to find in execution wide deviations from this idea (in theory).

It will then be said that he who once has power in his hands will not allow the people to prescribe laws for him; a state which once is able to stand under no external laws will not submit to the decision of other states questions of the way in which it seeks its rights against them; and one continent, which feels itself superior to another, even though the other does not interfere with it, will not neglect to increase its power by robbery or even conquest. Thus all theoretical plans of civil and international laws and laws of world citizenship vanish into empty and impractical ideas, while practice based on empirical principles of human nature, not blushing to draw its maxims from the usages of the world, can alone hope to find a sure ground for its political edifice.

If there is no freedom and no morality based on it, and everything which occurs or can occur happens by the mere mechanism of nature, certainly politics (which is the art of using this mechanism for ruling men) is the whole of practical wisdom, and the concept of right is an empty thought. But if we find it necessary to connect the latter with politics, and even to raise it to a limiting condition thereon, the possibility of their being united must be conceded. I can easily conceive of a moral politician, i.e., one who so chooses political principles that they are consistent with those of morality; but I cannot conceive of a political moralist, one who forges a morality in such a way that it conforms to the statesman's advantage.

When a remediable defect is found in the constitution of the state or in its relations to others, the principle of the moral politician will be that it is a duty, especially of the rulers of the state, to inquire how it can be remedied as soon as possible in a way conforming to natural law as a model presented by reason; this he will do even if it costs self-sacrifice. But it would be absurd to demand that every defect be immediately and impetuously changed, since the disruption of the bonds of a civil society or a union of world citizens before a better constitution is ready to take its place is against all politics agreeing with morality. But it can be demanded that at least the maxim of the necessity of such a change should be taken to heart by those in power so that they may continuously approach the goal of the constitution that is best under laws of right. A state may exercise a republican rule, even though by its present constitution it has a despotic sovereignty; until gradually the people becomes susceptible to the influence simply of the idea of the authority of law (as if it possessed physical power) and thus is found fit to be its own legislator (as its own legislation is originally established on law). If a violent revolution, engendered by a bad constitution, introduces by illegal means a more legal constitution, to lead the people back to the earlier constitution would not be permitted; but, while the revolution lasted, each person who openly or covertly shared in it would have justly incurred the punishment due to those who rebel. As to the external relations of states, a state cannot be expected to renounce its constitution even though it is a despotic one (which has the advantage of being stronger in relation to foreign enemies) so long as it is exposed to the danger of being swallowed up by other states. Thus even in the case of the intention to improve the constitution, postponement to a more propitious time may be permitted.*

---

* These are permissive laws of reason. Public law laden with injustice must be allowed to stand either until everything is of itself ripe for complete reform or until this maturity has been brought about by peaceable means; for a legal constitution, even though it be right to only a low de-

It may be that despotizing moralists, in practice blundering, often violate rules of political prudence through measures they adopt or propose too precipitately; but experience will gradually retrieve them from their infringement of nature and lead them on to a better course. But the moralizing politician, by glossing over principles of politics which are opposed to the right with the pretext that human nature is not capable of the good as reason prescribes it, only makes reform impossible and perpetuates the violation of law.

Instead of possessing the *practical science* they boast of, these politicians have only *practices;* they flatter the power which is then ruling so as not to be remiss in their private advantage, and they sacrifice the nation and, where possible, the whole world. This is the way of all professional lawyers (not legislators) when they go into politics. Their task is not to reason too nicely about the legislation but to execute the momentary commands on the statute books; consequently, the legal constitution in force at any time is to them the best, but when it is amended from above, this amendment always seems best too. Thus everything is preserved in its accustomed mechanical order. Their adroitness in fitting into all circumstances gives them the illusion of being able to judge constitutional principles according to concepts of right (thus not empirically but a priori). They make a great show of understanding *men* (which is certainly something to be expected of them, since they have to deal with so many) without understanding *man* and what can be made of him, for they lack the higher point of view of anthropological observation which is needed for this. If with these ideas they go into civil and international law, as reason prescribes it, they take this step in a spirit of chicanery, for they still follow their accustomed mechanical routine of despotically imposed coercive laws in a field where only concepts of reason can establish a legal compulsion according to the principles of freedom, and where for the first time a justly durable constitution is possible.

---

gree is better than none at all, the anarchic condition which would result from precipitate reform. Political wisdom, therefore, will make it a duty to introduce reforms which accord with the ideal of public law. But even when nature herself produces revolutions, political wisdom will not employ them to legitimize still greater oppression. On the contrary, it will use them as a call of nature for fundamental reforms to produce a lawful constitution founded upon principles of freedom, for only such a constitution is durable.

In this field the pretended practical man thinks he can solve the problem of establishing such a constitution without the rational idea but solely from the experience he has had with what was previously the most lasting constitution—a constitution which in many cases was opposed to law.

The maxims which he makes use of (though he does not divulge them) are, roughly speaking, the following sophisms:

1. *Fac et excusa.* Seize every favorable opportunity for usurping the right of the state over its own people or over a neighboring people; the justification will be easier and more elegant *ex post facto*, and the power can be more easily glossed over especially when the supreme power in the state is also the legislative authority which must be obeyed without argument. It is much more difficult to do the violence when one has first to wait upon the consideration of convincing arguments and to meet them with counterarguments. Boldness itself gives the appearance of inner conviction of the legitimacy of the deed, and the God of success is afterward the best advocate.

2. *Si fecisti, nega.* What you have committed, deny that it was your fault—for instance, that you have brought your people to despair and hence to rebellion. Rather assert that it was due to the obstinacy of your subjects; or, if you have conquered a neighboring nation, say that the fault lies in the nature of man, who, if not met by force, can be counted on to make use of it to conquer you.

3. *Divide et impera.* That is, if there are certain privileged persons in your nation who have chosen you as their chief (*primus inter pares*), set them at variance with one another and embroil them with the people. Show the latter visions of greater freedom, and all will soon depend on your untrammeled will. Or if it is foreign states that concern you, it is a pretty safe means to sow discord among them so that, by seeming to protect the weaker, you can conquer them one after another.

Certainly no one is now the dupe of these political maxims, for they are already universally known. Nor are they blushed at, as if their injustice were too glaring, for great powers blush only at the judgment of other great powers but not at that of the common masses. It is not that they are ashamed of revealing such principles (for all of them are in the same boat with respect to the morality of their maxims); they are ashamed only when these maxims fail, for they still have political honor which cannot be disputed—and this honor is the aggrandizement of their power by whatever means.*

All these twistings and turnings of an immoral doctrine of prudence in leading men from their natural state of war to a state of peace prove at least that men in both their private and their public relationships cannot reject the concept of right or trust themselves openly to establish politics merely on the artifices of prudence. Thus they do not refuse obedience to the concept of public law, which is especially manifest in international law; on the contrary they give all due honor to it, even when they are inventing a hundred pretenses and subterfuges to escape from it in practice, imputing its authority, as the source and union of all laws, to crafty force. Let us put an end to this sophism, if not to the injustice it protects, and force the false representatives of power to confess that they do not plead in favor of the right but in favor of might. This is revealed in the imperious tone they assume as if they themselves could command the right. Let us remove the delusion by which they and others are duped, and discover the supreme principle from which the intention to perpetual peace stems. Let us show that everything evil which stands in its way derives from the fact that the political moralist begins where the moral politician

* Even if we doubt a certain wickedness in the nature of men who live together in a state and instead plausibly cite lack of civilization, which is not yet sufficiently advanced, i.e., regard barbarism as the cause of those antilawful manifestations of their character, this viciousness is clearly and incontestably shown in the foreign relations of states. Within each state it is veiled by the compulsion of civil laws, because the inclination to violence between the citizens is fettered by the stronger power of the government. This relationship not only gives a moral veneer (*causae non causae*) to the whole but actually facilitates the development of the moral disposition to a direct respect for the law by placing a barrier against the outbreak of unlawful inclinations. Each person believes that he himself would hold the concept of law sacred and faithfully follow it provided he was sure that he could expect the same from others, and the government does in part assure him of this. Thereby a great step (though not yet a moral step) is taken toward morality, which is attachment to this concept of duty for its own sake and without regard to hope of a similar response from others. But since each one with his own good opinion of himself presupposes a malicious disposition on the part of all the others, they all pronounce the judgment that they in fact are all worth very little. We shall not discuss how this comes about, though it cannot be blamed on the nature of man as a free being. But since even respect for the concept of right (which man cannot absolutely refuse to respect) solemnly sanctions the theory that he has the capacity of conforming to it, everyone sees that he, for his part, must act according to it, however others may act.

would correctly leave off, and that, since he thus subordinates principles to the end (putting the cart before the horse), he vitiates his own purpose of bringing politics into agreement with morality.

To make practical philosophy self-consistent, it is necessary, first, to decide the question: In problems of practical reason, must we begin from its material principles, i.e., the end as the object of choice? Or should we begin from the formal principles of pure reason, i.e., from the principle which is concerned solely with freedom in outer relations and which reads, "So act that you can will that your maxim could become a universal law, regardless of the end"?

Without doubt it is the latter which has precedence, for as a principle of law it has unconditional necessity. On the other hand, the former is obligatory only if we presuppose the empirical conditions of the proposed end, i.e., its practicability. Thus if this end (in this case, perpetual peace) is a duty, it must be derived from the formal principle of the maxims of external actions. The first principle, that of the political moralist, pertaining to civil and international law and the law of world citizenship, is merely a problem of technique (*problema technicum*); the second, as the problem of the moral politician to whom it is an ethical problem (*problema morale*), is far removed from the other in its method of leading toward perpetual peace, which is wished not merely as a material good but also as a condition issuing from an acknowledgment of duty.

For the solution of the former, the problem of political prudence, much knowledge of nature is required so that its mechanism may be employed toward the desired end; yet all this is uncertain in its results for perpetual peace, with whatever sphere of public law we are concerned. It is uncertain, for example, whether the people are better kept in obedience and maintained in prosperity by severity or by the charm of distinctions which flatter their vanity, by the power of one or the union of various chiefs, or perhaps merely by a serving nobility or by the power of the people. History furnishes us with contradictory examples from all governments (with the exception of the truly republican, which can alone appeal to the mind of a moral politician). Still more uncertain is an international law allegedly erected on the statutes of ministries. It is, in fact, a word without meaning, resting as it does on compacts which, in the very act of being concluded, contain secret reservations for their violation.

On the other hand, the solution of the second problem, that of political wisdom, presses itself upon us, as it were; it is clear to everyone and puts to shame all affectation. It leads directly to the end, but, remembering discretion, it does not precipitately hasten to do so by force; rather, it continuously approaches it under the conditions offered by favorable circumstances.

Then it may be said, "Seek ye first the kingdom of pure practical reason and its righteousness, and your end (the blessing of perpetual peace) will necessarily follow." For it is the peculiarity of morals, especially with respect to its principles of public law and hence in relation to a politics known a priori, that the less it makes conduct depend on the proposed end, i.e., the intended material or moral advantage, the more it agrees with it in general. This is because it is the universal will given a priori (in a nation or in the relations among different nations) which determines the law among men, and if practice consistently follows it, this will can also, by the mechanism of nature, cause the desired result and make the concept of law effective. So, for instance, it is a principle of moral politics that a people should unite into a state according to juridical concepts of freedom and equality, and this principle is based not on prudence but on duty. Political moralists may argue as much as they wish about the natural mechanism of a mass of men forming a society, assuming a mechanism which would weaken those principles and vitiate their end; or they may seek to prove their assertions by examples of poorly organized constitutions of ancient and modern times (for instance, of democracies without representative systems). They deserve no hearing, particularly as such a pernicious theory may itself occasion the evil which it prophesies, throwing human beings into one class with all other living machines, differing from them only in their consciousness that they are not free, which makes them, in their own judgment, the most miserable of all beings in the world.

The true but somewhat boastful sentence which has become proverbial, *Fiat iustitia, pereat mundus* ("Let justice reign even if all the rascals in the world should perish from it"), is a stout principle of right which cuts asunder the whole tissue of artifice or force. But it should not be misunderstood as a permission to use one's own right with extreme rigor (which would conflict with ethical duty); it should be understood as the obligation of those in power not to limit or to extend anyone's right through sympathy or disfavor for others. This requires, first, an internal constitution of the state erected on pure principles of right, and, second, a convention of the state with other near or distant states (analogous to a universal state) for the legal settlement of their differences. This implies only that political maxims must not be derived from the welfare or happiness which a single state expects from obedience to them, and thus not from the end which one of them proposes for itself. That is, they must not be deduced from volition as the supreme yet empirical principle of political wisdom, but rather from the pure concept of the duty of right, from the *ought* whose principle is given a priori by pure reason, regardless of what the physical consequences may be. The world will by no means perish by a diminution in the number of evil men. Moral evil has the indiscerptible property of being opposed to and destructive of its own purposes (especially in the relationships between evil men); thus it gives place to the moral principle of the good, though only through a slow progress.

Thus objectively, or in theory, there is no conflict between morals and politics. Subjectively, however, in the selfish propensity of men (which should not be called "practice" as this would imply that it rested on rational maxims), this conflict will always remain. Indeed, it should remain, because it serves as a whetstone of virtue, whose true courage (by the principle, *tu ne cede malis, sed contra audentior ito*)[13] in the present case does not so much consist in defying with strong resolve evils and sacrifices which must be undertaken along with the conflict, but rather in detecting and conquering the crafty and far more dangerously deceitful and treasonable principle of evil in ourselves, which puts forward the weakness of human nature as justification for every transgression.

In fact, the political moralist may say: the ruler and people, or nation and nation, do each other no injustice when by violence or fraud they make war on each other, although they do commit injustice in general in that they refuse to respect the concept of right, which alone could establish perpetual peace. For since the one does transgress his duty against the other, who is likewise lawlessly disposed toward him, each gets what he deserves when they destroy each other. But enough of the race still remains to let this game continue into the remotest ages in order that posterity, someday, might take these perpetrators as

---

13. ["Yield not to evils, but go against the stronger" (*Aeneid* vi. 95).]

a warning example. Hence Providence is justified in the history of the world, for the moral principle in man is never extinguished, while with advancing civilization reason grows pragmatically in its capacity to realize ideas of law. But at the same time the culpability for the transgressions also grows. If we assume that humanity never will or can be improved, the only thing which a theodicy seems unable to justify is creation itself, the fact that a race of such corrupt beings ever was on earth. But the point of view necessary for such an assumption is far too high for us, and we cannot theoretically support our philosophical concepts of the supreme power which is inscrutable to us.

To such dubious consequences we are inevitably driven if we do not assume that pure principles of right have objective reality, i.e., that they may be applied, and that the people in a state and, further, states themselves in their mutual relations should act according to them, whatever objections empirical politics may raise. Thus true politics can never take a step without rendering homage to morality. Though politics by itself is a difficult art, its union with morality is no art at all, for this union cuts the knot which politics could not untie when they were in conflict. The rights of men must be held sacred, however much sacrifice it may cost the ruling power. One cannot compromise here and seek the middle course of a pragmatic conditional law between the morally right and the expedient. All politics must bend its knee before the right. But by this it can hope slowly to reach the stage where it will shine with an immortal glory.

APPENDIX II

OF THE HARMONY WHICH THE TRANSCENDENTAL CONCEPT OF PUBLIC RIGHT ESTABLISHES BETWEEN MORALITY AND POLITICS

IF, LIKE the teacher of law, I abstract from all the material of public law (i.e., abstract from the various empirically given relationships of men in the state or of states to each other), there remains only the form of publicity, the possibility of which is implied by every legal claim, since without it there can be no justice (which can only be conceived as publicly known) and thus no right, since it can be conferred only in accordance with justice. Every legal claim must be capable of publicity. Since it is easy to judge whether it is so in a particular case, i.e., whether it can be compatible with the principles of the agent, this gives an easily applied criterion found a priori in reason, by which the falsity (opposition to law) of the pretended claim (*praetensio iuris*) can, as it were, be immediately known by an experiment of pure reason.

Having set aside everything empirical in the concept of civil or international law (such as the wickedness in human nature which necessitates coercion), we can call the following proposition the transcendental formula of public law: "All actions relating to the right of other men are unjust if their maxim is not consistent with publicity."

This principle is to be regarded not merely as ethical (as belonging to the doctrine of virtue) but also as juridical (concerning the right of man). A maxim which I cannot divulge without defeating my own purpose must be kept secret if it is to succeed; and, if I cannot publicly avow it without inevitably exciting universal opposition to my project, the necessary and universal opposition which can be foreseen a priori is due only to the injustice with which the maxim threatens everyone. This principle is, furthermore, only negative, i.e., it only serves for the recognition of what is not just to others. Like an axiom, it is indemonstrably certain and, as will be seen in the following examples of public law, easily applied.

1. In the law of the state (*ius civitatis*) or domestic law, there is a question which many hold to be difficult to answer, yet it is easily solved by the transcendental principle of publicity. The question is: "Is rebellion a legitimate means for a people to employ in throwing off the yoke of an alleged tyrant (*non titulo, sed exercitio talis*)?" The rights of the people are injured; no injustice befalls the tyrant when he is deposed. There can be no doubt on this point. Nevertheless, it is in the highest degree illegitimate for the subjects to seek their rights in this way. If they fail in the struggle and are then subjected to severest punishment, they cannot complain about injustice any more than the tyrant could if they had succeeded.

If one wishes to decide this question by a dogmatic deduction of legal grounds, there can be much arguing pro and con; only the transcendental principle of the publicity of public law can free us of this prolixity. According to this principle, a people would ask itself before the establishment of the civil contract whether it dare to publish the maxim of its intention to revolt occasionally. It is clear that if, in the establishment of a constitution, the condition is made that the people may in certain cases employ force against its chief, the people would have to pretend to a legitimate power over him, and then he would not be the chief. Or if both are made the condition of the establishment of the state, no state would be possible, though to establish it was the purpose of the people. The illegitimacy of rebellion is thus clear from the fact that its maxim, if openly acknowledged, would make its own purpose impossible. Therefore, it would have to be kept secret.

This secrecy, however, is not incumbent upon the chief of the state. He can openly say that he will punish every rebellion with the death of the ring leaders, however much they may believe that he was the first to overstep the basic law; for when he knows he possesses irresistible power (which must be assumed to be the case in every civil constitution, because he who does not have enough power to protect the people against every other also does not have the right to command them), he need not fear vitiating his own purpose by publishing his maxims. If the revolt of the people succeeds, what has been said is still quite compatible with the fact that the chief, on retiring to the status of a subject, cannot begin a revolt for his restoration but need not fear being made to account for his earlier administration of the state.

2. We can speak of international law only under the presupposition of some law-governed condition, i.e., of the external condition under which right can really be awarded to man. For, being a public law, it contains in its very concept the public announcement of a general will which assigns to each his rights, and this *status iuridicus* must result from some compact which is not founded on laws of compulsion (as is the case of the compact from which a single state arises). Rather, it must be founded on a free and enduring association, like the previously mentioned federation of states. For without there being some juridical condition, which actively binds together the different physical or moral persons, there can be only private law; this is the situation met with in the state of nature. Now here there is a conflict of politics with morality (regarding the latter as a science of right), and the criterion of publicity again finds an easy application in resolving it, though only if the compact between the states has been made with the purpose of preserving peace between them and other states and not for conquest. The following cases of the antinomy between politics and morality occur (and they are stated with their solution).

a) "If one of these states has promised something to the other, such as aid, cession of some province, subsidies, and the like, and a case arises where the salvation of the state depends upon its being relieved of its promise, can it then, this is the question, consider itself in two roles: first as a sovereign (as it is responsible to no one in the state), and second as merely the highest official (who must give an account to the state)? From this dual capacity it would follow that in its latter role the state can relieve itself of what it has obliged itself to do in its former role." But if a state (or its chief) publicizes this maxim, others would naturally avoid entering an alliance therewith or ally themselves with others so as to resist such pretensions. This proves that politics with all its cunning would defeat its purpose by sincerity; therefore, that maxim must be illegitimate.

b) "If a neighboring power becomes formidable by its acquisitions (*potentia tremenda*) and thus causes anxiety, can one assume because it *can* oppress that it *will*? And does this give the lesser power, in union with others, a right to attack it without having first been injured by it?" A state which made known that such was its maxim would produce the feared evil even more certainly and quickly, for the greater power would steal a march on the smaller. And the alliance of the smaller powers would be only a feeble reed against one who knew how to apply the maxim *divide et impera*. This maxim of political expediency, if made public, would necessarily defeat its own purpose, and hence it is illegitimate.

c) "If a smaller state is so situated as to break up the territory of a larger one, and continuous territory is necessary to the preservation of the larger, is the latter not justified in subjugating the smaller and in incorporating it?" We easily see that the greater power cannot afford to let this maxim become known; otherwise the smaller states would very early unite, or other powers would dispute the prey, and thus publicity would render this maxim impracticable. This is a sign that it is illegitimate. It may be unjust to a very high degree, for a small object of injustice does not prevent the injustice from being very great.

3. I say nothing about the law of world citizenship, for its analogy with international law makes it a very simple matter to state and evaluate its maxims.

Thus in the principle of incompatibility between the maxims of international law and publicity we have a good distinguishing mark for recognizing the nonconformity of politics with morality (as a science of right). Now we need to know the condition under which these maxims agree with the law of nations, for we cannot infer conversely that the maxims which bear publicity are therefore just, since no one who has decidedly superior power needs to conceal his plans. The condition of possibility of international law in general is this: a juridical condition must first exist. For without this there is no public law, since all law which one may think of outside of this, in the state of nature, is merely private law. We have seen that a federation of states which has for its sole purpose the maintenance of peace is the only juridical condition compatible with the freedom of the several states. Therefore the harmony of politics with morals is possible only in a federative alliance, and the latter is necessary and given a priori by the principles of right. Furthermore, all politics has for its juridical basis the establishment of this harmony to its greatest possible extent, and without this end all its sophisms are but folly and veiled injustice. This false politics outdoes the best Jesuit school in casuistry. It has *reservatio mentalis,* wording public compacts with such expressions as can on occasion be interpreted to one's own advantage (for example, it makes the distinction between *status quo de fait* and *de droit*). It has *probabilism,* attributing hostile intentions to others, or even making probabilities of their possible superior power into legal grounds for destroying other, peaceful, states. Finally, it has the *peccatum philosophicum (peccatillum, bagatelle),* holding it to be only a trifle when a small state is swallowed up in order that a much larger one may thereby approach more nearly to an alleged greater good for the world as a whole.*

The duplicity of politics in respect to morality, in using one branch of it or the other for its purposes, furthers these sophistic maxims. These branches are philanthropy and respect for the rights of men, and both are duty. The former is a conditional

* The precedents for such maxims may be seen in Counsellor Garve's treatise, *On the Union of Morality with Politics* (1788).[14] This worthy scholar admits in the beginning that he is not able to solve the problem completely. But to approve of this union while admitting that one cannot meet all objections which may be raised against it seems to show more tolerance than is advisable toward those who are inclined to abuse it.

14. [Christian Garve (1742-98), *Abhandlung über die Verbindung der Moral mit der Politik oder einige Betrachtungen über die Frage, inwiefern es möglich sei, die Moral des Privatlebens bei der Regierung der Staaten zu beobachten* (Breslau, 1788).]

duty, while the latter is an unconditional and absolutely mandatory duty. One who wishes to give himself up to the sweet feeling of benevolence must make sure that he has not transgressed this absolute duty. Politics readily agrees with morality in its first branch (as ethics) in order to surrender the rights of men to their superiors. But with morality in the second branch (as a science of right), to which it must bend its knee, politics finds it advisable not to have any dealings, and rather denies it all reality, preferring to reduce all duties to mere benevolence. This artifice of a secretive politics would soon be unmasked by philosophy through publication of its maxims, if they only dared to allow the philosopher to publish his maxims.

In this regard I propose another affirmative and transcendental principle of public law, the formula of which is:

"All maxims which *stand in need* of publicity in order not to fail their end agree with politics and right combined."

For if they can attain their end only through publicity, they must accord with the public's universal end, happiness; and the proper task of politics is to promote this, i.e., to make the public satisfied with its condition. If, however, this end is attainable only by means of publicity, i.e., by removing all distrust in the maxims of politics, the latter must conform to the rights of the public, for only in this is the union of the goals of all possible.

The further development and discussion of this principle I must postpone to another occasion. But that it is a transcendental formula is to be seen from the exclusion of all empirical conditions (of the doctrine of happiness) as material of the law, and from the reference it makes to the form of universal lawfulness.

If it is a duty to make real (even if only through approximation in endless progress) the state of public law, and if there is well-grounded hope that this can actually be done, then perpetual peace, as the condition that will follow what has erroneously been called treaties of peace (but which in reality are only armistices) is not an empty idea. As the times required for equal steps of progress become, we hope, shorter and shorter, perpetual peace is a problem which, gradually working out its own solution, continuously approaches its goal.

VII

ON A SUPPOSED RIGHT TO LIE FROM ALTRUISTIC MOTIVES

IN THE journal *France*[1] for 1797, Part VI, No. 1, page 123, in an article entitled "On Political Reactions"[2] by Benjamin Constant,[3] there appears the following passage:

The moral principle, "It is a duty to tell the truth," would make any society impossible if it were taken singly and unconditionally. We have proof of this in the very direct consequences which a German philosopher has drawn from this principle. This philosopher goes so far as to assert that it would be a crime to lie to a murderer who asked whether our friend who is pursued by him had taken refuge in our house.*

The French philosopher on page 124 refutes this principle in the following manner:

It is a duty to tell the truth. The concept of duty is inseparable from the concept of right. A duty is that which in one being corresponds to the rights of another. Where there are no rights, there are no duties. To tell the truth is thus a duty; but it is a duty only in respect to one who has a right to the truth. But no one has a right to a truth which injures others.

1. [The journal *Frankreich im Jahre 1797. Aus den Briefen deutscher Männer in Paris*, published in Altona.]

2. [*Des réactions politiques* had appeared in 1796 and was translated in this journal.]

3. [Henri Benjamin Constant de Rebecque (1767–1830), the French writer, statesman, and orator.]

* "J. D. Michaelis[4] of Göttingen expressed this extraordinary opinion earlier than Kant. But the author of this essay has informed me that Kant is the philosopher spoken of in this passage."—K. F. CRAMER.†[5]

4. [Johann David Michaelis (1717–91), biblical scholar, professor in Göttingen.]

† That this was really said by me somewhere I hereby admit, though I cannot now remember the place.[6]—I. KANT.

5. [Karl Friedrich Cramer (1752–1807), the editor of *Frankreich*..., formerly professor of Greek and oriental languages and homiletics at Kiel, had been dismissed in 1794 because of his open sympathy for the Revolution.]

6. ["Such a place is not to be found in Kant's previous works."—HEINRICH MAIER (editor of the Academy edition of this work).]

The πρῶτον ψεῦδος in this argument lies in the sentence: "To tell the truth is a duty, but it is a duty only toward one who has a right to the truth."

It must first be noted that the expression, "to have a right to truth" is without meaning. One must rather say, "Man has a right to his own truthfulness (*veracitas*)," i.e., to the subjective truth in his own person. For to have objectively a right to truth would mean that it is a question of one's will (as in questions of what belongs to individuals generally) whether a given sentence is to be true or false. This would certainly produce an extraordinary logic.

Now the first question is: Does a man, in cases where he cannot avoid answering "Yes" or "No," have a right to be untruthful? The second question is: Is he not in fact bound to tell an untruth, when he is unjustly compelled to make a statement, in order to protect himself or another from a threatened misdeed?

Truthfulness in statements which cannot be avoided is the formal duty of an individual to everyone,* however great may be the disadvantage accruing to himself or to another. If, by telling an untruth, I do not wrong him who unjustly compels me to make a statement, nevertheless by this falsification, which must be called a lie (though not in a legal sense), I commit a wrong against duty generally in a most essential point. That is, so far as in me lies I cause that declarations should in general find no credence, and hence that all rights based on contracts should be void and lose their forcce, and this is a wrong done to mankind generally.

Thus the definition of a lie as merely an intentional untruthful declaration to another person does not require the additional condition that it must harm another, as jurists think proper in their definition (*mendacium est falsiloquium in praeiudicium alterius*). For a lie always harms another; if not some other particular man, still it harms mankind generally, for it vitiates the source of law itself.

This benevolent lie, however, can become punishable under civil law through an accident (*casus*), and that which escapes liability to punishment only by accident can also be condemned as wrong even by external laws. For instance, if by telling a lie

---

* I should not like to sharpen this principle to the point of saying, "Untruthfulness is a violation of duty to one's self." This principle belongs to ethics, but here we are concerned with a legal duty. [Ethics as a] theory of virtue sees in this transgression only worthlessness, which is the reproach the liar draws upon himself.

you have prevented murder, you have made yourself legally responsible for all the consequences; but if you have held rigorously to the truth, public justice can lay no hand on you, whatever the unforeseen consequences may be. After you have honestly answered the murderer's question as to whether his intended victim is at home, it may be that he has slipped out so that he does not come in the way of the murderer, and thus that the murder may not be committed. But if you had lied and said he was not at home when he had really gone out without your knowing it, and if the murderer had then met him as he went away and murdered him, you might justly be accused as the cause of his death. For if you had told the truth as far as you knew it, perhaps the murderer might have been apprehended by the neighbors while he searched the house and thus the deed might have been prevented. Therefore, whoever tells a lie, however well intentioned he might be, must answer for the consequences, however unforseeable they were, and pay the penalty for them even in a civil tribunal. This is because truthfulness is a duty which must be regarded as the ground of all duties based on contract, and the laws of these duties would be rendered uncertain and useless if even the least exception to them were admitted.

To be truthful (honest) in all declarations, therefore, is a sacred and absolutely commanding decree of reason, limited by no expediency.

Mr. Constant makes a thoughtful and correct remark on decrying principles so strict that they are alleged to lose themselves in such impracticable ideas that they are to be rejected. He says, on page 23, "In every case where a principle which has been proved to be true appears to be inapplicable, the reason is that we do not know the middle principle which contains the means of its application." He adduces (p. 121) the doctrine of equality as the first link of the social chain, saying (p. 122):

No man can be bound by any laws except those to the formulation of which he has contributed. In a very limited society this principle can be applied directly and needs no mediating principle in order to become a common principle. But in a society consisting of very many persons, another principle must be added to this one we have stated. This mediating principle is: the individuals can participate in the formulation of laws either in their own person or through their representatives. Whoever wished to apply the former principle to a large society without making use of the mediating principle would invariably bring about the destruction of the society. But this circumstance, which would only show the ignorance or the incompetence of the legislator, proves nothing against the principle.

He concludes (p. 125) that "a principle acknowledged to be true must never be abandoned, however obviously danger seems to be involved in it." (And yet the good man himself abandoned the unconditional principle of truthfulness on account of the danger which it involved for society. He did so because he could find no mediating principle which could serve to prevent this danger; and, in fact, there is no principle to be interpolated here.)

If we wish to preserve the names of the persons as they have been cited here, the "French philosopher" confuses the action by which someone does harm (*nocet*) to another in telling the truth when he cannot avoid making a statement, with the action whereby he does the other a wrong (*laedit*). It was only an accident (*casus*) that the truth of the statement harmed the occupant of the house; it was not a free act (in a juristic sense). For to demand of another that he should lie to one's own advantage would be a claim opposed to all lawfulness. Each man has not only a right but even the strict duty to be truthful in statements he cannot avoid making, whether they harm himself or others. In so doing, he does not do harm to him who suffers as a consequence; accident causes this harm. For one is not at all free to choose in such a case, since truthfulness (if he must speak) is an unconditional duty.

The "German philosopher" will not take as one of his principles the proposition (p. 124): "To tell the truth is a duty, but only to him who has a right to the truth." He will not do so, first, because of the ambiguous formulation of this proposition, for truth is not a possession the right to which can be granted to one and denied to another. But he will not do so chiefly because the duty of truthfulness (which is the only thing in question here) makes no distinction between persons to whom one has this duty and to whom one can exempt himself from this duty; rather, it is an unconditional duty which holds in all circumstances.

Now in order to proceed from a metaphysics of law (which abstracts from all empirical conditions) to a principle of politics (which applies these concepts to cases met with in experience), and by means of this to achieve the solution of a problem of politics in accord with the universal principle of law, the philosopher will enunciate three notions. The first is an axiom, i.e., an apodictically certain proposition which springs directly from the definition of external law (the harmony of the freedom of each with the freedom of all others according to a universal law). The second is a postulate of external public law (the will of all united according to the principle of equality, without which no one would have any freedom). Third, there is the problem of how it is to be arranged that, in a society however large, harmony may be maintained in accordance with principles of freedom and equality (namely, by means of a representative system). The latter will then become a principle of politics, the organization and establishment of which will entail decrees drawn from the practical knowledge of men, which will have in view only the mechanism of the administration of justice and how this may be suitably carried out. Law must never be accommodated to politics but politics always accommodated to law.

The author says, "A principle recognized as true (I add, recognized as an a priori and hence apodictic principle) must never be abandoned, however obviously danger seems to be involved in it." But one must only understand the danger not as a danger of accidentally doing a harm but only as a danger of doing a wrong. This would happen if I made the duty of being truthful, which is unconditional and the supreme juridical condition in testimony, into a conditional duty subordinate to other considerations. Although in telling a certain lie I do not actually do anyone a wrong, I formally but not materially violate the principle of right with respect to all unavoidably necessary utterances. And this is much worse than to do injustice to any particular person, because such a deed against an individual does not always presuppose the existence of a principle in the subject which produces such an act.

If one is asked whether he intends to speak truthfully in a statement that he is about to make and does not receive the question with indignation at the suspicion it expressed that he might be a liar, but rather asks permissions to consider possible exceptions, that person is already potentially a liar. That is because he shows that he does not acknowledge truthfulness as an intrinsic duty but makes reservations with respect to a rule which does not permit any exception, inasmuch as any exception would directly contradict itself.

All practical principles of right must contain rigorous truth, and the so-called "mediating principles" can contain only the more accurate definition of their application to actual cases (according to rules of policy), but they can never contain exceptions from the former. Such exceptions would nullify their universality, and that is precisely the reason that they are called principles.

VIII

SELECTIONS FROM THE METAPHYSICS OF MORALS

[PERPETUAL PEACE AS A MORAL AND POLITICAL IDEAL][1]

IF ONE cannot prove that a certain thing is, he may try to prove that it is not. But if he does not succeed in either (as is often the case), he can still ask whether he is interested in assuming the one or the other by hypothesis. He may do this from either a theoretical or a practical point of view. That is, he may do so in order merely to explain a certain phenomenon (as the astronomer's phenomenon of the retrogression and station of the planets) or in order to reach a certain end. In the latter case, this end may be either pragmatic (an end of art) or moral, i.e., an end of such kind that the maxim to propose it is itself duty. It is self-evident that the assumption (*suppositio*) of the practicability of that end is not made a duty, as it is a merely theoretical and moreover a problematical judgment; for there is no obligation to believe anything. But action in accordance with the idea of that end, even when there is not the least theoretical probability that it can be realized provided only that its impossibility cannot be demonstrated, is that to which a duty obligates us.

Now our moral-practical reason pronounces its irresistible veto: There ought not be war, neither that between me and thee in the state of nature nor that between us as states, which, though internally in a lawful condition, are externally in relation to each other in a lawless condition. For war is not the way in which each one should seek his rights. Thus the question no longer is whether perpetual peace is something or nothing and whether we delude ourselves in our theoretical judgment by assuming it to be something. Rather, we must act as if that thing, perpetual peace, existed—though it may not exist; we must endeavor to make it real and strive after the constitution (perhaps the republicanism of each and every state) which seems to us most likely

1. [The selection is the conclusion to Part II of the "Doctrine of Right" and is titled simply "Conclusion."]

to bring it to pass and to make an end to the disastrous warmaking to which all states without exception have directed their institutions as their chief end. And if the achievement of this purpose were to remain always only a pious wish, certainly in assuming a maxim of incessantly striving toward it we would not at least delude ourselves, for this is duty. But to assume that the moral law in us is deceptive would produce an abhorrent wish to dispense with all reason and to regard ourselves, by the nature of this wish, as subject to the same mechanism of nature as all other species of animals.

We can say that establishment of universal and enduring peace constitutes not just a part but rather the entire final end of jurisprudence within the limits of mere reason. Peace is the only condition under laws guaranteeing the mine and thine within a group of neighboring persons living together under a constitution whose rules are not derived from the experience of those who have fared best under it and whose experience, therefore, might serve as a norm for others. Rather, the rules must be derived by reason a priori from the ideal of a legal association of men under public laws generally, because all examples (which only illustrate and do not prove) are deceptive. Such rules, however, require a metaphysics, the necessity of which is carelessly conceded even by those who make fun of it.

This is seen, for example, when they say (as they often do), "The best constitution is one in which laws, not men, are sovereign." For what can be more metaphysically sublimated than this idea which, according to their own assertion, has the most assured objective reality and which is readily borne out by actual events? And this idea alone, if it is not taken in a revolutionary sense and made the basis of sudden change through violent overthrow of a previously existing wrong condition—this idea alone, I say, if it is sought for and realized by gradual reform in the light of firm principles, can uninterruptedly lead to the highest political good, perpetual peace.

EXPOSITION OF THE CONCEPT OF AN END WHICH IS ALSO A DUTY

WE CAN think of the relation of end to duty in two ways: either we can start from the end in order to discover the maxim of actions conforming to duty, or conversely we can commence with the latter to find the end which is also a duty.

Jurisprudence proceeds in the first way. It is left to everyone's free choice what end he proposes for his action. But the maxim of the action is determined a priori; that is, the freedom of the agent must be consistent with the freedom of every other agent according to a universal law.

Ethics, however, takes the opposite course. It cannot start from the ends which man may propose to himself and thereby decide the maxims he should adopt, i.e., decide his duty, for that would be to take empirical grounds for the maxims, and such grounds furnish no concept of duty, for this concept, the categorical ought, has its source only in pure reason. And even if the maxims were to be chosen in accordance with such ends (which are all selfish), we could not properly speak of the concept of duty at all. Thus in ethics the concept of duty must lead to that of ends, and the maxims with respect to the ends which we ought to set before ourselves must be founded on moral maxims.

Putting aside the question of what kind of end it is which is in itself a duty, and how such an end is possible, it is here necessary only to show that a duty of this kind is called a duty of virtue, and why it is so called.

To every duty there corresponds a right, as a warrant [to action] (*facultas moralis generatim*), but to every duty there is not a corresponding right of another person (*facultas iuridica*) to compel anyone; those which do are called legal duties specifically. Similarly, the concept of virtue corresponds to every ethical obligation, but not all ethical duties are for that reason duties of virtue. Those duties, in fact, which do not concern a certain end (the material, the object of choice) but only the formal element of the moral determination of the will (e.g., that the action which accords with duty must also be done from duty), are not duties of virtue. Only an end which is also duty can be called a duty of virtue. Therefore, there are several duties of virtue (and also various virtues), but there is only one duty of the former kind (a virtuous disposition), but it is valid for all actions.

The duty of virtue is essentially distinguished from juridical duty in that an external constraint is morally possible to the latter while the former rests only on free self-constraint. For finite holy beings (who cannot even be tempted to violate duty), there is no doctrine of virtue but merely a doctrine of morals, the latter being an autonomy of practical reason, while the former is also an autocracy of it. That is, it includes a consciousness of power to become master of one's inclinations to resist the law; even though this consciousness is not directly given, it is nevertheless correctly inferred from the moral categorical imperative. Thus human morality at its highest stage can still be nothing else than virtue, even if it be absolutely pure (wholly free from every incentive except that of duty). Even then it is commonly held to be an ideal which one should unceasingly approach, and which has been poetically personified under the name of the *wise man*.

Virtue, however, is not to be defined and esteemed merely as a perfected skill and (as Cochius[2] describes it in his prize essay) as a habit acquired by long practice of morally good actions. For if this habit is not a result of resolute, firm, and more and more purified principles, like any other mechanism of technical practical reason it is neither armed for all circumstances nor secured against the change which may be produced by new allurements. . . .

OF THE REASONS FOR CONCEIVING OF AN END WHICH IS ALSO A DUTY

An end is an object of free choice, the conception of which determines choice to an action by which the object is produced. Every action, therefore, has its end, and since no one can have an end without himself making the object of his choice the end, to have any end for an action is an act of freedom of the acting subject, not an effect of nature. But because this act which determines an end is a practical principle commanding not the means (and thus conditionally) but the end itself (and thus unconditionally), it is a categorical imperative of pure practical reason, and hence an imperative which combines the concept of duty with that of an end as such.

There must then be such an end and a categorical imperative corresponding to it. For, since there are free actions, there must be also ends to which, as objects, those actions are directed. But among these ends there must be some which are also, by their very concept, duties. For if there were no such ends, and since no action can be without some end, all ends for the practical reason would be valid only as means to other ends, and a cate-

2. [Leonhard Cochius (1717–79), court preacher and a member of the Berlin Academy, obtained the Academy prize in 1769 with his essay, *Über die Neigungen*.]

gorical imperative would be impossible. Thus ethics would be destroyed.

Here, therefore, we are not discussing the ends which man actually proposes because of the sensuous impulses of his nature, but the objects of free choice under its own laws, which objects he ought to make his end. We can call the former technical (subjective) and, properly speaking, pragmatic doctrine of ends involving the rule of prudence in the choice of ends, while the latter we must call the moral (objective) doctrine of ends. But this distinction is really superfluous here, since ethics is already clearly distinguished by its concept from the doctrine of nature (in this case, anthropology), in that the latter rests on empirical principles, whereas the moral doctrine of ends which concerns duties rests on a priori principles given in pure practical reason.

WHAT ARE THE ENDS WHICH ARE ALSO DUTIES?

They are: my own perfection [and] the happiness of others.

We cannot invert these and make our own happiness and the perfection of others into ends which should of themselves be duties for the same person.

For one's own happiness is an end which all men, by virtue of the impulses of their nature, do have, but this end can never be regarded without contradiction as duty. What each person already inevitably wills of himself does not belong under the concept of duty, for this is a constraint to a reluctantly adopted end. Thus it is a contradiction to say that one is obligated to promote his own happiness with all his power.

Similarly it is a contradiction to make the perfection of another my end and to regard myself as obligated to its promotion. For the perfection of another man as a person consists precisely in the fact that he is himself capable of setting before himself his own ends according to his own concepts of duty, and it is contradictory to require (i.e., to make it my duty) that I ought to do something which no one except himself can do.

EXPLANATION OF THESE TWO CONCEPTS

A. MY OWN PERFECTION

The word "perfection" is subject to many misconceptions. It is sometimes taken as a concept belonging to transcendental philosophy, namely, the concept of the totality of the manifold which, when taken together, constitutes a thing. Then again it is understood as belonging to teleology, meaning the harmony of the properties of a thing with an end. We may call perfection in the former sense quantitative (material), and in the latter, qualitative (formal) perfection. The former can be one only, for the totality of what belongs to a thing is one. There can be several of the latter in one thing, and it is the latter perfection which is here discussed.

When it is said of the perfection which belongs to man in general (properly, to mankind) that it is itself a duty that they make themselves an end, this perfection must be placed in that which can be an effect of their act and not in what is merely a gift of nature; otherwise it would not be duty. This perfection, therefore, can be nothing else than the cultivation of their power (or natural capacity) and will (moral character) to satisfy the requirements of all duty as such. The supreme element of the former is the understanding as the faculty of concepts, including those concerning duty.

First, it is a duty for him to work upward from the crudity of his nature, from animality (*quoad actum*) more and more toward humanity, by which alone he is capable of setting ends for himself. It is his duty to supply the defects of his knowledge by instruction and to correct his errors. To all this he is not merely counseled by technically practical reason with a view to his other purposes (of art), but the morally practical reason absolutely commands it of him and makes this end his duty in order for him to be worthy of the humanity that resides in him.

Second, it is his duty to cultivate his will to the purest disposition of virtue, to raise it to the point where the law becomes the incentive to his actions which accord with duty, and to obey the law from duty—this being inner morally practical perfection. As this is a feeling of the effect which the legislative will in him exercises on his capacity to act in accordance with the law, it is called the moral feeling. It is, as it were, a special sense (*sensus moralis*); often it is misused in a fanatical sense, as if it (like Socrates' genius) preceded reason or even could dispense with its judgment. Nevertheless, it is still moral perfection, making each particular end, which is also a duty, our object.

B. THE HAPPINESS OF OTHERS

To wish for and to seek happiness, i.e., contentment with one's condition in so far as one is certain of its continuance, is inevitable for human nature; but for this very reason it is not an end which is also a duty. Some still make a distinction between a moral and a physical happiness, the former consisting in the contentment with one's person and moral conduct and thus in what one does, the latter consisting in that which nature affords and hence in that which one enjoys as a gift. Without here censuring the misuse of the word (which indeed contains a contradiction), we must nevertheless note that only the former kind of feeling belongs under the present head, namely, perfection. For he who feels happy in the mere consciousness of his rectitude already possesses that perfection which in the preceding section was defined as the end which is also duty.

Thus if it is a question of happiness, which is to be my duty to effect as an end, it must be the happiness of other men, whose (permitted) end I thus make my own also. It remains for them to decide what they reckon as belonging to their happiness; but it is open to me to decline much that they reckon to it but which I do not regard as happiness, supposing that they have no right to demand it from me as their own. A plausible objection often made against the previously given division of duties consists in setting against that end an alleged obligation to take care of my own (physical) happiness and thus to make this natural and merely subjective end into a duty (an objective end). This requires to be cleared up.

Adversity, pain, and want are great temptations to transgress one's duty. Prosperity, strength, health, and welfare generally, because they stand opposed to the former influences, can thus, it seems, be regarded as ends which are also a duty, the duty, namely, to promote one's own happiness and not to make the happiness of others our end. But in this case happiness is not the end, for the morality of the subject is that to which happiness is merely the permitted means of removing hindrances to morality, since no one else has a right to demand that I sacrifice my not immoral ends. To seek prosperity for itself is not directly a duty, but indirectly it can very well be a duty, in order to guard against poverty, which is a great temptation to vice. But then it is not to be happy, but to maintain the integrity of my morality, that is my end and also my duty.

BIBLIOGRAPHICAL NOTE

This list is intended as a guide for the general reader who wishes to explore the extensive literature on Kant's ethics. In addition, most textbooks in the history of philosophy and in ethics devote one or more chapters to Kant, and these can be read with profit. Nor should the excellent articles on "Kant" and "Kantian Philosophy" in the fourteenth edition of the *Encyclopaedia Britannica* be overlooked.

A. GENERAL WORKS ON KANT

CAIRD, EDWARD. *The Critical Philosophy of Immanuel Kant*. 2 vols. New York: Macmillan Co., 1889. 2d ed., 1909. Pp. xxiv + 654 and xxix + 660.

Perhaps the most famous study of Kant in English, written from a Hegelian point of view. Kant's ethics is dealt with in Volume II.

CLARK, NORMAN. *An Introduction to Kant's Philosophy*. London: Methuen & Co., 1935. Pp. xv + 302.

A popular exposition, filling the gap between brief sketch and commentary. Part IV deals extensively with Kant's ethics.

LINDSAY, ALEXANDER DUNLOP. *Kant*. London: Oxford University Press, 1934. Pp. x + 316.

Concise, lucid, and closely reasoned, this work is a reliable guide for mature students.

PAULSEN, FRIEDRICH. *Immanuel Kant, His Life and Doctrine*. Translated by J. E. CREIGHTON and ALBERT LEFEVRE. New York: Charles Scribner's Sons, 1902. Pp. xix + 419.

A biography with a critical study from a eudemonistic point of view.

[SCHAUB, EDWARD L. (ed.).] *Immanuel Kant: Papers Read at Northwestern University on the Bicentenary of Kant's Birth*. Chicago: Open Court Publishing Co., 1925. Pp. 211.

Lectures on various phases of Kant's philosophy. Among them is G. T. W. Patrick's "The Need and Possibility of an Imperativistic Ethics."

WARD, JAMES. *A Study in Kant*. London: Cambridge University Press, 1923. Pp. vii + 206.

Ward approaches Kant from the standpoint of pluralistic idealism, thus seeing him more as a successor to Leibniz than as a forerunner to Hegel. This involves a more "individualistic" interpretation of the ethics than that found in Caird.

WELDON, T. D. *Introduction to Kant's Critique of Pure Reason.* Oxford: Clarendon Press, 1945. Pp. viii + 205.

A good introduction and commentary; important for the study of the theory of the empirical self.

WHITNEY, GEORGE TAPLEY, and BOWERS, DAVID F. (eds.). *The Heritage of Kant.* Princeton: Princeton University Press, 1939. Pp. xi + 426.

A series of critical studies on Kant's epistemology, ethics, aesthetics, and philosophy of religion. Among those on ethics are D. W. Gotschalk's "The Central Problem of the Kantian Ethic," W. O. Doescher's "Kant's Postulates of Practical Freedom," W. T. Jones's "Purpose, Nature, and the Moral Law," and W. M. Urban's "Kant and Modern Axiology." Every paper in this book deserves careful study.

B. KANT'S ETHICS IN GENERAL

Kant's Lectures on Ethics. Translated by LOUIS INFIELD, with an Introduction by J. MACMURRAY. London: Methuen & Co., 1930. Pp. xiii + 253.

Translated from a student's notes on Kant's lectures on practical philosophy in 1780–81, this volume is an elementary introduction to some phases of Kant's ethics, dealing especially with concrete cases.

FRIEDRICH, CARL JOACHIM. *Inevitable Peace.* Cambridge: Harvard University Press, 1948. Pp. xii + 294.

An elaborate study of the background of Kant's political theory and of the interrelations between his ethics and his theory of peace. The appendix contains a translation of *Perpetual Peace.*

SCHILPP, PAUL ARTHUR. *Kant's Precritical Ethics.* Evanston and Chicago: Northwestern University, 1938. Pp. xvi + 185.

A detailed analysis of Kant's ethics prior to the first *Critique*. Schilpp develops a "procedural" interpretation of Kant's formalism, holding that it was not a set of rigorous rules but simply a rational procedure in moral decisions.

SCHROEDER, H. H. "Some Common Misinterpretations of the Kantian Ethics," *Philosophical Review,* XLIX (1940), 424–46.

Refutes in considerable detail, by citation of relevant passages, the charges of empty formalism, sterile rigorism, and the like.

SCOTT, JOHN WAUGH. *Kant on the Moral Life: An Exposition of the Grundlegung.* London: Black & Co., 1924. Pp. viii + 182.

A running commentary on the *Foundations of the Metaphysics of Morals.*

C. THE CATEGORICAL IMPERATIVE

BROAD, C. D. *Five Types of Ethical Theory*. New York: Harcourt, Brace & Co., 1930. Pp. xxv + 288.

Chapter v discusses Kant. Broad develops the thesis that the categorical imperative is a "second-order principle," being the formula for other first-order categorical imperatives which have actual content.

CHROUST, A. H. "About a Fourth Formula of the Categorical Imperative in Kant," *Philosophical Review*, LI (1942), 600–605.

The *Metaphysics of Morals* (Cassirer ed., VII, 139) holds that man is to be treated only as an end and not as a means. This, Chroust argues, functions as a fourth formula of the imperative, and he applies it particularly to the problem of punishment.

EWING, A. C. "The Paradoxes of Kant's Ethics," *Philosophy*, XIII (1938), 40–56.

Discusses the necessity of considering circumstances, the relation of immorality to logical impossibility, the role of the consciousness of moral constraint, and the relation of moral conflict to virtue.

FIELD, G. C. "Kant's First Moral Principle," *Mind*, XLI (new ser., 1932), 17–36.

An evaluation of various criticisms of the categorical imperative.

JACKSON, REGINALD. "Kant's Distinction between Categorical and Hypothetical Imperatives," *Proceedings of the Aristotelian Society*, 1943–44, pp. 131–66.

PATON, H. J. *The Categorical Imperative: A Study in Kant's Moral Philosophy*. London: Hutchinson, [1946]; Chicago: University of Chicago Press, 1948. Pp. 283.

Paton's work is an exhaustive commentary on the *Foundations* and deals with much besides the categorical imperative. His argument is distinctive chiefly for the emphasis he places upon the necessity of direct insight into the moral principle and on the "necessary self-consciousness of practical reason."

RASHDALL, HASTINGS. *The Theory of Good and Evil: A Treatise on Moral Philosophy*. 2 vols. Oxford: Clarendon Press, 1924. Pp. xx + 312 and xv + 464.

Volume I, chapter v, treats of the categorical imperative, arguing that Kant is incorrect in believing that it enables us to decide right conduct without any appeal to experience. Rashdall, moreover, proposes several acceptable deviations from the categorical imperatives.

D. FREEDOM

HARTMANN, NICOLAI. *Ethics.* Translated by STANTON COIT. 3 vols. New York: Macmillan Co., 1932. Pp. 343, 476, and 288.

Volume III presents a solution to the antinomy of freedom which is the direct opposite of that in Jones (below). Hartmann develops the ontology of various levels of causes which interpenetrate in the phenomenal realm.

JONES, W. T. *Morality and Freedom in the Philosophy of Immanuel Kant.* London: Oxford University Press, 1940. Pp. vii + 178.

The concept of freedom is independent of that of noumenal causality. Kant occasionally used the latter concept, but it is not essential to his argument and is, in fact, incompatible with its final development.

PERRY, RALPH BARTON. "Kant's Abstract Freedom," *Philosophical Review,* IX (1900), 630–47.

Kant's concept of freedom is not applicable to the individual in the world but is an expression of the transcendent dependence of the entire system of the world. Perry suggests that "idealistic metaphysics has led to an abstract definition of freedom that fails utterly to do justice either to the common moral life or to the requirements of the idealist's own ethical interpretation."

E. MORALS AND RELIGION

Kant's Religion within the Limits of Reason Alone. Translated and edited by THEODORE M. GREENE and HOYT H. HUDSON. Chicago: Open Court Publishing Co., 1934. Pp. lxxxv + 200.

Not only the text but the excellent introduction by Greene should be read for Kant's moral theology.

ENGLAND, FREDERICK ERNST. *Kant's Conception of God: A Critical Exposition of Its Metaphysical Development Together with a Translation of the "Nova Dilucidatio."* With a Foreword by G. DAWES HICKS. London: Allen & Unwin, 1929. Pp. 256.

The theological implications of the "facts of the moral life" are discussed in chapter ix.

WEBB, CLEMENT C. J. *Kant's Philosophy of Religion.* Oxford: Clarendon Press, 1926. Pp. l + 218.

Lectures on the development of Kant's religious thought and moral theology, especially the immanentist theology of the *Opus Postumum.*

F. BIBLIOGRAPHIES

ADICKES, ERICH. *German Kantian Bibliography*. Boston: Ginn & Co., 1895–96. Pp. 623.

Friedrich Überwegs Grundriss der Geschichte der Philosophie. Berlin: Mittler, 1924.

Volume III contains extensive bibliographies on all phases of Kant scholarship.

BECK, LEWIS WHITE. "A Bibliography on Kant's Ethics, 1924–1944," *Delaware Notes* (University of Delaware), XVIII (1945), 23–43.

The literature since the latest edition of *Überweg*, together with some titles omitted from that work.

INDEX

A posteriori; *see* A priori
A priori: defined, 9, 21 ff.; in naturalism, 24; in phenomenology, 27; theoretical and practical, 46, 61, 71, 109, 126–27
Abbott, T. K., v n., vii, viii, xi, 30 n., 86 n., 148 n., 187 n.
Adickes, Erich, 48 n., 107 n., 198 n., 362
Altruism, 45, 82, 189, 346 ff.; *see also* Benevolence; Sympathy
Analogy of Experience, 33
Analytic, 129, 152–53, 195 ff.
Anaxagoras, 242
Anthropology, 52, 71
Antinomies, 11–12, 14, 31, 141, 217
Appearances, world of: in "two-world theory," 10, 13, 28, 34, 104 ff., 110–11, 113, 157, 174, 193, 201 ff., 207–8, 219; as "type" of intelligible world, 153, 178
Aristocracy, 313–14
Aristotle, 24, 231 n.
Armies, 308
Assent, 119, 243 ff.
Augustine, 269, 322 n.
Autonomy: definition of, 21, 90, 97; and dignity, 93, 96; and freedom, 32, 102, 105, 107, 144, 152; and God, 48; and interest, 114; as a juridical principle, 289, 312 n.; and moral sense, 26; and realm of ends, 90–91; as supreme moral principle, 97, 144

Baumann, J., 261 n.
Baumgarten, Alexander, 4
Beauty, 43
Beck, L. W., 362
Belief, 300 ff., 351; *see also* Faith
Benevolence, 20, 59–60, 82, 88, 98, 347–48; in Hutcheson, 26; and rights of man, 345; and worth, 92; *see aso* Altruism; Sympathy
Berkeley, George, 2
Boleyn, Ann, 253
Bouterwek, Friedrich, 328
Bowers, D. F., 359
Broad, C. D., vi n., 22 n., 360
Butler, Joseph, 44–45
Butler, Nicholas Murray, ix

Caird, Edward, 15, 358
Cassirer, Ernst, v, vi n., 4 n.
Categorical imperative, 6, 79, 83, 97, 360; application of, 22, 82–83, 350; definition of, 73, 76; and ends of action, 87, 94, 354; formulas of, 22 n., 80, 87, 89, 90, 94–95; and freedom, 108, 115; and intention, 76; as law of intelligible world, 95, 108; in politics, 337 ff.
Categories: of freedom, 11, 165, 174–75, 209; and noumena, 159, 164–65; of quantity, 94; as regulative ideas, 12, 163–64, 238; theoretical, 11, 165, 209; *see also* Causality; Modality
Causality, 12 ff., 34, 114, 127, 160 ff., 196, 200, 208 ff.; freedom as, 31, 121, 129, 152, 157, 173; and noumena, 36, 159 ff., 164–65, 361; of pure reason, 112, 173; *see also* Categories
Censorship, 286–87, 291–92, 303 ff.
Certainty, 272, 276 ff.
Character, 32–33, 40 ff., 106
Charles V, 139
Cheselden, William, 128
Choice, 29–30, 87, 174
Chroust, A. H., 360
Clark, Norman, 358
Clearness, 261 n.
Cochius, Leonhard, 354

[363]

Coit, Stanton, 27 n., 361
Commerce, 329
Common sense, 293
Compact, social, 6, 312
Conscience, 204
Consciousness, 275
Constant de Rebecque, Benjamin, 346
Constitution, 312 n.
Constraint, 72, 76, 84, 91
Contradiction, law of, 279
"Copernican Revolution," 10 ff., 20, 26
Cramer, K. F., 346 n.
Creation, 207–8
Creighton, J. E., vi n., 358
Critique of Judgment, 29, 34 ff., 43
Critique of Practical Reason, viii, x, 16 ff., 118 ff., 155; relation of, to *Critique of Pure Reason*, 34, 121, 129, 153, 162, 195 ff.; relation of, to *Foundations*, 54; significance of title of, 118
Critique of Pure Reason, viii, 3, 8 ff., 16 ff., 35, 120 ff., 203, 302 n.; see also *Critique of Practical Reason*
Crusius, C. A., 151, 278–79
Cynics, 230 n.

Darwinism, 24
Definition, 262 ff., 271 ff., 278
Democracy, 314–15
Descartes, René, 1, 2, 3 n., 297 n.
Design, 24, 34 ff., 56 ff.; see also Purpose; Teleology
Desire: definition of, 124 n., 266, 270; lower and higher faculty of, 133 ff.; manifold of, 174; object of, 132; and pleasure, 44–45, 123, 132 ff.
Despotism, 315
Dialectic, 65–66, 110, 129, 173, 209 ff.
Dignity, 92–93, 96, 292
Dissertation (1770), vi n., 4, 9
Distinctness, 261 n.
Doescher, W. O., 359
Duties: classification of, 20, 60, 80, 83, 87–88, 123, 255–56, 283; as ends, 40, 326, 351 ff.; of virtue, 353
Duty: apostrophe to, 193; apriority of, 19 ff., 66–67, 71, 83, 89; definition of, 61, 64, 68, 96, 144, 187; and good will, 58, 64; and legality, 59, 61, 221; and pleasure, 114, 220; and realm of ends, 91; and rights, 344, 353; and self-love, 66 f., 70 n., 79, 92; see also Obligation

Education, 71, 75, 251 ff., 305 n.
Empiricism, 15, 84, 128, 161, 179, 200
End(s): and categorical imperative, 94, 354; determined by reason, 85–86, 89; as duties, 40, 326, 351 ff., 354 ff.; final ends, 40, 86, 89, 92, 95; and the good, 171; humanity as, 23, 87–88, 356; material, 86, 93, 151; and means, 86, 94, 137 n., 283; as negative concept, 94; see also Realm of ends
England, F. E., 361
Enlightenment, 2, 286 ff., 305 n.
Epicureans, 51, 78 n., 135, 152, 195, 216, 219, 224, 229, 230 n., 243
Epicurus; see Epicureans
Equality, 6 f., 313 n., 350
Ethics: certainty in, 282 ff.; Christian, 3, 25, 60, 189–90, 192, 230 ff.; and happiness, 232–33; history of, 259; and metaphysics of morals, 17, 52, 69; and politics, 331 ff.; relationships of, 50 ff., 71, 353; and religion, 232–33; uses of, 65, 87–88
Evil, 34, 167–68, 242
Ewing, A. C., 360
Example, 68, 71, 78, 158, 192, 250 ff., 332

Fairclough, H. R., 120 n., 320 n.
Faith, 13–14, 46–47, 116, 229, 245 ff., 300
Fanaticism, 46, 192, 238, 259, 294, 297 n., 304
Farber, Marvin, 27 n.
Fatalism, 111

[364]

INDEX

Fictionalism, 13
Field, G. C., 360
Fontanelle, Bernard Le Bovier de, 184
Form, 138, 140
Formalism, 25, 27, 38, 40, 337–38
Formula, 22, 123 n.
Foundations of Metaphysics of Morals, vii, x, 5, 16, 19, 50 ff., 54–55, 122–23
Frederick II, 291, 315
Freedom: 29 ff., 361; and autonomy, 101 ff., 105, 107, 144, 152; and categorical imperative, 108, 115; categories of, 165, 174–75, 209; as causality, 29 ff., 121, 129, 152, 157, 173; of choice, 29–30; and concept of right, 332; consciousness of, 152; definition of, 101; of efficient cause, 36 n., 121, 158, 199–200, 209; enjoyment of, 222; and equality, 6, 350; and faith, 33; and form of law, 119, 140; and God, 119, 206–7, 210; and good will, 84; inexplicability of, 30, 32, 109–10, 113 ff., 156, 180; and judgment, 34; laws of, 102, 119; legal, 312 n.; positive and negative concepts of, 12–13, 29 ff., 47, 102, 118, 122, 141, 201 ff.; as postulate, 235 ff.; and purpose, 35 ff.; as *ratio essendi* of morality, 14, 29, 119 n., 140–41; and realm of ends, 91; as regulative idea, 38, 103, 113, 158; and use of reason, 111, 115, 129; *see also* Autonomy
Freedom of thought; *see* Censorship
Free thinking, 304
Friedrich, C. J., x, 359

Galilei, Galileo, 1
Garve, Christian, vii, 344 n.
God, 361; attributes of, 233 n., 240–41, 282; and autonomy, 48; belief in, 13, 47, 301, 323 n.; duties to, 255–56; existence of, 7–8, 16, 227 f., 235–36, 297 n.; and freedom, 119, 206, 210; and highest good, 68, 228, 246 ff.; Kingdom of, 231, 239; as ideal, 151; love of, 189 ff.; as moral law, 49; and natural right, 313 n.; need of, 298; and purpose, 323 n.; will of, 98, 283
Goldmann, Lucien, 39 n.
Good, the: 73, 177; definitions of, 167–68; and desire, 168 ff.; moral and natural, 26; and obligation, 28, 123, 171–72; and pleasure, 167; sensations of, 284; *see also* Highest good
Good, J. M., 261 n.
Good will: and autonomy, 101, 109; definition of, 94, 96; and duty, 58; and freedom, 84; and general will, 6; and holy will, 73, 96; and idea of perfection, 100; and respect, 92; as sole absolute good, 55–56
Gotschalk, D. W., 359
Government, form of, 315–16
Grace, 43
Greene, T. M., 34 n., 86 n., 361
Grillo, 157 n.
Grotius, Hugo, 317
Gutman, J., 4 n.

Happiness, 15, 22, 40, 77, 173, 198, 233; as end and duty, 60, 355 ff.; and end of nature, 56; and highest good, 215–16, 219, 227, 246; and imperatives, 40, 74 n., 77, 136, 148; and moral feeling, 99; in moral life, 43, 60, 170, 199; of others, 62, 88, 98, 146; and self-love, 133, 146; as system, 65, 77–78; and virtue, 217–18; worthiness for, 16, 23, 232, 357
Hartenstein, Gustav, 140 n., 148 n., 158 n., 173 n.
Hartmann, Nicolai, 27–28, 361
Harvey, William, 1
Hastie, W., ix, xi, 3 n.
Hedonism, 40, 44–45, 98; *see also* Happiness; Pleasure
Hegel, G. W. F., 19, 22, 358
Hegemony, 307, 309

[365]

Hegler, Alfred, 29 n.
Heisenberg principle, 33 n.
Hendel, C. W., 6
Henry VIII, 253
Herz, Marcus, 5 n., 42
Heteronomy, 28, 90, 97-98, 144, 173; and interest, 114; and natural necessity, 102; and object of will, 113; *see also* Autonomy
Hicks, G. D., 361
Highest good, 16, 45, 62, 72, 213 ff., 235, 246; as a priori, 119; and immortality, 226; and religion, 228, 232
Hobbes, Thomas, 1, 2, 25, 45
Hoernlé, R. F. A., 110 n.
Horace, 120
Hospitality, 320
Hudson, H. H., 34 n., 86 n., 361
Human nature, 5, 28 ff., 41 ff., 70 n., 84, 103, 332 f.
Humanity, as an end in itself, 23, 87-88, 356
Hume, David, 2-3, 8, 10-11, 24, 127, 160 ff., 165
Hutcheson, Francis, 5, 7, 8, 26, 99 n., 220 n., 285
Hypothesis, 48, 244, 300, 351

Idea of a Universal Cosmopolitical History, ix
Immortality, 16, 18, 118, 225-26, 235-36
Imperatives: classification of, 73-74, 76 ff., 79, 125, 131; definition of, 72-73, 131; and freedom, 16; and happiness, 40, 74 n., 77, 136, 148; and heteronomy, 97; and moral law, 143; *see also* Autonomy; Categorical imperative
Incentives, 86, 89, 180 ff., 186-87; moral, 42-43, 70-71, 116, 194; and motives, 86; and religion, 48 n.
Inclinations, 73 n., 84, 86, 182
Infield, Louis, x, 359
Inquiry (1764), vi, 4, 8, 21, 261 ff.
Intelligible world, 115-16, 152 ff., 163, 235, 296; and appearances, 10, 13, 28, 34, 106 ff., 174, 178, 193,
203, 207-8, 219; and categorical imperative, 95, 108; categories and, 159, 238; and highest good, 219; and Kingdom of God, 239; and personality, 193; and realm of ends, 95; *see also* Appearances, world of; Noumenon
Intention, 28, 76, 174, 179, 180 n., 249
Interest, 73, 225; and autonomy, 114; and imperatives, 89-90; and incentives, 89, 186; moral, 62 n., 115-16, 186-87, 250; in morality, 18, 116, 103-4, 256
Intuition, 25-26, 94, 106, 156, 196 ff., 209; intellectual, 38-39, 205, 226, 238-39

Jackson, Reginald, 360
Jacobi, F. H., vii-viii, 294, 302
Jentsch, Daniel, 123 n.
Jones, W. T., 36 n., 359, 361
Judgment, faculty of, 35, 65
Judgments: classification of, 8-9; and freedom, 29, 34; and imperatives, 77-78, 177
Juvenal, 143 n., 255, 257 n.

Kristeller, P. O., 4 n.
Kroeger, A. E., x
Kroner, Richard, 14 n., 49
Krüger, Gerhart, 7 n.
Kuhn, Helmut, v

Language, 328
Laws: classification of, 312 n.; international, 312 n., 316, 319-20, 337, 342-43; moral (*see* Moral law); natural, 15, 50, 72, 80, 137, 177-78, 311 n. (*see also* Natural law); permissive, 125 n., 310, 333; of war, 309, 317
League of Nations, 316 ff., 328
Lebensphilosophie, 47
Lectures on Ethics, Kant's, x, 359
Lefevre, Albert, vi n., 358
Legality, 59, 61, 180, 188, 221, 249
Leibniz, G. W. von, 2, 3, 203, 206 n., 257, 263, 358
Lessing, G. E., vii

INDEX

Lindsay, A. D., 358
Locke, John, 25
Logic, 50 ff.
Lucretius, 33 n., 261
Lying, 63–64, 98, 154, 346 ff.

MacMurray, J., 359
Maier, Heinrich, 322 n., 328 n., 346 n.
Malebranche, Nicolas de, 2
Mallet du Pan, Jacques, 316 n.
Man, as end, 39, 86, 193–94, 234
Mandeville, Bernard, 151
Manthey-Zorn, Otto, vii
Marcus Aurelius, 316 n.
Marxism, 24
"Material of rules," 22, 61, 93–94, 116, 132, 138, 145, 151–52, 283–84
Mathematics, 77, 127, 137 n., 161, 262 ff.
Maxim, 84, 187; definition of, 62 n., 80 n., 130; form of, 93; and moral law, 62 ff., 80 n.
Mead, G. H., 3
Mendelssohn, Moses, vi ff., 206, 292 n., 293, 297 n., 299 ff.
Menzer, Paul, x
Messer, August, 19 n.
Metaphysics: definition of, 51, 269; of law, 349, 352; limits of, 13, 47 ff.; method in, 262 ff.; of morals, 66 ff., 69–70, 85, 101, relation to ethics, 17, 52, 69–70, in Wolff, 53
Metaphysics of Morals, x, 17, 43, 80 n.
Methodology, 129, 249 ff.
Michaelis, J. D., 346 n.
Modality, 125 n., 175
Monarchy, 307, 315
Montaigne, Michel, 151
Moral feeling, 26, 41, 43, 98–99, 114, 151, 173, 183–84, 187, 221, 254, 285, 356
Moral law: apriority of, 52, 61, 68, 71, 76, 79, 83–84, 143; and concept of the good, 171–72; deduction of, 19, 152–53, 156 ff., 199–200; a fact of pure reason, 27, 29, 142,

157; and freedom, 119, 140–41, 157; the fundamental, 142; as God, 48; as imperative, 143; and maxim, 62 ff., 80; and natural law, 15, 50, 72, 80, 177; a principle of experience, 16; respect for, 62, 182; typic of 38, 94, 116, 176 ff.; see also Categorical imperative; Practical principles
Moral sense, 25 ff., 84, 99 n., 100, 150
Moral value, 24–25, 61
Morality: autonomy and, 12, 96–97; and ends, 92, 96; as a fact, 18, 24, 27 ff., 143, 157; interest in, 18, 103–4, 256; knowledge of, common, 19, 54–55, 63 ff., 72, 107, 147, 197, 252; and politics, 328, 331 ff., 340 ff.; as *ratio cognoscendi* of freedom, 14, 29, 119, 140 ff.; as respect for law, 183
Morals; *see* Ethics
Motives, 53, 86, 112, 180, 250
Mysticism, 179

National debt, 308
Natorp, P., 144 n., 145 n., 170 n.
Natural law, 311 n., 333
Natural right, 313 n., 315 n.
Nature: and freedom, 110, 201 ff.; as guarantor of peace, 322 ff.; and heteronomy, 100–101; and intelligible world, 95, 153 ff.; mechanism of, 93, 110, 201 ff., 205 ff.; as phenomena under law, 11, 80; philosophy of, 15; and purpose, 322 ff.; and realm of ends, 93; state of, 311 n., 312 n.; *see also* Appearances, world of; Laws, natural
Need: in Mendelssohn, 299; of pure reason, 119, 229, 244, 296–97, 304; and "right to assume," 119, 160, 166; theoretical and practical, 46, 298
Neo-Platonists, 302 n.
Newton, Sir Isaac, 1, 7, 10, 35, 261, 271
Nietzsche, F. W., 48–49
Northrop, F. S. C., 23 n.

[367]

Noumenon, 121, 153, 198; categories and, 121; causality of, 36, 159, 163 ff., 361; person as, 30–31, 113, 158, 219; and thing-in-itself, 13, 31, 106, 113 ff., 162–63, 219; *see also* Intelligible world

Obligation: definition of, 96, 143; as evidence of freedom, 32; a fact, 20, 27, 143, 157; and the good, 28, 123, 171–72; and holy will, 73, 96, 144, 189; and means and end, 283; and Wolff, 53; *see also* Duty
O'Brien, Helen, x
Observations on the Feeling of the Sublime and the Beautiful, 26–27, 221
On the Saying, "That May Be True in Theory...," 3 n., 6 n., 22 n., 41
On a Supposed Right To Lie from Altruistic Motives, x, 22 n., 346 ff.
Opus posthumum, 16 n., 48, 361
Organism, 36–37
Orientation, 294
"Ought," 27, 72, 104, 109, 131

Paton, H. J., 10 n., 20 n., 43 n., 89 n., 140 n., 360
Patrick, G. T. W., 358
Paulsen, Friedrich, vi n., 358
Peace, 306 ff., 351 ff.
Perfection, 98 ff., 126 n., 151, 173, 283
Perpetual Peace, viii–ix, 306 ff.
Perry, R. B., 361
Personality, 193–94
Persons: as noumena, 30–31, 113, 158, 219; respect for, 62 n., 87, 184 ff., 188 n.; and things, 86
Phenomenology, 25 ff.
Philosophers, 65, 306, 329–30
Philosophy: and ethics, 15, 17, 50, 65–66, 213, 260; limits of, 109 ff., 113, 247 ff.; and mathematics, 262 ff., 271 ff., 276 ff.; method in, 262 ff.; and peace, 329
Pietism, 3, 19
Pistorius, H. A., 123 n.
Plato, 199, 231 n., 243

Plautus, 126 n.
Pleasure: definition of, 124 n., 266; and desire, 44–45, 123 n., 132 ff.; and duty, 114, 220; and good, 167; and happiness, 40, 78 n.; and heteronomy, 173; and incentive, 40; and inner sense, 167; and interest, 73; *see also* Happiness; Hedonism
Politicians, 306, 333–34
Politics, 331 ff., 337–38, 340 ff., 349
Pope, Alexander, 7, 316 n.
"Popular philosophers," 4, 66 ff., 69
Positivism, 13, 46
Postulates, 126 n., 226, 234 ff., 243–44; and hypotheses, 48, 300
Practical principles, 86, 98–99, 130 ff., 138, 141, 254, 350
Practical reason; *see* Reason, practical
Price, 92–93
Priestley, Joseph, 204
Prolegomena, vii
Promises, 63, 78, 81, 88, 92, 132
Providence, 322 ff.
Prudence, 74 n., 75, 77, 131–32, 148, 331 ff.
Prussian Academy of Sciences, v, vi
Psychology, 85
Ptolemy, 10 n.
Publicity, criterion of, 6, 340 ff., 345
Pufendorf, Samuel von, 317
Punishment, 149–50, 170, 360
Purpose: faith in, 323 n.; and freedom, 35 ff.; of moral action, 61; in nature, 322–23; and theoretical reason, 246

Ramsay, G. G., 143 n., 256 n.
Randall, J. H., Jr., 4 n.
Rashdall, Hastings, 360
Rationalism, 10–11, 128, 179
Realm of ends, 91 ff., 95 ff.
Reason: and feeling, 42; and happiness, 57; as higher faculty of desire, 133 ff.; limits of, 7, 49, 109 ff., 116–17, 157, 247 ff.; private and public use of, 287–88; relation of,

[368]

to other faculties, 11, 34–35, 106, 124 n.; twofold legislation of, 15, 155, 164, 197

Reason, practical, 58, 71, 85, 113 ff.; antinomy of, 217 ff.; empiricism and mysticism of, 179; object of, 101, 112–13, 166; primacy of, 7, 12, 18, 128–29, 223 ff.; pure and empirical, 129; synthetical use of, 101; and theoretical reason, 15, 18, 128, 158 ff., 197, 223 ff.; and will, 15, 32, 72, 98

Reason, speculative, 10, 116, 155, 159 ff., 223 ff., 236 ff., 294, 299, 304

Reason, theoretical: dialectic of, 64 ff.; and metaphysics, 12–13, 293 ff.; and practical reason, 15, 18, 128, 158 ff., 197, 223 ff.; and purpose, 246

Regulative ideas, 12, 35, 39, 46 n., 158, 163, 238

Religion: definition of, 48, 232; differences of, 328 n.; enlightenment in, 289 ff.; immortality and, 226; as incentive, 48 n.; influence of, on Kant, 3

Religion within the Limits of Reason Alone, 43

Republic, 312–13, 316, 327; freedom of thought in, 291–92; of world, 319, 339

Respect, 181 ff., 221; definition of, 62 n.; for law, 61, 96, 186 ff.; and moral feeling, 41 n.; and obligation, 21; for persons, 62 n., 87, 184, 188 n., 194

Revelation, 301

Revolution, vii, ix, 3 n., 333, 341–42

Richardson, William, vi

Right, the, 6, 332, 340 ff.

Rights, 88, 312 n., 327, 340, 344 ff., 353

Romanticism, 2, 46

Ross, W. D., 22 n., 27

Rousseau, Jean Jacques, 2, 4 n., 5 ff., 327 n.

Satisfaction, 44

Sauvage, F. B. de, 275
Schaub, E. L., 358
Scheler, Max, 27–28
Schema, 11, 177, 293
Schiller, J. C. F. von, 19, 42–43
Schilpp, P. A., 5 n., 22 n., 78 n., 359
Schöndorffer, 165 n.
Schopenhauer, Arthur, 49
Schrecker, P., 3 n.
Schroeder, H. H., 359
Science, 1, 12, 24
Scott, J. W., 359
Selby Bigge, L. A., 25 n.
Self-contentment, 181, 219, 221–22
Self-evidence, 272
Selfishness, 181
Self-love, 66–67, 79, 133, 137, 146–47, 181–82
Semple, J. W., vii, xi
Seneca, 327 n.
Sensibility, 11, 107, 114
Shaftesbury, A. A. C., 5, 7, 25
Simpson, F. H., 19 n.
Skepticism, 13, 24, 47, 163
Smith, Adam, 5 n.
Smith, Mary Campbell, ix, 324 n.
Smith, Norman Kemp, 10 n.
Socrates, 5, 64, 356
Sophists, 5
Sovereignty, 314 ff., 317
Space, 265 ff., 272
Speculative reason; *see* Reason, speculative
Spener, P. J., 3
Spinoza, Baruch, vii, 1, 2, 34, 47, 207, 302
State, the, 307
Stoicism, 126, 151, 169, 192, 216, 219, 229–30
Storm and Stress, philosophers of, 47
Strife of Faculties, vii, 330 n.
Sublime, the, 96, 221, 258
Substance, 272
Suicide, 59, 81, 87, 154
Sulzer, J. G., 70 n.
Summum bonum; see Highest good

[369]

Supersensuous world; *see* Intelligible world
Swabey, M. C., vi n.
Swabey, W. C., vi n.
Sympathy, 60, 99, 189, 222; *see also* Altruism; Benevolence

Talent, 55–56, 81–82, 88
Technique of nature, 37
Teleology, 20 n., 35 ff., 40, 93 n.; *see also* Purpose
Theodicy, 340
Theology, 45 ff., 240 ff., 281 ff.
Theoretical reason; *see* Reason, theoretical
Thing-in-itself; *see* Noumenon
Things, 86, 184
Time, 11, 200 ff., 206 ff., 263, 266, 269
Tittel, G. A., 123 n.
Tolerance; *see* Censorship
Transcendental method, 18
Treaties, 306 ff., 318
Trueblood, B. F., ix
Truthfulness; *see* Lying
Tufts, J. H., 5 n.
Typic of Moral Law, 38, 94, 116, 176 ff.

Überweg, Friedrich, 362
Understanding, 11, 34–35, 106–7, 164; intuitive (*see* Intuition)
Universality, 21, 80, 93–94, 137; *see also* A priori
Urban, W. M., 359
Utilitarianism, 24

Vaucanson, A. von, 206
Virgil, 320, 339
Virtue, 41, 43, 67, 85, 144, 191, 217, 222; duties of, 353–54; as end, 356; as supreme good, 215–16
Voltaire, vii, 185
Voluntarism, 49
Vorländer, Karl, v, 3 n., 107 n., 122 n., 124 n., 157 n., 165 n., 166 n., 284 n.

War, 306 ff., 351–52; laws of, 309, 317; preventive, 343
Warburton, William, 269
Ward, James, 358
Wattel, 317
Webb, C. C. J., 361
Weiss, Paul, v
Weldon, T. D., 359
Wellek, René, vi n.
What Is Enlightenment? vii, 2, 286 ff.
What Is Orientation in Thinking? vii–viii, 5, 46, 293 ff.
Whitney, G. T., 359
Will: and choice, 32; content and form of, 61; definition of, 101–2; general, 6; of God, 98–99, 151, 284; holy, 73, 96, 144, 189 ff., 226; as legislative, 89 ff., 93; and practical reason, 15, 32, 72; *see also* Good will
Willich, A. F. M., vi n.
Windelband, Wilhelm, 5
Windisch-Grätz, J. K., 311 n.
Wizenmann, Thomas, 245 n., 294 n.
Wolff, Christian von, 4, 7, 9, 53, 151, 261 n., 263, 298 n.
World citizenship, 320 ff.
World republic, 319, 328